THE ALA
BOOK OF
LIBRARY
GRANT
MONEY

THE ALA BOOK OF LIBRARY GRANT MONEY

NINTH EDITION

Edited by Nancy Kalikow Maxwell

an imprint of

THE AMERICAN LIBRARY ASSOCIATION

CHICAGO   2014

Throughout her thirty-year library career, **Nancy Kalikow Maxwell** has partici-
pated in successful grant projects totaling more than ten million dollars, with
more than one million of those dollars flowing directly to the library. She is the
author of *Grant Money through Collaborative Partnerships* (ALA, 2012) and wrote
the chapter "Grant Writing in Retirement" that appears in the book *Writing After
Retirement: Tips by Successful Writers* (forthcoming, Scarecrow Press). Formerly
library director at Miami Dade College (Miami, Fla.) and Barry University (Miami Shores, Fla.), Maxwell currently owns and operates Kaliwell, Inc. (www
.librarygrants.org), a grant development company specializing in locating, writing, and evaluating library, educational, and other grants. She holds a master's
degree in library science from the University of Missouri-Columbia and a master's
degree in theology from Barry University in Miami Shores, Florida. She can be
reached at kaliwell@kaliwellinc.com.

© 2014 by the American Library Association

Printed in the United States of America

18 17 16 15 14   5 4 3 2 1

Extensive effort has gone into ensuring the reliability of the information in this book; however, the publisher makes no warranty, express or implied, with respect to the material
contained herein.

ISBNs: 978-0-8389-1211-9 (paper); 978-0-8389-9679-9 (PDF); 978-0-8389-9680-5 (ePub);
978-0-8389-9681-2 (Kindle). For more information on digital formats, visit the ALA Store
at alastore.ala.org and select eEditions.

Cover design by Kim Thornton. Cover image © Stokkete/Shutterstock, Inc.

Text composition in the Charis SIL typeface by Dianne M. Rooney.

♾ This paper meets the requirements of ANSI/NISO Z39.48-1992 (Permanence of Paper).

CONTENTS

INTRODUCTION

Congratulations. By finding this book and flipping to the introduction, you have advanced one step further than most people. Just about everyone who works in a library wants grant money, but few ever do anything to get some. When librarians learn that I am a grant writer, they invariably respond with, "Boy, does my library need a grant. We desperately need a new boiler, an updated circulation system, e-book readers, a new children's room," and so on. Or the honest ones (who hold a special place in my heart) will ignore their professional responsibilities and instead say, "I need a trip to Tahiti. Are there any grants for that?"

But no matter what they dream of, most never get past the "I want" stage. Those who do are frequently prompted by others. Someone (usually the boss) shoots them an e-mail with the subject "Grant Opportunity." "Something for us to think about," reads the message accompanying the announcement of new grant funding. But what most people think about is how much work a grant involves. They click delete and hope the boss forgets about it.

There is no denying that pursuing a grant is, indeed, additional work. A former supervisor of mine would not even entertain the notion of grant funding. "No grants, no grants," she would repeat like a mantra whenever I broached the subject. "We did that years ago. Way too much work." Another colleague told me that she would rather kill herself than write a grant. One library director considered turning down a job offer because it included administering a major federal grant. She did take the position, but vowed to never pursue another grant. Her resolve lasted only six months, when she received one of those previously mentioned grant announcement e-mails. Since it came not from her boss, but from the college president, she had no choice but to pursue another one.

Whether it is your idea (hopefully) or that of your boss (or the president), by obtaining and reading this book, you are at least investigating grant funding sources for your library. Once again, congratulations for getting this far. You go, girl (or boy).

But before you flip to your state's listings and begin scanning listings for that perfect funding source, you may want to read the rest of this introduction. You, like many potential grant developers, may not be what is known in the field as "grant ready."

Grant Readiness

Grant experts differ in the advice they provide grant seekers, but one recommendation they would all agree upon is that grant seekers must come to the grant development process prepared. Several steps should be taken beforehand. Readers of a certain age may remember those *Leave It To Beaver* shows, when the father would come home from work, take off his coat and pull up to the dinner table, ready to enjoy a delicious dinner. The meal magically appeared before him, with none of the wife's pervious toil or preparation in evidence. And so it can be for grant development. To the uninitiated it appears that a successful grant proposal blossoms effortlessly without any previous preparation. But this is deceiving.

An incredible amount of work is—or should—be done before beginning any grant search. The following are the most common components to assemble before launching a grant project.

Components to Becoming Grant-Ready

STRATEGIC PLAN

As the old adage has it, if you don't know where you are going, any road will get you there. Or, as they say in the US Army, "You can't hit a target you can't see." In order to "hit the target" of grant funding, a grant seeker must make sure the goals of the requesting institution fit those of the granting agency.

An organization's aims must be clearly stated in order for the funder to recognize if it matches their own. Fortunately, most libraries already have a strategic plan and mission statement in place. For some, the parent organization's overarching goals serve as the library's goals. For instance, if a college's mission is to *prepare* graduates for a successful culinary arts career then the library's mission may simply be *to provide support to prepare* successful culinary art students. Other libraries may similarly mirror the parent organization, but include specifics about how the parent will be served. For instance, the library mission may be to provide the library services, collections, and instructional and technical support needed for the organization to accomplish its mission, which is . . . (with the institution's mission repeated).

No matter what the strategic plan includes, the funder must be convinced that the library's stated goals and that of the funding agency are symbiotic. If the library does not have an updated strategic plan it will be difficult to demonstrate that the library is the appropriate organization to meet the funder's goals. On the other hand, when a library's clearly stated goals overlap with those of the funding agency, the chances of a proposal's success are enhanced immeasurably.

Especially powerful are instances when the same words in a library's strategic plan appear in the stated goals of the funding source. For instance, if one of the goals of the library is "to improve the effectiveness of nonprofit organizations in Polk County," and a funder issues a grant to provide computer training to make Polk County nonprofit employees more effective, the chances of crafting a successful proposal are excellent. However, if a library's goals are to serve the school's student population, a funding opportunity for staff development would be harder to demonstrate. A case can be made that student performance will be improved through teacher training, but it would be easier to justify if staff and faculty development appeared somewhere in the organization's official plan.

Before you search for any grant funding, it will behoove you to pull out your organization's strategic plan. Review the wording and keep the key phrases in mind as you review grant opportunities. If your organization does not have such a plan, you may want to postpone any grant searching until one is produced.

NEEDS ASSESSMENT

Unlike the strategic plan, which most libraries already have, few libraries approach a grant search with a thorough needs assessment in hand. Actually, the needs assessment encompasses two components: the assessment of library needs and an assessment of the user's need for the service or product. Both are explained below.

Library Needs Assessment

The first needs assessment that should be completed before a grant search begins is the identification of the library's top priorities for funding. Though this sounds easy, it is anything but. The answer to "What does the library need?" will be different depending on who is doing the answering. One of the major federal college grant programs is informally called "The President's Program" because it is intended to fund those projects deemed most important to the college president. As implied by its name, the priority for funding as seen by a college's chief executive may differ from—and is often at odds with—those of others on campus.

Library administrators are well aware of this discrepancy. Especially since libraries are not revenue-generating, few academic or municipal administrators see the construction of new library buildings as a top priority. Yet for many library directors, that would be the number one answer to what the library needs.

Even within the confines of the library, rarely does agreement exist about what the library needs. While a young adult librarian may see the paltry collection of DVDs as the biggest need, the technical services librarian may cry out for more part-time staff, while the library clerk sees a pressing need for student lockers.

"We need more computers."

"No we don't. We need more science journals."

"No, we need more parenting books. And why does Harry always get what he asks for?"

Coming to the grant search with such divergent clamors can be both unproductive and contentious. A better approach would be to come to the grant search with an agreed-upon list. Though it may be difficult to arrive at consensus beforehand, much time, not to mention staff dissention, could be avoided by hashing this out before beginning the funding search. Formally requesting priority items from staff, either via a written survey or e-mail request, would prove more effective than throwing out ideas while reviewing grant opportunities. You must know what you are seeking before you begin searching.

User Needs Assessment

Amassing a list of priorities in need of funding completes one-half of the assessment phase. But don't stop there. Approaching funders with only a list of staff-derived library needs will most likely prove unsuccessful. Few funders care to give to libraries based only on what the library employees want. Rather, they want to support those programs and services demanded by the library's users. The young adult librarian's assertion that the library needs more movies is less impressive than, "Ninety-three percent of eighth graders agreed with the statement, 'The library needs more movies on DVD.'" Providing quantified indicators is one of the best methods to demonstrate user need. Other avenues, such as focus group results, online feedback, or even suggestion box comments, can also be used to demonstrate need. No matter the method chosen, evidence that the potential population deems the product or service necessary should be presented to the grant funder. Once you can show what the library's users and staff need, you will be ready to move to the next stage of grant readiness.

PARTNERS

Once you know what is needed, the next step to becoming grant-ready is to identify the most appropriate institution to meet the stated need. Ask yourself what is the best organization to offer this program or service. If the answer is the library, give yourself a pat on the back; you have created a potentially grant-fundable project. If the answer is some other institution—for instance, the public school, the parks and recreation department, or the student services division—consider partnering with that group.

Even projects best accomplished by the library could be improved through collaborative partnerships. Many funding sources require a joint effort in order to qualify for funding. But even funding sources that do accept single-organization projects would most likely be strengthened if they included a cross-institutional collaboration. For ideas on where to find collaborative partnerships, see my book *Grant Money through Collaborative Partnerships* (ALA, 2012). (See my book even if you don't need partnership ideas!)

Before beginning your grant search, try to identify the logical agencies that would extend the program envisioned. For instance, if you decide to meet the needs of Spanish-language library users, organizations that already serve that population may be interested in joining your effort. Or think of organizations the library already works with. Are there groups that regularly meet in the library? Do you already have a comfortable working relationship with some agency director or department chair? Is there someone you *want* to have such a relationship with (for either personal or professional reasons)? Whatever the reason, you should think through the collaboration angle before searching for funding sources.

PROJECT SUMMARY

In the classic Talmudic story, the great sage Rabbi Hillel was asked to explain all of the Jewish Torah standing on one foot. "What is hateful unto you, do not do unto your neighbor.

That is the whole Torah, all the rest is commentary. Now, go and study." If Hillel can condense all of the five books of Moses to one statement, you should be able to summarize your proposed grant-funded project in one paragraph. If you cannot convey your idea in just a few sentences, keep working on it until you can repeat it standing on one foot.

And make sure the final synopsis is understandable to all readers. Ever since the financial derivatives disaster, investors are now warned, "If you can't explain it, don't buy it." The same holds true for grants and can be especially important for technology grants. Though I hate to admit it, I once worked on a grant proposal to create some kind of online student educational product that I never clearly understood. Throughout the proposal I referred to it as a "toolkit," hoping the funders would know what that meant. Evidently they didn't. The lack of clarity most likely contributed to the proposal being unsuccessful. Funders are unlikely to put money behind something that they don't understand. The goal is to describe the project so succinctly it can easily be understood by nontechnical readers in one or two sentences.

EVALUATION

Once you know what you want to do, you next need to ask, "How will you know when you have done it right?" The answer to that question will form the basis of the project evaluation, which constitutes the next required grant-readiness element. The ability to effectively and objectively assess the impact of any proposed project is a central requirement of grant funding. One former chief executive officer of the national Grant Professionals Association recommended including evaluation of a project in all grant proposals, whether or not requested in the grant application.

You will save time, both your own and that of the funding agency, by laying out the evaluation plan for your project before approaching the grant search. Many people find it helpful to work backwards from the evaluation to design the project. For instance, a proposed project to teach library users computer skills would, hopefully, enhance the ability of those participating to more effectively use computers. But "using computers" is such a broad concept, it could cover anything from manipulating a mouse to constructing complex search statements. To "go backwards" from the evaluation, you would start by asking what the successful participants would know or be able to do at the conclusion of the instruction.

More importantly, how will you—or any observer—know this knowledge has been obtained? Self-reported surveys, pre- and post-assessments, and observations are some of the methods that could be employed to evaluate the level of proficiency or knowledge gained. Thinking through this step first will enable the program to most effectively reach a successful outcome.

SUSTAINABILITY

The final step for pre-grant readiness is the creation of a sustainability plan. Though usually associated with the environmental movement, sustainability is also a term prevalent in the philanthropic world.

"Sustain" means "to provide for an institution by furnishing means or funds." Few funders are interested in supporting a project indefinitely and want to know how their initial support will be continued in the future. Much like venture capitalists, nonprofit and governmental funders want to benefit from the successful implementation of a new service or program. Though no money would accrue to the funder, they would rather be "paid back" in the long term by successfully providing users with a necessary product or service.

Before approaching any grant funder, it would be worth your time to consider how the project will be carried on once the initial appropriation is made. Will the project be incorporated into the library's existing services? Are you attempting to create a collaborative partnership that would be self-sustaining through member contributions? Are participant fees or scholarships available to sustain future programs? Perhaps donor contributions are possible. Whatever the means identified, the chances of success for any grant-funded project will be enhanced if a detailed sustainability plan can be presented from the very beginning.

If you cannot identify any method to continue the project beyond the grant award, you could still seek funding. However, the chances of success will be diminished without a solid sustainability plan. If nothing else, you can always claim that once the grant ends, you will seek additional grants. But it would be preferable to be creative and devise a more definitive plan. Once you have crafted a way to continue the program or service, and accomplished each of the components above, you can declare yourself grant-ready.

NEXT STEP FOR THE GRANT-READY

Once you have become grant-ready as detailed above, your next step is to consult the *ALA Book of Library Grant Money* for the appropriate funder or funders. The How to Use This Book section provides information about the elements of each entry and instruction on how best to use this book.

As you search the grant sources, pay special attention to funding opportunities in your state or that expressly give to your type of library or project. Pursuing opportunities for which you are not eligible or that are not within the parameters of the funder is a waste of both your and the giver's time. Keep in mind that you are seeking that perfect confluence of your library's needs with the funder's giving priorities.

NEED TO UPDATE FUNDER INFORMATION

Identifying a likely source of funds brings you one step closer to soliciting funds. But there remains one more important hurdle to scale before you send out any proposals. You will need to update and verify the funding opportunity information found here. Because of the lag time inherent in this—and any—print publication, the information found in this directory may be out-of date by the time it appears. Indeed, one could reasonably argue that many, if not most, of the funders' data elements will have changed during the book's publishing. There is a good chance the name and address of the funder will not have changed, but little else about the funder may be the same. Every fact about the grant giver needs to be verified.

Once you have the potential funder's name, the best place to consult for up-to-date giving guidelines is with the funder directly, preferably through the funder's website. Whenever available, website addresses are provided for this purpose. However, not all funders maintain websites. For those lacking websites, you could use the funder's address or phone number. Some funders prefer to be contacted by phone and some by mail. Which type of contact is preferred has been included in each entry whenever available.

Along with contacting the funder, updating and verifying the granting guidelines can be accomplished through a grants database or other secondary source. The Grant-Related Organizations and Resources section of this publication lists several grant sources that can be consulted to verify and update the information found here.

Some of the databases of funders require paid subscriptions or are free only to members of certain organizations. However, there are two important free sources to consider: the IRS and Foundation Center.

INTERNAL REVENUE SERVICE FORMS

Foundations are required to file information about their giving annually with the Internal Revenue Service. These required forms, called the IRS 990 Form, are excellent sources for verifying grant-giving organizations. Several sites, including the nonprofit Foundation Center (see below), provide free access to these IRS forms.

FOUNDATION CENTER'S COOPERATING COLLECTIONS

The nonprofit Foundation Center (www.foundationcenter .org) is an invaluable, free resource for grant seekers. Grant seekers can visit any of the organization's five comprehensive Library/Learning Centers or four hundred Cooperating Collections spread across the country—and the world—to conduct their grant research free of charge. At these locations, free online access is provided to two of the organization's comprehensive paid databases: Foundation Directory Online and Foundation Grants to Individuals Online. A list of these locations, which are usually located in libraries, community foundations, and educational institutions, can be found on the Foundation Center website. Along with free online access, these sites also provide collections of print resources and directories that will be helpful to all types of grant seekers.

Ready, Set, Begin

Once you have gone through the processes listed above to become grant-ready, have identified and verified potential sources, you will be ready to begin your grant search in earnest. Give yourself lots of space, time, and caffeinated beverages. Here's wishing you and your team luck as you search for library grant money.

HOW TO USE THIS BOOK

The *ALA Book of Library Grant Money*, ninth edition, is intended to provide the most likely funding sources for libraries. Here librarians, fund-raisers, and researchers will find quick, convenient access to information on the major US funding organizations supporting libraries. The indexes at the end of the book provide several methods to identify sources. As was mentioned previously, once a funding source is identified, the grant seeker is encouraged to verify details about funding opportunities before launching into crafting a grant request. Among the US philanthropic programs included are private foundations, corporate foundations, corporate direct givers, government agencies, library and nonprofit organizations.

Inclusion Criteria

All of the funders in this directory have either made grants to libraries within the last few reporting periods or have listed libraries as a possible recipient category. For foundation sources to be included in this edition, they must have given out at least $5,000 in grants per year or have assets of at least $100,000. The source must have given to libraries, expressed an interest in giving in libraries, or be included in databases or directories of library grant providers.

Excluded from these listing are sources that do not accept unsolicited grant requests or only give to preselected recipients. However, funders that have given to or indicated an interest in libraries in the past, but are currently not accepting applications, have been included with such information noted.

Also excluded are funders or organizations that primarily offer awards, prizes, or scholarships, rather than grants for which libraries could apply.

METHOD OF COMPILATION

More than two years of research has gone into the compilation of this resource. Data has been gathered from a myriad of sources. Among the major sources used to identify granting sources have been: the granting sources' websites, US government agencies, foundation databases, grants databases, nonprofit organizations, library publications, and publicly available IRS 990 forms.

DATA ELEMENTS

Among the types of funders are private foundations, corporate foundations, corporate direct givers, library and nonprofit organizations, and government agencies. Because the giving program of each type of giver differs, the specific information in each profile is not the same. As much as possible, each entry includes the pertinent information a grant seeker would need to begin researching the potential funder.

Whenever available, the following elements have been included for each funder:

Name

Address

Phone

Contact(s)

E-mail

Website

Type of Grant Maker

Founded (for Foundations)

Operating Locations/Geographic Preferences

Corporate Foundation Information (for Corporate Foundations)

Financial Summary

Grant Types

Typical Recipients/Subjects of Interest

Past Grant Recipients

Requirements and Restrictions

Application Procedures

Deadlines

Name

The main profile section is arranged alphabetically by the name of the funding source. Whenever possible, the last name of the funder is used. For instance, the Eli and Edythe Broad Foundation is listed under Broad. Corporate entries are listed under the name of the company and government sources appear under the name of the agency. A funding source that is a place name, such as the Community Foundation of Broward, is listed as Broward, Community Foundation. Grants given by units of the American Library Association will be found under American Library Association, arranged by giving unit.

For corporation names and corporate foundations that are personal names, the user is advised to locate the company by surname. For instance, J. C. Penney Company Fund is listed under Penney, J. C. Professional grants available from state library associations can be found alphabetically under the name of the state.

Address, Phone, Contacts

When available, the physical location of the funding source, phone number, and key contacts are provided for each funding source. Several foundations are so small they do not provide a mailing address, but only provide online information. Others list only a post office box address or bank contact, with no website or phone number given.

E-mail

When available, the e-mail addresses are provided for the key contact or granting source in general.

Website

Website addresses are provided both for the funding source and any grant-specific information. This vital source should be consulted before any further grant preparation is begun.

Type of Grant Maker

Each funding source is categorized as one of the following:

Foundation (meaning an independent foundation)

Community Foundation (supporting a limited area)

Corporate Foundation (sponsored by a commercial venture)

Corporation (for corporate givers providing support directly from the company rather than through a Corporate Foundation)

Government (for grants given by a governmental agency)

Library or Nonprofit Organization

Founded

The year founded is provided for foundations since the longevity of the granter may be helpful in assessing the potential funder.

Operating Locations/Geographic Preferences

Geographic restrictions are among the most important information provided. Companies frequently elect to support projects in the areas in which they do business. Community foundations only support the local area and many foundations frequently limit giving to one location, state, or region.

Corporate Foundation Information

Some companies establish a foundation through which they funnel charitable contributions. Background information on these types of funders is provided here.

Financial Summary

The synopsis of financial data for foundations includes the organization's assets and total giving. When available, the number of grants given and ranges of these awards are provided.

Grant Types

The types of support that most libraries seek through grants are program development or seed money (to begin a new project), continuing, operating, or general support (which is just plain old unrestricted money). Therefore, this information is included first. Granting sources that provide money for building or renovation, investment, or loans are also included when provided, as well as those that will fund capital campaigns or matching grants. Other types of support that are not as relevant to libraries, such as research or scholarships, have usually been omitted.

Typical Recipients/Subjects of Interest

Many funding sources, especially the larger foundations, identify specific social problems or priorities for giving. These topics are listed, along with any other overriding interests stated by the funder.

Past Grant Recipients

A sampling of representative grants issued by the organization is provided. Examples chosen for inclusion are intended to provide libraries with an understanding of the grant size, subject, and typical recipients. Whenever possible, grant projects that bear some similarity to library service are included. For instance, prior giving to a museum or historical society may indicate a predisposition to support library service. Projects that funded community services or children's or senior programs could be seen as likely sources for a public or school library request.

Requirements and Restrictions

Many funding sources state the types of projects they will not support, such as scholarship, religious institutions, political causes, or research. Major exclusions such as these are listed, but libraries are encouraged to research each giver for specific limitations currently in place.

Application Procedures

The key elements of the application process are provided, with a listing of the types of information that may be required for requests. However, as with all of the information above, additional sources should be checked— and rechecked—before any grant proposals are submitted.

Deadlines

When available, applicable deadlines for grant submissions have been included.

PROFILES

Abbott Fund

Headquarters

100 Abbott Park Rd., D379/AP6D
Abbott Park, IL 60064-3500
Phone: 847-937-7075
www.abbottfund.org
Contact: Cindy Schwab
E-mail: cindy.schwab@abbott.com
Type of Grant Maker: Corporate Foundation

Description

Founded: 1951

Operating Locations/Geographic Preferences: Giving on a national and international basis in areas of company operations, with emphasis on AR, CA, CT, Washington, DC, IL, IN, MA, NH, NY, OH, OR, PR, TX, VA, Afghanistan, Africa, Haiti, India, Kenya, and Tanzania; giving also to national and international organizations.

Corporate Foundation Information: Corporate foundation of Abbott Laboratories

Financial Summary

Assets: $205,032,015
Total Giving: $26,211,738
Grant Ranges: $2,770,000–$1,000

Grants Information

GRANT TYPES

General, operating and continuing support, building and renovation, program development, matching, management development, sponsorships

TYPICAL RECIPIENTS/SUBJECTS OF INTEREST

Education, health organizations, science, international/ foreign affairs, human services

PAST GRANT RECIPIENTS

Library or School Related

- Imperial Library Foundation, Imperial (NE), $25,000, general support
- Baylor College of Medicine International Pediatric AIDS Initiative, Houston (TX), BIPAI Network Partnership, $2,770,000

General

- Project HOPE—The People-to-People Health Foundation, Millwood (VA), AFI Nutrition, $841,600
- Art Institute of Chicago, Chicago (IL), Modern Wing, $750,000
- Kohl Children's Museum of Greater Chicago, Glenview (IL), for Science Focused Traveling Exhibit, $600,000.

REQUIREMENTS AND RESTRICTIONS

Abbott Fund giving has 3 components: Community Vitality, Science Education, and Improving Access to Health Care. Libraries, universities, museums and health and human welfare organizations are included in the first component.

Abbott Fund is not currently accepting unsolicited grant applications.

However, at certain times unsolicited applications are accepted for grants relating to community health and well-being, science education and community outreach. Future opportunities will be posted on this website.

During periods when the Abbott Fund is accepting unsolicited grant applications as specified above, requests must be made online. See the website for details.

APPLICATION PROCEDURES

See website for eligibility test and submission guidelines

Deadlines: See website

Abbott Laboratories

See Abbott Fund

ACHELIS FOUNDATION

767 3rd Ave., 4th Fl.
New York, NY 10017-9029
Phone: 212-644-0322

www.achelis-bodman-fnds.org

Contact: John B. Krieger, Secy. and Exec. Dir.; Carmel Mazzola

E-mail: main@achelis-bodman-fnds.org

Type of Grant Maker: Foundation

Description

Founded: 1940

Operating Locations/Geographic Preferences: Giving primarily in the New York, NY area

Financial Summary

Assets: $37,602,002
Total Giving: $1,400,600
Number of Grants: 48
Grant ranges: $100,000–$400

Grants Information

GRANT TYPES

General support, program development, matching

TYPICAL RECIPIENTS

Children/youth services, education, economically disadvantaged, health care

PAST GRANT RECIPIENTS

Library or School Related

- New York Society Library, Edith Wharton Exhibition, $15,000
- Pierport Morgan Library, General Operating Support, $25,000
- New York Academy of Medicine Library, GIRLS (Get Into Real Life Science) Project

General

- Wildlife Conservation Society, Oceans Wonders, $250,000

REQUIREMENTS AND RESTRICTIONS

Generally, no support for political organizations, small art, dance, music, or theater groups, national health or mental health organizations, housing, international projects, government agencies, public schools (except charter schools), or nonprofit programs and services significantly funded or wholly reimbursed by the government. No grants to individuals, or for annual appeals, dinner functions, fund-raising events, capital campaigns, deficit financing, or film or travel

APPLICATION PROCEDURES

Do not send CDs, DVDs, discs or tapes, or proposals; see website for application guidelines and procedures.

Applicants should submit the following:

1. Timetable for implementation and evaluation of project
2. Results expected from proposed grant
3. Copy of IRS Determination Letter
4. Copy of most recent' annual report/audited financial statement/990
5. How project's results will be evaluated or measured
6. Listing of board of directors, trustees, officers and other key people and their affiliations
7. Detailed description of project and amount of funding requested
8. Copy of current year's organizational budget and/or project budget

ADC Foundation

See TE Foundation

ADOBE FOUNDATION

625 Townsend
San Francisco, CA 94103
Phone: 408-536-3993

www.adobe.com/aboutadobe/philanthropy/
commgivingprgm.html

Does not accept applications. Only contributes to preslected organizations.

AEGON TRANSAMERICA FOUNDATION

4333 Edgewood Rd., N.E.
Cedar Rapids, IA 52499-3210
Phone: 319-355-8511

www.aegonins.com/AEGONTransamericaFoundation.aspx

E-mail: shaegontransfound@aegonusa.com

Type of Grant Maker: Corporate Foundation

Description

Founded: 1994

Operating Locations/Geographic Preferences: Primarily in areas of company operations, with emphasis on Little Rock, AR, Los Angeles, CA, St. Petersburg, FL, Atlanta, GA, Cedar Rapids, IA, Louisville, KY, Baltimore, MD, Harrison, NY, Exton, PA, Bedford and Plano, TX.

Corporate Foundation Information: Corporate foundation for AEGON USA, Inc., Life Investors Insurance Co. of America, Transamerica Financial Life Insurance Co.

Financial Summary

Assets: $116,259,265
Total Giving: $5,416,302
Number of Grants: 327
Grant Ranges: $500,000–$100

Grants Information

GRANT TYPES

Program development, general support, building/renovation

TYPICAL RECIPIENTS/SUBJECTS OF INTEREST

Arts and culture, civic and community, education and literacy, health and welfare. Special emphasis on programs to promote financial literacy, financial security, and financial education

PAST GRANT RECIPIENTS

Library or School Related

- Enoch Pratt Free Library of Baltimore City, Baltimore (MD), general support, $10,000
- National Czech and Slovak Museum and Library, Cedar Rapids (IA), general support, $100,000

General

- University of Iowa Foundation, Iowa City (IA), general support, $500,000
- United Way of East Central Iowa, Cedar Rapids (IA), general support, $225,000

REQUIREMENTS AND RESTRICTIONS

No support for athletes or athletic organizations, fraternal organizations, political parties or candidates, religious or social organizations. No grants to individuals, or conference, seminars, or trips, courtesy or goodwill advertising, fellowships, K–12 school fund-raisers or events, or political campaigns.

APPLICATION PROCEDURES

Visit website for company facility addresses. Applicants should submit the following:

1. Name, address and phone number of organization
2. Contact person
3. Detailed description of project and amount of funding requested
4. Copy of IRS Determination Letter
5. Brief history of organization and description of its mission
6. Listing of board of directors, trustees, officers and other key people and their affiliations
7. Copy of most recent annual report/audited financial statement/990
8. Statement of problem project will address
9. Population served
10. Qualifications of key personnel

11. How project's results will be evaluated or measured
12. Copy of current year's organizational budget and/or project budget
13. How project will be sustained once grant-maker support is completed
14. Listing of additional sources and amount of support
15. Plans for cooperation with other organizations, if any

AHMANSON FOUNDATION

9215 Wilshire Blvd.
Beverly Hills, CA 90210-5501
Phone 310-278-0770

www.theahmansonfoundation.org

Contact: Yvonne deBeixedon, Grants Admin.

E-mail: info@theahmansonfoundation.org

Type of Grant Maker: Foundation

Description

Founded: 1952

Operating Locations/Geographic Preferences: Giving primarily in southern CA, with emphasis on the Los Angeles area

Financial Summary

Assets: $948,985,204
Total Giving: $43,419,929
Number of Grants: 546
Grant Ranges: $2,000,000–$1,000; average: $75,000–$1,000,000

Grants Information

GRANT TYPES

General support, building/renovation, land acquisition

TYPICAL RECIPIENTS/SUBJECTS OF INTEREST

Emphasis on education at all levels, libraries, museums, the arts and humanities, health and medicine, and a broad range of human service programs. Adult education, including literacy and basic skills, education, reading; elementary school/education; health care; children/young adults

PAST GRANT RECIPIENTS

Library or School Related

- Independent School Alliance for Minority Affairs, Los Angeles (CA), minority student placement program, $35,000

General

- Teach for America, New York (NY).
- Los Angeles Corps Program, $250,000
- Boys and Girls Club of Hollywood, Hollywood (CA). Repairs to roof and renovation, $70,000
- Great Beginnings for Black Babies, Inglewood (CA). Relocation expenses, $50,000

REQUIREMENT AND RESTRICTIONS

No support for religious organizations for sectarian purposes, or advocacy or political organizations. No grants to individuals, or generally for continuing support, endowed chairs, annual campaigns, deficit financing, professorships, internships, film production, media projects, general research and development, workshops, studies, surveys, operational support of regional and national charities, underwriting, or exchange programs.

APPLICATION PROCEDURES

Submission Guidelines: Fax or e-mail requests not accepted. Application form not required. Applicants should submit:

1. Signature and title of chief executive officer
2. Brief history of organization and description of its mission
3. Descriptive literature about organization
4. Detailed description of project and amount of funding requested
5. Copy of current year's organizational budget and/or project budget

Deadlines: None

Air Products and Chemicals, Inc.

Headquarters

Corporate Giving Program
7201 Hamilton Blvd.
Allentown, PA 18195-1501
Phone: 610-481-4911

www.airproducts.com/social_responsibilities

Contact: Laurie Gostley-Hackett, Mgr., Community Rels. and Philanthropy

E-mail: gostlelj@airproducts.com

Type of Grant Maker: Corporation

Description

Founded: 1940

Operating Locations/Geographic Preferences: Giving primarily in areas of company operations and Allentown, PA

Corporate Information: In addition to its foundation (see Air Products Foundation) company also makes charitable contributions to nonprofit organizations directly.

Financial Summary

N/A

Grants Information

GRANT TYPES

Program development, matching, general and operating support, volunteering, donated equipment

TYPICAL RECIPIENTS/SUBJECTS OF INTEREST

Education (including higher education), arts, economic development, human services

APPLICATION PROCEDURES

Contact Corporate Relations Department at headquarters or nearest company facilities for giving procedures

Deadlines: none

AIR PRODUCTS FOUNDATION

7201 Hamilton Blvd.
Allentown, PA 18195
Phone: 610-481-4911

www.airproducts.com/company/Sustainability/
corporate-citizenship.aspx

Contact: Timothy J. Hold, Pres.

E-mail: corprela@airproducts.com

Type of Grant Maker: Corporate Foundation

Description

Founded: 1979

Operating Locations/Geographic Preferences: Giving on a national basis in areas of company operations.

Corporate Foundation Information: Corporate foundation of Air Products and Chemicals, Inc. (see listing)

Financial Summary

Assets: $63,190,460
Total Giving: $3,770,653

Grants Information

GRANT TYPES

General and operating support, annual campaigns, matching

TYPICAL RECIPIENTS/SUBJECTS OF INTEREST

Education, arts and culture, environment, health, safety and sustainability, human services and community development

PAST GRANT RECIPIENTS

General

- United Way, $25,000
- American Red Cross, Washington, DC, $25,000

REQUIREMENTS AND RESTRICTIONS

Applicants must have tax-exempt status. No grants to individuals, sectarian or denominational organizations, political organizations, veterans organizations, service clubs, or labor groups.

APPLICATION PROCEDURES

Application form not required. See website for details.

Deadlines: May 15

AKC Fund

Headquarters

6 W. 48th St., 10th fl.
New York, NY 10038
Phone: 212-812-4362
Fax: 212-812-4395

Currently supporting trustee-sponsored projects only. Unsolicited requests for funds not accepted.

Alaska State Library

Headquarters

PO Box 110571
333 Willoughby Avenue, 8th floor
Juneau, AK 99811-0571
Phone: 907-465-2920
Fax: 907-465-2151

www.library.state.ak.us

E-mail: asl@alaska.gov or asl.historical@alaska.gov

Type of Grant Maker: Government

Description

PUBLIC LIBRARY ASSISTANCE GRANTS

Alaska public libraries and combined school public libraries may apply for the Public Library Assistance grant each year. In order to receive this grant, the library must continue to meet a variety of ongoing eligibility requirements. Grant funds may be used to pay staff, purchase library materials, or pay for any other daily operating cost of the library.

INTERLIBRARY COOPERATION GRANTS

Each year, the State Library funds a limited number of grants which have statewide significance or direct impact on library users. Libraries of all types are encouraged to submit applications for interlibrary cooperation grants. Grants have been awarded for a wide variety of projects, such as reading incentive programs, automation projects, computers and printers for public use, and the development of special programs for patrons. To see the broad range of grants awarded in recent years, please look at the summaries of interlibrary cooperation, regional services, and netlender reimbursement grants.

CONTINUING EDUCATION GRANTS

In order to help public libraries meet the continuing education requirement for the Public Library Assistance Grant, the State Library encourages staff in public or combined school public libraries to apply for continuing education grants, an ongoing grant program that reimburses the cost of training. Every library director must attend at least 6 hours of training once every two years

for her library to remain eligible for the public library assistance grant. Public libraries that are currently receiving the Public Library Assistance Grant program may apply for financial assistance for two events, conferences, or courses per fiscal year. The proposed CE opportunities must be approved in advance by the State Library Continuing Education Coordinator. Actual costs, not to exceed $1,000 for in-state training and $1,500 for out-of-state training, will be reimbursed.

REQUIREMENT AND RESTRICTIONS

Vary according to program

APPLICATION PROCEDURES

See website

Deadlines: April

Alcoa Foundation

Headquarters

Alcoa Corporate Ctr.
201 Isabella St.
Pittsburgh, PA 15212-5858
Phone: 412-553-2348

www.alcoa.com/global/en/community/foundation.asp

E-mail: alcoafoundation@alcoa.com

Type of Grant Maker: Corporate Foundation

Description

Founded: 1952

Operating Locations/Geographic Preferences: Giving on a national and international basis in areas of company operations, with emphasis on New York, NY, Pittsburgh, PA, Africa, Asia, Australia, Canada, Caribbean, Central America, Europe, Mexico, and South America.

Corporate Foundation Information: Supported by Aluminum Co. of America and Alcoa Inc. (see listing)

Financial Summary

Assets: $435,170,273
Total Giving: $16,222,038
Number of Grants: 1,057
Grant Ranges: $778,404–$100

Grants Information

GRANT TYPES

Program development, annual campaigns, building and renovation, continuing support, matching, sponsorships, employee volunteering

TYPICAL RECIPIENTS/SUBJECTS OF INTEREST

Education, the environment and sustainable design

GIVING PROGRAMS INCLUDE

Education

With special emphasis on education, training programs, and teaching in the areas of science, technology, engineering, and math; environment, including environmental awareness.

Empowerment

To develop life and professional skills in youth and promote self-sufficiency and sustainable livelihood, with special emphasis on programs designed to increase diversity by engaging girls, women, and other underrepresented groups.

Advancing Sustainability Research Initiative

With special emphasis on research focusing on energy and environmental economics; materials science and engineering; natural resource management; and sustainable design.

Alcoa Global Service Leaders Scholarship

Alcoa Sons and Daughters Scholarship Program

Alcoans Coming Together In Our Neighborhoods (ACTION)

Providing grants of up to $3,000 to nonprofit organizations with which a team of five or more employees of Alcoa volunteers at least 4 hours on a community service project.

Bravo!

Awarding $250 grants to nonprofit organizations and non-governmental organizations with which employees of Alcoa volunteer at least 50 hours.

PAST GRANT RECIPIENTS

Library or School Related

- City Year, Boston (MA). For South Bronx Team Sponsorship Program, $225,000

General

- American Association of University Women, Torrance (CA). For Tech Trek Science Camp for Girls, $22,500

- Change the Equation, Washington, DC. For Change the Equation, Science, Technology, Engineering and Mathematics (STEM) program, $75,000

REQUIREMENTS AND RESTRICTIONS

No support for political or lobbying organizations, sectarian or religious organizations not of direct benefit to the entire community, private foundations, or trust funds. No grants to individuals or for endowments, capital campaigns, debt reduction, or general operating support, fund-raising events or sponsorships, trips, conferences, seminars, festivals, one-day events, documentaries, videos, or research projects/programs, or indirect or overhead costs.

APPLICATION PROCEDURES

Submit proposal to nearest company facility

Deadlines: Contact nearest company facility

ALCOA, INC.

Corporate Contributions Program
Corporate Center
390 Park Ave.
New York, NY 10022-4608
Phone: 212-836-2600

www.alcoa.com/global/en/community/foundation

Type of Grant Maker: Corporation

Description

Founded: 1888

Corporate Information: In addition to its foundation (see Alcoa Foundation), company also makes charitable contributions to nonprofit organization directly.

Operating Locations/Geographic Preferences: Given on a national and international basis in areas of company operations.

Financial Summary

Total Giving: $16,889,826

Grants Information

GRANT TYPES

General and operating support

TYPICAL RECIPIENTS/SUBJECTS OF INTEREST

Education, economic and community development, environment

APPLICATION PROCEDURES AND DEADLINES

Contact nearest company location through website:
www.alcoa.com/global/en/about_alcoa/map/globalmap
.asp?lc=16&country=United_States

Aldridge, Tom S. and Marye Kate Charitable & Educational Trust

Headquarters

3035 N.W. 63rd St., Ste. 207N
Oklahoma City, OK 73116-3606

www.aldridgefoundation.org

Contact: Robert S. Aldridge, Dir.

E-mail: aldro@accessacg.net

Type of Grant Maker: Foundation

Description

Founded: 1995

Operating Locations/Geographic Preferences: Giving primarily in Escambia and Santa Rosa counties, FL, Pottawatomie, Grady, Oklahoma and Cleveland counties, OK, and Hunt, Raines and Brazoria counties, TX.

Financial Summary

Assets: $3,308,555
Total Giving: $86,700

Grants Information

GRANT TYPES

Matching, continuing support

TYPICAL RECIPIENTS/SUBJECTS OF INTEREST

Education and child development

PAST GRANT RECIPIENTS

Library or School Related

- Lone Oak Library, $10,000, continuing support

General

- Selmon living lab, furniture, $1,000
- UCO Dancing with Downs, $2,000

REQUIREMENTS AND RESTRICTIONS

No grants to individuals, or for construction or repairs, retirement of debt, day to day operations, or fund-raising activities.

APPLICATION PROCEDURES

Agencies requesting a grant should submit a concept letter in duplicate no later than April 30. This concept letter of two typewritten pages or less must include:

- Verification of 501(c)(3) status
- Purpose and goals
- Number of persons to benefit
- Name and qualifications of person(s) responsible
- Amount requested to fund program
- Matching funds and their source
- A program evaluation guideline

After review, agency may be asked to submit full proposal.

Deadline: April 30

Alexander, Joseph Foundation, Inc.

Headquarters

110 E. 59th St.
New York, NY 10022-1304

Contact: Robert Weintraub, Pres.

Type of Grant Maker: Foundation

Description

Founded: 1960

Operating Locations/Geographic Preferences: Giving primarily in New York, NY

Financial Summary

Assets: $14,595,577
Total Giving: $679,500

Grants Information

GRANT TYPES

Program development, annual and capital campaigns, general and operating support, building and renovation

TYPICAL RECIPIENTS/SUBJECTS OF INTEREST

Higher education, health organizations and medical research, optic nerve research, social services, and Jewish organizations.

PAST GRANT RECIPIENTS

Library or School Related

- Albert Einstein College of Medicine of Yeshiva University, Bronx (NY), $25,000

General

- Jewish Museum, New York (NY), $15,000
- International Center of Photography, New York (NY), $5,000

REQUIREMENTS AND RESTRICTIONS

None listed.

APPLICATION PROCEDURES

Send letter requesting application guidelines.

Deadlines: None

Allegheny Foundation

Headquarters

1 Oxford Ctr.
301 Grant St., Ste. 3900
Pittsburgh, PA 15219-6401
Phone: 412-392-2900

www.scaife.com/alleghen.html

Contact: Matthew A. Groll, Exec. Dir.

Type of Grant Maker: Foundation

Description

Founded: 1953

Operating Locations/Geographic Preferences: Giving primarily in western PA, with emphasis on Pittsburgh

Financial Summary

Assets: $49,479,642
Total Giving: $5,284,000
Number of Grants: 54
Grant Ranges: $1,250,000–$4,500

Grants Information

GRANT TYPES

Program development, general and operating support, seed money

TYPICAL RECIPIENTS/SUBJECTS OF INTEREST

Historic preservation, education, and community development.

PAST GRANT RECIPIENTS

General

- Westmoreland Museum of American Art, Greensburg (PA). For general operating support, $150,000
- Pittsburgh History and Landmarks Foundation, Pittsburgh (PA). For program support, $500,000
- River City Brass Band, Pittsburgh (PA). For general operating support, $50,000
- Commonwealth Education Organization, Pittsburgh (PA). For program support, $25,000

REQUIREMENTS AND RESTRICTIONS

No grants to individuals, or for endowment funds, event sponsorship, capital campaigns, renovations, government agencies, scholarships, fellowships, or loans.

APPLICATION PROCEDURES

Initial inquiries to the Foundation should be in letter form signed by the organization's President, or authorized representative, and have the approval of the Board of Directors. The letter should include a concise description of the specific program for which funds are requested. Additional information must include a budget for the program and for the organization, the latest audited financial statement and annual report. A copy of the organization's current ruling letter evidencing tax exemption under Section 501(c)(3) of the Internal Revenue Service Code is required. Additional information may be requested if needed for further evaluation.

Grant application letters should be addressed to:

Mr. Matthew A. Groll
Executive Director
Allegheny Foundation

One Oxford Centre
301 Grant St., Suite 3900
Pittsburgh, PA 15219-6401

Deadlines: None

Allen Foundation (Paul G. Family)

Headquarters

505 5th Ave., S., Suite 900
Seattle, WA 98104-3821
Phone: 206-342-2039

Pgafamilyfoundation.org

Contact: Lisa Arnold, Grants Manager

E-mail: info@pgafmilyfoundation.org

Type of Grant Maker: Foundation

Description

Founded: 2005

Operating Locations/Geographic Preferences: Pacific Northwest, including AK, ID, MT, OR and WA

Financial Summary

Assets: $17,000,000
Total Giving: $14,690,000
Number of Grants: 200
Grant Range: $1,000,000–$100; Average
    $200,000–$45,000

Grants Information

GRANT TYPES

Program development, building/renovation, capital campaign

TYPICAL RECIPIENTS/SUBJECTS OF INTEREST

Strengthen the role of public libraries in connecting people to information, help librarians increase use of public library services and cultivate interest in book-centered programs

PAST GRANT RECIPIENTS

Library or School Related

- Univ. of Washington, Asset-building programs, $300,000

General

- Idaho Foodbank Warehouse, Building project, $230,000
- Boise Art Museum, Exhibition, $40,000

REQUIREMENTS AND RESTRICTIONS

Application is by invitation only. However, organizations are encouraged to contact the foundation website to see if their projects are within the parameters of the foundation.

ALLIANT ENERGY FOUNDATION, INC. (SEE ALSO ALLIANT ENERGY CORP.)

4902 N. Biltmore Ln., Ste. 1000
Madison, WI 53707-1007
Phone: 608-458-4483

www.alliantenergy.com/Community/
    CharitableFoundation/index.htm

Contact: Julie Bauer, Exec. Dir.

E-mail: foundation@alliantenergy.com

Type of Grant Maker: Corporate Foundation

Description

Founded: 1984

Operating Locations/Geographic Preferences: Giving limited to areas of company operations in IA, MN, and WI.

Corporate Foundation Information: Supported by Alliant Entergy Corp., Wisconsin Power and Light Co. and Interstate Power and Light Co.

Financial Summary

Assets: $17,141,338
Total Giving: $3,224,240

Grants Information

GRANT TYPES

Program development, annual campaigns, building and renovation, continuing support, matching, employee volunteering, seed money

TYPICAL RECIPIENTS/SUBJECTS OF INTEREST

Civic, culture and art, education, community development, environment, and human needs.

PAST GRANT RECIPIENTS

Library or School Related

- Iowa Public Television Foundation's Reading Road Trip, $10,000
- University of Iowa Foundation, Iowa City (IA), $400,000
- University of Wisconsin System, Madison (WI), $400,000
- Iowa College Foundation, Des Moines (IA), $100,000

REQUIREMENTS AND RESTRICTIONS

No support for athletes or teams, fraternal or social clubs, third-party funding groups, religious organizations not of direct benefit to the entire community, or discriminatory organizations. No grants to individuals (except for scholarships), or for advertising, door prizes, raffle tickets, dinner tables, golf outings or sponsorships of organized sports teams or activities; sporting events or tournaments, endowments, registration fees for fund-raising events, books, magazines or professional journal articles, political activities, salaries, facilities costs or general operating expenses, capital campaigns, or "bricks and mortar" projects.

APPLICATION PROCEDURES

See website for online eligibility quiz and application forms and information

Deadlines: Jan. 15, May 15, and Sept. 15 for Community Grants; Dec. 23 to Feb. 15 for Community Service Scholarships; None for Hometown Challenge Grant

Altman Foundation

Headquarters

521 5th Ave., 35th Floor
New York, NY 10175-3599
Phone: 212-682-0970

www.altmanfoundation.org

Contact: Karen L. Rosa, V.P. and Exec. Dir

E-mail: info@altman.org

Type of Grant Maker: Foundation

Description

Founded: 1913

Operating Locations/Geographic Preferences: NY state, especially boroughs of New York City

Financial Summary

Assets: $245,000,000
Total Giving: $11,000,000
Number of Grants: 160
Grant Ranges: $275,000–$5,000; average $25,000–$250,000

Grants Information

GRANT TYPES

Program development, capacity building, investments/loans

TYPICAL RECIPIENTS/SUBJECTS OF INTEREST

Arts and Culture, education, health, strengthening communities, nonprofit services

PAST GRANT RECIPIENTS

Library or School Related

- Queens Borough Public Library, Language Instruction, Family Literacy, Youth Workforce, $450,000
- Literacy Assistance Center, Health Family Initiative, $237,500

General

- Cooper-Hewitt Museum, design education, $170,000

REQUIREMENTS AND RESTRICTIONS

No grants to individuals, building funds, capital equipment, galas or fund-raising events

APPLICATION PROCEDURES

No applications via e-mail or in person. Applicants should submit:

1. Copy of IRS determination letter
2. Copy of annual report/audited statement
3. List of board of directors
4. Current year budget or project budget
5. Additional sources of support

Deadlines: None

Amado, Maurice Foundation

Headquarters

3940 Laurel Canyon Blvd., No. 809
Studio City, CA 91604-3709
Phone: 818-980-9190

www.mauriceamadofdn.org

Contact: Pam Kaizer, Exec. Dir.

E-mail: pkaizer@mauriceamadofdn.org

Type of Grant Maker: Foundation

Description

Founded: 1961

Operating Locations/Geographic Preferences: None listed

Financial Summary

Assets: $25,755,503
Total Giving: $1,115,000
Number of Grants: 51
Grant Ranges: $426,000–$1,000

Grants Information

GRANT TYPES

Program development, continuing, general and operating support

TYPICAL RECIPIENTS/SUBJECTS OF INTEREST

Education and activities that promote Sephardic Jewish culture and heritage.

PAST GRANT RECIPIENTS

Library or School Related

- Stanford University Library, for the purchase of the Rifat Bali collection of 20th-century Sephardic Judaica published in Turkey, consisting of 700 monographic and serial titles, mostly in Turkish but also in French, English, Hebrew and Judeo-Spanish.
- University of Southern California, Los Angeles (CA), $12,000
- Brooklyn Kindergarten Society, Brooklyn (NY), $10,000

General

- Center for Jewish History, New York (NY), $50,000
- Jewish Community Center of Houston, Houston (TX), $80,000

REQUIREMENTS AND RESTRICTIONS

No grants to individuals. Grants are made only to qualified tax-exempt 501(c)(3) organizations.

APPLICATION PROCEDURES

Applicants should send an initial e-mail letter of inquiry to the Foundation at inquiry@mauriceamadofdn.org. This e-mail should include:

1. Background and purpose of your organization
2. Short description of the specific program or project for which the organization is requesting funds
3. Dollar amount of the request
4. The subject line of the e-mail should read: "Grant Inquiry"

If the Foundation is interested in your project, you will be sent instructions on how to submit a grant proposal.

PROGRAM/PROJECT DESCRIPTION

If requesting support for a project or program the following is also required:

1. Project goals
2. Description of specific project activities
3. Intended audience
4. Timeline
5. Project budget
6. Staff and their qualifications
7. Evaluation plan

Deadlines: March 15, August 31

American Association of Law Libraries

Headquarters

105 W. Adams St., Suite 3300
Chicago, IL 60603
Phone: 312-939-4764
Fax: 312-431-1097

www.aallnet.org/main-menu/Member-Resources/grants

E-mail: support@aall.org

Type of Grant Maker: Library Organization

Description

AALL ANNUAL MEETING/ WORKSHOP GRANTS

The AALL Grants Program provides financial assistance to experienced law librarians who are actively involved in AALL or its chapters and to newer law librarians or graduate students who hold promise of future involvement in AALL and the law library profession. Funds are provided by AALL, AALL individual members, and vendors.

Grants cover registration costs at either the Annual Meeting or workshops associated with the Annual Meeting. Individuals eligible for the Experienced Member Grant are active members with five or more years of AALL or AALL chapter membership. Individuals eligible for the Student/ New Member Grant are active members with less than five years of AALL or AALL chapter membership or student members of AALL or an AALL chapter.

QUALIFICATIONS

An applicant must meet all of the following criteria to be considered for the award:

- be a member or student member of AALL or an AALL chapter;
- not have received a grant in the past three years; and
- submit a timely and complete application.

*If circumstances prevent a recipient from using the grant, it reverts to the Committee; however, the recipient remains eligible to apply another year.

APPLICATION PROCEDURES

Submit one application package with the following items:

- a complete, legible application form;
- two letters of recommendation that comment on your potential to contribute to AALL and the field of law librarianship and address your need for the grant; and
- a current résumé is strongly suggested.
- Applications and letters of recommendation must be on 8 1/2" x 11" paper.

Send to:

Grants Committee Chair
American Association of Law Libraries
105 W. Adams St., Suite 3300
Chicago, IL 60603

Deadline: April 1

AALL/BLOOMBERG CONTINUING EDUCATION GRANTS PROGRAM

The purpose of the AALL/Bloomberg Continuing Education Grants Program (CEGP) is to encourage program development and promote sharing among AALL entities.

The AALL/Bloomberg grants program is open to AALL HQ, chapters, SISs, member institutions, caucuses, and individual AALL members. The grants can assist in providing ongoing quality continuing education programming outside of the AALL annual meeting. These programs that are supported by the grant must be able to be distributed to a wider audience. The grant can assist program content (speakers, venue, etc.) or the method of a wider distribution (podcast, webinar, etc.). The grant funds cannot be used for food, gifts or purchases not related to the actual program.

APPLICATION PROCEDURES

Apply online.

Deadlines: vary

MINORITY LEADERSHIP DEVELOPMENT AWARD

Leadership Development Award was created in 2001 to nurture leaders for the future and to introduce minority law librarians to leadership opportunities within the Association. The Award shall consist of the following benefits: travel, lodging and registration expenses for one recipient to attend the Annual Meeting of AALL; an experienced AALL leader to serve as the recipient's mentor for at least one year; and an opportunity to serve on an AALL committee during the year following the monetary award.

Upon submission of the application, an applicant must meet all of the following criteria to be considered for the award:

- Be a member of a minority group as defined by current US government guidelines;
- Have a strong academic record and have earned a Master's degree in Library/Information Science;
- Have no more than 5 years of professional (post-MLS or post-JD) library or information service work experience;
- Be a current member of AALL at the time application is submitted;
- Have been a member of AALL for at least 2 years or have 2 years of full-time, professional law library work experience; and
- Demonstrate leadership potential.

APPLICATION PROCEDURES

Submit an application package containing:

- Completed application form.
- A current résumé or c.v.
- Three letters of recommendation from individuals who can evaluate your law library employment experience or relevant graduate education commenting on your present and potential contributions to AALL and the field of law librarianship.

- A brief essay on how belonging to a minority group has influenced your career to date and on how the profession benefits from encouraging the leadership development of law librarians from minority groups.
- A brief essay on what leadership means to you and how this grant will help you to realize your personal leadership goals.

Send package to address below:

> Chair, Committee on Diversity
> American Association of Law Libraries
> 105 W Adams St. Suite 3300
> Chicago, IL 60603

Deadline: April 1.

AALL RESEARCH FUND: AN ENDOWMENT ESTABLISHED BY LEXISNEXIS®

On July 17, 2000, the American Association of Law Libraries (AALL) announced the formation of the AALL Research Fund, an endowment established with a $100,000 pledge from LexisNexis®. The fund provides a secure financial base, enabling the AALL Research Committee to carry out the Association's Research Agenda. That agenda encompasses research in the major topic areas of provision of legal information services, law library collections, legal research, the profession of law librarianship, and law library administration.

The Research Fund provides grants to library professionals who seek to conduct research that is critical to the profession.

AALL/WOLTERS KLUWER LAW & BUSINESS GRANT PROGRAM

This grant was first established in 1996 as the AALL/ Aspen Law & Business Research Grant with a generous contribution of $50,000 from Aspen Law & Business to sponsor research that will have a practical impact on the law library profession and inspire products and changes in the marketplace. The grant was renamed the AALL/Wolters Kluwer Law & Business Grant Program in 2007.

APPLICATION PROCEDURES AND DEADLINES

See website

American Association of University Women

Headquarters

AAUW
1111 Sixteenth St. NW
Washington, DC 20036
Phone: 202-785-7700, 800-326-AAUW
www.aauw.org
E-mail: connect@aauw.org
Type of Grant Maker: Nonprofit Organization

Financial Summary

Total Giving: $225,000
Number of Grants: 27

Description

Community Action Grants provide seed money to women, AAUW branches, AAUW state organizations, and local community-based nonprofit organizations for innovative programs or nondegree research projects that promote education and equity for women and girls.

PAST GRANT RECIPIENTS

Library or School Related

- Agnes Scott College, for GEMS (Generating Excellence in Math and Science) program to encourage more women to pursue study and careers in math and science.
- Carthage College, Jeffery Elementary School of the Kenosha Unified School District.
- Kenosha Literacy Council to provide an instructional program to develop the mathematical problem-solving and 21st-century literacy skills of students at Carthage, Jeffery, and in the school district.
- Del Norte Schools, Del Norte (CO), for Science Ambassadors to encourage young women to pursue STEM careers.

REQUIREMENTS AND RESTRICTIONS

Recipients must be US citizens or permanent residents.

APPLICATION PROCEDURES AND DEADLINES

Available at: www.aauw.org/learn/fellowships_grants/index.cfm

American Library Association, Association for Library Collections and Technical Services (ALCTS)

Headquarters

50 E. Huron St.
Chicago IL 60611
Phone: 800-545-2433

www.ala.org/alcts/awards/grants/onlinegrant

Type of Grant Maker: Library Organization

Description

Online Course Grant for Library Professionals from Developing Countries

NUMBER OF GRANTS

1 free seat per ALCTS online continuing educational course session

REQUIREMENTS AND RESTRICTIONS

Available to librarians and information professionals from developing countries.
   Applicants must:

- Have a degree in library or information science (e.g., a 4-year undergraduate degree or a master's), or
   be enrolled in a library or information science
      program in a developing country, or
   be working as a librarian or information professional
      in a developing country.
- Be a legal national from a qualifying developing country.
- Have working knowledge of English.
- Have technical abilities to participate in an online course:
   Computer skills: be comfortable with Internet
      browsers such as Internet Explorer, Mozilla
      Firefox, etc.; a word processing program, such
      as Microsoft Word, Word Perfect, etc.; be able to
      send e-mails with attachments; copy and paste
      text; download and save a file, install a program or
      plug-in; quickly learn a new program using online
      tutorial or Help section;
   Regular unlimited access to a computer (at least a
      Pentium II-based PC or a G3 PowerMac machine;

A reliable high-speed Internet connection (Broadband
   or DSL, or at least 56k modem);
Antivirus software installed and kept up-to-date on a
   computer.
   Also look for technical requirements at course
   description as they may vary from course to
   course. Send e-mail to jreese@ala.org if you have
   any questions.
Financial need in assistance due to insufficient or lack
   of funding for professional development from your
   employer.
- Legal nationals from developing countries studying abroad are not eligible for this grant.

APPLICATION PROCEDURES

Registration for ALCTS grants will open after the annual schedule of courses becomes available. The IRC Committee creates the registration schedule and decides on the number of sessions open for simultaneous registration. Registration will stay open for at least 30 but no more than 45 days.

DEADLINES

For course sections beginning between February and August may be submitted between December 5 and January 6.

American Library Association, Association for Library Service to Children (ALSC)

Headquarters

50 E. Huron St.
Chicago, IL 60611-2795
Phone: 800-545-2433, x2163
Fax: 312-280-5271

www.ala.org/alsc

Type of Grant Maker: Library Organization

Grants Information

BOOKAPALOOZA PROGRAM

Number of Grants: 3
   Offers select libraries a collection of materials that will help transform their collection and provide the opportunity for these materials to be used in their community in creative and innovative ways.

Each year the ALSC office receives almost 3,000 newly published books, videos, audio books, and recordings from children's trade publishers. The materials are primarily for children age birth through fourteen and are submitted to ALSC award and media evaluation selection committees for award and notables consideration. After each ALA Midwinter Meeting in January, these materials (published in the preceding year) need to be removed from the ALSC office to make room for a new year of publications.

The Bookapalooza Program finds new homes for these materials. Libraries selected will receive a Bookapalooza collection of materials to be used in a way that creatively enhances their library service to children and families.

REQUIREMENTS AND RESTRICTIONS

- Applicants must be personal members of ALSC as well as ALA. Organizational members are not eligible.
- Libraries must be located in the United States.
- Libraries must work directly with children.
- All entries must include the application cover sheet, and information about the library as described in the How to Apply section below and in the application.
- The application must be signed by the director of the public library, the superintendent of schools, the building-level administrator, or the director of the institution.
- Applicants must agree to accept all the materials provided by the ALSC office, with the understanding that the collection of materials is targeted primarily for children age birth through fourteen and covers a wide range of formats including but not limited to picture books, early readers, nonfiction, and audiovisual material.
- Shipping and handling charges for shipment of the Bookapalooza collection are the responsibility of the libraries selected. For the purpose of estimating shipping costs, winning collections are anticipated to weigh as much as 600 pounds and include as many as 25 cartons. Shipping rates may range from $200–$500 when shipped at book rate

APPLICATION PROCEDURES

See website for application.

Deadline: December 1

LOUISE SEAMAN BECHTEL FELLOWSHIP

Grant Amount: $4,000
Number of grants: 1

Allows qualified children's librarian to spend a total of four weeks or more reading and studying at the Baldwin Library of the George A. Smathers Libraries, University of Florida, Gainesville. The Baldwin Library contains a special collection of 85,000 volumes of children's literature published mostly before 1950.

REQUIREMENTS AND RESTRICTIONS

Applicants must:

- Be personal members of ALSC as well as ALA; organizational members are not eligible
- Currently be working in direct service to children, or retired members who complete their careers in direct service to children, for a minimum of eight years
- Have a graduate degree from an ALA-accredited program
- Be willing to write a report about his/her study; the report will be submitted to the ALSC Office, for distribution to the Bechtel Committee and for possible inclusion in Children and Libraries, and to the Director of the Smathers Libraries and the Director of the Center for the Study of Children's Literature and Media at the University of Florida
- If selected, retired Fellowship winners would agree to present a minimum of three public programs based on their research project to librarians/teachers, children, or the general public

APPLICATION PROCEDURES

See website for online application.

Deadline: December 30

ALSC/BWI SUMMER READING PROGRAM GRANT

Grant Range: $3,000

To encourage reading programs for children in public libraries. Submit plan and outline submitted for a theme-based summer reading program in a public library. Innovative proposals involving children with physical or mental disabilities are encouraged.

REQUIREMENTS AND RESTRICTIONS

Applicants must:

- Be personal members of ALSC as well as ALA; organizational members are not eligible
- Submit program ideas that are open to all children (birth–14 years)
- Submit program ideas take place at a public library

APPLICATION PROCEDURES

See website for online application.

Deadline: December 1

ALSC/CANDLEWICK PRESS "LIGHT THE WAY" GRANT

Grant Range: $3,000

To assist a library in conducting exemplary outreach to underserved populations through a new program or an expansion of work already being done. Special population children may include those who have learning or physical differences, those who are speaking English as a second language, those who are in a nontraditional school environment, those who are in non-traditional family settings (such as teen parents, foster children, children in the juvenile justice system, and children in gay and lesbian families), and those who need accommodation services to meet their needs.

APPLICATION PROCEDURES

See website for online application

Deadline: November 15

MAUREEN HAYES AUTHOR/ ILLUSTRATOR AWARD

Grant Range: $4,000

To bring together children and nationally recognized authors/illustrators by funding an author/illustrator visit to a library.

REQUIREMENTS AND RESTRICTIONS

Applicants must be personal members of ALSC as well as ALA; organizational members are not eligible.

APPLICATION PROCEDURES

To be announced

American Library Association, Association of College and Research Libraries (ACRL)

Headquarters

50 E. Huron St.
Chicago, IL 60611-2795
Phone: 800-545-2433, x2523
Fax: 312-280-2520

www.ala.org/acrl/awards/researchawards/nijhoffstudy

E-mail: acrl@ala.org

Type of Grant Maker: Library Organization

Grant Information

WESS DE GRUYTER EUROPEAN LIBRARIANSHIP STUDY GRANT

Grant Range: 2,500 Euros

To support research on the acquisition, organization, or use of library resources from or relating to Europe. Current or historical subjects may be treated.

REQUIREMENTS AND RESTRICTIONS

Applicant must be a member of ACRL and employed as a librarian or information professional in a university, college, community college, or research library in the year prior to application for the award.

APPLICATION PROCEDURES

Application must include the following:

- A proposal, maximum of five (5) pages, double-spaced
- A tentative travel itinerary of up to thirty (30) days, including the proposed countries and institutions to be visited and the preferred period of study/travel
- A travel budget, including estimated round-trip coach airfare, transportation in Europe, lodging expenses, and meal costs
- A current curriculum vitae

Electronic submissions are required. E-mail the application to Casey Kinson at ckinson@ala.org. If sending multiple files, each file name must contain the applicant's name. Submissions will be acknowledged via e-mail.

Deadline: December 7

American Library Association, Association of Library Trustees, Advocates, Friends, and Foundations (ALTAFF)

Headquarters

50 E. Huron St.
Chicago, IL 60611-2795
www.ala.org/united

Type of Grant Maker: Library Organization

Grants Information

ALTAFF/Gale Outstanding Trustee Conference Grant

Grant Amount: $850
Number of Grants: 1

Enables a public library trustee who has demonstrated qualitative interests and efforts in supportive service of the local public library to attend the ALA Annual Conference.

REQUIREMENTS AND RESTRICTIONS

- Personal membership in ALA and the Trustee Section of ALTAFF at the time of application and through the time when the award is disbursed.
- Current service as a member of a local public library board.
- No previous attendance at an ALA Annual Conference.

APPLICATION PROCEDURES

Apply online and attach a brief statement of exhibited interest and activities resulting in their subsequent appointment/election as a public library Trustee. Include in this statement reasons for wishing to attend an ALA Annual Conference and how this relates to your library-related goals and philosophy. Include a list of all relevant library activities and experience, including professional associations (local, state, and national) of which you are a member.

Deadline: January 13

ALTAFF/LexisNexis Outstanding Friend Conference Grant

Grant Amount: $850, plus conference registration
Number of Grants: 1

REQUIREMENTS AND RESTRICTIONS

The awardee will be required to write an article chronicling their experience at the conference for *The Voice*.

APPLICATION PROCEDURES

Apply online.
Deadline: April 15

Baker & Taylor Awards for Friends Groups and Library Foundations

Grant Amount: $1,000

Awards are given for a specific project culminating in the year prior to application, or based on the full scope of the group's activities during that year. Applications are judged on the following:

- Planning: Friends/Foundation, library, and community involvement, use of resources, appropriateness of the activity, and measurable goals and objectives.
- Implementation: Use of resources, public relations, task monitoring, and broad membership involvement.
- Evaluation: Assessment of activity or program, measurable results.
- Innovation: New idea or implementation, creative involvement of people, fresh use of public relations.
- Community Involvement: Broad support by the community in planning and implementation.

APPLICATION PROCEDURES

Apply online.
Deadline: May 1

ALA President's Award for Advocacy

Grant Amount: $1,000
Number of Grants: 1

Awarded to a statewide advocacy campaign for the development of a program or programs for Friends and Trustees at the state library association conference.
The winning advocacy campaign must:

- Be conducted statewide.
- Result in either an increase in state funding for libraries, or a decrease or elimination of a proposed reduction in state funding for libraries.
- Use Capwiz or a similar interactive database to communicate with state legislators.
- Show significant participation by citizens in making the case for libraries.
- Have been conducted in the previous year.

APPLICATION PROCEDURES

Include the following supporting documents: a one- to two-page description of the statewide advocacy effort, including the specific goal of the campaign, who led the campaign, how citizens were involved, the avenues employed to make the case (e.g., e-mails, phone calls, letters, petitions, postcards, public service announcements, visits to legislators), the approximate number of citizens and librarians involved, and the results; newspaper clippings and other public recognition; materials used in the campaign.

Deadline: March 15

American Library Association, American Association of School Librarians (AASL)

Headquarters

50 E. Huron St.
Chicago IL 60611-2795
Phone: 800-545-2433
www.ala.org/aasl/aaslawards/aaslawards
Type of Grant Maker: Library Organization

Grants Information

AASL RESEARCH GRANT

Sponsored by Capstone
Number of grants: 2
Grant ranges: up to $2,500

The AASL Research Grant is given to up to two school librarians, library educators, library information science students, or education professors to conduct innovative research aimed at measuring and evaluating the impact of school library programs on learning and education. The study should have the potential to serve as a model for future school library research, and researchers should furnish documentation of the results of their work. Special consideration will be given to pilot research studies that employ experimental methodologies.

The AASL Research Grant Committee will evaluate applications on the basis of the following criteria:

1. Potential to measure and/or evaluate the impact of school library programs on learning and education.
2. Originality of the research project and methodology
3. Potential for replication
4. Demonstrated ability of the applicant(s) to undertake and successfully complete the project
5. Evidence that sufficient time and resources have been allocated to the effort
6. Support and commitment (financial and otherwise) by institutions and organizations to the project
7. Clarity and completeness of the proposal
8. Personal résumé of individual applicant attached
9. Personal membership in ALA/AASL at the time of application by the applicant

APPLICATION PROCEDURES

Apply online. For more information, contact Melissa Jacobsen, 800-545-2433, ext. 4381, Manager, Professional Development
Deadline: February 1

ABC-CLIO LEADERSHIP GRANT

Sponsored by ABC-CLIO

Grant Ranges: Up to $1,750

The ABC-CLIO Leadership Grant is given to school library associations that are AASL affiliates for planning and implementing leadership programs at the state, regional, or local levels.

Possibilities include programs that:

- Involve new members;
- Train ongoing leaders;
- Prepare school librarians to be building or district level leaders;
- Encourage collaboration among organizations.

New ideas and approaches to leadership are encouraged.

All applications for the grant will be judged against the following criteria:

1. Program objectives are clear
2. Nature and importance of desired leadership qualities are specified
3. Intended participant group is well defined
4. Plan of action and calendar are included
5. Budget is well planned
6. Evaluation plan is valid and follow-up activities are appropriate
7. Program has merit for replication by other affiliates

REQUIREMENTS AND RESTRICTIONS

Applicant must be a current member of the AASL Affiliate Assembly.

APPLICATION PROCEDURES

Apply online. For more information, contact Melissa Jacobsen, 800-545-2433, x4381, Manager, Professional Development
Deadline: February 1

BEYOND WORDS: DOLLAR GENERAL SCHOOL LIBRARY RELIEF FUND

Sponsored by Dollar General, in collaboration with the American Library Association (ALA), the American Association of School Librarians (AASL) and the National Education Association (NEA). This grant is a school library disaster relief fund for public school libraries in the states served by Dollar General. The fund will provide grants to public schools whose school library program has been affected by a disaster. Grants are to replace or supplement books, media and/or library equipment in the school library setting.

Grants will be awarded to public school libraries that have sustained substantial damage or hardship due to a natural disaster (tornado, earthquake, hurricane, flood, avalanche, mudslide), fire or an act recognized by the federal government as terrorism. The goal is to provide funding for books, media, and/or library equipment that support learning in a school library environment. The impact can be through direct loss or through an increase in enrollment due to displaced/evacuee students.

REQUIREMENTS AND RESTRICTIONS

Applicants must be:

- A public school with a pre-existing school library
- Within 36 months from the date of the disaster
- 20 miles from a Dollar General Store
- Replacing or supplementing books, media or library equipment (note furniture and shelving are not permissible purchases with grant funds)
- A certified school librarian, or is there a certified school librarian at the campus, district or regional level that will be involved with purchasing decisions
- Able to spend the funds within 180 days of receipt
- Able to submit a report, with receipts, to show how the funds were allocated

APPLICATION PROCEDURES

Apply online. For more information, contact Allison Cline, Deputy Executive Director, acline@ala.org.

Deadlines: None

INNOVATIVE READING GRANT

Sponsored by Capstone

Grant Range: $2,500

The AASL Innovative Reading Grant supports the planning and implementation of a unique and innovative program for children which motivates and encourages reading, especially with struggling readers.

The AASL Innovative Reading Grant Committee will evaluate the grant based on the following criteria:

1. Applicant must be a personal member of AASL.
2. The potential to measure and evaluate a literacy project that promotes the importance of reading and facilitates the learners' literacy development by supporting current reading research, practice, and policy
3. Reading program must be specifically designed for children (grades K–9) in the school library setting
4. Program must encourage innovative ways to motivate and involve children in reading. Existing commercial programs will not be considered

5. Project should demonstrate potential to impact student learning, especially reading
6. Originality of project and methodology
7. Potential for replication of the program should be apparent
8. Demonstration of the ability of the applicant(s) to undertake and successfully complete the project
9. A project plan that includes a timeline, budget, and clarity of purpose
10. Research should be evidence-based and scholarly in nature
11. Rankings based on a rubric that correlates with the ratings sheet.

This award is to be for a successful reading project that demonstrates the potential for reading improvement in grades K–9. (A program that promotes the importance of reading and facilitates the learners' literacy development by supporting current reading research, practice, and policy.) That can show improvement of reading in the students it is applied to. The grant recipient may be invited to present a program at a future AASL National Conference after the study has been completed and the results known. The grant recipient may be invited to write an article for *Knowledge Quest* that delineates their reading incentive project and demonstrate their successes, trials, and recommendations for improving so others can replicate the project.

APPLICATION PROCEDURES

Apply online. For more information, contact Melissa Jacobsen, 800-545-2433, ext. 4381, Manager, Professional Development.

Deadline: February 1

American Library Association, Federal and Armed Forces Libraries Round Table (FAFLRT)

Headquarters

50 E. Huron St.
Chicago, IL 60611-2795

www.ala.org/faflrt/initiatives/awards/
conference-sponsorship

Type of Grant Maker: Library Organization

Description

Grant Range: $1,000

Federal Librarians Adelaide Del Frate Conference Sponsorship Award is given to a library school student who has an interest in working in a Federal Library. The student will receive an award of $1,000 for annual conference registration fee, transportation, and other expenses related to attendance at the next ALA Annual Meeting.

REQUIREMENTS AND RESTRICTIONS

Grant limited to students who are currently enrolled in any ALA-accredited library school, who do not already have an ALA accredited degree, and who have expressed an interest in some aspect of Federal librarianship are eligible.

Applicants must be full- or part-time students at the time of application.

APPLICATION PROCEDURE

Students nominate themselves for this award and a letter of reference from a Federal librarian, a library school professor, etc., may be sent to the Awards Committee Chair in support of an application

Deadline: Mid-April

American Library Association, Freedom to Read Foundation (FTRF)

Headquarters

50 E. Huron St.
Chicago, IL 60611-2795
Phone: 800-545-2433, x4226
Fax: 312-280-4227
E-mail: ftrf@ala.org
Type of Grant Maker: Library Organization

Grants Information

LEGAL AND FINANCIAL GRANTS

Through the provision of financial and legal assistance to libraries and librarians, the Foundation attempts to eliminate the difficult choice between practical expediency and principle in the selection and distribution of library materials. Persons committed to defending the freedom to read should be given an assurance that their commitment will not result in legal convictions, financial loss or personal damage.

The Foundation will challenge the constitutionality of those laws which can inhibit librarians from including in their collections and disseminating to the public any work which has not previously been declared illegal.

JUDITH KRUG FUND BANNED BOOKS WEEK EVENT GRANTS

The first project of the Judith F. Krug Memorial Fund is to disburse grants to organizations to assist them in staging "Read-Outs" or other events during Banned Books Week. (A Banned Books Week Read-Out is an event at which people gather to read from books that have been banned or challenged over the years, in order to celebrate the freedom to read.)

APPLICATION PROCEDURES

Applicants must provide planning and budget outlines for their projects; agree to record the event, if selected; and provide a written narrative afterward, for use by the Freedom to Read Foundation and American Library Association. For more information, contact Jonathan Kelley at jokelley@ala.org or 800-545-2433, x4226; or Nanette Perez at nperez@ala.org or 800-545-2433, x4221.

Deadline: May

LEROY C. MERRITT HUMANITARIAN FUND

To support, maintenance, medical care, and welfare of librarians who, in the Trustees' opinion, are:

- Denied employment rights or discriminated against on the basis of gender, sexual orientation, race, color, creed, religion, age, disability, or place of national origin; or
- Denied employment rights because of defense of intellectual freedom; that is, threatened with loss of employment or discharged because of their stand for the cause of intellectual freedom, including promotion of freedom of the press, freedom of speech, the freedom of librarians to select items for their collections from all the world's written and recorded information, and defense of privacy rights.

APPLICATION PROCEDURES

If you are in need of assistance, please submit an online application. For more information, contact the Merritt Fund at 800-545-2433, x4226 or at merrittfund@ala.org.

GORDON M. CONABLE CONFERENCE SCHOLARSHIP

Annual award that allows a library school student or new professional to attend ALA's Annual Conference.

Grant Amount: Provides for conference registration, transportation, housing for six nights, and per diem expenses. In return, the recipient will be expected to attend various FTRF and other intellectual freedom meetings and programs at conference, consult with a mentor/board member, and present a report about their experiences and thoughts.

REQUIREMENTS AND RESTRICTIONS

Students currently enrolled in a library and information studies degree program, and new professionals (those who are three or fewer years removed from receiving a library school degree) are eligible to receive the Conable Scholarship. Those interested must submit an application including two references and an essay detailing their interest in intellectual freedom issues and how conference attendance will help further that interest. Applicants also are asked to attach a résumé, particularly those who are working professionals.

APPLICATION PROCEDURES

The application requires a résumé, two references, and an essay of up to 500 words describing your interest in intellectual freedom issues and how you will use your attendance at an ALA conference to further your interest during and after the conference. E-mail ftrf@ala.orgor call 800-545-2433, x4226 with any questions.

Deadline: April

American Library Association, H. W. Wilson Library Staff Development Grant

Headquarters

50 E. Huron St.
Chicago, IL 60611-2795
Phone: 800-545-2433

Type of Grant Maker: Library Organization

Grants Information

Grant Range: $3,500

Annual award given to a library organization whose application demonstrates greatest merit for a program of staff development designed to further the goals and objectives of the library organization.

REQUIREMENTS AND RESTRICTIONS

A library organization is defined as:

- individual library
- library system
- group of cooperating libraries
- state governmental agency
- local, state, or regional association

Staff development is defined as: "a program of learning activities that is developed by the library organization and develops the on-the-job staff capability and improves the abilities of personnel to contribute to the overall effectiveness of the library organization."

APPLICATION PROCEDURES

Application guidelines online.

Send six (6) copies of the application and (6) copies of supporting material to:

ALA Awards Program
Governance Office
50 E. Huron St.
Chicago, IL 60611

Contact:

Cheryl Malden (Staff Liaison, July 1, 2008, to June 30, 2015)
cmalden@ala.org
Phone: 312-280-3247
Fax: 312 944-3897

Deadlines: December 1.

American Library Association, International Relations Office

Headquarters

50 E. Huron St.
Chicago, IL 60611-2795

www.ala.org/offices/iro/awardsactivities/awardsgrants

E-mail: intl@ala.org

Type of Grant Maker: Library Organization

Grants Information

BOGLE PRATT INTERNATIONAL TRAVEL FUND

Sponsored by the Bogle Memorial Fund and the Pratt Institute School of Information and Library Science.

Grant Range: $1,000

REQUIREMENTS AND RESTRICTIONS

Given to an ALA personal member to attend their first international conference. An international conference may be defined as a conference sponsored by an international organization or a conference held in a country other than your home country.

APPLICATION PROCEDURE

See website for online application, which should be sent to:

International Relations Office
American Library Association
50 E. Huron St.
Chicago, IL 60611-2795
E-mail: intl@ala.org

Deadlines: January 1

HONG KONG BOOK FAIR FREE PASS PROGRAM FOR LIBRARIANS

Selected librarians from the United States and Canada who collect Chinese language materials are provided with 4 nights of hotel accommodation and free book fair registration to attend the Hong Kong Book Fair.

REQUIREMENTS AND RESTRICTIONS

Applicants must be personal members of ALA who work in the area of Chinese-language acquisitions or are working to build their Chinese-language collections to better serve their community of users.

APPLICATION PROCEDURES

Online application available in April. Send completed application by fax (312-280-4392) or e-mail (intl@ala.org).

Deadlines: See application

ALA-FIL FREE PASS PROGRAM

ALA and the Guadalajara International Book Fair are partnering to provide support for ALA members to attend the Guadalajara International Book Fair (FIL).

The program provides:

- 3 nights at the Hotel Guadalajara Plaza López Mateos (six nights if you share a room with a colleague who is also part of the program)
- 3 continental breakfast
- FIL Registration, courtesy of FIL
- $100 toward the cost of airfare, courtesy of ALA. The Guadalajara Book Fair is offering an additional $100 to the first 100 applicants who submit their airfare confirmation.

Free passes will be awarded to 150 librarians who work in the area of Spanish-language acquisitions and/or are working to build their Spanish-language collection to better serve their community and users.

REQUIREMENTS AND RESTRICTIONS

Applicants must be ALA Personal Members.

APPLICATION PROCEDURES

See website.

For more information or to apply for the free pass program, contact:

David Unger
FIL New York
Division of Humanities NAC 5/225
The City College of New York
New York, NY 10031
Phone: 212-650-7925
Fax: 212-650-7912
E-mail: filny@aol.com

Deadlines: August 13

American Library Association, Library Leadership & Management Association (LLAMA)

Headquarters

50 East Huron St.
Chicago, IL 60611-2795
Phone: 800-545-2433, x5032
Fax: 312-280-2169

www.ala.org/llama/awards

E-mail: llama@ala.org

Type of Grant Maker: Library Organization

Grants Information

LLAMA JOHN COTTON DANA LIBRARY PUBLIC RELATIONS AWARD

Grant Amount: $10,000
Number of Grants: 8

Provided in conjunction with the H. W. Wilson Foundation, the American Library Association and EBSCO Publishing honors outstanding library public relations, whether a summer reading program, a year-long centennial celebration, fund-raising for a new college library, an awareness campaign or an innovative partnership in the community.

APPLICATION PROCEDURES

Apply online.

Deadline: February 1

American Library Association, New Members Round Table (NMRT)

Headquarters

50 E. Huron St
Chicago, IL 60611-2788

www.ala.org/nmrt/initiatives/applyforfunds/applyfunds

Type of Grant Maker: Library Organization

Grants Information

NMRT PROFESSIONAL DEVELOPMENT GRANT

Sponsored by 3M

The purpose of the NMRT Professional Development Grant is to encourage professional development and participation by new ALA members in national ALA and NMRT activities.

The annual grant covers round-trip airfare, lodging, conference registrations fees and some incidental expenses.

REQUIREMENTS AND RESTRICTIONS

Applicants must be personal ALA/NMRT members who are working within the territorial United States.

APPLICATION PROCEDURES

Apply online. For more information, contact:

Kimberly L. Redd
E-mail: klredd@ala.org
Phone: 312-280-4279
Fax: 312-280-3256

Deadlines: December 1

SHIRLEY OLOFSON MEMORIAL AWARD COMMITTEE

Grant Range: $1,000

Award is intended to help defray costs to attend the ALA Annual Conference.

REQUIREMENTS AND RESTRICTIONS

Applicants must be members of ALA and NMRT; active within the library profession; show promise or activity in the area of professional development; have valid financial need; and have attended no more than five ALA annual conferences.

APPLICATION PROCEDURES

Apply online.

Deadlines: See application.

American Library Association, Office for Diversity

Headquarters

50 E. Huron St.
Chicago, IL 60611-2795
Phone: 800-545-243, x5295

www.ala.org/advocacy/diversity/
diversityresearchstatistics/diversityresearch

Type of Grant Maker: Library Organization

Grants Information

ANNUAL DIVERSITY RESEARCH GRANT PROGRAM

Number of Grants: 3

Grant Ranges: $2,000 annual award for original research and a $500 travel grant to attend and present at ALA Annual Conference.

Grant recipients will be expected to compile the results of their research into a paper and will be asked to present and publish the final product in conjunction with the American Library Association. Grant proposals may address any diversity topic that speaks to critical gaps in the knowledge of diversity issues within library and information science. Grant applicants may also e-mail diversity@ala.org to request a list of proposal topic suggestions.

REQUIREMENTS AND RESTRICTIONS

Applicants must be a current member of the American Library Association.

APPLICATION PROCEDURES

1. Proposals are only accepted during the open call for applications (from the conclusion of the ALA Midwinter Meeting to April 30th). A cover letter with name, primary contact information, and ALA member ID of the researcher(s) must be included.
2. A concise abstract of the project (no more than 200 words).
3. Description of the project (of no more than 5 pages in length) detailing:
   • Justification and needs for the research project
   • Research objectives
   • Design, methodology and analysis of the project
   • Expected outcomes and benefits
4. Budgetary plan and timeline, including other sources of support sought for the project.
5. A one-page vita for each of the researchers involved in the project.
6. Electronic submissions are preferred. All proposal elements should be collated and should be submitted in a single Word document attachment via e-mail to diversity@ala.org.

Deadlines: See application information.

American Library Association, Office for Research & Statistics

Headquarters

50 E. Huron St.
Chicago, IL 60611-2795
Phone: 800-545-2433, x4283 or 312-280-4273

www.ala.org/offices/ors/orsawards/awards

Contact: Kathy Rosa, Director

E-mail: krosa@ala.org

Type of Grant Maker: Library Organization

Grants Information

CARROLL PRESTON BABER RESEARCH GRANT

Grant Range: Up to $3,000

Annual grant given to one or more librarians or library educators who will conduct innovative research that could lead to an improvement in services to any specified group(s) of people. The project should aim to answer a question that is of vital importance to the library community and the researchers should plan to provide documentation of the results of their work. The Jury would welcome proposals that involve innovative uses of technology and proposals that involve cooperation between libraries, between libraries and other agencies, or between librarians and persons in other disciplines.

REQUIREMENTS AND RESTRICTIONS

Must be an ALA member. Projects that involve both a practicing librarian and a researcher are welcome.

APPLICATION PROCEDURES

Send via e-mail one completed application cover sheet and proposal with budget to the ALA Staff Liaison. File formats accepted are MS Word 2003 or newer, and PDF. Please do not fax or mail.

Deadline: December 14

LOLETA D. FYAN GRANT

Grant Ranges: up to $5,000

Grant given for the development and improvement of public libraries and the services they provide.

The project(s):

1. must result in the development and improvement of public libraries and the services they provide;
2. must have the potential for broader impact and application beyond meeting a specific local need;
3. should be designed to effect changes in public library services that are innovative and responsive to the future; and
4. should be capable of completion within one year.

REQUIREMENTS AND RESTRICTIONS

Applicants can include but are not limited to: local, regional or state libraries, associations or organizations, including units of the American Library Association; library schools; or individuals.

APPLICATION PROCEDURES

Online application and information available. Send via e-mail one completed application cover sheet and proposal with budget to the ALA Staff Liaison listed below. File formats accepted are MS Word 2003 or newer, and PDF. Please do not fax or mail.

Deadline: December 14

American Library Association, Public Information Office (PIO)

Headquarters

50 E. Huron St.
Chicago, IL 60611-2795

www.ala.org/conferencesevents/celebrationweeks/
natlibraryweek/nlwgrant

Type of Grant Maker: Library Organization

Grant Range: $3,000

Grants Information

SCHOLASTIC LIBRARY PUBLISHING NATIONAL LIBRARY WEEK GRANT

Cosponsored by Scholastic Library Publishing, a division of Scholastic and administered by the Public Awareness Committee.

Award grant to support a single library's public outreach efforts during National Library Week. Proposals will be judged on the basis of how well they meet criteria, including: creativity, originality, clarity of planning and potential for generating widespread public visibility and support for libraries. Commitment to ongoing public awareness activities and allocation of resources (staff, materials, time) also are considered.

Proposals must:

- Incorporate the National Library Week theme, "Communities matter @ your library®."
- Uses the @ your library® brand according to registered trademark guidelines on all related promotional materials.
- Involve at least one other community organization.

REQUIREMENTS AND RESTRICTIONS

Open to US libraries of all types.

APPLICATION PROCEDURES

Apply online. For more information, contact Megan McFarlane, 312-280-2148, mmcfarlane@ala.org.

Deadline: September 30

American Library Association, Public Library Association

Headquarters

50 E. Huron St.
Chicago, IL 60611-2795

www.ala.org/pla/awards

Type of Grant Maker: Library Organization

Grants Information

DEMCO NEW LEADERS TRAVEL GRANT

To enhance the professional development and improve the expertise of public librarians new to the field by making possible their attendance at major professional development activities.

This grant has been established to enable PLA Members new to the profession and who have not had the opportunity to attend a major PLA continuing education event in the last five years to do so. Eligible events are PLA Results Boot Camp; PLA Conference; and other PLA events, such as preconferences or institutes, held in conjunction with ALA Annual Conference or ALA Midwinter Meeting.

Grant Ranges: Up to $1,500

REQUIREMENTS AND RESTRICTIONS

- Applicant must be a current member of the Public Library Association.
- Applicant must have been a practicing librarian (with an MLS from an accredited institution) for five years or less.
- Applicant cannot be a current officer or member of the PLA Board of Directors.
- Applicant cannot be a current member of the New Leaders Travel Grant Jury.
- Applicant's supervisor or supervising authority cannot be a current member of the New Leaders Travel Grant Jury.
- Applicant cannot have attended a major PLA continuing education program in the last five years due to limited or nonexistent funding for professional travel at his or her institution.

APPLICATION PROCEDURES

To submit an application for this award, please visit the PLA Awards Online Application.

Deadlines: See website.

ROMANCE WRITERS OF AMERICA LIBRARY GRANT

To provide a public library the opportunity to build or expand its romance fiction collection and/or host romance fiction programming. Presented by the Public Library Association and the Romance Writers of America.

Grant Amount: $4,500 to be used toward the purchase of romance fiction, author honorariums and travel expenses, and other applicable program expenses.

REQUIREMENTS AND RESTRICTIONS

Any size public library.

APPLICATION PROCEDURES

To submit an application for this award, please visit the PLA Awards Online Application.

Deadlines: See website.

American Library Association, Publishing Department

Headquarters

50 E. Huron St.
Chicago, IL 60611-2795
Phone: 800-545-2433, x5416

www.ala.org/awardsgrants/awards/42/apply

Type of Grant Maker: Library Organization

Grants Information

CARNEGIE-WHITNEY GRANT

Grant Ranges: Up to $5,000 awarded annually.

Number of Grants: vary

Program Description: Provides grants for the preparation and publication of popular or scholarly reading lists, indexes and other guides to library resources that will be useful to users of all types of libraries.

The grants may be used for print and electronic projects of varying lengths.

Grants are awarded to individuals; local, regional or state libraries, associations or organizations, including units, affiliates and committees of the American Library Association, or programs of information and library studies/science. International applicants welcome.

APPLICATION PROCEDURES

Send the Application Cover Sheet and proposal electronically to mbolduc@ala.org. Proposals must include the following components:

- The Application Cover Sheet.
- Résumé for each person responsible for the project, including list of publications.
- For each applicant, two letters from professional references attesting to the ability of the applicants(s) to carry out the project.
- A statement of purpose that provides a clear and concise description of the project, the scope of subjects covered and the intended audiences.
- A plan of work that includes a schedule for completion and addresses research, compilation, and writing activities.
- A plan for the timely publication or dissemination of the work, including a weblink to the final product.
- A budget that itemizes and justifies costs.

Narrative

- Need: What problem, issue or concern will be addressed by this project?
- Purpose: What do you hope to achieve by undertaking this project? Include in your answer both the anticipated immediate impact of the project and its potential for the future.
- Target audience: Who is the audience for this project? Why?
- Planned activities: Outline what you intend to do and when you intend to do it. Include a time line or calendar. Remember that the project should be completed within two years. Be as specific as possible.
- Plans for sharing the results of your project: Describe how you intend to share the results of the project with others in the library field. Sharing of results can take place after the end of the project.
- Evaluation: How will you know if the project is successful?
- Describe the knowledge and experience of the people who will be doing the project. Please state specifically why they are qualified for this project.
- The budget should include all costs that can be specifically identified with the proposal and should show both costs being covered by other sources and the amount being requested from the Carnegie-Whitney Grant.

Deadline: None

American Library Association, Reference and User Services Association (RUSA)

Headquarters

50 E. Huron St.
Chicago, IL 60611-2795

Phone: 312-280-4395

E-mail: rusa@ala.org

Type of Grant Maker: Library Organization

Grants Information

EMERALD RESEARCH GRANT AWARDS

To individuals seeking support to conduct research in business librarianship. The funds may be used at the discretion of the award recipients.

Grant Amount: $5,000

REQUIREMENTS AND RESTRICTIONS

Award recipient must be an ALA member or at least one member of a collaborative team must be an ALA member. Recipients may be asked to present their findings at a public BRASS event within two years of receiving the award (at the discretion of the BRASS Executive Committee). Recipients will also be required to acknowledge the Emerald Research Grant when publishing or presenting their research.

APPLICATION PROCEDURES

Submit a detailed proposal to the committee chair. See website for details.

Deadline: December 15

American Library Association, Young Adult Library Services Association (YALSA)

Headquarters

American Library Association
50 E. Huron St.
Chicago, IL 60611-2795

Grants Information

YALSA CONFERENCE GRANTS

Grant Amounts:

$1,000 each are funded by Baker & Taylor (2 grants)

$1,000—YALSA's Leadership Endowment and is the Dorothy Broderick Student Conference Scholarship for travel to the conference for one graduate student

Awarded to librarians who work for or directly with young adults in a public or school library or library agency to enable librarians to attend the Annual Conference for the first time.

Deadline: December 1

BWI/YALSA COLLECTION DEVELOPMENT GRANT

Grant Amount: $1,000 for collection development to two YALSA members who represent a public library, and who work directly with young adults ages 12 to 18.

Deadlines: December 1

ABC-CLIO/GREENWOOD/YALSA SERVICE TO YOUNG ADULTS ACHIEVEMENT AWARD

Grant Amount: $2,000

Recognizes the national contributions of a YALSA member who has demonstrated unique and sustained devotion in two or more of the following areas to young adult services: promoting literature or programming for young adults, conducting and publishing research about young adults, mentoring other professionals in the field, or for notable efforts in the work of the Young Adult Library Services Association. The purpose of the cash award will be to enable the recipient to further his or her good work in the field of young adult librarianship.

Deadline: December 1

MAE AWARD FOR BEST LITERATURE PROGRAM FOR TEENS

Grant Amount: $500 to the winner and an additional $500 to the winner's library or library agency.

To honor a member of YALSA who has developed an outstanding reading or literature program for young adults.

Deadline: December 1

FRANCES HENNE/YALSA/ VOYA RESEARCH GRANT

Grant Amount: $1,000

To provide seed money for small-scale projects which will encourage research that responds to the YALSA Research Agenda.

Deadline: December 1

GREAT BOOKS GIVEAWAY COMPETITION

Each year the YALSA office receives approximately 1,200 newly published children's, young adult and adult books, videos, CDs and audio cassettes for review. YALSA and the cooperating publishers annually offer one year's worth of review materials as a contribution to a library in need. Applications must be received in the YALSA office by the first business day of December each year. The estimated value of this collection is $25,000.

APPLICATION PROCEDURES

See website for details.

American Society for Information Science and Technology

Headquarters

1320 Fenwick Lane, Suite 510
Silver Spring, MD 20910
Phone: 301-495-0900
Fax: 301-495-0810
www.asis.org/awards.html
E-mail: asis@asis.org
Type of Grant Maker: Library Organization

Grants Information

Grant Range: $1,000

HISTORY FUND RESEARCH AWARD GRANT

This grant will be awarded for the best research support proposal. All topics relevant to the history of information science and technology may be proposed. The proposal should state: the central topic or question to be researched, qualifications of the researcher (brief vita should be included), a budget, and how the funds will be expended.

APPLICATION PROCEDURES

Submit proposal to www.softconf.com/asist2/History (choose the "Research Award" category).

Deadlines: May 1

American Theological Library Association

Headquarters

300 South Wacker Drive, Suite 2100
Chicago, IL 60606-6701
Phone: 888-665-ATLA
Outside North America: 312-454-5100
Fax: 312-454-5505
www.atla.com/Members/programs/awards/Pages/
default.aspx
Type of Grant Maker: Library Organization

Description

PUBLICATION GRANT

The American Theological Library Association (ATLA) awards publication grants each year to one or more recipients to aid in the development of a scholarly work that advances some aspect of theological librarianship or provides bibliographic access to a significant body of literature within theological or religious studies. The committee especially encourages proposals from persons undertaking their first major project in this area. The goal of projects proposed should be peer-reviewed publication (e.g., in the *ATLA Journal, Theological Librarianship,* or in one of the book series it publishes with The Scarecrow Press). ATLA reserves first right of refusal of publication for all projects receiving grants.

Grant Range: up to $4,000 for reimbursable expenses, which could include:

a) Travel expenses for the purpose of research, writing, or collaborating with colleagues
b) Research and clerical assistance
c) Specialized software (e.g., EndNote©) and/or equipment (e.g., scanner)
d) Services such as photocopying, interlibrary loan, mailings, or copyediting

REQUIREMENTS AND RESTRICTIONS

Grants are open to both members and nonmembers of ATLA.

APPLICATION PROCEDURE

Complete and submit an ATLA Publication Grant Application as an attachment to an e-mail to the Member Representative, memberrep@atla.com.

Acceptable formats include Microsoft Word 2007 or earlier versions, PDF, and RTF. If you cannot send the application by e-mail according to the above criteria, please mail your application to Publications Grant, ATLA, 300 South Wacker Drive, Suite 2100, Chicago, IL 60606-6701.

The two letters of reference specified on the application form should also be sent by e-mail under the same guidelines as for the application. Letters of reference will not be accepted unless sent directly from the e-mail address of the person writing the reference. If letters of reference cannot be sent by e-mail according to the above criteria, they should be mailed to Barbara Kemmis, ATLA, 300 South Wacker Drive, Suite 2100, Chicago, IL 60606-6701.

Deadlines: February 1

CONSULTATION GRANTS

The American Theological Library Association provides funds for library consultations. This service is designed to help theological libraries and their administrations assess library operations and facilitate planning. This service is intended to offer practical guidance to theological libraries anticipating building programs, reorganization of administration, assessment of personnel and resources, visits from accrediting agencies, acquisition and utilization of computer and newer technologies, or expansion of other library resources or services.

Grant Range: Pays an honorarium to the consultant of $400 for a one-day visit, or $800 for a two-day visit.

APPLICATION PROCEDURES

The library, in concert with the dean, president, academic vice-presidents, or provost, will submit an official request for the ATLA Consultation Service. The request should detail the objectives and purpose of the consultation.

Applications are to be mailed to:
Member Representative
American Theological Library Association
300 South Wacker Drive, Suite 2100
Chicago, Illinois 60606-6701

For more information, contact the director of member services at memberrep@atla.com.

Deadlines: None

CONTINUING EDUCATION PROGRAM GRANTS

ATLA provides continuing education grants for programs for both regional groups associated with ATLA, and

individual institutional libraries, to create educational programming.

Grant Ranges: Up to $1,000 per category below

REQUIREMENTS AND RESTRICTIONS

Two categories of grants are available:

1. Regional groups associated with ATLA
2. Institutional Members of ATLA, whether or not in a regional group

Grant funds may be requested for all types of expenses related to speakers. No grants for individuals or for lunch/break expenses or parking fees. Suggested honoraria are full day, $400–$450, half day, $200–$250, one- to two-hour workshops, $150–$250. Exceptions should be noted in the application.

APPLICATION PROCEDURES

Complete online form, which can be submitted via mail or e-mail

Deadlines: None

AMETEK Foundation, Inc.

Headquarters

1100 Cassatt Rd.
Berwyn, PA 19312-1177

Contact: Kathryn E. Sena, Secy.-Treas.

Type of Grant Maker: Corporate Foundation

Description

Founded: 1960

Operating Locations/Geographic Preferences: Giving primarily in areas of company operations and organizations that have received volunteer or financial contributions from employees

Corporate Foundation Information: Supported by Ametek, Inc.

Financial Summary

Assets: $4,779,024
Total Giving: $1,148,870
Number of Grants: 79
Grant Ranges: $108,444–$1,000

Grants Information

GRANT TYPES

Program development, annual campaigns and endowments, general and operating support, matching, building and renovation, equipment

TYPICAL RECIPIENTS/SUBJECTS OF INTEREST

Education, health, civic and social needs

GRANT RECIPIENTS

Library or School Related

- Alamance Burlington School District, 100 Book Challenge, $108,444
- Binghamton School, District, 100 Book Challenge, $46,000
- Panther Valley School District, 100 Book Challenge, $54,100
- Alamance Community College, $5,000

General

- Abilities, Inc. of Florida, $15,000
- Science Center of Pinellas County, $5,000

REQUIREMENTS AND RESTRICTIONS

None listed

APPLICATION PROCEDURES

Call 610-647-2121 for recording of application information.
    No formal guidelines or annual report is published. Send letter with following information to Catherine Sena:

- Verification of organizational IRS status
- Mission and purpose of organization
- Summary of project, amount requested
- Rationale for project
- Benefits to population served
- Name of contact

Deadlines: February 28, September 30

Amsterdam Foundation, Gustave G. and Valla

Headquarters

135 S. 19th St., Ste. 200
Philadelphia, PA 19103-4907
Phone: 215-665-0989

Contact: Barb Deaner, Mgr.
Type of Grant Maker: Foundation

Description

Founded: 2001
Operating Locations/Geographic Preferences: Primarily in PA

Financial Summary

Assets: $394,733
Total Giving: $158,153
Number of Grants: 22
Range of Grants: $35,000–$3

Grants Information

TYPICAL RECIPIENTS/SUBJECTS OF INTEREST

Libraries, higher education, arts, Jewish agencies, medical care

PAST GRANT RECIPIENTS

General

- Jewish Federation of Greater Philadelphia, Philadelphia (PA), $5,000
- Opera Company of Philadelphia, Philadelphia (PA), $5,000
- United Way, $3,300
- Philadelphia Museum of Art, Philadelphia (PA), $3,300

REQUIREMENTS AND RESTRICTIONS

No grants to individuals

APPLICATION PROCEDURES

Application form required. Applicants should submit an initial approach letter and copy of IRS Determination letter.

Andersen Corp. (*See also* Andersen Corporate Foundation)

Headquarters

100 Fourth Avenue North
Bayport, MN 55003

www.andersenwindows.com

Contact: Susan Roeder, Corporate Affairs Manager

Type of Grant Maker: Corporation

Description

Founded: 1903

Operating Locations/Geographic Preferences: Giving to organizations located in communities where Andersen Corporation operates and headquarters region (metro St. Paul/Minneapolis, St. Croix Valley including western Wisconsin) and national organizations whose missions relate to shelter, architecture and design or the building industry.

Corporation Information: In addition to Andersen Corporate Foundation (see listing), company makes contributions to nonprofit organizations.

Grants Information

GRANT TYPES

Cash donation, sponsorships, volunteer support, product donations

RECIPIENTS/SUBJECTS OF INTEREST

Health and human services, civic, education, safety, recreation, veterans, arts, shelter and environmental organizations.

 Focuses on:

- Shelter
- Architecture and Design
- Building Industry
- Community

REQUIREMENTS AND RESTRICTIONS

No support for:
1. Individuals
2. Religious organization fund-raising
3. Political/lobbying organizations
4. Travel for individuals or groups
5. Fund-raising events or activities, social events or goodwill advertising except where Andersen employees are participating
6. For-profit organizations

APPLICATION PROCEDURES

Contribution requests must be typewritten on the organization's letterhead. If organization meets basic criteria, please send a letter of inquiry to:

Susan Roeder
Corporate Affairs Manager
Andersen Corporation
100 Fourth Avenue North
Bayport, MN 55003

Deadlines: None

Andersen Corporate Foundation (*See also* Andersen Corp.)

Headquarters

White Pine Bldg.
342 5th Ave. N., Ste. 200
Bayport, MN 55003-1201
Phone: 651-275-4450

www.srinc.biz/bp/index.html

Contact: Chloette Haley, Prog. Off.

E-mail: andersencorpfdn@srinc.biz

Type of Grant Maker: Corporate Foundation

Description

Founded: 1941

Operating Locations/Geographic Preferences: Giving primarily in Washington County, Minnesota and portions of Western Wisconsin. Secondarily, the East Metro area of St. Paul. Foundation has expanded its giving to the many communities where Andersen has facilities and employees, including Menomonie, Wisconsin; Des Moines, Iowa; Dubuque, Iowa; Page County, Virginia; Marion, Ohio and North Brunswick, New Jersey.

Corporate Foundation Information: Supported by Andersen Corp. (see listing).

Financial Summary

Assets: $41,176,016
Total Giving: $1,849,900

Grants Information

GRANT TYPES

Capital, projects, and general operating support

TYPICAL RECIPIENTS/SUBJECTS OF INTEREST

Affordable Housing

Health and Safety

Education and Youth Development

Focusing on:

Programs for public and private schools that are not funded in the general operating budget, and a responsible, independent group oversees allocation of the funds

Programs that focus on science, technology, engineering and mathematics

Preservation of environmental quality

After school programs, drug prevention, career planning

Human Services

Civic Support

Focusing on:

Community assets such as public radio or public television, and museums

Cultural organizations (performing arts, visual arts, and music) that make a significant contribution to the life of the community

PAST GRANT RECIPIENTS

Library or School Related

- Bayport Public Library, Bayport (NM), for general support, $45,000
- Partnership Plan for Stillwater Area Schools, Stillwater (MN), for Math and Science Partnership Plan programs, $40,000
- Let's Talk Science, London (Canada). For Wings of Discovery Program, $15,000

General

- YMCA of Greater Saint Paul, Minneapolis (MN), for YMCA Camp and Branch programs, $50,000
- Minnesota Children's Museum, St. Paul (MN), for Earth World Gallery, $20,000

REQUIREMENTS AND RESTRICTIONS

No lead gifts. No grants to organizations that are in competition with each other to provide the same service to the community. No support for endowments or individuals.

APPLICATION PROCEDURES

Review online materials prior to submitting an application.

Deadlines: April 15, July 15, October 15, and December 15

Andersen Foundation, Fred C. and Katherine B.

Headquarters

PO Box 80

Bayport, MN 55003

Contact: Mary Gillstrom, V.P., Secy. and Dir.

Type of Grant Maker: Foundation

Description

Founded: 1959

Operating Locations/Geographic Preferences: Giving on a national basis for higher education, locally in MN and western WI for others

Financial Summary

Assets: $466,414,465

Number of Grants: 215

Grant Ranges: $2,250,000–$1,000

Grants Information

GRANT TYPES

Program development, general support, capital campaigns

TYPICAL RECIPIENTS

Higher education institutions that do not accept state or federal funding; youth, elderly and health programs in local areas.

PAST GRANT RECIPIENTS

Library or School Related

- University of Minnesota, Minneapolis (MN), general operating support, $2,250,000
- Gardner-Webb University, Boiling Springs (NC), general support, $250,000
- Union University, Jackson (TN), general support, $250,000

General

- Gundersen Lutheran Medical Foundation, La Crosse (WI), program support, $1,125,000
- Boy Scouts of America, Saint Paul (MN), program support, $235,000

- Lakeview Memorial Hospital Association, Stillwater (MN), program support, $70,000
- Minnesota Children's Museum, Saint Paul (MN), program support, $50,000

REQUIREMENTS AND RESTRICTIONS

No support for federally funded colleges, universities, or endowment programs. No grants to individuals.

APPLICATION PROCEDURES

Applicants should submit:

1. IRS Determination Letter
2. Annual report/audited financial statement/990
3. Description of project and amount of funding request

Deadlines: March 11, July 15, and October 14

Annenberg Foundation

Headquarters

2000 Ave. of the Stars, Ste. 1000
Los Angeles, CA 90067-4704
Phone: 310-209-4560
Fax: 310-209-1631

www.annenbergfoundation.org

Contact: Leonard Aube, Exec. Dir

E-mail: info@annenbergfoundation.org

Type of Grant Maker: Foundation

Description

Founded: 1989

Operating Locations/Geographic Preferences: Giving on a national and international basis, with an emphasis on southern CA.

Financial Summary

Assets: $1,718,656,943
Total Giving: $74,728,193
Number of Grants: 383
Grant Ranges: $500–$50,000; average grants from $10,000–$250,000

GRANT TYPES

General operations, program support

TYPICAL RECIPIENTS/SUBJECTS OF INTEREST

- Arts, Culture and Humanities
- Animal Welfare
- Civic and Community
- Environment
- Education
- Human Health & Wellness
- Military Veterans

PAST GRANT RECIPIENTS

Library or School Related

- Library Foundation of Los Angeles, Los Angeles (CA), to support literacy programs, $30,000
- Friends of Foundation de France, Inc., New York (NY), for the La Bibliotheque nationale de France's (National Library of France) acquisition of the Saint Catherine manuscript, $8,681
- University of Southern California, Los Angeles (CA), to design and construct Annenberg Academic Building, $50,000,000

General

- EnCorps, San Francisco (CA), to increase number of math and science teachers in California's public middle and high schools, $1,000,000

REQUIREMENTS AND RESTRICTIONS

No support for political activities. No grants to individuals. Requests for capital campaigns and multiyear commitments are discouraged.

APPLICATION PROCEDURES

Begin by downloading online VISION+ Guidelines. Online application and financial form required.

Deadlines: None

Aon Foundation

Headquarters

200 E. Randolph
Chicago, IL 60601-6419
Phone: 312-381-3555
Fax: 312-381-6166

www.aon.com/usa/about-aon/community-involvement.jsp

Contact: Carolyn Barry Frost, Pres. and Treas.

E-mail: aon_foundation@aon.com

Type of Grant Maker: Corporate Foundation

The Aon Foundation is currently reviewing grant proposals by invitation only. Organizations with demonstrated successes in the foundation's areas of interest will be contacted and asked to submit a proposal. Please note that any unsolicited letters of inquiry or proposals will not be reviewed.

Argyros Foundation

Headquarters

949 S. Coast Dr., No. 600
Costa Mesa, CA 92626-7734
Phone: 714-481-5000

Contact: Carol Campbell, Treas. and Tr.

Type of Grant Maker: Foundation

Description

Founded: 1979

Operating Locations/Geographic Preferences: Giving limited to Orange County, CA.

Financial Summary

Assets: $94,550,775
Total Giving: $9,337,796
Number of Grants: 100
Grant Ranges: $2,357,940–$275

Grants Information

GRANT TYPES

Program development

TYPICAL RECIPIENTS/SUBJECTS OF INTEREST

Arts and cultural programs, education, health care, youth development, and human services

PAST GRANT RECIPIENTS

Library or School Related

- George W. Bush Presidential Library, $1,000,000
- Library of Congress, Open World Leadership Center, $500,000

General

- South Coast Repertory Theater, Costa Mesa (CA), $1,050,000
- Orange County Museum of Art, Newport Beach (CA), $25,000

REQUIREMENTS AND RESTRICTIONS

No grants to individuals

APPLICATION PROCEDURES

Applicants should submit:

1. Statement of problem project will address
2. Copy of IRS Determination Letter
3. Brief history of organization and description of its mission

Deadline: June 1

Arizona State Library, Archives and Public Records

Headquarters

Library Development Division
1101 W. Washington St.
Phoenix, AZ 85007
Phone: 602-926-3604, 800-255-5841
Fax: 602-256-7995

www.lib.az.us/lsta

Type of Grant Maker: Government

Grants Information

Library Services and Technology Act (LSTA) funds are intended to help libraries develop central roles as community builders. LSTA funds are used to promote improvements in services to all types of libraries; to facilitate access to, and sharing of, resources; and to achieve economical and effective delivery of service for the purpose of cultivating an educated and informed citizenry.

LSTA funds are targeted for statewide library services and support a wide array of programs from family literacy to providing broad access to sophisticated databases. This program develops the role of libraries as "information brokers," helping to make resources and services, which are often prohibitively expensive, more readily available. LSTA also supports efforts to recruit and educate librarians. LSTA funds are available as grants to individual libraries.

APPLICATION PROCEDURES

Guidelines and application packet are posted online when available.

For information, contact the LSTA Consultant 602-926-3604 or 1-800-255-5841 (Arizona only).

Deadlines: Posted with application information.

Arkansas Department of Rural Services

Headquarters

101 E. Capitol, Ste. 202
Little Rock, AK 72201
Phone: 501-682-6011, 888-787-2527
Fax: 501-682-6014

www.state.ar.us/drs/drsgrants.html

E-mail: Rural.Arkansas@arkansas.gov

Type of Grant Maker: Government

Grants Information

Rural Community Development Grant Program/Rural Fire Protection Grant Program

Funds can be used for a variety of purposes, such as: library shelving, baseball/softball fields, community centers, walking tracks, park and playground equipment, pavilions, picnic tables, fire stations, additional bays for existing stations, turn-out gear, communications equipment, fire trucks.

Grant Ranges: Up to $15,000

REQUIREMENTS AND RESTRICTIONS

Applicants must be from incorporated towns of less than 3,000 in population and unincorporated rural areas.

APPLICATION PROCEDURES

Applications accepted August through March.

Deadlines: August 17, December 7, March 15

RURAL SERVICES BLOCK GRANT PROGRAM

Funds can be used for new construction or renovations, such as: community centers, fire stations, or multipurpose buildings, and the purchase of fire trucks

Grant Ranges: Up to $75,000

REQUIREMENTS AND RESTRICTIONS

Applicants must be incorporated towns and rural communities with a population of less than 3,000 and the community population must be at least 51% low to moderate income. See online list to determine a community's eligibility.

APPLICATION PROCEDURES

See website for guidelines and application forms.

Deadline: December 7

Arnold Fund

Headquarters

1201 W. Peachtree St., Ste. 4200
Atlanta, GA 30309-3469

Type of Grant Maker: Foundation
Unsolicited requests for funds not accepted.

Arrillaga, John Foundation

Headquarters

2450 Watson Ct.
Palo Alto, CA 94303-3216
Phone: 650-618-7000

Contact: John Arrillaga, Pres.

Type of Grant Maker: Foundation

Description

Founded: 1978

Operating Locations/Geographic Preferences: Giving primarily in CA, with some emphasis on Stanford.

Financial Summary

Assets: $31,330,396
Total Giving: $5,354,062

Grants Information

GRANT TYPES

Program development and continuing support

TYPICAL RECIPIENTS/SUBJECTS OF INTEREST

Higher education, arts, health, human services.

PAST GRANT RECIPIENTS

Library or School Related

- Menlo School, Atherton (CA), for gym construction, $2,000,000
- Castilleja School, Palo Alto (CA), School Courtyard Project, $250,000

General

- Menlo Park, City of, Menlo Park (CA), to construct Burgess Gym, $3,000,000
- San Francisco Ballet, Annual Fund, $25,000

REQUIREMENTS AND RESTRICTIONS

None listed.

APPLICATION PROCEDURES

Send letter with:

1. Descriptive literature about organization
2. Additional materials/documentation

Deadline: None

Arronson Foundation

Headquarters

c/o Joseph C. Kohn, Esq.
2400 One Reading Ctr., Ste. 2100
Philadelphia, PA 19107-3304

Type of Grant Maker: Foundation

Description

Founded: 1957

Operating Locations/Geographic Preferences: Giving primarily in Philadelphia, PA.

Financial Summary

Assets: $4,404,715
Total Giving: $130,475

Grants Information

GRANT TYPES

Seed money, annual and capital campaigns and endowments, building and renovations

TYPICAL RECIPIENTS/SUBJECTS OF INTEREST

Jewish organizations and education, particularly higher education, performing arts, cultural programs, hospitals and hospices, nursing and medical research, women's issues, and family planning.

PAST GRANT RECIPIENTS

Library or School Related

- Children's Literacy Initiative, Philadelphia (PA), $2,500
- Community College of Philadelphia, Philadelphia (PA), $4,800

General

- American Swedish Historical Museum, Philadelphia (PA), $5,000
- Arden Theater Company, Philadelphia (PA), $2,500

REQUIREMENTS AND RESTRICTIONS

None listed.

APPLICATION PROCEDURES

Send letter.

Deadlines: None

Art Libraries Society of North American (ARLIS/NA)

Headquarters

7044 S. 13th St.
Oak Creek, WI 53154
Phone: 414-908-4954, x116
Fax: 414-768-8001

www.arlisna.org/about/awards/awards_index.html

H. W. WILSON FOUNDATION RESEARCH AWARD

Grant Ranges: Up to $3,000

Program Description: To support research activities by ARLIS/NA individual members in the fields of librarianship, visual resources curatorship, and the arts. The award encourages the professional development of the membership in their capacities as information intermediaries and as subject specialists in the arts.

Projects may focus on research which benefits the profession of art and visual resources librarianship, as well as the broader world of librarianship, through such means as compilation and dissemination of information, translation of original scholarship, analysis of our professions, or the enhancement of access to information. In addition, eligible projects include those which result in original scholarship in the arts (literary, performing, architectural, visual, etc.) or aspects of visual and material culture.

REQUIREMENTS AND RESTRICTIONS

Available to ARLIS/NA individual members (including special Individual membership categories, "honorary," "student," "retired," and "unemployed"). Applicants must have been an Individual ARLIS/NA member for at least one year prior to the deadline for a submitted grant application. Group projects undertaken by not more than four principal participants are eligible, at least half of whom must meet the above ARLIS/NA Individual membership criteria. Institutional members, Official Groups, Committees, Chapters, Divisions, and Sections of the Society are not eligible to apply to this Research Fund (special funding for group projects may be available through other channels within the Society). Current members of the ARLIS/NA Executive Board and the Research Committee are not eligible.

APPLICATION PROCEDURES

See website for application guidelines. Additional copies available from:

Kathy Edwards
Art and Architecture Librarian
Emery A. Gunnin Architecture Library
2-112 Lee Hall, Clemson University
Clemson, SC 29634
Phone: 864-656-4289
E-mail: kathye@clemson.edu

Cara List
Art and Architecture Librarian
Architecture and Allied Arts Library
5249 University of Oregon
Eugene, OR 97405-5249
Phone: 541-346-2200
E-mail: clist@uoregon.edu

Deadlines: February 3

CONFERENCE ATTENDANCE AWARD

Number of Grants: 1
Grant Ranges: $1,000

Program Description: To encourage participation in ARLIS/NA by assisting conference attendance by committee members, chapter officers, and moderators of divisions, sections, and round tables.

REQUIREMENTS AND RESTRICTIONS

Individual member who serves as a committee member, group moderator, and/or chapter officer.

APPLICATION PROCEDURES

See website for forms

MERRILL WADSWORTH SMITH TRAVEL AWARD IN ARCHITECTURE LIBRARIANSHIP

Grant Ranges: $1,000

Program Description: To encourage participation of members active in the field of Architecture Librarianship, Visual Resources Professionals in Architecture-dominated collections, Archivists, and students interested in Architecture Librarianship who could not attend the conference without financial assistance.

REQUIREMENTS AND RESTRICTIONS

ARLIS/NA members who are actively, but not necessarily exclusively, involved with the field of architecture in visual and/or print collections including librarians, visual resources curators, archivists, and students.

APPLICATION PROCEDURES

See website for forms.

ANDREW CAHAN PHOTOGRAPHY AWARD

Grant Ranges: $1,000

Program Description: To encourage participation of members active in the field of photography who could not attend the conference without financial assistance.

REQUIREMENTS AND RESTRICTIONS

Members who are actively involved in the field of photography through reference, research, or bibliographic work.

APPLICATION PROCEDURES

See website for forms.

AskArt Conference Attendance Award

Grant Ranges: $1,000

Program Description: To encourage participation of members active in the field of American art research and bibliography who could not attend the conference without financial assistance.

REQUIREMENTS AND RESTRICTIONS

Members who are actively involved in the field of American art through reference, research, bibliographic work, the overseeing of significant art research collections, or who are researching subjects or themes related to American art.

APPLICATION PROCEDURES

See website for forms

Student Conference Attendance Award

Grant Ranges: $1,000

Program Description: To encourage participation in ARLIS/NA by assisting students considering a career in art librarianship or visual resources to attend the annual ARLIS/NA conference.

Eligibility: Student members who are active participants in ARLIS/NA and are currently enrolled in an accredited graduate program in Library Studies and/or Information Studies or have recently graduated (within 12 months of graduation).

APPLICATION PROCEDURES

See website for forms

Student Diversity Award for Conference Attendance

Grant Ranges: $1,000

Program Description: To encourage multicultural students considering a career in art librarianship or visual resources to participate in the activities of ARLIS/NA.

REQUIREMENTS AND RESTRICTIONS

Students from a traditionally underrepresented group who are currently enrolled in an accredited graduate program in Library Studies and/or Information Studies or have recently graduated (within 12 months of graduation).

APPLICATION PROCEDURES

See website.

Howard & Beverly Joy Karno Award

Grant Ranges: $1,000

Program Description: To encourage professional development of art librarians who work to advance the study of Latin American art through interaction with ARLIS/NA colleagues and conference participation.

REQUIREMENTS AND RESTRICTIONS

Art librarians residing in Latin America or Art Librarians residing in North America working with significant Latin American art/architecture research collections or researching subjects or themes related to Latin American art/architecture.

APPLICATION PROCEDURES

See website for forms

Judith A. Hoffberg Student Award for Conference Attendance

Grant Ranges: $1,000

Program Description: To encourage students considering a career in art librarianship or visual resources to participate in the activities of ARLIS/NA.

REQUIREMENTS AND RESTRICTIONS

Students who are currently enrolled in an accredited graduate program in Library Studies and/or Information Studies or have recently graduated (within 12 months of graduation).

APPLICATION PROCEDURES

See website for forms

Samuel H. Kress Foundation Award for European Travel

Grant Range: N/A

Program Description: To support and encourage ARLIS/NA participation, collaboration, and professional development at European conferences.

REQUIREMENTS AND RESTRICTIONS

ARLIS/NA members in good standing who have had a paper accepted at a European conference or program relevant to the field of art librarianship or visual resources curatorship.

APPLICATION PROCEDURES

See website for forms.

Deadline: March 15

Asplundh Family Public Foundation

Headquarters

708 Blair Mill Rd.
Willow Grove, PA 19090-1701
Phone: 215-784-4200

Type of Grant Maker: Foundation

Description

Founded: 1953

Operating Locations/Geographic Preferences: Giving primarily in PA.

Financial Summary

Assets: $43,490,927
Total giving: $2,801,950
Number of Grants: 22
Grant Ranges: $417,750–$300

Grants Information

GRANT TYPES

General support

TYPICAL RECIPIENTS/SUBJECTS OF INTEREST

Christian higher education and schools, arts, education and health organizations

PAST GRANT RECIPIENTS

Library or School Related

- Columbia College, New York (NY), $78,900
- Queens University of Charlotte, Charlotte (NC), $6,000
- Academy of the New Church, Bryn Athyn (PA), $1,000,000

General

- General Church of the New Jerusalem, Bryn Athyn (PA), $50,000
- Abington Art Center, Jenkintown (PA), $25,000

REQUREMENTS AND RESTRICTIONS

No grants to individuals

APPLICATION PROCEDURES

Send letter with name, address and phone number of organization, history, mission, project description and amount requested.

Deadlines: None

Association of Jewish Libraries

Headquarters

PO Box 1118
Teaneck NJ 07666
Phone: 201-371-3255

www.jewishlibraries.org/main/AboutAJL/
    AwardsGrants.aspx

Type of Grant Maker: Library Organization

Grant Information

STUDENT SCHOLARSHIP

Grant Range: $1,000
Number of Grants: 1

Awarded to a student attending or planning to attend a graduate school of library and information science. Prospective candidates should have an interest in, and demonstrate a potential for, pursuing a career in Judaica librarianship.

REQUIREMENTS AND RESTRICTIONS

Students accepted in an ALA-accredited library school or equivalent (see application form for details) for the next academic year or students planning to continue their studies into the next academic year.

Evidence must be presented showing acceptance from a graduate school of library and information science, or evidence that indicates that studies will continue through the next academic year.

Applicants must provide documentation showing participation in Judaic studies at an academic or less formal level and/or experience working in Judaica libraries.

Applicants are also asked to submit a brief statement highlighting the extent of their participation in Judaic studies, in libraries, and other relevant experiences and relating how they feel their involvement in such activities might be reflected in their future career in library and information science.

APPLICATION PROCEDURES

Complete the application form online and forward it by e-mail, and submit necessary documentation via regular mail to:

Shulamith Berger
Curator of Special Collections
Yeshiva University
500 W. 185th St.
New York, NY 10033
Phone: 212-960-5451
E-mail: sberger@yu.edu

Deadline: April 4

Association of Research Libraries

Headquarters

21 Dupont Circle NW, Suite 800
Washington, DC 20036
Phone: 202-296-2296
Fax: 202-872-0884

www.arl.org/arl/index.shtml

Type of Grant Maker: Library Organization

Grants Information

LIBQUAL+® IN-KIND GRANT

Grant Amount: $3,200.
Number of Grants: Vary

Program Description: Award given for participation in LibQUAL survey. Recipients will be based on the following criteria:

1. Financial need. Applicants with the greatest financial need, who also meet the other criteria, will be given priority.
2. Contribution to the growth of LibQUAL+®. The LibQUAL+® Team continues to have strong interest in expanding the reach and scope of the survey in terms of how the survey is applied in different environments. Institutions whose participation would represent a new library type, a new language translation, a new country, or would otherwise increase the diversity of the LibQUAL+® project are particularly encouraged

to apply. The team is seeking institutions whose participation will provide the team with the best opportunity to further its understanding of library service quality.
3. Improvements in local service and quality. The ability of the participating library to both improve overall services and contribute to the quality of service provided to students and faculty at the institution will be considered.

APPLICATION PROCEDURES

Submit the following:

- A three- to five-page narrative explaining their unique situation and how they meet the criteria above (approximately 1,500 to 2,500 words)
- A brief paragraph describing their institution (less than 500 words)
- The name, phone number, e-mail address, and mailing address of the contact person for the application
- A short biography of the person applying on behalf of the institution

Applications will be accepted via e-mail to libqual@arl.org, by fax to 202-872-0884, or by mail to:

LibQUAL+® Grant Award
Association of Research Libraries
21 Dupont Circle, Suite 800
Washington, DC 20036-1543

Deadlines: June 17 and December 16

AT&T Foundation

Headquarters

208 S. Akard, Ste. 100
Dallas, TX 75202-4206

Fax: 210-351-2599

www.att.com/gen/landing-pages?pid=7735

Contact: Laura P. Sanford, Pres.

E-mail: foundation@att.com

Type of Grant Maker: Corporate Foundation

Description

Founded: 1984

Operating Locations/Geographic Preferences: Giving on a national basis in areas of company operations.

Corporate Foundation Information: Supported by AT&T Inc., Southwestern Bell Corp. and SBC Communications Inc.

Financial Summary

Assets: $45,095,569
Total Giving: $18,567,032

Grants Information

GRANT TYPES

Program development, matching, employee volunteering, equipment

TYPICAL RECIPIENTS/SUBJECTS OF INTEREST

Education, community needs and sustainability.

Special emphasis on programs designed to address the high school dropout crisis while strengthening student success and workforce readiness.

PAST GRANT RECIPIENTS

Library or School Related

- Walnut Creek Library, Walnut Creek, (CA), $3,000
- Library Association of Ringwood, Ringwood (NJ), $1,000
- Dallas Public Library, $1,456
- Herrick District Library, Holland (MI), $600
- Detroit Public Library, Detroit (MI), $700
- Regional Library of Hot Spring, Hot Springs (AR), $500
- Desert Foothills Library, Cave Creek (AZ), $250
- Grinnell Library, Wappingers Fall (NY), $500
- Seminole County Public Schools, Sanford (FL) in 2010. For the Teach Forward-Pay Forward, $89,000

APPLICATION PROCEDURES AND DEADLINES

See website.

Atherton, Leburta Foundation

Headquarters

c/o Bank of Hawaii
PO Box 3170, Dept. 715
Honolulu, HI 96802-3170
Type of Grant Maker: Foundation

Description

Founded: 1997
Operating Locations/Geographic Preferences: CA, HI

Financial Summary

Assets: $13,618,666
Total Giving: $543,800
Number of Grants: 26
Grant Ranges: $50,000–$1,000

Grants Information

GRANT TYPES

Program and operating support

TYPICAL RECIPIENTS/SUBJECTS OF INTEREST

Education and human services

PAST GRANT RECIPIENTS

Library or School Related

- Long Beach Public Library, Program support, $25,000
- La Pietra-Hawaii School for Girls, Honolulu (HI), for program support, $25,000
- Punahou School, Honolulu (HI), for operating support, $25,000

General

- Food Basket, Hilo (HI), for program support, $35,000
- Hospice Hawaii, Honolulu (HI), $30,000

REQUIREMENTS AND RESTRICTIONS

None

APPLICATION PROCEDURES

Send letter.
Deadlines: None

Atran Foundation, Inc.

Headquarters

23-25 E. 21st St., 3rd Fl.
New York, NY 10010-6207
Phone: 212-505-9677

Contact: Diane Fischer, Pres.

Type of Grant Maker: Foundation

Description

Founded: 1945

Operating Locations/Geographic Preferences: Giving primarily in New York, NY.

Financial Summary

Assets: $14,481,272
Total Giving: $610,000

Grants Information

GRANT TYPES

Program development, continuing, general and operating support, endowments, conferences, annual campaigns

TYPICAL RECIPIENTS/SUBJECTS OF INTEREST

Research relating to labor and labor relations, art, science, literature, economics, and sociology

PAST GRANT RECIPIENTS

Library or School Related

- Columbia University Memorial Library, $60,500
- New York Public Library, $4,000
- Medem Library, New York (NY), $10,000
- Columbia University, New York (NY), $50,500
- Brandeis University, Waltham (MA), $50,000

General

- Workers Defense League, New York (NY), $13,000

REQUIREMENTS AND RESTRICTIONS

No grants to individuals.

APPLICATION PROCEDURES

Send proposal with the following:

1. Listing of additional sources and amount of support
2. Copy of current year's organizational budget and/or project budget
3. Detailed description of project and amount of funding requested
4. Copy of IRS Determination Letter
5. Statement of problem project will address
6. How project will be sustained once grant-maker support is completed
7. Timetable for implementation and evaluation of project

Deadline: September 30

Autry Foundation

Headquarters

4383 Colfax Ave.
Studio City, CA 91604-2837
Phone: 818-752-7770

Contact: Jacqueline Autry, Pres.

Type of Grant Maker: Foundation

Description

Founded: 1974

Operating Locations/Geographic Preferences: Giving primarily in the Los Angeles, CA area, and Riverside and Orange counties.

Financial Summary

Assets: $18,313,675
Total Giving: $399,686
Number of Grants: 26
Grant Ranges: $125,000–$100

Grants Information

GRANT TYPES

General support

TYPICAL RECIPIENTS/SUBJECTS OF INTEREST

Giving primarily for hospital and human services, however, some previous support has been given to libraries.

PAST GRANT RECIPIENTS

General

- Eisenhower Medical Center Foundation, Rancho Mirage (CA), for general support, $500,000
- People Assisting the Homeless, Los Angeles (CA), for general support, $50,000
- Los Angeles Zoo and Botanical Gardens, Los Angeles (CA), $6,900
- Boy Scouts of America, Sherman Oaks (CA), for general support, $4,000
- Los Angeles Opera Company, Los Angeles (CA), for general support, $1,000

REQUIREMENTS AND RESTRICTIONS

No grants to individuals.

APPLICATION PROCEDURES

Send letter on organization letterhead.

Deadlines: None

Avery Arts Foundation, Milton and Sally

Headquarters

c/o Radin, Glass & Co., LLP
360 Lexington Ave.
New York, NY 10017-6502

Fax: 212-595-2840

Contact: March A. Cavanaugh, Pres.

Type of Grant Maker: Foundation

Description

Founded: 1983
Operating Locations/Geographic Preferences: Giving primarily in NY.

Financial Summary

Assets: $2,530,084
Total Giving: $429,750

Grants Information

GRANT TYPES

General support

TYPICAL RECIPIENTS/SUBJECTS OF INTEREST

Art education, with emphasis on the visual arts

PAST GRANT RECIPIENTS

Library or School Related

- Pitzer College, Claremont (CA), $30,000
- Hobart and William Smith Colleges, Geneva (NY), $17,000
- Bard College, Annandale on Hudson (NY), $15,000
- State University of New York College at Purchase, Purchase (NY), $15,000
- Studio Elementary School, New York (NY), $10,000

General

- Metropolitan Museum of Art, New York (NY), $10,000

REQUIREMENTS AND RESTRICTIONS

No support for religious or political organizations or to individuals.

APPLICATION PROCEDURES

Send letter to:

300 Central Park W.
Apt. 16J
New York, NY 10024

Deadlines: None

Aylward Family Foundation

Headquarters

PO Box 409
Neenah, WI 54957-0409

Phone: 920-725-7000

Contact: E.W. Alyward, Pres.

Contributes only to preselected organizations. Applications not accepted.

Azadoutioun Foundation

Headquarters

c/o Gravestar, Inc.
160 2nd St.
Cambridge, MA 02142-1515

Contact: Laurie Le Blanc

Type of Grant Maker: Foundation

Description

Founded: 1985

Operating Locations/Geographic Preferences: United States

Financial Summary

Assets: $4,724,135
Total Giving: $309,145
Number of Grants: 5
Grant Ranges: $251,770–$5,000

Grants Information

GRANT TYPES

General and operating support, program development

TYPICAL RECIPIENTS/SUBJECTS OF INTEREST

Education and human services, especially Armenian

PAST GRANT RECIPIENTS

General

- Armenia Tree Project, Watertown (MA), $169,500
- Armenian Assembly of America, Washington (DC), $39,600
- Direct Cultural Access, New York, general support, $7,500
- Armenian Library and Museum of America (MA), general support, $50,000

REQUIREMENTS AND RESTRICTIONS

No grants to individuals or loans.

APPLICATION PROCEDURES

Send letter to:

10 Madison Ave.
Groveland, MA 01834-1143

Deadlines: None

BankAtlantic Foundation, Inc.

Headquarters

2100 W. Cypress Creek Rd.
Fort Lauderdale, FL 33309-1823
Phone: 954-940-5058
Fax: 954-940-5030

www.bankatlantic.com/bafoundation

Contact: Marcia Barry-Smith, Secy. and Exec. Dir.

E-mail: mbarrysmith@bankatlantic.com

Type of Grant Maker: Corporate Foundation

Description

Founded: 1994

Operating Locations/Geographic Preferences: Giving limited to areas where company has a presence in FL.

Corporate Foundation Information: Supported by

- BankAtlantic, F.S.B.
- The Annenberg Foundation
- BankAtlantic
- BankAtlantic Bancorp, Inc.

Financial Summary

Assets: $2,537,931
Total Giving: $425,875
Number of Grants: 144
Grant Ranges: $30,000–$61

Grants Information

GRANT TYPES

Program development, continuing, general and operating support

TYPICAL RECIPIENTS/SUBJECTS OF INTEREST

Education, arts and culture, human services, and community development

PAST GRANT RECIPIENTS

Library or School Related

- Broward Public Library Foundation, fort Lauderdale (FL), $20,000
- Broward County School District, fort Lauderdale (FL), $25,000
- Dade Public Education Fund, Miami (FL), $20,000

General

- Leadership Broward Foundation, fort Lauderdale (FL), $10,000
- Urban League of Broward County, fort Lauderdale (FL), $10,000
- Fort Lauderdale Children's Theater, fort Lauderdale (FL), $8,500

REQUIREMENTS AND RESTRICTIONS

No funds for:

- Capital improvement or building campaign
- Courtesy or goodwill advertising in benefit publications
- Endowment campaigns
- Fund-raising events or purchase of tickets

- Funds for travel expenses
- Hospitals or medical research
- Individual K–12 schools
- National health-related organizations
- Organizations or projects of national scope
- Organizations without 501(c)(3) status
- Political or lobbying organizations
- Programs or organizations operating outside the state of Florida
- Religious, veteran, or fraternal organizations
- School athletic teams, cheerleading squads, bands, choirs, etc.
- Social functions or sporting events
- Individuals

APPLICATION PROCEDURES

Applications must be in writing and addressed to:

Marcia Barry-Smith
Executive Director
Phone: 954-940-5058
BankAtlantic Foundation
2100 West Cypress Creek Road
Fort Lauderdale, FL 33309

Faxed applications will not be considered.

Applications must include:

- Name, address and telephone number of the organization
- Director's name
- Brief history of the organization
- Project description, including the need or issue to be addressed by the project
- Anticipated benefits of the project
- Total amount requested
- Dates of proposed project
- Operating budget
- Program budget, including funds you have already raised for the program
- Identification of additional revenue sources
- List of current corporate and foundation funding sources, with amounts contributed
- Project director's name, address, and telephone number— if different from above
- Project location
- Copy of 501(c)(3) letter
- Copy of Charitable Solicitation License; for information, call 1-800-435-7352
- List of board members and their affiliations
- List of any funding that you may have received from BankAtlantic in the same calendar year
- Signature of executive director acknowledging application

Deadlines: Requests are decided upon twice a year and reviewed in the order received.

Bardes Fund

Headquarters

4730 Madison Rd.
Cincinnati, OH 45227-1426
Phone: 513-533-6228

Unsolicited requests for funds not accepted.

Barker Foundation Inc.

Headquarters

PO Box 328
Nashua, NH 03061-0328
Contact: Douglas M. Barker, Treas.
Type of Grant Maker: Foundation

Description

Founded: 1954
Operating Locations/Geographic Preferences: Giving primarily in NH.

Financial Summary

Assets: $5,005,118
Total Giving: $157,095

Grants Information

GRANT TYPES

Program development, general, operating and continuing support, annual and capital campaigns, building and renovation, equipment

TYPICAL RECIPIENTS/SUBJECTS OF INTEREST

Youth, health associations, and social services

PAST GRANT RECIPIENTS

General

- Bedford Historical Society, Bedford (NH), $5,000
- Big Brothers Big Sisters of Greater Nashua, Nashua (NH), $1,500

- Bishop Guertin High School, Nashua (NH), $3,500
- Boys & Girls Club of Greater Nashua, Nashua (NH), $5,000
- Boy Scouts of America, Troop #12, Hollis (NH), $1,000
- Bridgewater Public Safety, Bridgewater (NH), $2,095
- Camp Allen, Bedford (NH), $2,000
- CareGivers, Nashua (NH), $3,000
- Center for Wildlife, Cape Neddick (ME), $5,000
- Community Hospice House, Merrimack (NH), $25,000

REQUIREMENTS AND RESTRICTIONS

No grants to individuals.

APPLICATION PROCEDURES

Submit a one-page concept paper in writing, including:

1. Copy of IRS Determination Letter
2. Listing of board of directors, trustees, officers and other key people and their affiliations
3. Detailed description of project and amount of funding requested.

Deadlines: None

Barker, Coeta and Donald Foundation

Headquarters

PO Box 936
Rancho Mirage, CA 92270-0936
Phone: 760-340-1162

Contact: Joan K. Damiani, Exec. Admin.

Unsolicited requests for funds not accepted.

Barker Welfare Foundation

Headquarters

PO Box 2
Glen Head, NY 11545-0002
Phone: 516-759-5592
Fax: 516-759-5497

www.barkerwelfare.org

Contact: Sarane H. Ross, Pres.

E-mail: SusanDeMaio@barkerwelfare.org

Type of Grant Maker: Foundation

Description

Founded: 1934

Operating Locations/Geographic Preferences: Giving primarily in Chicago, IL, Michigan City, IN, and New York, NY, Grants to Chicago agencies are by invitation only.

FINANCIAL SUMMARY

Assets: $76,766,238
Total Giving: $2,342,174
Number of Grants: 254
Grant Ranges: $150,000–$500

Grants Information

GRANT TYPES

General, operating and continuing support, annual and capital campaigns, building and renovation, equipment

TYPICAL RECIPIENTS/SUBJECTS OF INTEREST

Libraries, youth and families, museums and the fine and performing arts, child welfare and youth agencies, health services and rehabilitation, welfare, aid to the handicapped, family planning, the environment, recreation, and elderly

PAST GRANT RECIPIENTS

Library or School Related

- Chicago Public Library, Teacher in the Library, $15,000
- New York Public Library, Teen Center $25,000
- New York Public Library, Children's Room, $12,500
- Julliard School, Music Technology Center, $12,500

General

- Coalition for Hispanic Families, After School Arts and Literacy, $6,000

REQUIREMENTS AND RESTRICTIONS

No support for political activities, start-up organizations, national health, welfare, or education agencies, institutions or funds, including private or public schools.

No grants to individuals or for endowment funds, seed money, emergency funds, deficit financing, scholarships, fellowships, medical or scientific research, films or videos, conferences, or loans.

APPLICATION PROCEDURES

See website for application guidelines.

Deadlines: February 1 and August 1

BARKER, J.M.R. FOUNDATION

1350 Avenue of the Americas
New York, NY 10019
Phone: 978- 282-4776

No giving since 2008

Barnes Group Foundation Inc.

Headquarters

123 Main St.
Bristol, CT 06010-0489

www.barnesgroupinc.com/about_foundation.php

Type of Grant Maker: Corporate Foundation

Description

Founded: 1973

Operating Locations/Geographic Preferences: Giving primarily in areas of company operations, with emphasis on CT.

Corporate Foundation Information: Supported by Barnes Group, Inc.

FINANCIAL SUMMARY

Assets: $4,710 (as listed in 2010)
Total Giving: $1,104,796

Grants Information

GRANT TYPES

General and operating support, annual campaigns, building and renovation, employee volunteering and matching

TYPICAL RECIPIENTS/SUBJECTS OF INTEREST

Education, arts and culture, environment, health, cancer, youth services, and civic affairs

APPLICATION PROCEDURES
CONTACT FOUNDATION

Barrington Foundation, Inc. (Also known as the Greater Barrington Foundation)

   7-11 S. Broadway, Ste. 200
   White Plains, NY 10601-3520

Unsolicited requests for funds not accepted. However, Foundation has supported selected libraries in the past.

Barstow Foundation

Headquarters

c/o Chemical Bank & Trust Co.
235 E. Main St.
Midland, MI 48640-5137
Phone: 989-839-5305

Contact: John E. Kessler, Secy.

Type of Grant Maker: Foundation

Description

Founded: 1967

Operating Locations/Geographic Preferences: Giving primarily in MI; giving also in states where trustees reside, including AZ, CA, and TX.

Financial Summary

Assets: $6,257,692
Total Giving: $135,000

Grants Information

GRANT TYPES

Program development, general and operating, capital campaigns

TYPICAL RECIPIENTS/SUBJECTS OF INTEREST

Arts and humanities, civic, education, environment, health, social services

PAST GRANT RECIPIENTS

General

- Hands Extended Loving People, Ludington (MI), $10,000
- Asheville Community Band, Asheville (NC), $2,000
- Food Bank of East Michigan, Flint (MI) $4,000
- Enterprise Community Partners, Columbia (MD), $5,000

REQUIREMENTS AND RESTRICTIONS

No grants to individuals

APPLICATION PROCEDURES

Send letter with brochures or descriptive literature about organization

Deadlines: July 31

Barth, Theodore H. Foundation, Inc.

Headquarters

45 Rockefeller Plz., 20th Fl., Ste. 2006
New York, NY 10111-0100
Contact: Ellen S. Berelson, Pres.
E-mail: barthfoundation@earthlink.net
Type of Grant Maker: Foundation

Description

Founded: 1953
Operating Locations/Geographic Preferences: Giving primarily in New York, NY, and Washington, DC; also MA and VA

Financial Summary

Assets: $24,714,455
Total Giving: $1,063,250
Number of Grants: 79
Grant Ranges: $110,000–$1,000

Grants Information

GRANT TYPES

Program development, continuing, general and operating support, annual campaigns, endowments, seed money

TYPICAL RECIPIENTS/SUBJECTS OF INTEREST

Education, arts and humanities, civic, environment, health, religion, science, social services

PAST GRANT RECIPIENTS

Library or School Related

- Morgan Library, New York (NY), $5,000
- New York Public Library, New York (NY), $7,500
- Clark University, Worcester (MA), $15,000
- Framingham State University, Framingham (MA), $3,250

General

- National Book Foundation, New York (NY), $25,000
- Brooklyn Museum, Brooklyn (NY), $5,000
- New York City Ballet, New York (NY), $17,500
- Roundabout Theater Company, New York (NY), $10,000

REQUIREMENTS AND RESTRICTIONS

No grants to individuals or for capital projects.

APPLICATION PROCEDURES

Send letter.
Deadlines: None

Bay State Federal Savings Charitable Foundation

Headquarters

55 Cambridge Pkwy.
Cambridge, MA 02142-1234
Phone: 617-225-2822
Fax: 617-225-6945
www.baystatecharitable.com
Contact: Jill W. Power, Corp. Secy.
E-mail: info@baystatecharitable.com
Type of Grant Maker: Corporate Foundation

Description

Founded: 1997
Operating Locations/Geographic Preferences: Giving primarily in MA, with emphasis on the Boston area.
Corporate Foundation Information: Supported by:

- Bay State Bancorp, Inc.
- Bay State Federal Savings Bank.

Financial Summary

Assets: $8,574,563
Total Giving: $360,891
Number of Grants: 301
Grant Ranges: $5,000–$100

Grants Information

GRANT TYPES

General support

TYPICAL RECIPIENTS/SUBJECTS OF INTEREST

Projects to expand home ownership opportunities and to support community organizations

PAST GRANT RECIPIENTS

Library or School Related

- Hudson Catholic High School, Hudson (MA), $25,000
- Presentation School Foundation, Brighton (MA), $75,000

General

- New England Center for Children, Southborough (MA), $13,000

REQUIREMENTS AND RESTRICTIONS

No grants to individuals.

APPLICATION PROCEDURES

Send application package or written letter with 501(c)(3) IRS approval

Address application to:

Denise Renaghan,
Bay State Federal Savings Charitable Foundation
55 Cambridge Parkway
Cambridge, MA 02142

Deadlines: None

Bechtel, Jr. Foundation, S. D.

Headquarters

PO Box 193809
San Francisco, CA 94119-3809
Phone: 415-284-8570

www.sdbjrfoundation.org

Contact: Kay Barthold, Grants Mgr.

E-mail: sdbjr.@sdbjrFoundation.org

Type of Grant Maker: Foundation

Description

Founded: 2005

Operating Locations/Geographic Preferences: Giving primarily in the San Francisco Bay, CA, area

Financial Summary

Assets: $231,750,977
Total Giving: $26,154,837
Number of Grants: 365 grants
Grant Ranges: $2,500,000–$1,000

Grants Information

GRANT TYPES

Program development, general support, building/renovation, capital campaigns, capacity building, research

TYPICAL RECIPIENTS/SUBJECT OF INTEREST

Citizenship development; youth development; access to healthcare; nutrition and fitness; Science; Technology; Engineering and Math (STEM) education; water management; wetlands protection; parks sustainability, energy security and sustainability

PAST GRANT RECIPIENTS

Library or School Related

- Massachusetts Institute of Technology, Cambridge (MA), program support, $840,000
- Pennsylvania State University, University Park (PA), program support, $45,000

General

- Boy Scouts of America National Council, Irving (TX), capital support, $2,500,000
- Community Hospital Foundation, Monterey (CA), capital support, $1,000,000
- Monterey Bay Aquarium Foundation, Monterey (CA), capital support, $1,000,000
- Museum of Science, Boston (MA), program support, $267,000

APPLICATION PROCEDURES

Approach with a letter, not exceeding two pages, focusing on program areas. Upon review of the letter a full proposal may be invited.

Bender Foundation, Inc.

Headquarters

1120 Connecticut Ave. N.W., Ste. 1200
Washington, DC 20036-3932
Phone: 202-828-9000

Contact: Julie Bender Silver, Pres.

E-mail: benderfoundation@blakereal.com

Contributes only to preselected organizations. Applications not accepted.

Benenson, Frances & Benjamin Foundation, Inc.

Headquarters

708 3rd Ave., 28th Fl.
New York, NY 10017-4232
Contact: Bruce W. Benenson
Type of Grant Maker: Foundation

Description

Founded: 1983
Operating Locations/Geographic Preferences: United States

Financial Summary

Assets: $35,264,351
Total Giving: $2,362,044

Grants Information

GRANT TYPES

Continuing support and endowments

TYPICAL RECIPIENTS/SUBJECTS OF INTEREST

Education, human services, arts and culture, health care, and community development

PAST GRANT RECIPIENTS

Library or School Related

- Yale University, New Haven (CT), $500,000

General

- United Negro College Fund, Fairfax (VA), $5,000
- American Civil Liberties Union Foundation, $50,000
- Metropolitan Opera, New York (NY), $25,000
- New York Civil Liberties Union Foundation, New York (NY), $20,000

REQUIREMENTS AND RESTRICTIONS

No grants to individuals

APPLICATION PROCEDURES

Send letter with description of project and amount of funding requested
Deadlines: None

Berks County Community Foundation

Headquarters

237 Court St.
Reading, PA 19601
Phone: 610-685-2223
www.bccf.org
Contact: Kevin K. Murphy, Pres.; for grants: Richard C. Mappin, V.P., Grant-making
E-mail: info@bccf.org
Type of Grant Maker: Community Foundation

Description

Founded: 1994
Operating Locations/Geographic Preferences: Giving limited to Berks County, PA

Financial Summary

Assets: $49,428,689
Total Giving: $3,257,998

Grants Information

GRANT TYPES

Program development, capital campaigns, matching, consulting services, seed money

TYPICAL RECIPIENTS/SUBJECTS OF INTEREST

Historic preservation, education, youth, aging, arts, cultural awareness, economic development, health care

PAST GRANT RECIPIENTS

Library or School Related

- Kutztown University Foundation, Kutztown (PA), general support, $3,000
- Albright College, Reading (PA), general support, $34,800
- Drexel University, Philadelphia (PA), health center needs assessment, $30,000
- United Berks Community Television, Reading (PA), for web-based Community Information Hub, $252,500

General

- Reading, City of, Reading (PA), park solar lighting, $22,000
- United Way of Berks County, Reading (PA), general support, $13,000
- YMCA of Reading and Berks County, Reading (PA), Living the Legacy Campaign, $7,000

REQUIREMENTS AND RESTRICTIONS

No support for religious organizations from discretionary funds. No grants for operational support.

APPLICATION PROCEDURES

Visit foundation website. Applicants should submit:

1. Name, address and phone number of organization
2. Detailed description of project and amount of funding requested
3. Contact person

Deadlines: Vary

Bingham, William 2nd Betterment Fund

Headquarters

c/o Christine O'Donnell, Bank of America, N.A.
1 Bryant Park
NY1-100-28-05
New York, NY 10036-6715
Phone: 646-855-1011

www.megrants.org/betterment.htm

Contact: Christine O'Donnell, V.P., Bank of America, N.A.

E-mail: betterment@ustrust.com

Type of Grant Maker: Foundation

Description

Operating Locations/Geographic Preferences: Maine

Financial Summary

Assets: $32,749,588
Total Giving: $1,815,840
Number of Grants: 104
Grant Ranges: $250,000–$670

Grants Information

GRANT TYPES

General support, capital campaigns

TYPICAL RECIPIENTS/SUBJECTS OF INTEREST

Education, economics, environment, health care

PAST GRANT RECIPIENTS

Library or School Related

- Gould Academy, Bethel (ME), capital campaign, $250,000
- University of Maine, Orono (ME), Maine Youth Fitness Project, $26,000
- Franklin County Community College Network, Farmington (ME), operating support, $10,000

General

- Haystack Mountain School of Crafts, Deer Isle (ME), endowment, $40,000
- Cobscook Bay Resource Center, Eastport (ME), operating support, $15,000
- Medical Care Development, Augusta (ME), school-based health centers, $15,000
- Franco-American Heritage Center at Saint Mary's, Lewiston (ME), operating support, $10,000

REQUIREMENTS AND RESTRICTIONS

No support for religious activities or programs or grants to individuals.

APPLICATION PROCEDURES

Only full proposals accepted for review. No letters of inquiry or pre-submission proposal review. See guidelines available on website. Applicants should submit:

1. Copy of IRS Determination Letter
2. Detailed description of project and amount of funding requested

Deadlines: January 31, April 30, and September 30

Blood-Horse Charitable Foundation, Inc.

Headquarters

3101 Beaumont Centre Cir., Ste. 100
Lexington, KY 40513-1959

Phone: 859-278-2361

Contact: Stacy V. Bearse, Secy.

Type of Grant Maker: Foundation

Description

Founded: 1988

Operating Locations/Geographic Preferences: Giving primarily in KY.

Financial Summary

Assets: $0 (market value)
Total giving: $1,550

Grants Information

GRANT TYPES

General and operating support

TYPICAL RECIPIENTS/SUBJECTS OF INTEREST

Museums, organizations involved with equestrianism and human services

REQUIREMENTS AND RESTRICTIONS

No grants to individuals.

APPLICATION PROCEDURES

Send letter. Apply to address:

    PO Box 919003
    Lexington, KY 40591-9003

Applicants should submit:

1. Copy of IRS Determination Letter
2. Detailed description of project and amount of funding requested

Deadline: April

Blowitz-Ridgeway Foundation

Headquarters

1701 E. Woodsfield Rd., Ste. 201
Schaumburg, IL 60173-5127
Phone: 847-330-1020
Fax: 847-330-1028

www.blowitzridgeway.org

Contact: Serena L. Moy, Admin.; Laura Romero, Prog. Assoc.

E-mail: laura@blowitzridgeway.org

Type of Grant Maker: Foundation

Description

Founded: 1984

Operating Locations/Geographic Preferences: Giving generally limited to IL

Financial Summary

Assets: $20,459,843
Total Giving: $1,338,503

Grants Information

GRANT TYPES

Program development, capital campaigns, continuing, general and operating support, investments and loans

TYPICAL RECIPIENTS/SUBJECTS OF INTEREST

Health, mental and physical disability, and social services, with emphasis on children and youth

PAST GRANT RECIPIENTS

Library or School Related

- Josephinum Academy, $15,000
- Queen of Peace High School, $10,000

General

- Art Encounter, for its "Hats Off to Art: Creative Community Building with Older Adults" program, $10,000
- Better Boys Foundation, for YouthLab Program, $5,000
- Big Brothers/Big Sisters of Metro Chicago for mentoring program, $5,000
- Cabrini Green Tutoring Program, for operating support, $10,000

REQUIREMENTS AND RESTRICTIONS

No support for government agencies, religious purposes, or organizations that subsist mainly on third-party funding. No grants to individuals, or for production or writing of audiovisual materials.

APPLICATION PROCEDURES

Applicants outside the state of Illinois are asked to please contact the Foundation prior to submitting an application.

See website for online applications.

Inquiries for further information should be addressed to:

Serena L. Moy
Administrator
Blowitz-Ridgeway Foundation
1701 E. Woodfield Road, Suite 201
Schaumburg, IL 60173

Deadlines: None

Blue Bell Foundation

Headquarters

1525 W. WT Harris Blvd.
Charlotte, NC 28288-5709
Phone: 910-373-3412

Type of Grant Maker: Corporate Foundation

Description

Founded: 1944

Operating Locations/Geographic Preferences: Giving primarily in areas of company operations, with emphasis on NC.

Corporate Foundation Information: Supported by:

- Blue Bell, Inc.
- Wrangler Apparel Corp.

Financial Summary

Assets: $5,648,106
Total Giving: $274,226

Grants Information

GRANT TYPES

General and operating support, employee matching

TYPICAL RECIPIENTS/SUBJECTS OF INTEREST

Education, arts and culture, health, athletics, human services, and community development

PAST GRANT RECIPIENTS

Library or School Related

- Wake Forest University, Winston-Salem (NC), $2,000
- Georgia Tech, $1,500
- Triad Catholic Schools, $1,200
- High Point University, $2,000
- Tennessee Scholars, $2,000

General

- Summit House, Greensboro (NC), $3,000
- Habitat for Humanity, $2,000
- Girl Scouts Carolinas Peaks, $5,000

REQUIREMENTS AND RESTRICTIONS

No support to individuals.

APPLICATION PROCEDURES

Send proposal to:

c/o Sam Tucker
V.P., Human Resources
PO Box 21488
Greensboro, NC 27420

Deadlines: None

Blue Shield of California Foundation (*Also known as California Physicians' Service Foundation*)

Headquarters

50 Beale St., 14th Fl.
San Francisco, CA 94105-1819
www.blueshieldcafoundation.org

Contact: Gwyneth Tripp, Grant Admin.

E-mail: bscf@blueshieldcafoundation.org

Type of Grant Maker: Corporate Foundation

Description

Founded: 1981

Operating Locations/Geographic Preferences: Giving limited to CA.

Corporate Foundation Information: Blue Shield of

California Foundation is funded entirely by contributions from Blue Shield of California, a not-for-profit health plan founded by physicians.

Financial Summary

Assets: $52,881,521
Total Giving: $28,141,951
Number of Grants: 458
Grant Ranges: $1,500,000–$1,000

Grants Information

GRANT TYPES

Program development, general support (only for invited organizations), capacity building

TYPICAL RECIPIENTS/SUBJECTS OF INTEREST

Foundation programs include:

- Blue Shield Against Violence
- Clinic Leadership Institute
- Health Care and Coverage
- Strong Field Project (in collaboration with other organizations) to build a network of domestic violence service providers

PAST GRANT RECIPIENTS

Library or School Related

- University of California, San Francisco (CA), for Clinic Leadership Institute, $491,000

General

- Women's Foundation of California, San Francisco (CA), for Blue Shield Against Violence Strong Field Projects program, $1,500,000
- National Family Justice Center Alliance, San Diego (CA), for California Family Justice Initiative, $924,000
- Youth Radio, Oakland (CA), for Boss of Me Youth Media Campaign, $255,000

APPLICATION PROCEDURES

Online questionnaire and letter of inquiry form

Deadlines: January 6, April 27, and August 3

Baker, George F. Trust

Headquarters

c/o Citibank, N.A.
1 Court Sq., 29th Fl.
Long Island City, NY 11120
Phone: 800-770-8444

Type of Grant Maker: Foundation

Description

Founded: 1937

Operating Locations/Geographic Preferences: Giving primarily in CT, FL, MA, and NY

Financial Summary

Assets: $5,740,020
Total Giving: $1,149,885
Number of Grants: 29
Grant Ranges: $200,000–$100

Grants Information

GRANT TYPES

General and operating support, matching

TYPICAL RECIPIENTS/SUBJECTS OF INTEREST

Education, arts, hospitals and human services

PAST GRANT RECIPIENTS

Library or School Related

- Society of Four Arts, Palm Beach (FL), $2,000
- Harvard Business School, Baker Library, Cambridge (MA), $350,000
- Salisbury School, Salisbury (CT), $100,000
- Georgetown University, Washington (DC), $50,000

General

- Fishers Island Community Center, Fishers Island (NY), $10,000
- YMCA of the Palm Beaches, West Palm Beach (FL), $5,000

APPLICATION PROCEDURES

Send letter to:

> c/o Miss Rocio Suarez
> Exec. Dir.
> 477 Madison Ave., Ste. 1650
> New York, NY 10022

Letter should include:

1. Signature and title of chief executive officer
2. Copy of IRS Determination Letter
3. Detailed description of project and amount of funding requested
4. Listing of additional sources and amount of support

Deadlines: None

Baker, R.C. Foundation

Headquarters

PO Box 6150
Orange, CA 92863
Phone: 714-750-8987

No giving recorded since 2007

Bakewell Foundation

Headquarters

7800 Forsyth Blvd., 8th Fl.
St. Louis, MO 63105-3311
Phone: 314-862-5555

Contact: Richard W. Meier, Secy.

Type of Grant Maker: Corporate Foundation

Description

Founded: 1987

Operating Locations/Geographic Preferences: Giving primarily in CA, CO, FL, MO, and WY.

Corporate Foundation Information: Supported by Bakewell Corp.

Financial Summary

Assets: $6,525,040
Total Giving: $282,600
Number of Grants: 8
Grant Ranges: $150,000–$100

Grants Information

GRANT TYPES

General and operating support

TYPICAL RECIPIENTS/SUBJECTS OF INTEREST

Museums, hospitals, and organizations involved with higher education and sustainability research

PAST GRANT RECIPIENTS

Library or School Related

- University of Southern California, Los Angeles (CA), $125,000

General

- Heartland Museum, Clanon (IA), $2,500
- Neighborhood Health Clinic, Naples (FL), $2,500

REQUIREMENTS AND RESTRICTIONS

None

APPLICATION PROCEDURES

Send proposal detailing description of project and amount of funding requested.

Deadlines: None

Balfour, Lloyd G. Foundation

Headquarters

c/o Bank of America, N.A., Philanthropic Solutions
225 Franklin St., 4th Fl.
Boston, MA 02110-2801

www.bankofamerica.com/grant-making

Contact: Miki C. Akimoto, V.P., Bank of America, N.A., Philanthropic Solutions

E-mail: miki.akimoto@baml.com

Type of Grant Maker: Corporate Foundation

Description

Founded: 1973

Operating Locations/Geographic Preferences: Giving primarily in New England, with emphasis on Attleboro, MA

Corporate Financial Information: Supported by Balfour Corp.

Financial Summary

Assets: $101,121,784
Total Giving: $4,233,196
Number of Grants: 54
Grant Ranges: $472,540–$7,000

Grants Information

GRANT TYPES

Program development and general and operating support

TYPICAL RECIPIENTS/SUBJECTS OF INTEREST

Education, health, human services; especially college readiness, access, and success for underserved populations in New England.

PAST GRANT RECIPIENTS

Library or School Related

- Citizen Schools, Boston (MA), for High School Success and College Readiness program, $125,000
- Indiana University, Bloomington (IN), for scholarship fund, $200,000
- Boston Foundation, Boston (MA), for general support for Achieving the Dream, program to help more community college students succeed, $472,540
- Massachusetts Institute of Technology, Cambridge (MA), for MIT OEOP for underserved middle and high school students in New England, $125,000

General

- Grant-makers for Education, Portland (OR), for operating funds, $7,000

REQUIREMENTS AND RESTRICTIONS

No grants to individuals.

APPLICATION PROCEDURES

To discuss the application process or for questions, contact:

Miki C. Akimoto
Vice President
U.S. Trust
Phone: 866-778-6859

E-mail: miki.akimoto@baml.com
225 Franklin St., 4th Fl.
MA1-225-04-02
Boston, MA 02110

Deadlines: Rolling

Baltimore Community Foundation

Headquarters

2 E. Read St., 9th Fl.
Baltimore, MD 21202-6903
Phone: 410-332-4171

www.bcf.org

Contact: Maya Smith, Prog. Asst.

E-mail: questions@bcf.org

Type of Grant Maker: Community Foundation

Description

Founded: 1972

Operating Locations/Geographic Preferences: Giving primarily in Baltimore City and Baltimore County, MD.

Financial Summary

Assets: $157,851,613
Total giving: $21,724,587

Grant Information

GRANT TYPES

Program development, management development, capacity building, income development, seed money

TYPICAL RECIPIENTS/SUBJECTS OF INTEREST

Subjects: Adult education, literacy and basic skill, education, neighborhood development, aging and youth

PAST GRANT RECIPIENTS

Library or School Related

- Trinity College, Hartford (CT), $200,000
- Morgan State University Foundation, Baltimore (MD), $3,500
- Baltimore School for the Arts Foundation, Baltimore (MD), $161,000

General

- Johns Hopkins Hospital, Baltimore (MD), $1,000,000
- Baltimore Museum of Art, Baltimore (MD), $200,000
- Community Assistance Network, Baltimore (MD), for Crisis Intervention Initiative, $400,000

REQUIREMENTS AND RESTRICTIONS

No support for religious or sectarian purposes. No grants to individuals (except for scholarships), or for capital campaigns, annual fund campaigns, or event sponsorships.

APPLICATION PROCEDURES

See website for application guidelines. Applications begin with a brief letter of inquiry; Prog. Officer may request a full proposal upon review of the letter.

Deadlines: None for letters of inquiry

Baltimore Equitable Insurance Foundation

Headquarters

100 N. Charles St., Ste. 640
Baltimore, MD 21201-1794
Phone: 410-727-1794
Fax: 410-539-1073

Contact: Timothy J. Swartz, Pres. and Treas.

Type of Grant Maker: Corporate Foundation

Description

Founded: 1990

Operating Locations/Geographic Preferences: Giving limited to the Baltimore, MD area.

Corporate Foundation Information: Supported by the Baltimore Equitable Society

Financial Summary

Assets: $5,207,236
Total Giving: $197,500
Number of Grants: 11
Grant Ranges: $65,000–$1,000

Grants Information

GRANT TYPES

Program development, general and operating support

TYPICAL RECIPIENTS/SUBJECTS OF INTEREST

Elementary education, health, human services, and community development

PAST GRANT RECIPIENTS

Library or School Related

- Pot Spring Elementary, Timonium (MD), $1,000

General

- Maryland Historical Society, Baltimore (MD), $12,000
- Fire Museum of Maryland, Lutherville (MD), $10,000
- Women's Housing Coalition, Baltimore (MD), $7,500

REQUIREMENTS AND RESTRICTIONS

No grants to individuals.

APPLICATION PROCEDURES

Contact foundation for application form.

Deadlines: January 1, April 1, July 1, and October 1

Bamberger, Ruth Eleanor and John Ernest Bamberger Memorial Foundation

Headquarters

136 S. Main St., Ste. 418
Salt Lake City, UT 84101-1690
Phone: 801-364-2045

www.ruthandjohnbambergermemorialfdn.org

Contact: Eleanor Roser, Chair

E-mail: bambergermemfdn@qwestoffice.net

Foundation is not accepting any requests from new organizations at this time.

Bandai Foundation

Headquarters

5551 Katella Ave.
Cypress, CA 90630-5002

www.bandai.com/about/foundation.php

Type of Grant Maker: Corporate Foundation

Description

Founded: 1995

Operating Locations/Geographic Preferences: Giving primarily in CA, Washington, DC and NY.

Corporate Foundation Information: Supported by Bandai Corp.

Financial Summary

Assets: $9,373,993
Total Giving: $483,290
Number of Grants: 32
Grant Ranges: $40,000–$45

Grants Information

GRANT TYPES

General support

TYPICAL RECIPIENTS/SUBJECTS OF INTEREST

Children's education and children with AIDS

PAST GRANT RECIPIENTS

Library or School Related

- Columbia University Low Memorial Library, New York (NY), $2,000
- Orange County High School of Arts, Santa Ana (CA), $920

General

- Children's Institute, Los Angeles (CA), $10,000
- Japanese American Cultural Center, Los Angeles (CA), $4,000

REQUIREMENTS AND RESTRICTIONS

None

APPLICATION PROCEDURES

Complete online application and submit it to:

Bandai Foundation
5551 Katella Avenue
Cypress, California 90630

Deadlines: September 15

Booth Ferris Foundation

Headquarters

c/o JPMorgan Private Bank, Philanthropic Svcs.
PO 227237 TX1-2963
Dallas, TX 75222-7237
Fax: 212-464-2305

foundationcenter.org/grant-maker/boothferris

Contact:

Contact for Parks and Gardens, Arts and Culture: Jonathan Horowitz, Prog. Off.

Contact for Education: Erin K. Hogan, V.P.

Contact for Strengthening NYC's Nonprofit Sector: Connie Brandeis, Prog. Off.

E-mail: jonathan.g.horowitz@jpmchase.com

Type of Grant Maker: Foundation

Description

Founded: 1957

Operating Locations/Geographic Preferences: Giving limited to the New York, NY metropolitan area for the arts, K–12 education, and civic and urban affairs; broader giving area for higher education

Financial Summary

Assets: $195,578,487
Total Giving: $8,085,508
Number of Grants: 99
Grant Ranges: $200,000–$10,000

Grants Information

GRANT TYPES

Capital campaigns, management development and capacity building

TYPICAL RECIPIENTS/SUBJECTS OF INTEREST

Education, especially smaller colleges and independent secondary schools. Some support for urban programs, social service agencies, and cultural activities

PAST GRANT RECIPIENTS

- Teachers College Columbia University, New York (NY), $200,000
- Urban Education Exchange, New York (NY), for technology improvement initiative for the New York City program, $100,000.
- Columbia University, New York (NY), General Support, $100,000
- Florida Southern College, Lakeland (FL), General Support, $75,000

General

- Lincoln Center for the Performing Arts, New York (NY), for purchase of the Atrium's audio and acoustical equipment, $200,000
- Elaine Kaufman Cultural Center, New York (NY), for a key card access security system, $150,000

REQUIREMENTS AND RESTRICTIONS

No support for federated campaigns, community chests, social services and cultural institutions from outside the New York metropolitan area, or for work with specific diseases or disabilities. No grants to individuals, or for research; generally no grants to educational institutions for scholarships, fellowships, or unrestricted endowments or loans.

APPLICATION PROCEDURES

Submit online application at: www.jpmorgan.com/pages/jpmorgan/private_banking/foundations/online_grant_application/guidelines_to_apply.

Deadlines: February 1 for Civic Affairs, Education and Arts/Culture grants; May 31, Parks Gardens grants

Borchard, Albert & Elaine Foundation, Inc.

Headquarters

22055 Clarendon St., Ste. 210
Woodland Hills, CA 91367-6355
Phone: 818-888-2871
Fax: 818-888-2872

www.borchardfoundation.org
E-mail: info@borchardfoundation.org
Type of Grant Maker: Foundation

Description

Founded: 1978

Operating Locations/Geographic Preferences: Giving primarily in CA.

Financial Summary

Assets: $24,116,420
Total Giving: $1,108,088
Number of Grants: 64
Grant Ranges: $100,000–$2,500

Grants Information

GRANT TYPES

Program support, research, scholarships

TYPICAL RECIPIENTS/SUBJECTS OF INTEREST

- Elimination of poverty
- Human services
- Youth development
- Health and medicine
- Education
- Arts
- Environment

PAST GRANT RECIPIENTS

Library or School Related

- University of Southern California, Research position for Pasternak collection, $10,000
- Stetson University College of Law, for Elder Law Professorial Lecture, $25,000

General

- Los Rios Foundation, Creative writing program, $20,000
- Southern Center for Human Rights, Atlanta (GA), for internship program, $25,000

REQUIREMENTS AND RESTRICTIONS

No grants to individuals.

APPLICATION PROCEDURES

Submit letter of inquiry online. The letter of inquiry narrative should be limited to 250 words (not including current 501(c)(3) letter). This brief submission must include:

- Information about your organization's mission, activities, and annual budget
- Region and population served
- Total amount requested from Foundation and how funds to be used
- Project needs, goals, leadership and duration

Deadlines: February 1 and August 1

Boston Foundation, Inc.

Headquarters

75 Arlington St., 10th Fl.
Boston, MA 02116-3936
Phone: 617-338-1700

www.tbf.org

Contact: David Trueblood, Dir., Public Rels.; for grants: Corey L. Davis, Grants Mgr.

E-mail: info@tbf.org

Type of Grant Maker: Community Foundation

Description

Founded: 1915

Operating Locations/Geographic Preferences: Giving limited to Greater Boston, MA area

Financial Summary

Assets: $859,510,000
Total Giving: $77,521,000

Grants Information

GRANT TYPES

Program development, seed money, matching, investments/loans, consulting services

TYPICAL RECIPIENTS/SUBJECTS OF INTEREST

Public education, college student graduation, economic advancement of low-income families, health, violence reduction, civic improvement

PAST GRANT RECIPIENTS

Library or School Related

- Saint Vincent College, general support, $1,250,000

General

- Boston Ballet, general support, $1,000,000
- Action for Boston Community Development, $330,000
- Artists for Humanity, general support, $4,000
- United Way, North Shore, general support, $10,000

REQUIREMENTS AND RESTRICTIONS

No support for religious purposes, city or state government agencies or departments, private schools, municipalities, or national or international programs. No grants to individuals, or for scientific or academic research, books or articles, films, radio, or television programs, equipment, travel, endowments, scholarships, fellowships, conferences, or symposia or capital campaigns.

APPLICATION PROCEDURES

Letter of inquiry. Visit website for application guidelines

Deadlines: February, May, August, November

Bradley Foundation, Inc., Lynde and Harry

Headquarters

1241 N. Franklin Pl.
Milwaukee, WI 53202-2901
Phone: 414-291-9915

www.bradleyfdn.org

Contact: Daniel P. Schmidt, V.P., Progs.

Type of Grant Maker: Foundation

Description

Founded: 1942

Operating Locations/Geographic Preferences: Primarily Milwaukee, WI, but also gives on national and international basis

Financial Summary

Assets: $561,556,697
Total Giving: $42,346,950
Number of Grants: 716
Grant Ranges: $3,000,000–$500

Grants Information

GRANT TYPES

Program development, continuing and general support, building/renovation, investment/loans, research

TYPICAL RECIPIENTS/SUBJECTS OF INTEREST

Civil society, citizenship, public policy, cultural and education programs, social service, health, education

PAST GRANT RECIPIENTS

Library or School Related

- Encounter for Culture and Education (NY), Encounter Books, $1,000,000
- Charter School Growth Fund, Broomfield (CO), $3,000,000
- Ohio State University, fellowship program, $25,000

General

- National Association of Scholars, Princeton (NJU), general support, $40,000
- Milwaukee Symphony Orchestra, general support, $510,000
- National Strategy Information Center, Washington (DC), general support, $350,000
- Centre for Social Justice, London (England), general support, $40,000

REQUIREMENTS AND RESTRICTIONS

No grants for denominational projects, individuals or endowments

APPLICATION PROCEDURES

Submit inquiry letter and intended project to the organization. If the foundation determines the project to be within its current program interest, the applicant will be invited to submit a formal proposal.

Deadlines: February 1, May 1, August 1 and November 1

Bremer Foundation, Otto

Headquarters

445 Minnesota St., Ste. 2250
St. Paul, MN 55101-2107
Phone: 651-227-8036

www.ottobremer.org

Contact: Danielle Cheslog, Grants Mgr.; Kari Suzuki, Dir., Opers.

E-mail: obf@ottobremer.org

Type of Grant Maker: Foundation

Description

Founded: 1944

Operating Locations/Geographic Preferences: Minneapolis/St. Paul metropolitan area

Financial Summary

Assets: $713,359,200
Total Giving: $24,143,328
Number of Grants: 684
Grant Ranges: $330,000–$1,000

Grants Information

GRANT TYPES

Program development, general and continuing support, building, capacity building, capital campaigns, seed money

TYPICAL RECIPIENTS/SUBJECTS OF INTEREST

Public libraries, nonprofit organizational development, economic development, civic and social participation

PAST GRANT RECIPIENTS

General

- Amery Area Senior Citizen, general support, $25,000
- Community Action Partnership, Minot (ND), emergency grants, $43,000
- Asian Women United of Minnesota, capacity building, $20,000
- ABC for Rural Health, Balsam Lake (WI), health care access, $20,000

APPLICATION PROCEDURES

See website. Applicants should submit the following:

1. How project will be sustained once grant-maker support is completed
2. Signature and title of chief executive officer
3. Results expected from proposed grant
4. Qualifications of key personnel
5. Statement of problem project will address
6. Name, address, and phone number of organization
7. Copy of IRS Determination Letter
8. Brief history of organization and description of its mission

9. Copy of most recent annual report/audited financial statement/990
10. How project's results will be evaluated or measured
11. Listing of board of directors, trustees, officers and other key people and their affiliations
12. Detailed description of project and amount of funding requested
13. Contact person
14. Copy of budget and/or project budget
15. Listing of additional sources and amount of support

Deadlines: June 17, August 19 and October 14

Bretzlaff Foundation, Inc.

Headquarters

4795 Caughlin Pkwy., Ste. 100
Reno, NV 89519-0994
Phone: 775-333-0300

Contact: Michael J. Melarkey, Secy.

Type of Grant Maker: Foundation

Description

Founded: 1988

Operating Locations/Geographic Preferences: Giving primarily in Honolulu, HI and Reno, NV.

Financial Summary

Assets: $17,616,961
Total Giving: $787,000
Number of Grants: 31
Grant Ranges: $200,000–$1,000

Grants Information

GRANT TYPES

General and operating support, building and renovation, endowments, equipment

TYPICAL RECIPIENTS/SUBJECTS OF INTEREST

Higher education, youth, the arts, health care, and the environment

PAST GRANT RECIPIENTS

Library or School Related

- Stanford University, Stanford (CA), for scholarship endowment, $60,000
- University of Nevada, Reno (NV), $50,000
- University of San Francisco, San Francisco (CA), for scholarship endowment, $30,000

General

- Nevada Museum of Art, Reno (NV), for endowment, $50,000
- KNPB Channel 5 Public Broadcasting, Reno (NV), $25,000
- Hawaii Theater Center, Honolulu (HI), $20,000
- Reno Philharmonic Association, Reno (NV), for operational support, $15,000

REQUIREMENTS AND RESTRICTIONS

No grants to individuals.

APPLICATION PROCEDURES

Send letter with literature about organization and detailed description of project and amount of funding requested.

Deadlines: None

Bridgestone Americas Trust Fund (*Formerly* The Bridgestone/Firestone Trust Fund)

Headquarters

535 Marriott Dr.
Nashville, TN 37214-5092
Phone: 615-937-1415
Fax: 615-937-1414

www.bridgestone-firestone.com/trustfund.asp

Contact: Bernice Csaszar, Admin.

E-mail: bfstrustfund@bfusa.com

Type of Grant Maker: Corporate Foundation

Description

Founded: 1952

Operating Locations/Geographic Preferences: Giving on a national basis, with emphasis on areas of company operations in AR, IN, OH, and TN; giving also to regional and national organizations.

Corporate Foundation Information: Supported by:

- Firestone Tire and Rubber Co.
- Bridgestone/Firestone, Inc.
- Bridgestone Americas Holding, Inc.
- Bridgestone Americas, Inc.

Financial Summary

Assets: $17,094,926
Total Giving: $2,559,817
Number of Grants: 807
Grant Ranges: $207,500–$50

Grants Information

GRANT TYPES

Program development, annual and capital campaigns, building and renovation, continuing, general and operating support, matching, emergency funds, sponsorships, endowments

TYPICAL RECIPIENTS/SUBJECTS OF INTEREST

Arts and culture, agriculture, housing development, disaster relief, automotive safety, human services, and the automotive industry. Special emphasis on education, the environment and conservation, and children.

PAST GRANT RECIPIENTS

Library or School Related

- University of Tennessee, Knoxville (TN), College of Business Technology Fund, $10,000
- Prescott Elementary School, Prescott (AR), $20,000

General

- National Inventors Hall of Fame, Akron (OH), Camp Invention, Nashville Tennessee Schools, $2,000
- Akron Community Service Center, Akron (OH), Science and Engineering Scholarships, $3,000
- Boy Scouts, Akron (OH), Pathfinder Program $6,000
- Nashville Ballet, Nashville (TN), $15,00

REQUIREMENTS AND RESTRICTIONS

No support for partisan political organizations, discriminatory organizations, or religious organizations not of direct benefit to the entire community. No grants to individuals, loans or for debt reduction, equipment, land acquisition, or publications.

APPLICATION PROCEDURES

Send proposal to nearest company facility. Send proposals to the foundation for national organizations.

Proposals should be no longer than 2 pages and include:

1. Population served
2. Copy of IRS Determination Letter
3. Brief history of organization and description of its mission
4. Copy of most recent annual report/audited financial statement/990
5. How project's results will be evaluated or measured
6. Listing of board of directors, trustees, officers and other key people and their affiliations
7. Detailed description of project and amount of funding requested
8. Copy of current year's organizational budget and/or project budget
9. Listing of additional sources and amount of support

Deadlines: None

Bright Family Foundation

Headquarters

1620 N. Carpenter Rd., Bldg. B
Modesto, CA 95351-1155

Contact: Calvin E. Bright, Pres.; Carol B. Tougas, Secy.-Treas.

Type of Grant Maker: Foundation

Description

Founded: 1986

Operating Locations/Geographic Preferences: Giving primarily in Stanislaus County (CA), within a 20-mile radius of Modesto

Financial Summary

Assets: $8,014,112
Total Giving: $314,850
Number of Grants: 32
Grant Ranges: $50,000–$250

Grants Information

GRANT TYPES

General, operating and scholarships

TYPICAL RECIPIENTS/SUBJECTS OF INTEREST

Education and medical services

PAST GRANT RECIPIENTS

Library or School Related

- Stanislaus County Library, Modesto (CA), $3,000
- Brigham Young University, Provo (UT), $5,000
- Modesto Junior College, Modesto (CA), $42,000
- California State University, Stanislaus, Turlock (CA), $30,000

General

- Memorial Hospital Foundation, Modesto (CA), $20,000
- Parent Resource Center, Modesto (CA), $10,000

REQUIREMENTS AND RESTRICTIONS

None

APPLICATION PROCEDURES

Send letter on organization letterhead and include:

1. Copy of IRS Determination Letter
2. Detailed description of project and amount of funding requested

Deadlines: November 1

Bristol-Myers Squibb Foundation, Inc.

Headquarters

345 Park Ave., 3rd Fl.
New York, NY 10154-0004
Phone: 212-546-4000

www.bms.com/foundation/Pages/home.aspx

Contact: John L. Damonti, Pres.

Type of Grant Maker: Corporate Foundation

Description

Founded: 1982

Operating Locations/Geographic Preferences:
Giving primarily in areas of company operations:

- Devens, Massachusetts
- Hopewell, New Jersey
- Mount Vernon, Indiana
- New Brunswick, New Jersey
- New York, New York
- Plainsboro, New Jersey
- Princeton, New Jersey
- Syracuse, New York
- Wallingford, Connecticut
- West Windsor, New Jersey
- Also: Africa, China, Europe, India, Japan, Sub-Saharan Africa, Taiwan, and Thailand.

Corporate Foundation Information: Supported by Bristol-Myers Squibb Co.

Financial Summary

Assets: $145,418,399
Total Giving: $35,357,136
Number of Grants: 175
Grant Ranges: $4,500,000–$1,250

Grants Information

GRANT TYPES

Program development, seed money, continuing, general and operating support, matching, employee volunteering, management development, technical assistance, in-kind gifts

TYPICAL RECIPIENT/SUBJECTS OF INTEREST

Programs to reduce health disparities around the world. Special emphasis on programs designed to improve the health outcomes of populations disproportionately affected by HIV/AIDS in Africa; hepatitis in Asia; type-2 diabetes; mental health and well-being in the United States; and cancer in Europe.

PAST GRANT RECIPIENTS

Library or School Related

- Duke University, Research Grant, $500,000

General

- Pharmacists Association, Together on Diabetes, $1,960,000
- National Science Resources Center, Washington (DC), for RxeSearch—An Educational Journey, $500,000
- West Alabama Mental Health Center, Demopolis (AL), for outreach to Alabama Black Belt, $100,000

REQUIREMENTS AND RESTRICTIONS

No support for political, fraternal, social, or veterans' organizations, religious or sectarian organizations not of direct benefit to the entire community, or federated campaign-supported organizations. No grants to individuals or for endowments, capital campaigns, debt reduction, conferences, sponsorships or independent medical research, or specific public broadcasting or films or loans.

APPLICATION PROCEDURES

Complete online application; download letter of inquiry form and e-mail for Mental Health & Well-Being in the U.S.; download application form and e-mail for Together on Diabetes; complete online application for Secure the Future—Technical Assistance and Skills Transfer Program

Deadlines: December

Broad Foundation, Eli and Edythe

Headquarters

10900 Wilshire Blvd., 12th Fl.
Los Angeles, CA 90024-6532
Phone: 310-954-5050

www.broadfoundation.org

E-mail: info@broadfoundation.org

Type of Grant Maker: Foundation

Description

Founded: 1999

Operating Locations/Geographic Preferences: Giving on a national basis.

Financial Summary

Assets: $1,689,097,000
Total Giving: $145,971,000

Grants Information

GRANT TYPES

Investments and loans

TYPICAL RECIPIENTS/SUBJECTS OF INTEREST

Major programs include: Broad Art Loan, Broad Center for the Management of School Systems, Broad Education Program, Broad Institute for School Boards, Broad Medical Research and Broad Price for Urban Education

PAST GRANT RECIPIENTS

Library or School Related
- Broad Center for the Management of School Systems, Los Angeles (CA), for training public school system leaders, $4,500,000
- Excellent Education Development, Los Angeles (CA), for Camino Nuevo High School expansion, $86,000

General
- Broad Institute, Cambridge (MA), for Broad Institute endowment and support, $100,000,000
- University of Southern California, Los Angeles (CA), for The Eli and Edythe Broad Center for Regenerative Medicine and Stem Cell Research, $5,000,000
- Los Angeles Philharmonic Association, Los Angeles (CA), for general support, $29,300

REQUIREMENTS AND RESTRICTIONS

No grants to individuals.

APPLICATION PROCEDURES

See website for each program's policies and guidelines. Applicants should submit:

1. Detailed description of project and amount of funding requested
2. Copy of current year's organizational budget and/or project budget

Deadlines: None

Brooklyn Community Foundation

Headquarters

45 Main St., Ste. 409
Brooklyn, NY 11201-1093
Phone: 718-750-2310

www.brooklyncommunityfoundation.org

Contact: Marilyn G. Gelber, Pres.

E-mail: info@brooklyncommunityfoundation.org

Type of Grant Maker: Community Foundation

Description

Founded: 1998

Operating Locations/Geographic Preferences: Giving limited to Brooklyn, NY

Financial Summary

Assets: $63,649,280
Total Giving: $3,330,498
Number of Grants: 200

Grants Information

GRANT TYPES

Program development, general support, building and renovation, capital campaigns, land acquisition, investments and loans, seed money

TYPICAL RECIPIENTS/SUBJECTS OF INTEREST

Major program areas include: Arts for All, Caring Neighbors, Community Development, Education and Youth Achievement, and Green Communities

PAST GRANT RECIPIENTS

Library or School Related

- Pratt Institute, Brooklyn (NY), $100,000
- New York City College of Technology of the City University of New York Foundation, Brooklyn (NY), $100,000

General

- Brooklyn Museum, Brooklyn (NY), $200,000
- Prospect Park Alliance, Brooklyn (NY), $25,000
- Educators for Children, Youth and Families, Brooklyn (NY), $20,000
- Rush Philanthropic Arts Foundation, New York (NY), $10,000

REQUIREMENTS AND RESTRICTIONS

No support for religious purposes. No grants to individuals, or for tickets for dinners, golf outings, or fund-raising events.

APPLICATION PROCEDURES

Online requests only. See website for application guidelines.

Deadlines: January 1–January 31; and July 1–July 31

Brooks, Gladys Foundation

Headquarters

1055 Franklin Ave., Ste. 208
Garden City, NY 11530-2903
www.gladysbrooksfoundation.org
Contact: Jessica L. Rutledge
Type of Grant Maker: Foundation

Description

Founded: 1981

Operating Locations/Geographic Preferences: Giving generally limited to CT, DE, FL, IL, IN, LA, MA, MD, ME, NH, NJ, NY, OH, PA, RI, TN, and VT.

Financial Summary

Assets: $34,323,820
Total Giving: $1,050,000
Number of Grants: 18
Grant Ranges: $200,000–$5,000

Grants Information

GRANT TYPES

Endowments, building and renovation, equipment

TYPICAL RECIPIENTS/SUBJECTS OF INTEREST

Giving in the following program areas:

Libraries: Library grant applications will be considered for endowments, construction and equipment.

Education: Support generally for: a) educational endowments to fund scholarships based solely on leadership and academic ability of the student; b) endowments to support salaries of educators who confine their activities primarily to classroom instruction in the liberal arts, mathematics, and the sciences during the academic year; and c) erection or endowment of buildings, wings, or additions thereto of buildings for educational purposes.

Hospitals and Clinics: Support generally for projects that demonstrate one or more of the following: a) a new health need; b) better efficiency in health care; or c) reduced health costs with better patient outcomes.

PAST GRANT RECIPIENTS

Library or School Related

- Weeks Memorial Library, Lancaster (NY), for endowment, $50,000
- New York Academy of Medicine, for library technology, $15,000
- Mt. Washington Observatory, Library, $25,000
- Canterbury School, New Milford (CT), $100,000
- Columbia University, New York (NY), $100,000
- Kingsborough Community College, Brooklyn (NY), $100,000

General

- Helen Keller Services for the Blind, Brooklyn (NY), $100,000
- Indian River Hospital Foundation Inc., Vero Beach (FL), $100,000

REQUIREMENTS AND RESTRICTIONS

No grants to individuals, or for research or salaries.

APPLICATION PROCEDURES

Online application required.

No application will be considered if all questions have not been answered.

Do not alter the space allotments on the application.

Electronic submissions of the application and supporting documents is not acceptable.

Deadlines: June 1

Brown Foundation, Inc.

Headquarters

2217 Welch Ave.
Houston, TX 77019-5617
Phone: 713-523-6867

www.brownfoundation.org

Contact: Nancy Pittman, Exec. Dir.

E-mail: bfi@brownfoundation.org

Type of Grant Maker: Foundation

Description

Founded: 1951

Operating Locations/Geographic Preferences: Giving primarily in TX, with emphasis on Houston.

Financial Summary

Assets: $1,115,833,756
Total Giving: $49,970,108
Number of grants: 669
Grant Ranges: $1,856,628–$1,000

Grants Information

GRANT TYPES

Program development, continuing and general support, building and renovation, capital campaigns

TYPICAL RECIPIENTS/SUBJECTS OF INTEREST

Education, arts, community service, children and youth

PAST GRANT RECIPIENTS

General

- Teach for America, Houston (TX), for program expansion, $370,000
- Houston Zoo, Houston (TX), for capital campaign, $325,000
- Planned Parenthood of Houston, for operating support, $154,000

REQUIREMENTS AND RESTRICTIONS

No support for political organizations, private foundations, or religious organizations for religious purposes. No grants to individuals, or for operating deficits, debt retirement, testimonial dinners, marketing, fund-raising events, or loans.

APPLICATION PROCEDURES

Guidelines and form available upon request. Applicants should submit the following:

1. Copy of IRS Determination Letter
2. Copy of most recent annual report/audited financial statement/990
3. Listing of board of directors, trustees, officers and other key people and their affiliations
4. Copy of current year's organizational budget and/or project budget
5. Listing of additional sources and amount of support

Deadlines: None

Brundage, Charles E. and Edna T. Charitable, Scientific and Wildlife Conservation Foundation

Headquarters

c/o McElroy, Deutsch, Mulvaney & Carpenter, LLP
3 Gateway Ctr., 100 Mulburry St.
Newark, NJ 07102-4079
Phone: 973-622-7711

Contact: Francis X. O'Brien, Secy.

Type of Grant Maker: Foundation

Description

Founded: 1955

Operating Locations/Geographic Preferences: Giving primarily in NJ; some giving also in MA, MN, NH, NY, and VT.

Financial Summary

Assets: $3,834,221
Total Giving: $194,500
Number of Grants: 43
Grant Ranges: $35,000–$500

Grants Information

GRANT TYPES

Program development, capital campaigns, endowments, general and operating support

TYPICAL RECIPIENTS/SUBJECTS OF INTEREST

Arts and humanities, civic, education, health, science and social services

PAST GRANT RECIPIENTS

Library or School Related

- Canaan Town Library, Canaan (NH), $6,000
- St. Philips Academy, Newark (NJ), $3,500
- Blake School, Hopkins (MN), $8,000

General

- New Jersey Symphony Orchestra, Newark (NJ), $35,000
- Newark Museum, Newark (NJ), $35,000
- Enfield Shaker Museum, Enfield (NH), $6,000

REQUIREMENTS AND RESTRICTIONS

No grants to individuals.

APPLICATION PROCEDURES

Send letter.

Deadlines: None

Buell, Temple Hoyne Foundation

Headquarters

1666 S. University Blvd., Ste. B
Denver, CO 80210-2834
Phone: 303-744-1688
Fax: 303-744-1601

www.buellfoundation.org

Contact: Susan J. Steele, Exec. Dir.

E-mail: info@buellfoundation.org

Type of Grant Maker: Foundation

Description

Founded: 1962

Operating Locations/Geographic Preferences: Giving limited to CO

Financial Summary

Assets: $235,966,225
Total Giving: $8,054,369
Number of Grants: 310
Grant Ranges: $410,000–$800

Grants Information

GRANT TYPES

Program development, operating support, capital improvements (for early childhood programs), and technical assistance

TYPICAL RECIPIENTS/SUBJECTS OF INTEREST

Early childhood education and development and teen pregnancy prevention.

PAST GRANT RECIPIENTS

Library or School Related

- Denver Public Library, Read Aloud Program, $25,000
- South Chaffee Co. Reg. Lib., Early Childhood Council, $21,800
- Loveland Public Library, Every Child Read, $15,000
- Grand Junction Imagination Library, operating support, $5,000
- Gunnison Co. Library, Literacy Action, $5,000

General

- Friends of the Haven, Denver (CO), for capital campaign for Baby Haven Therapeutic Early Childhood Education Center, $75,000
- Wray Community Child Care Center, Wray (CO), for general operating support, $20,000

REQUIREMENTS AND RESTRICTIONS

No support for political organizations. Generally, no support for medical programs. No grants to individuals, or for past operating deficit, or retirement of debt. Generally, no grants for testimonial dinners, multiyear awards, events, annual campaigns, membership drives, emergency needs, conferences, endowments or loans.

APPLICATION PROCEDURES

All requests must be consistent with Foundation mission and guidelines and made in writing to the offices of the Foundation. Grant seekers are encouraged to call with any questions.

Deadlines: Generally January 15 and the first business day of May and September.

Build-A-Bear Workshop Foundation, Inc.

Headquarters

1954 Innerbelt Business Center Dr.
Saint Louis, MO 63114-5760
Phone: 314-423-8000
www.buildabear.com
Contact: Maxine Clark, Pres.

E-mail: giving@buildabear.com
Type of Grant Maker: Corporate Foundation

Description

Founded: 2003
Operating Locations/Geographic Preferences: United States
Corporate Foundation Information: Supported by Build-A-Bear Workshop, Inc.

Financial Summary

Assets: $1,014,694
Total Giving: $1,841,995

Grants Information

GRANT TYPES

Individual Project grants—generally for one-time purchases or to fulfill a short-term need, such as the purchase of books, materials or equipment.

Organization Program grants—to fund start-up or operational costs for ongoing programs. Examples include funds for research, educational programs or financial assistance for children and families in need.

TYPICAL RECIPIENTS/SUBJECTS OF INTEREST

Children and families in the areas of: Health and wellness, literacy or education, animals, including wildlife, the environment or environmental education

PAST GRANT RECIPIENTS

Library or School Related

- St. Louis Public Library, St. Louis (MO)
- Waukegan Public Library Foundation, Waukegan (IL)
- Washington County School Supply Drive, Bartlesville (OK)

General

- Autism Speaks, Princeton (NJ), $188,670
- American Red Cross, Washington (DC), $159,000
- Children's Heart Fund, Lincolnshire (IL), $231,000

REQUIREMENTS AND RESTRICTIONS

No support for:

- Annual Appeals or Capital Campaigns
- Construction or "New Facility" expenses
- Fund-raising or Event Sponsorships

- Political Activities
- Religious organizations for religious purposes

APPLICATION PROCEDURES

See website for online application.

Deadlines: None

Burroughs Wellcome Fund

Headquarters

21 T. W. Alexander Dr.
PO Box 13901
Research Triangle Park, NC 27709-3901
Phone: 919-991-5100

www.bwfund.org

Contact: Russell Campbell III, Comms. Off.

E-mail: info@bwfund.org

Type of Grant Maker: Foundation

Description

Founded: 1955

Operating Locations/Geographic Preferences: United States and Canada

Financial Summary

Assets: $633,871,299
Total Giving: $19,946,661
Number of Grants: 717
Grant Ranges: $275,087–$400

Grants Information

GRANT TYPES

Program development and research

TYPICAL RECIPIENTS/SUBJECTS OF INTEREST

In the early years of the foundation, all of the income was devoted to research in medicine and the sciences and the maintenance of research museum and libraries in those fields.

Current funding programs include: Career Awards at the Scientific Interface; Career Awards in the Medical Sciences, and research initiatives, science and philanthropy and the student science enrichment program.

PAST GRANT RECIPIENTS

Library or School Related

- Marine Biological Laboratory, Woods Hole (MA), for Biology of Parasitism Course, $681,000
- University of Pennsylvania, Philadelphia (PA), for development of Pan Fungal data resource, $250,000
- West Marion Elementary School, Marion (NC), for G.O.A.L.—Get Outside And Learn, $180,000
- Durham Academy, Durham (NC), for MONS (Mars Outreach for NC Students), $179,000

General

- Shodor Education Foundation, Durham (NC), for Computing MATTERS: Sowing the Seeds of SUCCEED, $180,000
- Foundation for the Carolinas, Charlotte (NC), for Sixth Grade Science Sleuths, $177,350

REQUIREMENTS AND RESTRICTIONS

No grants to individuals, or for building or endowment funds, equipment, operating budgets, continuing support, annual campaigns, deficit financing, publications, conferences, matching gifts or loans.

APPLICATION PROCEDURES

See website for application information.

Deadlines: Vary, depending on the program.

Bush, Barbara Foundation for Family Literacy

Headquarters

c/o Community Foundation for the National Capital Region
1201 15th St., N.W., Ste. 420
Washington, DC 20005-2842
Phone: 202-955-6183
Fax: 202-955-5492

www.barbarabushfoundation.com

Contact: Kiev Richardson, Prog. Off.

E-mail: info@barbarabushfoundation.com

Tallassee, FL Office:
516 N. Adams St.
Tallahassee, FL 32301
Phone: 850-562-5300

Type of Grant Maker: Foundation

Description

Founded: 1989

Operating Locations/Geographic Preferences: Giving on national basis

Financial Summary

Assets: $6,925,557
Total Giving: Approx $600,000
Grant Ranges: $50,000–$65,000

Grants Information

GRANT TYPES

Program development

TYPICAL RECIPIENTS/SUBJECTS OF INTEREST

Literacy skills for adult primary care givers and their children.

PAST GRANT RECIPIENTS

Library or School Related

- Dallas Public Library, Dallas (TX), Literacy program, $22,500
- George Bush Presidential Library, College Station (TX), Literacy program, $75,000
- Houston Indep. School District, Houston (TX), Literacy program, $25,000
- Univ. of S.C., Columbia (SC), Literacy program, $63,000

REQUIREMENTS AND RESTRICTIONS

No grants to individuals.

APPLICATION PROCEDURES

Check website in January, when grant guidelines are published.

Deadlines: February

Bush, Laura Foundation for America's Libraries

Headquarters

c/o Community Foundation for the National Capital Region
1201 15th St., N.W., Ste. 420

Washington, DC 20005-2842
Phone: 202-263-4774
www.laurabushfoundation.org
Contact: Alicia Reid
E-mail: laurabushfoundation@cfncr.org
Type of Grant Maker: Foundation

Description

Founded: 2001

Operating Locations/Geographic Preferences: Giving on a national basis, including Puerto Rico and the U.S. Virgin Islands.

Financial Summary

Grant Ranges: $6,000 average

Grants Information

GRANT TYPES

Grant requests may support library book collections and magazine/serial copies and subscriptions

TYPICAL RECIPIENTS/SUBJECTS OF INTEREST

School libraries. The purpose of the foundation is to enhance the book collections of school libraries across the country. Grants are given to update, extend, and diversify book collections of school libraries.

REQUIREMENTS AND RESTRICTIONS

Grants are made to individual schools only; eligible schools must have a minimum of 50 percent of its student body qualifying for federal Free or Reduced Lunch program funds.

Requests for staffing, shelving, furniture, equipment, software, videos, classroom book sets, or any kind of book guides, tests, or exams will not be honored.

APPLICATION PROCEDURES

Check website in September, when guidelines are published.

Deadlines: Usually December 1

Cafritz Foundation, Morris and Gwendolyn

Headquarters

1825 K St. N.W., Ste. 1400
Washington, DC 20006-1202
Phone: 202-223-3100

www.cafritzfoundation.org

Contact: Rose Ann Cleveland, Exec. Dir.

E-mail: info@cafritzfoundation.org

Type of Grant Maker: Foundation

Description

Founded: 1948

Operating Locations/Geographic Preferences: Giving limited to the Washington, DC, area and the surrounding counties in MD and VA, specifically Prince George's and Montgomery counties (MD), and Arlington and Fairfax counties, and the cities of Alexandria and Falls Church, VA.

Financial Summary

Assets: $634,908,564
Total Giving: $21,595,739
Number of Grants: 573
Grant Ranges: $500,000–$250

Grants Information

GRANT TYPES

Program development, general support, capacity building, matching

TYPICAL RECIPIENTS/SUBJECTS OF INTEREST

Education, arts, humanities, community service, health and the environment

PAST GRANT RECIPIENTS

General

- Community of Hope, Washington, DFC, for health and resource center, $600,000
- Teach for America, Washington (DC), for general support, $500,000
- Community Foundation for the National Capital Region, Washington (DC), for general support, $250,000

- First Time Computers, Washington (DC), for general support $35,000

REQUIREMENTS AND RESTRICTIONS

No grants to individuals, or for emergency funds, deficit financing, endowments, demonstration projects, or loans.

APPLICATION PROCEDURES

Applicants should submit:

1. Signature and title of chief executive officer
2. Statement of problem project will address
3. Brief history of organization and description of its mission
4. Copy of most recent annual report/audited financial statement/990
5. Detailed description of project and amount of funding requested
6. Copy of current year's organizational budget and/or project budget

Deadlines: March 1, July 1, and November 1

California Community Foundation

Headquarters

221 S. Figueroa St., Ste. 400
Los Angeles, CA 90012
Phone: 213-413-4130
Fax: 213-383-2046

www.calfund.org

E-mail: info@ccf-la.org

Type of Grant Maker: Community Foundation

Description

Founded: 1915

Operating Locations/Geographic Preferences: Giving limited to Los Angeles County, CA

Financial Summary

Assets: $1,242,402,000
Total Giving: $117,608,000

Grants Information

GRANT TYPES

Capital campaigns, consulting services, continuing, general and operating support, matching, program development, investments and loans, technical assistance, management development, technical assistance

TYPICAL RECIPIENTS/SUBJECTS OF INTEREST

Giving areas include:

- Arts
- CCF Fellowship for Visual Arts
- Centinela Medical Funds
- Civic Engagement
- Education:
    Focus on increasing K–5 student performance in math and literacy in Los Angeles County among low-income, minority and English learner students
- Fedco Teacher Grants
- Health Care
- Housing and Neighborhoods
- Human Development
- Management Support Organizations
- Program-Related Investments
- Scholarships

PAST GRANT RECIPIENTS

Library or School Related

- West Hollywood, West Hollywood (CA), $25,000
- Southern California Library for Social Studies and Research, Los Angeles (CA), $25,000
- Huntington Library and Art Gallery, $87,500
- Klein Stock Market Museum and Library, $127,500
- Library Foundation of Los Angeles, $215,000

General

- East L.A. Community Corporation, Los Angeles (CA), $100,000
- Social and Public Art Resource Center, Venice (CA), $95,000

REQUIREMENTS AND RESTRICTIONS

No support for sectarian purposes. No grants to individuals (except fellowships for artists or scholarships), or for annual campaigns, equipment, endowment funds, debt reduction, operating budgets, re-granting, fellowships, films, conferences, dinners, or special events.

APPLICATION PROCEDURES

See foundation website for online application forms and guidelines

Deadlines: Vary

California Endowment

Headquarters

1000 N. Alameda St.
Los Angeles, CA 90012-1804
Phone: 800-449-4149

www.calendow.org

E-mail: questions@calendow.org

Type of Grant Maker: Foundation

Description

Founded: 1996

Operating Locations/Geographic Preferences: Giving primarily in CA

Financial Summary

Assets: $3,745,324,056
Total Giving: $124,777,309
Number of Grants: 1,381
Grant Ranges: $5,000,000–$75

Grants Information

GRANT TYPES

General support, investments, loans, capacity building

TYPICAL RECIPIENTS/SUBJECTS OF INTEREST

Grants must align with Healthy Happens Here Program or Building Healthy Communities plan or 4 Big Results. Goal of the Health Happens in Neighborhood program is to contribute to the rise of neighborhoods with parks, grocery stores, bike paths and safe places to walk, run, work and play

PAST GRANT RECIPIENTS

Library or School Related

- Charles R. Drew University of Medicine and Science, Los Angeles (CA), for Technical Assistance, $5,000,000
- University of California, Los Angeles (CA), for California Health Interview Survey, $3,000,000

General

- Youth UpRising, Oakland (CA), for Building Healthy Communities through Youth Leadership, $1,500,000
- Pacific News Service, San Francisco (CA), for Youth-Led

Media for Community Health, $1,000,000
- Liberty Hill Foundation, Los Angeles (CA), for Improving Health through Small Grants, $994,000
- Social Advocates for Youth San Diego, San Diego (CA), for Hub Collaborative, $771,700

REQUIREMENTS AND RESTRICTIONS

No support for political purposes, research, clinical services, scholarships, deficits, media, construction

APPLICATION PROCEDURES

- Online letter of inquiry
- Check website for requests for proposal announcements

California State Library

Headquarters

PO Box 942837
Sacramento, CA 94237-0001
Phone: 916-654-0266
Fax: 916-654-0064

www.library.ca.gov

E-mail: csl-adm@library.ca.gov

Type of Grant Maker: Government

Grants Information

LIBRARY SERVICES AND TECHNOLOGY ACT

LSTA funding is used each year to support three key areas:

1. Statewide initiatives that provide libraries with the opportunity to support their local communities with programs and information services.
2. A competitive grant process to provide local libraries with funding to development programs and innovative initiatives.
3. Services and access to resources available through the California State Library.

APPLICATION PROCEDURES

See online documents for restrictions and procedures. For questions or concerns regarding LSTA, contact:

California State Library
Stacey A. Aldrich, State Librarian of California
900 N St.
Sacramento, CA 95814-4813
Phone: 916-653-5217
Fax: 916-653-8443
E-mail: lsta@library.ca.gov

LIBRARY BOND ACT OF 2000

The California State Library administers the Library Bond Act of 2000, Proposition 14, which provided $350 million of state bond funding for public library construction and renovation. All grant funding has been allocated at this time.

CALIFORNIA CIVIL LIBERTIES PUBLIC EDUCATION PROGRAM (CCLPEP)

This state-funded grant project is administered by the California State Library.

Due to the State budget situation, CCLPEP funding has been eliminated at this time.

CALIFORNIA CULTURAL AND HISTORICAL ENDOWMENT

The California Cultural and Historical Endowment was established at the California State Library in 2003 to raise the profile and scope of California's historic and cultural preservation program in an era of cultural homogeneity and dwindling historic structures.

At this time CCHE has no additional grant funds available.

Campbell Soup Foundation

Headquarters

1 Campbell Pl.
Camden, NJ 08103-1799
Phone: 856-342-4800

www.campbellsoupcompany.com/community_center.asp

Contact: Jerry S. Buckley, Chair

E-mail: community_relations@campbellsoup.com

Type of Grant Maker: Corporate Foundation

Description

Founded: 1953

Operating Locations/Geographic Preferences: Giving primarily in areas of company operations in Davis, Sacramento, and Stockton, CA, Bloomfield and Norwalk, CT, Lakeland, FL, Downers Grove, IL, Marshall, MI, Maxton, NC, South Plainfield, NJ, Napoleon, Wauseon, and Willard, OH, Denver and Downingtown, PA, Aiken, SC, Paris, TX, Richmond, UT, Everett, WA, and Milwaukee, WI, with emphasis on Camden, NJ.

Corporate Foundation Information: Supported by Campbell Soup Co.

Financial Summary

Assets: $16,735,504
Total Giving: $1,569,821

Grants Information

Program development, building and renovation, matching, employee volunteering, general and operating support

TYPICAL RECIPIENTS/SUBJECTS OF INTEREST

Hunger relief, wellness, education, and community revitalization

PAST GRANT RECIPIENTS

Library or School Related

- Univ. of Mass, Amherst, $3,000
- Union College, $2,500
- Haverford School, $1,000
- Catholic Partnership Schools, $5,500
- King's Christian School, $500

General

- Zoological Society of Philadelphia, Philadelphia (PA), $25,000
- Philadelphia Children's Alliance, Philadelphia (PA), $2,000

REQUIREMENTS AND RESTRICTIONS

No support for religious organizations not of direct benefit to the entire community, political organizations, or units of government. No grants to individuals (except for employee-related scholarships), or for events or sponsorships.

APPLICATION PROCEDURES

See website for guidelines and online eligibility quiz
Deadlines: None

Carlson, Curtis L. Family Foundation

Headquarters

550 Tonkawa Rd.
Long Lake, MN 55356-9724
Phone: 952-404-5605
Fax: 952-404-5051

www.clcfamilyfoundation.com

Contact: C. David Nelson, Exec. Dir.

Type of Grant Maker: Foundation

Description

Founded: 1959

Operating Locations/Geographic Preferences: Giving primarily in MN.

Financial Summary

Assets: $80,124,000
Total Giving: $3,994,184
Number of Grants: 273
Grant Ranges: $298,000–$25

Grants Information

GRANT TYPES

Operating and general support, matching

TYPICAL RECIPIENTS/SUBJECTS OF INTEREST

Education, at-risk children, mentoring, community

PAST GRANT RECIPIENTS

Library or School Related

- Friends of the Minneapolis Public Library, Minneapolis (MN), for General Operating Support
- University of Minnesota Foundation, Minneapolis (MN), for General Operating Support for The Center for Integrative Leadership; Capital Support for Herbert M. Hanson Hall
- University of St. Thomas, St. Paul (MN), for Program Support for *VISION* Scholarships

General

- Minneapolis Institute of Arts, Minneapolis (MN), for General Operating Support for Minnesota Children's Museum

- Minnesota Orchestral Association, Minneapolis (MN), for General Operating Support

REQUIREMENTS AND RESTRICTIONS

No grants to individuals (including scholarships), or for endowment funds, dinners, benefits, conferences, travel, athletic events, or endowments.

APPLICATION PROCEDURES

Online application required. See website.

Deadlines: January 1, April 1, or July 1

Carnahan-Jackson Foundation

Headquarters

9-11 East Fourth St.
Jamestown, NY 14701
Phone: 716-483-1015
Fax: 716-483-6556

www.chautauquagrants.org/Funders/
CarnahanJacksonFoundation/tabid/287/Default.aspx

E-mail: stephen@sellstromlaw.com

Type of Grant Maker: Foundation

Description

Operating Locations/Geographic Preferences: United States, especially in Chautauqua County, NY, particularly in the Jamestown area.

Financial Summary

Total Grants: $587,155
Grant Ranges: $150,000–$1,000

Grants Information

GRANT TYPES

General support, capital campaigns, project development

TYPICAL RECIPIENTS/SUBJECTS OF INTEREST

Religious, charitable, scientific, testing for public safety, literary, or educational purposes, or for the prevention of cruelty to children or animals

Giving focus on:

- Scholarships
- Libraries
- Basic Human Needs
- Educational Institutions

PAST GRANT RECIPIENTS

Library or School Related

- Houghton College, Houghton (NY), $50,000
- Jamestown Community College, Jamestown (NY), $50,000
- Berry College, Mount Berry (GA), $15,000

General

- WCA Hospital, Jamestown (NY), $50,000
- YWCA, $35,000
- Chautauqua Striders Youth Development Coalition, Jamestown (NY), $15,000

REQUIREMENTS AND RESTRICTIONS

None

APPLICATION PROCEDURES

Written grant application with supporting documentation required. Grant guidelines detailing the format for the grant application and the required supporting documentation may be obtained from the Carnahan Jackson Foundation offices.

Deadlines: April 30, September 30

Carnegie Corporation of New York

Headquarters

437 Madison Ave.
New York, NY 10022-7003
Fax: 212-754-4073

Contact: Nicole Howe Buggs, Dir., Grants Management

Type of Grant Maker: Foundation

Description

Founded: 1911

Operating Locations/Geographic Preferences: Higher Education and Libraries in Africa and Public Libraries in South Africa

Other programs: United States

Financial Summary

Assets: $2,534,623,009
Total Giving: $126,171,879

Grants Information

GRANT TYPES

Program development, conferences, continuing, general and operating support, technical assistance

TYPICAL RECIPIENTS/SUBJECT OF INTEREST

- Urban and Higher Education
- Higher Education and Libraries in Africa
- Strengthening Democracy/Immigrant Civic Integration
- International Peace and Security

PAST GRANT RECIPIENTS

Library or School Related

- ALA, Chicago (IL), for Carnegie Medal for Best Fiction and Best Non-Fiction Award, $300,000
- Library and Information Assoc of South Africa, for South African library and information services, $1,500,000
- City of Johannesburg Library and Information Services, for model city library, $2,000,000
- Bibliotheca Alexandrina, Islam Initiative, $1,000,000

General

- Yale University Press, Islam Initiative, $500,000
- Cooper Hewitt Museum, Digitize archives, $250,000

REQUIREMENTS AND RESTRICTIONS

No funds for:

- Individuals
- Endowments, buildings or fund-raising drives, including fund-raising dinners
- Political campaigns, to support political activities or to lobby for or against particular pieces of legislation
- Existing deficits
- Scholarships
- Churches or other religious organizations

APPLICATION PROCEDURES

Letter of Inquiry must be submitted online at website
Deadlines: None

Carpenter Foundation, E. Rhodes & Leona B.

Headquarters

1735 Market St., Ste. 3420
Philadelphia, PA 19103-2921
Phone: 215-979-3222
www.erlbcarpenterfoundation.org
Contact: Joseph A. O'Connor, Jr., Exec. Dir.
E-mail: admin@carpenterfoundation.us
Type of Grant Maker: Foundation

Description

Founded: 1975
Operating Locations/Geographic Preferences: Giving primarily in MA, NC, NY, PA, TX, and Richmond, VA (for performing arts only)

Financial Summary

Assets: $203,472,692
Total Giving: $10,015,664
Number of grants: 302
Grant Ranges: $500,000–$1,000; average: $5,000–$200,000

Grants Information

GRANT TYPES

Program development, construction

TYPICAL RECIPIENTS/SUBJECTS OF INTEREST

Performing arts organizations in the Richmond, VA, area; education, graduate theological institutions; museums, Asian art, and health care, particularly hospices

PAST GRANT RECIPIENTS

Library or School Related

- Hebrew College, Newton Centre (MA), for scholarships, $60,000
- Johns Hopkins University, Baltimore (MD), for new wing, $714,000

General

- United Church of Christ, Burlington (NC), for Pastoral Leadership, $200,000
- Barksdale Theater, Richmond (VA), for performances, $40,000

REQUIREMENTS AND RESTRICTIONS

No support for private secondary education, no grants to individuals, or endowments

APPLICATION PROCEDURES

No specific form is required; however, an application must be prefaced by a maximum 50-word synopsis of the project and the amount of funding requested. A letter application is sufficient and must include:

1. The amount requested.
2. The specific project or program for which funding is requested.
3. A detailed budget for that project or program, including any charges for general administrative overhead.
4. A brief history of and the purpose of the requesting organization.
5. Financial statements of the requesting organization for its current and the immediately preceding fiscal year.
6. A copy of the organization's IRS ruling that it is described in Internal Revenue Code Section 501(c)(3) and is not a private foundation under Code Section 509(a).

Deadlines: January 31, July 31

Carvel, Thomas & Agnes Foundation

Headquarters

35 E. Grassy Sprain Rd.
Yonkers, NY 10710-4612
Phone: 914-793-7300

Contact: William E. Griffin, Pres.

Type of Grant Maker: Foundation

Description

Founded: 1976

Operating Locations/Geographic Preferences: Giving primarily in Westchester County, NY.

Financial Summary

Assets: $37,553,106
Total Giving: $1,952,450
Number of Grants: 100
Grant Ranges: $500,000–$1,000

Grants Information

GRANT TYPES

Program development, building and renovation, matching

TYPICAL RECIPIENTS/SUBJECTS OF INTEREST

Health care, arts, children, youth and social services, and higher education

PAST GRANT RECIPIENTS

Library or School Related

- Seton Hall University, South Orange (NJ), $50,000
- Fordham University, New York (NY), $5,000

General

- Hudson River Museum of Westchester, Yonkers (NY), $65,000
- Park Performing Arts Center, Union City (NJ), $25,000
- Historic Hudson Valley, Tarrytown (NY), $10,000

REQUIREMENTS AND RESTRICTIONS

No support for political and international organizations.

APPLICATION PROCEDURES

Send letter with organizational budget and/or program budget

Deadlines: October 1

Carver, Roy J. Charitable Trust

Headquarters

202 Iowa Ave.
Muscatine, IA 52761-3733
Phone: 563-263-4010
Fax: 563-263-1547

www.carvertrust.org

Contact: Troy K. Ross Ph.D., Exec. Admin.

E-mail: info@carvertrust.org

Type of Grant Maker: Foundation

Description

Founded: 1982

Operating Locations/Geographic Preferences: Giving primarily in IA, with some funding in IL

Financial Summary

Assets: $284,980,743
Total Giving: $12,572,742
Number of Grants: 90
Grant Ranges: $5,400,000–$4,700

Grants Information

GRANT TYPES

Building and renovation, program development, equipment, conferences, seed money, capital campaigns

TYPICAL RECIPIENTS/SUBJECTS OF INTEREST

Carver Iowa Public Library Grant Program: Direct support for the establishment, expansion and enhancement of community-based library facilities and services. Grants of up to $60,000 are generally awarded for construction, renovation and/or furnishings and equipment needs, including technology-based initiatives that link libraries across multiple sites. Projects emphasizing library patronage among youth are especially encouraged. The trust does not provide grants specifically targeted to making libraries handicapped accessible and has traditionally avoided awarding grants to support the creation of Iowa Communications Network (ICN) classrooms within new or existing library facilities. Trust does not provide funding for joint school/community library projects or facilities.

Carver Medical and Scientific Research Initiative Awards Program

Carver Scholars Program

Elementary and Secondary Education: Focusing on elementary and secondary education to provide strategic assistance to enhance instruction in the core areas of language arts, science and mathematics. Within this very broad program area projects as diverse as teacher training, development of new curricular models, and the improvement of alternative classroom facilities have received substantial trust support. Of special interest have been efforts devoted to the unique academic needs of at-risk or underserved youth, as well as initiatives that hold the potential for impacting K–12 education at the state or regional level.

Excellence in Education: Honoring students, staff and faculty within the Muscatine Community School District with recognition awards and scholarships.

Higher Education: Supporting projects that strengthen institutions and offer innovative learning opportunities to students enrolled in baccalaureate and graduate programs throughout the grant-making region of Iowa and parts of Illinois. Typically, funding is awarded to capital or programmatic initiatives that seek to substantively improve instruction or increase access to educational resources, with the goal of better preparing students for future academic and professional challenges. Projects incorporating interdisciplinary approaches and demonstrating the potential for lasting impact among a diverse range of students are especially encouraged.

Medical and Scientific Research

Youth: Focusing on projects designed to complement curriculum-based education and encourage individual development and physical well-being, with a significant portion of support has been directed toward the efforts of organizations working with disadvantaged youth and their families.

Youth Recreational Program

PAST GRANT RECIPIENTS

Library or School Related

- Atkins Public Library, Construction, $60,000
- Bedford Public Library, Heating System, $7,400
- Clarksville Public Library, Construction of addition, $60,000
- Exira Public Library, Library expansion, $60,000
- Kothe Memorial Library, Library expansion $60,000
- Lewis Public Library, New Construction, $60,000
- North Liberty, Library expansion, $60,000
- Sherrard Public Library District, for children's materials, $6,300

General

- Iowa Juvenile Home Fund, for library activities, $11,850

REQUIREMENTS AND RESTRICTIONS

No support for religious activities or political organizations. No grants to individuals, or for endowments, fund-raising benefits, program advertising, annual operating support.

APPLICATION PROCEDURES

To determine if a proposed project coincides with an area of Trust interest and to avoid unnecessary labor for a potential applicant, the Carver Trust encourages initial written or electronically transmitted inquiries to info@ carvertrust.org before submission of a formal request. Letters of inquiry should be no longer than two pages and should not be accompanied by videotapes, detailed financial reports or other supporting documents.
The following information should be included in the initial letter of inquiry:

- A brief background on your organization, including a history of its existence, the size of staff and board and the type of service provided.
- A succinct description of the project, what it is designed to achieve, and how this will be accomplished.
- A proposed budget for the total cost of the project and the amount you intend to request from the Trust. If possible, identify the particular budget items for which you would be requesting Trust support. Specify other potential or committed sources of funding for the project.
- A statement describing why participation of the Carver Trust is vital to the success of the project. Indicate any past history with the Trust or any contacts you have made with Trust staff or others leading to your decision to approach the Trust for funding.

All letters of inquiry should be directed to:

Troy K. Ross, Ph.D.
Executive Administrator
Roy J. Carver Charitable Trust
202 Iowa Avenue
Muscatine IA 52761-3733

Deadlines: February 15, May 15, August 15, and November 15

Cassett, Louis N. Foundation

Headquarters

1 Penn Ctr., Ste. 1220
Philadelphia, PA 19103-1834
Phone: 215-563-8886

Contact: Malcolm B. Jacobson

Type of Grant Maker: Foundation

Description

Founded: 1946

Operating Locations/Geographic Preferences: Giving primarily in FL and Philadelphia, PA.

Financial Summary

Assets: $9,619,936
Total Giving: $421,260
Number of Grants: 168
Grant Ranges: $15,000–$750

Grants Information

GRANT TYPES

Building, renovation and annual campaigns

TYPICAL RECIPIENTS/SUBJECTS OF INTEREST

Cultural programs, social service and health agencies, and Jewish organizations

PAST GRANT RECIPIENTS

Library or School Related
- Abington Township Public Library, Abington (PA), $10,000
- Free Library of Philadelphia, $3,000
- Carnegie Mellon University, $2,500

General
- National Association for Children of Alcoholics, $10,000
- JHM Center for Literacy, $1,500

REQUIREMENTS AND RESTRICTIONS

No grants to individuals or for endowment funds

APPLICATION PROCEDURES

Send letter with brief history of organization and description of its mission, detailed description of project and amount of funding requested

Deadlines: None

Catholic Library Association

Headquarters

205 W. Monroe St., Ste. 314
Chicago, IL 60606-5061
Phone: 312-739-1776, 855-739-1776
Fax: 312-739-1778
www.cathla.org/scholarships-a-grants/

Type of Grant Maker: Library Organization

Grants Information

SISTER SALLY DALY MEMORIAL GRANT

Grant Range: $1,500
Number of Grants: 1

To enable a new member of CLA's Children's Library Services Section to attend the annual convention.

APPLICATION PROCEDURES

Applications may be downloaded or obtained by writing to:

Sister Sally Daly Memorial Grant
Catholic Library Association
205 West Monroe St., Suite 314
Chicago, IL 60606-5061

Deadlines: February 1

JOHN T. CORRIGAN, CFX MEMORIAL CONTINUING EDUCATION GRANT

To assist the national organization and local chapters and sections in providing quality, economically priced, and accessible educational programs for CLA members and the larger public. Programs selected should not duplicate other existing educational offerings but fill a specific need for our organization. These programs can be part of the national convention, a local chapter meeting or sponsored as a separate event. At times, the Committee may collaborate with other library organizations in offering an educational conference.

APPLICATION PROCEDURES

Applications may be downloaded or obtained by writing to:

John T. Corrigan Grant
Catholic Library Association
205 West Monroe St., Suite 314
Chicago, IL 60606-5061

Deadlines: December 1

Cedar Rapids Community Foundation, Greater

Headquarters

324 3rd St. SE
Cedar Rapids, IA 52401-1841
Phone: 319-366-2862

www.gcrcf.org

Contact: For grants: Karla Twedt-Ball, V.P., Progs.

E-mail: info@gcrcf.org

Type of Grant Maker: Community Foundation

Description

Founded: 1949

Operating Locations/Geographic Preferences: Giving limited to the greater Cedar Rapids and surrounding Linn County, IA, area

Financial Summary

Assets: $95,646,126
Total Giving: $7,715,331
Number of Grants: 155
Grant Ranges: $1,725,000 and under

Grants Information

GRANT TYPES

Program development, renovation, capital campaigns, emergency funds, matching, seed money

TYPICAL RECIPIENTS/SUBJECTS OF INTEREST

The foundation serves Linn County and funds four program areas: Arts and Culture, Community Development and the Environment, Education, and Health and Human Services.

PAST GRANT RECIPIENTS

Library or School Related

- Cedar Rapids Public Library, Cedar Rapids (IA), for general support, $17,000
- Coe College, Cedar Rapids (IA), for general fund, $166,700

General

- Cedar Rapids Museum of Art, Cedar Rapids (IA), for general support, $388,000
- Chamber of Commerce Foundation of Cedar Rapids Area, Cedar Rapids (IA), for Arts Festival, Job and Small Business Recovery, Flood Recovery and Reinvestment Director, $358,800
- Planned Parenthood of East Central Iowa, Cedar Rapids (IA), for general support, $32,600

REQUIREMENTS AND RESTRICTIONS

No support for religious activities of religious organizations, no grants to individuals, no grants for capital campaigns, endowment campaigns, one-time events, fund-raising, equipment, scientific research, debt retirement, or deficit financing.

APPLICATION PROCEDURES

See website for application Cover Sheet for Community Fund grants and additional instructions per grant type. Application form required. Applicants should submit:

1. Timetable for implementation and evaluation of project
2. Signature and title of chief executive officer
3. Results expected from proposed grant
4. Qualifications of key personnel
5. Statement of problem project will address
6. Population served
7. Name, address and phone number of organization
8. Copy of IRS Determination Letter
9. Brief history of organization and description of its mission
10. Geographic area to be served
11. How project's results will be evaluated or measured
12. Descriptive literature about organization
13. What distinguishes project from others in its field
14. Listing of board of directors, trustees, officers and other key people and their affiliations
15. Detailed description of project and amount of funding requested
16. Plans for cooperation with other organizations, if any
17. Contact person
18. Copy of current year's organizational budget and/or project budget
    Initial approach: Telephone

Deadlines: February 15, June 15, and October 17

Cengage Learning (also known as Gale Cengage)

Headquarters

10650 Toebben Drive
Independence, KY 41051
Phone: 800-354-9706

www.cengage.com

Contact: Lindsay Brown, Director, Corporate Communications

E-mail: lindsay.brown@cengage.com

Type of Grant Maker: Corporate Foundation

Description

Operating Locations/Geographic Preferences: None stated. For location of local representative, see website: www.cengage.com/contact/locations.

Financial Summary

Not available.

Grants Information

GRANT TYPES

Cash award given for TEAMS Award

TYPICAL RECIPIENTS/SUBJECTS OF INTEREST

- Teacher and Media Specialists
- TEAMS Award—Teachers and Media Specialists Influencing Student Achievement
- Winners awarded annually.

PAST GRANT RECIPIENTS

Library or School Related

- Winter Park Elementary School, for art, music and physical education collaboration with media specialist, $2,500
- Patrick F. Taylor Science and Technology academy, for student research skills, $2,500
- Skyline High School, for Media Center and English collaboration, $2,500

REQUIREMENTS AND RESTRICTIONS

Collaboration required between teachers and media specialists to promote learning and increase student achievement

APPLICATION PROCEDURES

See website.

Deadlines: See website

Central Minnesota Community Foundation

Headquarters

101 S. 7th Ave., Ste. 100
Saint Cloud, MN 56301
Phone: 320-253-4380

www.communitygiving.org

Contact: Steven R. Joul, President; Greta Stark-Kraker, Office Manager; for grants and scholarships: Susan Lorenz, Program Officer

E-mail: info@communitygiving.org

Type of Grant Maker: Community Foundation

Description

Founded: 1985

Operating Locations/Geographic Preferences: Giving primarily in Benton, Sherburne, and Stearns counties, MN

Financial Information

Assets: $52,844,720
Total Giving: $5,302,394
Number of Grants: 112

Grants Information

GRANT TYPES

Program development, renovation, seed money

TYPICAL RECIPIENTS/SUBJECTS OF INTEREST

Education, arts, environment, public affairs, youth, health care

PAST GRANT RECIPIENTS

Library or School Related

- Great River Regional Library, Saint Cloud (MN), for new library equipment, collection materials, and software licenses, $211,700
- Trinity International University, Deerfield (IL), $0,000

General

- United Way of Central Minnesota, Saint Cloud (MN), for youth programs, Feed our Families Event, leadership training, and Red River Flood Relief, $206,900
- Saint Cloud, City of, Saint Cloud (MN), for Munsinger Gardens support, capital improvements, and maintenance, $162,500
- Boys and Girls Clubs of Central Minnesota, Saint Cloud (MN), for Go Girl Go Program, Partner for the Future, and East Side Club Capital Campaign, $153,800
- Redeemer Lutheran Church, Willmar (MN), for general fund, $66,500
- Trinity Broadcasting Network, Tustin (CA), for general operating support, $20,000

REQUIREMENTS AND RESTRICTIONS

No support for religious organizations for direct activities, or for fraternal organizations, societies, or orders. No grants to individuals (except for designated scholarship funds), or for medical research, general operating expenses, national fund-raising, telephone solicitations, travel, capital campaigns, endowments, or debt retirement or deficit financing.

APPLICATION PROCEDURES

See website for application guidelines, deadlines. Applicants should submit:

1. How project will be sustained once grant-maker support is completed
2. Signature and title of chief executive officer
3. Results expected from proposed grant
4. Qualifications of key personnel
5. Statement of problem project will address
6. Population served
7. Name, address and phone number of organization
8. Copy of IRS Determination Letter
9. Brief history of organization and description of its mission
10. Geographic area to be served
11. Copy of most recent annual report/audited financial statement/990
12. How project's results will be evaluated or measured
13. Listing of board of directors, trustees, officers and other key people and their affiliations
14. Detailed description of project and amount of funding requested
15. Contact person
16. Copy of current year's organizational budget and/or project budget
17. Listing of additional sources and amount of support

Deadlines: Vary

Champlin Foundations

Headquarters

2000 Chapel View Blvd., Ste. 350
Cranston, RI 02920-3040
Phone: 401-944-9200

www.champlinfoundations.org

Contact: Keith H. Lang, Exec. Dir.

Type of Grant Maker: Foundation

Description

Founded: 1932

Operating Locations/Geographic Preferences: Giving primarily in RI.

Financial Information

Assets: $395,225,090
Total Giving: $17,074,565
Number of Grants: 174
Grant Ranges: $1,700,000–$1,200

Grants Information

GRANT TYPES

Renovation, land acquisition, capital campaigns, matching

TYPICAL RECIPIENTS/SUBJECTS OF INTEREST

Giving primarily for conservation; higher, secondary, and other education, including libraries; cultural activities, including historic preservation, social and family services, youth and health

PAST GRANT RECIPIENTS

Library or School Related

- Brown University, Providence (RI), for construction of the library and other projects, $1,700,000
- Ocean State Libraries, Warwick (RI), for technology for the Consortium and individual member libraries, $97,900
- Rhode Island School of Design, Providence (RI), for HVAC improvements, $250,000
- Society for the Preservation of New England Antiquities, Boston (MA), for improvements to buildings at Casey Farm, $150,000

General

- Nature Conservancy in Rhode Island, Providence (RI), for Rhode Island Open Space Conservation Program, $775,000
- Rhode Island Zoological Society, Providence (RI), for new Hasbro Children's Zoo, $750,000
- YMCA of Greater Providence, Providence (RI), for major renovations to and expansion of the Kent County branch, $645,000

REQUIREMENTS AND RESTRICTIONS

No support for churches, housing, mental health counseling centers or senior centers. No grants to individuals; or for program or operating expenses, administrative facilities, equipment, books, films, videos, plays, or for multiyear grants.

APPLICATION PROCEDURES

Application form not required. Applicants should submit:

1. Copy of IRS Determination Letter
2. Detailed description of project and amount of funding requested
3. Copy of current year's organizational budget and/or project budget
4. Listing of additional sources and amount of support

Deadlines: March 1 and April 30

Chatlos Foundation, Inc.

Headquarters

PO Box 915048
Longwood, FL 32791-5048
Phone: 407-862-5077
www.chatlos.org
Contact: William J. Chatlos, C.E.O. and Pres.
E-mail: info@chatlos.org
Type of Grant Maker: Foundation

Description

Founded: 1953
Operating Locations/Geographic Preferences: National

Financial Summary

Assets: $67,887,339
Total Giving: $2,369,323
Number of Grants: 308
Grant Ranges: average: $1,000–$50,000

Grants Information

GRANT TYPES

Program development, operating support, matching

TYPICAL RECIPIENTS/SUBJECTS OF INTEREST

Higher education, religious causes, hospitals, health agencies, social services, and child welfare

PAST GRANT RECIPIENTS

Library or School Related

- Davis College Johnson City (NY), to upgrade facilities, $100,000
- University of Pennsylvania, Philadelphia (PA), for clinical trials, $89,320
- Northwestern College Saint Paul (MN), for scholarship support, $10,000

General

- Orlando Health Foundation, Orlando (FL), for expansion of trauma and emergency services, $125,000
- Foundation Fighting Blindness, Columbia (MD), for public health education program, $100,000
- Wycliffe Bible Translators, Orlando (FL), for consultant development project, $20,000

REQUIREMENTS AND RESTRICTIONS

No support for individual church congregations, primary or secondary schools, the arts, or for organizations in existence for less than two years. No grants to individuals, or for seed money, deficit financing, endowment funds, medical research, conferences, bricks and mortar, or multiyear grants. No loans.

APPLICATION PROCEDURES

See website for proposal instructions. Application form may be requested in writing or printed from the foundation website. Application form required. Applicants should submit:

1. Copy of IRS Determination Letter
2. Copy of current year's organizational budget and/or project budget
3. Detailed description of project and amount of funding requested

Deadlines: None

Chicago Community Trust

Headquarters

225 N. Michigan
Chicago, IL 60601
Phone: 312-616-8000

www.cct.org

Contact: Ms. Sandy Phelps, Grants Mgr.

E-mail: info@cct.org

Type of Grant Maker: Community Foundation

Description

Founded: 1915

Operating Locations/Geographic Preferences: Giving primarily in Cook County and the adjacent 5 counties

Financial Summary

Assets: $1,582,884,555
Total Giving: $104,309,814

Grants Information

GRANT TYPES

Program development, continuing support, building and renovation, capital campaigns, capacity building, matching

TYPICAL RECIPIENTS/SUBJECTS OF INTEREST

- Arts and Culture
- Chicago Community Trust Fellowship
- Economic Development
- Education
- Environment and Natural Resources
- Health
- Housing
- Human Relations
- Hunger
- Public and Nonprofit Organizations
- Sustainability
- Workforce

PAST GRANT RECIPIENTS

Library or School Related

- University of Illinois at Chicago, Chicago (IL), for mathematics instruction, $777,000
- Consortium on Chicago School Research, Chicago (IL), for research on student outcomes, $133,000

General

- Chicago Community Foundation, Chicago (IL), for Arts Work Fund, $250,000
- Children's Memorial Foundation, Chicago (IL), for Consortium to Lower Obesity, $200,000
- Legal Assistance Foundation of Metropolitan Chicago, $20,000

REQUIREMENTS AND RESTRICTIONS

No support for sectarian purposes or support of single-disease oriented research, treatment or care. No grants to individuals or for reducing operating deficits or liquidating existing debt, or for writing, publishing, producing or distributing audio, visual or printing material, or for conducting conferences, festivals, exhibitions or meetings.

APPLICATION PROCEDURES

See website for strategic grant opportunities, guidelines, RFPs and to access online application system. Application form required.

Deadlines: Vary

Chinese American Librarians Association

Headquarters

c/o Lian Ruan, Ph.D.
Director/Head Librarian
Illinois Fire Service Institute
University of Illinois at Urbana-Champaign
11 Gerty Drive
Champaign, IL 61820
http://cala-web.org/node/203

Type of Grant Maker: Library Organization

Grants Information

SALLY C. TSENG'S PROFESSIONAL DEVELOPMENT GRANT

To support program and research related activities by CALA members. Proposals must focus on program and research in library and information science for which the applicant is highly qualified and which would result in the advancement of the individual's professional status, knowledge, and contributions to the community. Proposals will be evaluated by the criteria identified in these guidelines.

REQUIREMENTS AND RESTRICTIONS

1. Must be CALA members of Chinese descendants in good standing (CALA membership for 3 or more consecutive years with academic honesty, professional achievements and contributions) who are currently working full time in libraries are eligible to apply.
2. The applicants must demonstrate interests in research and professional development by presenting papers or reports at conferences, institutes or workshops sponsored by the American Library Association, the Chinese American Librarians Association, the China Society of Library Science and other similar professional organizations.
3. CALA members who received this grant must wait for another five years to apply for it again.

APPLICATION PROCEDURES

Submit application to the Chair of the Sally C. Tseng Professional Development Grant Committee with copy to:

Sally Tseng, Ex-Officio
E-mail: sctseng888@yahoo.com

The applicant(s) must submit one (1) complete set of their application electronically in Word and/or PDF files via e-mail attachments.

Deadlines: March 15

Chisholm Foundation

Headquarters

544 Central Ave.
PO Box 39442
Laurel, MS 39440-3955
Phone: 601-426-3378
www.chisholmfoundation.org

E-mail: info@chisholmfoundation.org

Type of Grant Maker: Foundation

Description

Founded: 1960

Operating Locations/Geographic Preferences: Giving primarily in MS, New York, NY and WA.

Financial Summary

Assets: $22,999,657
Total Giving: $1,738,200
Number of Grants: 132
Grant Ranges: $100,000–$500

Grants Information

GRANT TYPES

Program development, general support, endowments, matching

TYPICAL RECIPIENTS/SUBJECTS OF INTEREST

Higher and regular education, arts, health, and human services

PAST GRANT RECIPIENTS

Library or School Related

- Smith College, Northampton (MA), for Science Engineering Initiative, $65,000
- Millsaps College, Jackson (MS), for Chair in Arts and Science, $50,000
- Saint Paul's School, Concord (NH), for Alexander Saint-Amand Fund, $25,000

General

- Lauren Rogers Museum of Art, Laurel (MS), for exhibition, $20,000
- Second Stage Theater, New York (NY), $50,000
- Manhattan Institute for Policy Research, $60,000

REQUIREMENTS AND RESTRICTIONS

No grants to individuals

APPLICATION PROCEDURES

See website for application information

Cincinnati Foundation, Greater

Headquarters

200 W. 4th St.
Cincinnati, OH 45202-2602

www.gcfdn.org

Contact: Shiloh Turner, V.P., Community Investment; for grants: Kay Pennington, Community Investment Coord.

E-mail: info@gcfdn.org

Type of Grant Maker: Community Foundation

Description

Founded: 1963

Operating Locations/Geographic Preferences: Giving limited to southeastern IN, northern KY, and the greater Cincinnati, OH area

Financial Summary

Assets: $443,097,111
Total Giving: $62,620,127

Grants Information

GRANT TYPES

Program development, renovation, capital campaign, emergency fund, matching, seed money

TYPICAL RECIPIENTS/SUBJECTS OF INTEREST

Arts and culture, community progress, environmental needs, education, health, and social and human services, including youth agencies
    Programs include:

- Cultural Vibrancy
- Economic Opportunity
- Educational Success
- Environmental Stewardship
- Health and Wellness
- Jacob E. Davis Volunteer Leadership Award
- Job Creation
- Strong Communities:
- Summertime Kids Mini-Grant

PAST GRANT RECIPIENTS

General

- Community Learning Fund, for learning centers in the public schools, $500,000
- Cincinnati Center City Development, Cincinnati (OH), for park revitalization, $100,000
- Middletown House of Hope for the Homeless, Middletown (OH), for capital campaign, $50,000

APPLICATION PROCEDURES

See website for online application and guidelines.
Applicants should submit:

1. Timetable for implementation and evaluation of project
2. Results expected from proposed grant
3. Population served
4. Name, address, and phone number of organization
5. Geographic area to be served
6. How project's results will be evaluated or measured
7. Detailed description of project and amount of funding requested
8. Contact person
9. Copy of current year's organizational budget and/or project budget

Deadlines: For requests $25,000 or less: February 15, May 15, August 15, and November 15

Citizens Charitable Foundation

Headquarters

53 State St., 8th Fl.
Boston, MA 02109-2802
www.citizensbank.com/community/default.aspx
Type of Grant Maker: Corporate Foundation

Description

Founded: 1967

Operating Locations/Geographic Preferences: Giving on a national basis in areas of company operations, with emphasis on CT, DE, MA, ME, NH, NJ, NY, PA, RI, and VT.

Corporate Financial Information: Citizens Charitable Foundation is a charitable contributions vehicle of Citizens Financial Group, Inc., RBS Citizens, N.A. and Citizens Bank of Pennsylvania

Financial Summary

Assets: $15,742,201
Total Giving: $17,662,404
Number of Grants: 3,272
Grant Ranges: $300,000–$50

Grants Information

GRANT TYPES

Program development, public relations, capital campaigns, general support

TYPICAL RECIPIENTS/SUBJECTS OF INTEREST

Support is focused on housing, community development and basic human needs

PAST GRANT RECIPIENTS

General

- United Way of Massachusetts Bay, Boston (MA), for general operating support, $300,000
- YMCA of the U.S.A., Chicago (IL), for general operating support, $100,000
- Metropolitan Career Center, Philadelphia (PA), for general operating support, $66,600
- After School Matters, Chicago (IL), for general operating support, $40,000

REQUIREMENTS AND RESTRICTIONS

No support for discriminatory organizations, single disease/issue information or research organizations, religious organizations, labor, fraternal, or veterans' organizations, political organizations, governmental or quasi-governmental public agencies or organizations, grant-makers, or public or private educational institutions. No grants to individuals, or for annual campaigns, political projects, debt reduction, conferences or seminars, endowments, trips or tours, advertising or fund-raising activities, or historic preservation; no loans.

APPLICATION PROCEDURES

Prospective applicants must take the charitable grant eligibility quiz on the website, which also provides additional information. Applicants should submit:

1. Principal source of support for project in the past
2. Name, address and phone number of organization
3. Copy of IRS Determination Letter
4. Brief history of organization and description of its mission
5. Copy of most recent annual report/audited financial statement/990
6. How project's results will be evaluated or measured
7. Listing of board of directors, trustees, officers and other key people and their affiliations
8. Detailed description of project and amount of funding requested
9. Copy of current year's organizational budget and/or project budget

Deadlines: None

Clark, Robert Sterling Foundation, Inc.

Headquarters

135 E. 64th St.
New York, NY 10065-7045
Phone: 212-288-8900
www.rsclark.org
Contact: Margaret C. Ayers, C.E.O. and Pres.
E-mail: rscf@rsclark.org
Type of Grant Maker: Foundation

Description

Founded: 1952

Operating Locations/Geographic Preferences: Giving primarily in New York State

Financial Summary

Assets: $90,894,758
Total Giving: $4,153,970
Number of Grants: 89
Grant Ranges: $150,000–$1,000; average: $5,000–$150,000

Grants Information

GRANT TYPES

Program development, continuing support, operating support, management and capacity building

TYPICAL RECIPIENTS/SUBJECTS OF INTEREST

Reproductive rights, international arts and cultural engagement
   Major programs include:

- Public Institutions Program
- Ensuring Access to Comprehensive Reproductive Health Information and Services
- International Cultural Engagement

PAST GRANT RECIPIENTS

General

- Brooklyn Academy of Music, Brooklyn (NY), for dance tour, $200,000
- Planned Parenthood Federation of America, New York (NY), for public policy litigation and law program, $150,000
- American Civil Liberties Union Foundation, New York (NY), for litigation, legal analysis, advocacy and public education, $100,000
- National Performance Network, New Orleans (LA), for U.S. artists in Latin America and the Caribbean, $100,000

REQUIREMENTS AND RESTRICTIONS

No grants to individuals, or for annual campaigns, seed money, emergency funds, deficit financing, capital or endowment funds, general support or scholarships.

APPLICATION PROCEDURES

Applicants should submit:

1. How project will be sustained once grant-maker support is completed
2. Results expected from proposed grant
3. Qualifications of key personnel
4. Copy of IRS Determination Letter
5. Copy of most recent annual report/audited financial statement/990
6. How project's results will be evaluated or measured
7. Listing of board of directors, trustees, officers and other key people and their affiliations
8. Detailed description of project and amount of funding requested
9. Copy of current year's organizational budget and/or project budget
10. Listing of additional sources and amount of support
11. Additional materials/documentation

Deadlines: None

Cleveland Foundation

Headquarters

1422 Euclid Ave., Ste. 1300
Cleveland, OH 44115-2001
Phone: 216-861-3810
www.clevelandfoundation.org
Contact: Ronald B. Richard, C.E.O.
E-mail: rrichard@clevefdn.org
Type of Grant Maker: Community Foundation

Description

Founded: 1914

Operating Locations/Geographic Preferences: Giving limited to the greater Cleveland, OH, area, with primary emphasis on Cleveland, Cuyahoga, Lake, and Geauga counties

Financial Summary

Assets: $1,888,630,534
Total Giving: $94,560,803
Number of Grants: 2,560
Grant Ranges: $4,500,000–$50

Grants Information

GRANT TYPES

Program development, capital campaigns, matching, investments and loan, seed money

TYPICAL RECIPIENTS/SUBJECTS OF INTEREST

Major program areas include: arts and culture, civic affairs, economic development, education, the environment, health, and social services.

Special initiatives include: neighborhoods and housing, strengthening mid-size arts organizations, public school improvement, early childhood, successful aging, and economic transformation.

PAST GRANT RECIPIENTS

Library or School Related

- Cleveland State University Foundation, Cleveland (OH), for planning of Partnership for Enhancing Urban Health, $250,000

General

- Gordon Square Arts District, Cleveland (OH), for renovations for Cleveland Public Theater, $250,000
- Neighborhood Progress, Cleveland (OH), for operating support of Strategic Investment Initiative, $4,500,000
- Community Re-Entry, Cleveland (OH), for Cleveland Peacemakers Alliance Outreach Project, $400,000
- Cleveland Foundation, Cleveland (OH), for public awareness support for Cleveland Metropolitan School District's Transformation Plan, $300,000

REQUIREMENTS AND RESTRICTIONS

Special note for libraries: No support for community services such as library or welfare services, fire and police protection, or government staff positions. However, no restrictions exist for other types of libraries. No support for sectarian or religious activities, No grants to individuals, endowments, operating costs, debt reduction, fund-raising campaigns, publications, films and audiovisual materials, memberships, travel for bands, sports teams, classes and similar groups; no capital support for planning, construction, renovation, or purchase of buildings, equipment and materials, land acquisition, or renovation of public space.

APPLICATION PROCEDURES

Organizations must submit inquiries and applications electronically. See website.

Deadlines: None

Coastal Community Foundation of South Carolina

Headquarters

90 Mary St.
Charleston, SC 29403-6230
Phone: 843-723-3635
www.coastalcommunityfoundation.org
Contact: George C. Stevens, C.E.O.
E-mail: info@coastalcommunityfoundation.org
Type of Grant Maker: Community Foundation

Description

Founded: 1974
Operating Locations/Geographic Preferences: Giving in coastal counties of SC: Beaufort, Berkeley, Charleston, Colleton, Dorchester, Georgetown, Hampton and Jasper.

Financial Summary

Assets: $154,468,810
Total Giving: $9,881,331
Grant Ranges: scholarships from $500 to $5,000. *See* website for others

Grants Information

GRANT TYPES

Program development, building and renovation, capital campaigns, general support, seed money, land acquisition

TYPICAL RECIPIENTS/SUBJECTS OF INTEREST

Primarily for education, human services and environment

PAST GRANT RECIPIENTS

Library or School Related

- University of Virginia, Charlottesville (VA), for scholarship, $2,000

General

- South Carolina Coastal Conservation League, Charleston (SC), for GrowFood Carolina, $300,000
- Audubon South Carolina, Harleyville (SC), $161,000

- Sisters of Charity Ministry Development Corporation, Columbia (SC), for Healthy Learners program, $50,000
- Charleston Area Therapeutic Riding, Johns Island (SC), $4,500

APPLICATION PROCEDURES

See website for application forms and additional guidelines. Applicants should submit:

1. Signature and title of chief executive officer
2. Results expected from proposed grant
3. Statement of problem project will address
4. Population served
5. Copy of IRS Determination Letter
6. Geographic area to be served
7. How project's results will be evaluated or measured
8. Detailed description of project and amount of funding requested
9. Copy of current year's organizational budget and/or project budget
10. Listing of additional sources and amount of support

Deadlines: Vary

Cohen Foundation, Sam L.

Headquarters

50 Foden Rd., Ste. 5
Portland, ME 04106-1718
Phone: 207-871-5600

www.samlcohenfoundation.org

Contact: Nancy Brain, Exec. Dir.; Stephanie Eglinton, Prog. Off.

E-mail: nbrain@samlcohenfoundation.org

Type of Grant Maker: Foundation

Description

Founded: 1983

Operating Locations/Geographic Preferences: Giving primarily in York and Cumberland counties in southern ME

Financial Summary

Assets: $38,535,508
Total Giving: $1,514,653
Number of Grants: 71
Grant Ranges: $125,000–$2,000

Grants Information

GRANT TYPES

Program development, general support, management development, capacity building, matching

TYPICAL RECIPIENTS/SUBJECTS OF INTEREST

Nonprofit organizations of benefit to citizens of southern Maine, York and Cumberland counties

PAST GRANT RECIPIENTS

Library or School Related

- Osher Map Library, Portland (ME), Education Outreach, $25,000
- Naples Public Library, Community Technology Access, $7,500
- Maine School Library, Reader to Reader, $5,000

General

- Community Financial Literacy, Portland (ME), Operating support, $10,000
- Great School Partnerships, Portland (ME), $25,000
- Learning Works, After School Program, $25,000

APPLICATION PROCEDURES

See website for application information and current guidelines

Deadlines: See website

Collins Foundation

Headquarters

1618 S.W. 1st Ave., Ste. 505
Portland, OR 97201-5706
Phone: 503-227-7171

www.collinsfoundation.org

Contact: Cynthia G. Addams, Exec. V.P.

E-mail: information@collinsfoundation.org

Type of Grant Maker: Foundation

Description

Founded: 1947

Operating Locations/Geographic Preferences: Giving limited to OR, with emphasis on Portland

Financial Summary

Assets: $179,038,460
Total Giving: $7,467,058
Number of Grants: 261
Grant Ranges: $300,000—$1,500

Grants Information

GRANT TYPES

Investments and loans, building and renovation, matching, capital campaigns

TYPICAL RECIPIENTS/SUBJECTS OF INTEREST

Higher education, youth, hospices and health agencies, social welfare, the arts and cultural programs

PAST GRANT RECIPIENTS

Library or School Related

- Foundations for a Better Oregon, Portland (OR), for Chalkboard Project to improve K–12 public education, $286,500
- Humboldt School and Jefferson High School, Self Enhancement, Inc., Portland (OR), for achievement program to low-income students in grades 3-12, $110,000

General

- Oregon Historical Society, Portland (OR), for new permanent exhibit, $200,000
- Women's Coalition of Josephine County, Grants Pass (OR), for violence-prevention educator position for middle school and high school students, $20,000
- Shadow Project, Portland (OR), for program to improve educational outcomes for children in special education classrooms, $17,500

REQUIREMENTS AND RESTRICTIONS

No support for individual religious institutions. No grants to individuals, or for endowments, operational deficits, financial emergencies, debt retirement, or annual fund-raising activities.

APPLICATION PROCEDURES

Do not send proposals electronically. See website for submission guidelines. Applicants should submit:

1. How project will be sustained once grant-maker support is completed
2. Signature and title of chief executive officer
3. Population served
4. Copy of IRS Determination Letter
5. Brief history of organization and description of its mission
6. Copy of most recent annual report/audited financial statement/990
7. Listing of board of directors, trustees, officers and other key people and their affiliations
8. Detailed description of project and amount of funding requested
9. Contact person
10. Copy of current year's organizational budget and/or project budget
11. Listing of additional sources and amount of support

Deadlines: None

Colorado State Library

Headquarters

201 East Colfax Ave.
Room 309, Denver, CO 80203
Phone: 303-866-6900
Fax: 303-866-6940
www.cde.state.co.us/cdelib/index.htm

Type of Grant Maker: Government

Grants Information

LSTA GRANTS

Provided by the Colorado State Library to assist libraries and library-related agencies develop or enhance programs and projects that enable Coloradans to receive improved library services.

Total Giving: $300,000

Grant Ranges: Vary. Projects that have a local impact, involving a library plus one additional organization, may request a maximum of $20,000.

REQUIREMENTS AND RESTRICTIONS

Grant funds are available to officially recognized Colorado libraries, library-related agencies or organizations. This includes school (public, charter, nonprofit private); public, academic, and special libraries; BOCES; library consortium; and library professional organizations. Applicants must have sufficient staffing ability and fiscal capability to successfully implement, complete, and evaluate results at the conclusion of the project.

APPLICATION PROCEDURES

See website for application guidelines and application procedures.

For more information, contact:

Jean Heilig
Fiscal Officer & LSTA Coordinator
Colorado State Library
201 East Colfax Ave, Room 309
Denver, CO 80203-1799
Phone: 303-866-6731
Fax: 303-866-6940
E-mail: heilig_j@cde.state.co.us

Deadlines: August 1

MINI-GRANTS FOR STATEWIDE SUMMER READING PROGRAM

Grant Amount: $200
Number of Grants: Approx. 70

To support and promote the 2012 Collaborative Summer Library Program (CSLP) statewide Summer Reading Program in their local communities. Priority is given to libraries below 10,000 Legal Service Area (LSA) population and libraries in non-metro locations.

APPLICATION PROCEDURES

When available, information about applying is posted online.

Deadlines: To be announced

Columbus Foundation and Affiliated Organizations

Headquarters

1234 E. Broad St.
Columbus, OH 43205-1453
Phone: 614-251-4000

www.columbusfoundation.org

Contact: Raymond J. Biddiscombe, V.P., Finance

E-mail: tcfinfo@columbusfoundation.org

Type of Grant Maker: Community Foundation

Description

Founded: 1943

Operating Locations/Geographic Preferences: Giving limited to central OH

Financial Summary

Assets: $1,061,039,486
Total Giving: $96,119,215

Grants Information

GRANT TYPES

Program development, building and renovation, capital campaign, continuing support, matching, land acquisition, seed money

TYPICAL RECIPIENTS/SUBJECTS OF INTEREST

Education, arts and humanities, urban affairs, conservation, environment, health, mental health, developmentally disabled, and social service agencies

Funding programs include:

- Community Improvement Project
- Fund for Financial Innovation:
- Fund for Innovative Operations
- Fund for Targeting Needs

PAST GRANT RECIPIENTS

Library or School Related

- Just Think, Columbus (OH), for a free STEM curriculum to school systems in Franklin county and contiguous counties, $5,000
- Ohio State University Foundation, Columbus (OH), $1,900,000

General

- Franklin County Genealogical and Historical Society, Columbus (OH), for capital campaign, $900,000
- Mid-Columbia Symphony Society, Richland (WA), $5,000

REQUIREMENTS AND RESTRICTIONS

No support for religious purposes, or for projects normally the responsibility of a public agency. No grants to individuals, or generally for budget deficits, conferences, scholarly research, or endowment funds.

APPLICATION PROCEDURES

See website for information. Application form required.

Deadlines: Vary

Commonwealth Fund

Headquarters

1 E. 75th St.
New York, NY 10021-2692
Fax: 212-606-3500

www.commonwealthfund.org

Contact: Andrea C. Landes, Dir., Grants Mgmt.

Type of Grant Maker: Foundation

Description

Founded: 1918

Operating Locations/Geographic Preferences: United States

Financial Summary

Assets: $604,222,668
Total Giving: $16,060,432
Number of Grants: 268
Grant Ranges: $650,000–$903

Grants Information

GRANT TYPES

Types of Support: Program development, matching

TYPICAL RECIPIENTS/SUBJECTS OF INTEREST

Healthcare, especially improving quality and access and research

PAST GRANT RECIPIENTS

Library or School Related

• University of New Mexico, for rural medical clinical resources in three states, $220,000

General

• Qualis Health, Seattle (WA), for Transforming Safety-Net Clinics into Patient-Centered Medical Homes, $1,500,000

REQUIREMENTS AND RESTRICTIONS

No support for religious organizations for religious purposes, or basic biomedical research. No grants to individuals general planning or ongoing activities, existing deficits, endowment or capital costs, construction, renovation, equipment, conferences, symposia, major media projects, or documentaries

APPLICATION PROCEDURES

Application Information: Online application form preferred, but letters submitted via regular mail or fax will be accepted. Applicants should submit:

1. Timetable for implementation and evaluation of project
2. Results expected from proposed grant
3. Qualifications of key personnel
4. Statement of problem project will address
5. Population served
6. Name, address and phone number of organization
7. Detailed description of project and amount of funding requested
8. Contact person
9. Copy of current year's organizational budget and/or project budget
10. List of company employees involved with the organization

Connecticut Library Association

Headquarters

234 Court St.
Middletown, CT 06457
Phone: 860-346-2444
Fax: 860-344-9199

www.ctlibraryassociation.org/about.php

E-mail: cla@ctlibrarians.org

Type of Grant Maker: Library Organization

Grants Information

PEG (PROGRAM FOR EDUCATIONAL GRANTS)

Grant Range: $2,500

To help members of the Connecticut Library Association improve their knowledge and skills. PEG funds some expenses for continuing education programs, workshops, seminars, courses, institutes, and other activities.

REQUIREMENTS AND RESTRICTIONS

Any personal member of the Connecticut Library Association may apply for a PEG award. Applicants must be members at the time the program/event occurs and at other steps during the PEG process.

APPLICATION PROCEDURES

Grant application required. The form should be mailed or faxed to the PEG Chair.

For more information, contact:

Peter Ciparelli, PEG Chair
Killingly Public Library
25 Westcott Rd.
Danielson, CT 06239
Phone: 860-779-5383
Fax: 860-779-1823
E-mail: pciparelli@biblio.org

Deadlines: September 1, November 1, January 2 and July 1

Connecticut State Library

Headquarters

231 Capitol Avenue
Hartford, CT 06106
Phone: 860-757-6500, 866-886-4478

www.webjunction.org/partners/connecticut/ct-services/grants.html

Type of Grant Maker: Government

Grants Information

CONNECTICUT STATE PUBLIC LIBRARY CONSTRUCTION PROGRAM

Grant Ranges: $6,666–1,000,000

Provides grants for public library construction projects that create usable space (e.g., new buildings, additions, and renovations—known as Category #1 grants), and for projects that improve existing space (e.g., handicapped accessibility, correcting building and fire code violations, remodeling to accommodate new technologies, and energy conservation—known as Category #2 grants).

REQUIREMENTS AND RESTRICTIONS

All public libraries in the state of Connecticut are eligible.

APPLICATION PROCEDURES

See online "Library Construction Grant Program, An Explanation of the Program and the Application Process" (PDF) for more information.

Deadlines: August 30

LIBRARY SERVICES AND TECHNOLOGY ACT (LSTA)

Grant Ranges: Vary. (The amount of LSTA funds available for grants depends on each year's LSTA budget.)

The Advisory Council on Library Planning and Development determines grant categories based on goals in the LSTA Five Year Plan, 2013–2017. Starting in fiscal year 2012, directed grants will be made available on a rotating basis between programs for multi-language populations, programs for older adults, services to people with disabilities, and programs for young adults.

REQUIREMENTS AND RESTRICTIONS

In order to apply for an LSTA grant, a library must attend one session of a procedural workshop. The Division strongly recommends that the attendee be the same person who is writing the grant.

APPLICATION PROCEDURES

Attend procedural workshop and submit appropriate forms.

For more information, contact:

Douglas Lord, Division of Library Development
Middletown Library Service Center
786 South Main St.
Middletown, CT 06457
860-704-2204 or 800-437-2313 (fax: 860-704-2228)
douglas.lord@ct.gov

Deadlines: March

STATE AID GRANTS TO CONNECTICUT PUBLIC LIBRARIES

Grant Range: $1,200 to each library, plus additional amounts for equalization based on town AENGLC (Adjusted Equalized Net Grand List Per Capita) rankings and for incentive based on each town's per capita library expenditures.

Total Giving: $207,692 in 2011–2012

Each principal public library in the state that meets the eligibility requirements may apply for and receive an annual state aid grant. A principal public library is one which has been so designated by the local municipal governing board. A municipality may have more than one public library, but may designate only one library as its principal public library.

State aid funds must be used for general library purposes, which are defined in the state statutes as all functions of a public library, including the purchase of land or the construction, alteration or remodeling of buildings. In addition, state aid funds must be expended within two years of receipt, unless a library has applied to the State

Library Board and received authority to carry over funds beyond the two year limit.

REQUIREMENTS AND RESTRICTIONS

Eligibility requirements: All principal public libraries in the state of Connecticut that electronically submit a locked Public Library Annual Statistical Report and Application for State Aid with the State Library by the deadline, participate in Connecticard, provide equal access to library materials without charging individuals residing in the town for borrower cards or for use of the library's basic collections and services, do not discriminate, certify that the library's annual tax levy or appropriation has not been reduced to an amount which is less than the average amount levied or appropriated for the library in the preceding three years.

APPLICATION PROCEDURES

The application form is combined with the Public Library Annual Statistical Report which each of the state's 194 public libraries is requested to submit.

Deadline: November 15

Cord Foundation

Headquarters

418 Flint St.
Reno, NV 89501-2008

Contact: Joseph S. Bradley
Type of Grant Maker: Foundation

Description

Founded: 1962
Operating Locations/Geographic Preferences: Giving primarily in northern NV and the rural counties of NV

Financial Summary

Assets: $69,532,084
Total Giving: $3,640,500

Grants Information

GRANT TYPES

Program development, building and renovation, general support, matching

TYPICAL RECIPIENTS/SUBJECTS OF INTEREST

Secondary and higher education, colleges and universities, social services and youth organizations, and cultural organizations

PAST GRANT RECIPIENTS

Library or School Related

- Proctor R. Hug High School, Reno (NV), for weight room, $20,000
- University of Nevada Reno Foundation, Reno (NV), for medical school, $20,000

General

- Reno, City of, Reno (NV), for YMCA project, $250,000
- Auburn Automotive Heritage, Auburn (IN), for branding process, $50,000
- Alzheimer's Association, Reno (NV), for caregiver support services, $25,000
- Tru Vista Foundation, Reno (NV), for Family Needs Program, $25,000

REQUIREMENTS AND RESTRICTIONS

No support for religious organizations for sectarian purposes. No grants to individuals, or for continuing support.

APPLICATION PROCEDURES

Application form not required. Applicants should submit:

1. Copy of IRS Determination Letter
2. Brief history of organization and description of its mission
3. Copy of most recent annual report/audited financial statement/990
4. How project's results will be evaluated or measured
5. Listing of board of directors, trustees, officers and other key people and their affiliations
6. Detailed description of project and amount of funding requested
7. Copy of current year's organizational budget and/or project budget
8. Listing of additional sources and amount of support

Deadlines: None

Crown Family Philanthropies (*Also known as* Arie and Ida Crown Memorial)

Headquarters

222 N. LaSalle St., Ste. 2000
Chicago, IL 60601-1109
Phone: 312-750-6671

www.crownmemorial.org

Contact: Caren Yanis, Exec. Dir.

E-mail: aicm@crown-chicago.com

Type of Grant Maker: Foundation

Description

Founded: 1947

Operating Locations/Geographic Preferences: Giving primarily in metropolitan Chicago, IL, with some giving in NY

Financial Information

Assets: $470,489,043
Total Giving: $22,895,293
Number of Grants: 580
Grant Ranges: $1,000,000–$3

Grants Information

GRANT TYPES

Program development, building and renovation, general and continuing support, capital campaigns, matching

TYPICAL RECIPIENTS/SUBJECTS OF INTEREST

Arts and culture, civic affairs, education, environment, health, human services, and Jewish causes

PAST GRANT RECIPIENTS

Library or School Related

- Family Book Club, Ann Arbor (MI), $10,000
- Northwestern University, Evanston (IL), $25,000
- Solomon Schechter Day School, Northbrook (IL), $75,000
- Chicago Public Schools, Chicago (IL), $5,000

General

- Holocaust Education Foundation, Chicago (IL), $500,000
- Yellowstone to Yukon Conservation Initiative, Canmore (Canada), $150,000
- Urban Gateways: Center for Arts Education, Chicago (IL), $25,000
- Arts Alliance Illinois, Chicago (IL), $15,000

REQUIREMENTS AND RESTRICTIONS

No support for government-sponsored programs, or to organizations with budgets under $200,000. No grants to individuals, or for film, video, exhibitions, conference, associations or coalitions.

APPLICATION PROCEDURES

See website for guidelines. Applicants should submit:

1. Copy of IRS Determination Letter
2. Detailed description of project and amount of funding requested
3. Copy of current year's organizational budget and/or project budget

Deadlines: see website

Cummings Foundation, Nathan

Headquarters

475 10th Ave., 14th Fl.
New York, NY 10018-9715
Phone: 212-787-7300

www.nathancummings.org

Contact: Simon Greer, C.E.O. and Pres.

E-mail: contact@nathancummings.org

Type of Grant Maker: Foundation

Description

Founded: 1949

Operating Locations/Geographic Preferences: United States

Financial Summary

Assets: $415,102,143
Total giving: $19,944,000
Number of Grants: 308
Grant Ranges: $975,000–$200

Grants Information

GRANT TYPES

Program development, general and continuing support, seed money

TYPICAL RECIPIENTS/SUBJECTS OF INTEREST

Arts, culture, communities, ecology, social justice, Jewish tradition

PAST GRANT RECIPIENTS

Library or School Related

- American University, Washington (DC), for Best Practices in Climate Change, $100,000

General

- Community Catalyst, Boston (MA), for pooled Affordable Care Act Implementation Fund, $500,000
- New Israel Fund, New York (NY), for Women and the Environment: Agents of Change in Israel, $950,000

APPLICATION PROCEDURES

Application form required. Applicants should submit:

1. Timetable for implementation and evaluation of project
2. Qualifications of key personnel
3. Statement of problem project will address
4. Name, address and phone number of organization
5. Copy of IRS Determination Letter
6. Brief history of organization and description of its mission
7. Listing of board of directors, trustees, officers and other key people and their affiliations
8. Detailed description of project and amount of funding requested
9. Contact person
10. Copy of current year's organizational budget and/or project budget
11. Listing of additional sources and amount of support

Deadlines: None

Cummins Foundation

Headquarters

500 Jackson St., M.C. 60633
Columbus, IN 47201-6258
Phone: 812-377-3114
Fax: 812-377-7897

www.cummins.com

Contact: Tracy Souza, Pres. and Secy.

E-mail: Cummins.Foundation@cummins.com

Type of Grant Maker: Corporate Foundation

Description

Founded: 1954

Operating Locations/Geographic Preferences: Giving primarily in areas of company operations, with emphasis on Lake Mills, IA, the Columbus and Seymour, IN, areas, Fridley, MN, Jamestown, NY, Rocky Mount, NC, Findlay, OH, Charleston, SC, Cookeville, Memphis, and Nashville, TN, El Paso, TX, Stoughton, WI and in Brazil, China, India, Mexico, and South Africa; giving also to national organizations.

Corporate Foundation Information:

- Cummins Engine Co., Inc.
- Fleetguard, Inc.
- Cummins Inc.

Financial Summary

Assets: $22,316,934
Total Giving: $7,258,872
Number of Grants: 198
Grant Ranges: $910,511–$16

Grants Information

GRANT TYPES

Program development, annual campaigns, building and renovation, continuing, general and operating support, emergency funds, matching, technical assistance, sponsorships

TYPICAL RECIPIENTS/SUBJECTS OF INTEREST

Education, the environment, social justice, and programs to improve communities in which Cummins does business

PAST GRANT RECIPIENTS

Library or School Related

- Allen Co. Public Library, Ft. Wayne (partner agency), Lincoln Collection of Indiana collection preservation, $25,000
- Library Project, Children's libraries in China, $50,000; Computer labs in China, $22,000
- Whitakers Public Library, Whitakers (NC), Renovation, $79,000

General

- Literacy Network, English as Second Language, $39,500
- Community Education Coalition, Connersville (IN), for Early Childhood Education Initiative, $125,000
- Foundation for Youth, contest winner, $400

REQUIREMENTS AND RESTRICTIONS

No support for sectarian religious organizations, political candidates, or medical or disease-related organizations. No grants to individuals, or for capital campaigns, business start-up needs or political causes, loans or product donations.

APPLICATION PROCEDURES

Send proposal with:

1. Results expected from proposed grant
2. Qualifications of key personnel
3. Statement of problem project will address
4. Copy of IRS Determination Letter
5. How project's results will be evaluated or measured
6. Listing of board of directors, trustees, officers and other key people and their affiliations
7. Detailed description of project and amount of funding requested
8. Copy of current year's organizational budget and/or project budget

Deadlines: None

CVS Caremark Charitable Trust, Inc.

Headquarters

1 CVS Dr.
Woonsocket, RI 02895-6146
Phone: 401-770-4561

cvscaremark.com/community/our-impact/
community-grants

Contact: Eileen Howard Boone, V.P.

E-mail: communitymailbox@cvs.com

Type of Grant Maker: Corporate Foundation

Description

Founded: 1992

Operating Locations/Geographic Preferences: United States and Puerto Rico, primarily in areas of company operations

Corporate Foundation Information:

- Supported by CVS Pharmacy, Inc.
- CVS Corp.
- Melville Corp.

Financial Summary

Not available

Grants Information

GRANT TYPES

Program development, building and renovation, management development, employee volunteering

TYPICAL RECIPIENTS/SUBJECTS OF INTEREST

Children with disabilities and health care. Provides grants to support academic enrichment programs at public schools and grants to support organizations that provide access to health care and health education for at-risk and underserved populations

PAST GRANT RECIPIENTS

Library or School Related

- Rhode Island Quality Institute for program funding, $500,000
- Southern Methodist University, for scholarship aid, $4,000

General

- Easter Seals Metropolitan Chicago for program funding, $300,000
- Rehabilitation, Education and Advocacy for citizens with Disabilities, Dallas (TX) for program support, $10,000

REQUIREMENTS AND RESTRICTIONS

No grants for general operating support, fund-raising, sponsorships, endowments or capital campaigns.

APPLICATION PROCEDURES

Form required; see website

Deadlines: Grant requests accepts January 1–October 31

Dallas Foundation

Headquarters

Reagan Place at Old Parkland
3963 Maple Ave., Ste. 390
Dallas, TX 75219
Phone: 214-741-9898

www.dallasfoundation.org

Contact: Mary M. Jalonick, President; for grants: Laura J.
Smith, Dir., Community Philanthropy

E-mail: info@dallasfoundation.org

Type of Grant Maker: Community Foundation

Description

Founded: 1929

Operating Locations/Geographic Preferences: Giving
primarily to the City and County of Dallas, TX

Financial Summary

Assets: $175,000,000
Total Giving: $32,075,750
Number of Grants: 147
Grant Ranges: $1 million–$439

Grants Information

GRANT TYPES

Program development, building and renovation, capital
campaigns, general and operating support, matching

TYPICAL RECIPIENTS/SUBJECTS OF INTEREST

Community Impact Grants provided for education, social
services, healthcare, and the arts.

Field-of-Interest Grants in the areas of arts, critical
needs, animal welfare, older adults, low-income children,
abused and neglected children, disabled children, blind
or deaf children, children with debilitating diseases and
African-American citizens.

Safety Net Funding Cycle for organizations providing
services in Dallas County.

PAST GRANT RECIPIENTS

Library or School Related

- Southern Methodist University, Dallas (TX), for
  showcases in New York for theater students, $840,000

- University of Texas, Austin (TX), $656,000
- Cornell University, Ithaca (NY), $48,500

General

- Foundation for Community Empowerment, Dallas, TX,
  for Road to Broad, $431,000
- Highland Park United Methodist Church, Dallas, TX,
  $272,000
- Catholic Charities Diocese of Dallas, Dallas, TX, for
  Elderly Services program, $30,000

REQUIREMENTS AND RESTRICTIONS

No support for religious purposes. No grants to individuals
or for endowments, research, operating budgets, annual
campaigns, debt retirement, or underwriting of fund-raising
events.

APPLICATION PROCEDURES

See website for guidelines per grant type. Applicants should
submit:

1. Timetable for implementation and evaluation of project
2. Results expected from proposed grant
3. Brief history of organization and description of its
   mission
4. How project's results will be evaluated or measured
5. Detailed description of project and amount of funding
   requested
6. Copy of current year's organizational budget and/or
   project budget

Deadlines: August 1 for letters of inquiry and October 8
for full proposals for Community Impact grants; March 1
for Field-of-Interest fund grants; rolling basis for Safety Net
Fund grants

Daniel Foundation of Alabama

Headquarters

510 Office Park Dr., Ste. 210
Birmingham, AL 35223
Phone: 205-874-3523

danielfoundationofalabama.com

Contact: Maria S. Kennedy, Secy.-Treas. and Exec. Dir.

E-mail: info@df-al.com

Type of Grant Maker: Foundation

Description

Founded: 1978

Operating Locations/Geographic Preferences: Giving primarily in AL.

Financial Summary

Assets: $122,027,901
Total Giving: $5,725,875
Number of Grants: 328
Grant Ranges: $600,000–$10

Grants Information

GRANT TYPES

General and operating support, capital campaigns; endowments

TYPICAL RECIPIENTS/SUBJECTS OF INTEREST

Educational programs, arts and culture, civic and community programs, and medical care and research

PAST GRANT RECIPIENTS

Library or School Related

- Birmingham-Southern College, Birmingham (AL), for Urban Environmental Lab Park, $150,000
- Auburn University, Auburn (AL), for Professorship, $75,000

General

- Bethel Community Learning Center, Birmingham (AL), for STAGES Program, $10,000
- Birmingham Museum of Art Foundation, Birmingham (AL), for Art Fund, $200,000
- Pioneer Museum of Alabama, Troy (AL), for general operating expenses, $7,500
- Birmingham Zoo, Birmingham (AL), for Phase 1 of Elephant Trails, $200,000
- KID One Transport System, Birmingham (AL), for general operating support, $10,000

REQUIREMENTS AND RESTRICTIONS

No grants to individuals, or for fund-raising events or start-up costs and/or seed money for new organizations.

APPLICATION PROCEDURES

Guidelines must be requested each time prior to submitting a proposal.

Deadlines: 15th of the month prior to board meeting

Dell Foundation, Michael and Susan

Headquarters

PO Box 163867
Austin, TX 78716-3867

www.msdf.org

E-mail: info@msdf.org

Type of Grant Maker: Foundation

Description

Founded: 1999

Operating Locations/Geographic Preferences: Giving on a local (central TX), regional, national and international basis (international emphasis is on India)

Financial Summary

Assets: $934,701,114
Total Giving: $93,673,023
Number of Grants: 329
Grant Ranges: $9,500,000–$261

Grants Information

GRANT TYPES

Visit the programs page of the website for types of grants funded

TYPICAL RECIPIENTS/SUBJECTS OF INTEREST

Education, children's health, safety, youth development and early childhood care
   Program areas include:

- Dell Scholars Program
- Early Childhood Care
- Education
- Health: International Safety
- Supporting the Community
- Youth Development

PAST GRANT RECIPIENTS

Library or School Related

- University of Texas, Austin (TX), for capital campaign for Computer Science Building, $2,000,000
- University of Texas System, Austin (TX), for Dell Pediatric Research Institute, $9,500,000

- California Charter Schools Association, Los Angeles (CA), for Phase III of Performance Management Project for California Charter Schools, $200,000

General

- National Math and Science Initiative, Dallas (TX), for expansion of UTeach Texas, $688,500
- Teach for America, New York (NY), for Phase II US National Growth Funding, $2,000,000
- Advanced Placement Strategies, Austin (TX), for Phase III of Texas High School Project, (THSP): Improving AP Access and Impact, $1,600,000
- National Academy of Sciences, Washington (DC), for HBO Weight of the Nation obesity program $860,000

REQUIREMENTS AND RESTRICTIONS

No support for:

- Individuals
- Medical research projects
- Event fund-raisers or sponsorships
- Lobbying of any kind
- Endowments

APPLICATION PROCEDURES

See website for guidelines and requirements before submitting any full proposals. If the foundation finds that the preliminary grant request fulfills its mission, grant seekers will be notified.

Denver Foundation

Headquarters

55 Madison St., 8th Fl.
Denver, CO 80206
Phone: 303-300-1790

www.denverfoundation.org

Contact: David J. Miller, C.E.O.; Bill Inama, Grants Mgr.

E-mail: information@denverfoundation.org

Type of Grant Maker: Community Foundation

Description

Founded: 1925

Operating Locations/Geographic Preferences: Giving limited to Adams, Arapahoe, Boulder, Broomfield, Denver, Douglas, and Jefferson Counties, CO.

Financial Summary

Assets: $576,008,818
Total Giving: $69,012,161

Grants Information

GRANT TYPES

Program development, building and renovation, matching, general and operating support, capital campaigns, investments and loans, seed money

TYPICAL RECIPIENTS/SUBJECTS OF INTEREST

Grants primarily for education, civic, health, human services, and arts and cultural programs and strengthening neighborhoods
    Program areas include:

- Arts and Culture
- Civic and Education
- Health
- Human Services
- Strengthening Neighborhoods—Small Grants Program

PAST GRANT RECIPIENTS

Library or School Related

- Denver Public Library Friends Foundation, Denver (CO), for Library's Mi Biblioteca, Mi Futuro initiative, which provides programming to help new immigrants and non-English speakers, $330,000
- University of Colorado, Denver (CO), $3,500

General

- Denver Scholarship Foundation, Denver (CO), for general support, $20,800,000
- Free for All Concert Fund, Cambridge (MA), for general operating support, $1,722,000
- Wildlife Experience, Parker (CO), for general operating support, $1,000,000
- Craig Hospital Foundation, Englewood (CO), for Neurological Music Therapy Program, $5,000

REQUIREMENTS AND RESTRICTIONS

No support for government agencies, parochial or religious schools, or organizations that further religious doctrine. No grants to individuals (except for scholarships), or for sponsorships, debt liquidation, debt retirement, endowments or other reserve funds, membership or affiliation campaigns, dinners, or special events, research, publications, films, travel, or conferences, symposiums, workshops, or individual medical procedures, medical, scientific, or academic research, creation or installation of art objects, or multiyear funding requests.

APPLICATION PROCEDURES

See website for application guidelines. Applicants should submit the following:

1. Role played by volunteers
2. Timetable for implementation and evaluation of project
3. How project will be sustained once grant-maker support is completed
4. Signature and title of chief executive officer
5. Results expected from proposed grant
6. Qualifications of key personnel
7. Population served
8. Name, address and phone number of organization
9. Copy of IRS Determination Letter
10. Brief history of organization and description of its mission
11. Copy of most recent annual report/audited financial statement/990
12. How project's results will be evaluated or measured
13. Listing of board of directors, trustees, officers and other key people and their affiliations
14. Detailed description of project and amount of funding requested
15. Plans for cooperation with other organizations, if any
16. Contact person
17. Copy of current year's organizational budget and/or project budget
18. Listing of additional sources and amount of support

Deadlines: February 1, June 1, and October 1

Deutsche Bank Americas Foundation

Headquarters

60 Wall St., NYC60-2112
New York, NY 10005-2858
Phone: 212-250-0539

www.db.com/us/content/en/1066.html

Contact: Gary S. Hattem, Pres.

Type of Grant Maker: Corporate Foundation

Description

Founded: 1986

Operating Locations/Geographic Preferences: Giving on a national basis in areas of company operations with emphasis on NY, Canada, and Latin America

Corporate Foundation Information:

- Founded by Bankers Trust Co.
- BT Capital Corp.
- Deutsche Bank Americas Holding Corp.

Financial Summary

Assets: $22,686,138
Total Giving: $15,069,241

Grants Information

GRANT TYPES

Program development, general, continuing and operating support, volunteer services, investments and loans, employee matching program

TYPICAL RECIPIENTS/SUBJECTS OF INTEREST

Promotion of the arts, education, and community development

PAST GRANT RECIPIENTS

General

- Staten Island Institute of Arts and Sciences, Staten Island (NY), for Arts and Enterprise Stabilization Program, $25,000
- Harlem Stage, New York (NY), for Art and Enterprise Stabilization Program, $75,000
- Asian Americans for Equality, New York (NY), for College Ready Communities—Collaboration with the Brotherhood Sister Sol/Coalition for Education Justice, $300,000
- City Futures, New York (NY), for Center for Urban Future, $25,000

REQUIREMENTS AND RESTRICTIONS

No support for political parties or candidates, veterans', military, or fraternal organizations, United Way agencies not providing a fund-raising waiver, professional or trade associations, or discriminatory organizations. No grants to individuals, or for endowments, capital campaigns, legal advocacy, or religious purposes

APPLICATION PROCEDURES

Letters of intent not more than 3 pages in length submitted first. A full proposal may be requested at a later date. Applicants should submit:

1. Copy of IRS Determination Letter
2. Brief history of organization and description of its mission
3. Detailed description of project and amount of funding requested

Deadlines: None

Dime Bank Foundation, Inc.

Headquarters

c/o Dime Bank
290 Salem Tpke.
Norwich, CT 06360-6456
Phone: 860-859-4300

https://dime-bank.com/dime-foundation.php

Contact: Cheryl A. Calderado, V.P.

E-mail: ccalderado@dime-bank.com

Type of Grant Maker: Corporate Foundation

Description

Founded: 1998

Operating Locations/Geographic Preferences: New London County-Connecticut and Westerly/Pawcatuck-Rhode Island

Corporate Foundation Information: Supported by Dime Savings Bank of Norwich and Dime Bank

Financial Summary

Assets: $3,013,283
Total Giving: $148,044
Number of Grants: 41
Grant Ranges: $10,000–$308

Grants Information

GRANT TYPES

Building and renovation, capital campaigns, general and operating support, equipment, matching

TYPICAL RECIPIENTS/SUBJECTS OF INTEREST

Affordable housing

Basic human services for those considered most at-risk; with emphasis on children, families, and/or the elderly at low-income levels

Cultural enrichment programs, especially among disadvantaged populations

Development/education, job training, or promotion of literacy, especially preventative programs that encourages self-sufficiency

PAST GRANT RECIPIENTS

Library or School Related

• Westerly Public Library, Capital improvements, $5,000

General

• Ocean Community YMCA, capital campaign, $20,000
• Sea Research Foundation, Mystic (CT), $4,500
• Catholic Charities, Norwich (CT), $5,000
• Habitat for Humanity of Southeastern Connecticut, New London (CT), $5,000

REQUIREMENTS AND RESTRICTIONS

No grants to individuals

APPLICATION PROCEDURES

Online form required. See website.
For more information, contact Cheryl Calderado, 860-859-4300 or e-mail at ccalderado@dime-bank.com.

Deadlines: None

Dodge, Cleveland H. Foundation, Inc.

Headquarters

420 Lexington Ave., Ste. 2331
New York, NY 10170-2332
Phone: 212-972-2800
Fax: 212-972-1049

www.chdodgefoundation.org

Contact: Phyllis M. Criscuoli, Exec. Dir.

E-mail: info@chdodgefoundation.org

Type of Grant Maker: Foundation

Description

Founded: 1917

Operating Locations/Geographic Preferences: Giving primarily to institutions and agencies in New York City and the Near East.

Financial Summary

Assets: $39,591,625
Total Giving: $982,003

Grants Information

GRANT TYPES

Building and renovation, matching, endowments, equipment

TYPICAL RECIPIENTS/SUBJECTS OF INTEREST

Most grants in the United States for higher and secondary education, youth agencies and child welfare, and cultural programs

PAST GRANT RECIPIENTS

Library or School Related

- New York Public Library, New York (NY), $5,000
- Camden Public Library, Camden (ME), $250
- Rockport Public Library, Rockport (ME), $250
- Haverhill Public Library, Haverhill (PA), $1,000

General

- New York Botanical Garden, New York (NY), $5,000
- Planned Parenthood, New York (NY), $5,000
- American Museum of Natural History, New York (NY), $5,000

REQUIREMENTS AND RESTRICTIONS

Does not:

- Support individuals through scholarships or other aid.
- Support institutions dealing mainly with medical research or health care and training.
- Support school, colleges and universities excepting those which the Foundation has consistently supported over a long period of time, or to match gifts made under matching plans.
- Make loans.
- Manage programs or projects

APPLICATION PROCEDURES

Send letter and include:

1. Copy of IRS Determination Letter
2. Brief history of organization and description of its mission
3. Copy of most recent annual report/audited financial statement/990
4. Detailed description of project and amount of funding requested
5. Copy of current year's organizational budget and/or project budget

Deadlines: January 15, April 15, and September 15

Dodge, Geraldine R. Foundation, Inc.

Headquarters

14 Maple Ave.
PO Box 1239
Morristown, NJ 07962-1239
Phone: 973-540-8442

www.grdodge.org

Contact: Christopher J. Daggett, C.E.O. and Pres.

E-mail: info@grdodge.org

Type of Grant Maker: Foundation

Description

Founded: 1974

Operating Locations/Geographic Preferences: Giving primarily in NJ, with support for the arts limited to NJ, and support for other local projects limited to the Morristown area; some giving to national organizations for projects in NJ

Financial Summary

Assets: $260,461,020
Total Giving: $10,500,000
Number of Grants: 353

Grants Information

GRANT TYPES

Program development, general, operating and continuing support, matching, seed money

TYPICAL RECIPIENTS/SUBJECTS OF INTEREST

Proposals are invited from organizations that:

1. Enhance the cultural richness of the community and contribute to New Jersey's creative economy.
2. Provide educational opportunities both inside and outside of the classroom for young people with limited access to educational excellence.
3. Promote healthy ecosystems and sustainable communities in New Jersey.
4. Use traditional and new media to educate the public about issues and promote new paradigms towards a creative, sustainable New Jersey.

PAST GRANT RECIPIENTS

Library or School Related

- Unity Charter School, Morristown (NJ), for school expansion to new facility, $95,000
- Big Picture Company, Providence (RI), for design of new Newark high school focused on the environment and sustainability and infusion of arts into curriculum of all BPL schools in Newark, $40,000

General

- Trust for Public Land, New York (NY), for development and stewardship of parks and playgrounds in Newark and NJ, $350,000
- Cloud Institute for Sustainability Education, New York (NY), for NJ Learns, to develop sustainability models in New Jersey schools and communities, $250,000
- Newark Museum, Newark (NJ), for general operating support and exhibition and education initiatives, $125,000

REQUIREMENTS AND RESTRICTIONS

No support for religious, higher education, health, or conduit organizations. No grants to individuals, for capital projects, equipment purchases, indirect costs, endowment funds, deficit financing, or scholarships.

APPLICATION PROCEDURES

See website for guidelines and information. Applicants should submit the following:

1. Timetable for implementation and evaluation of project
2. How project will be sustained once grant-maker support is completed
3. Results expected from proposed grant
4. Qualifications of key personnel
5. Statement of problem project will address
6. Population served
7. Brief history of organization and description of its mission
8. Copy of most recent annual report/audited financial statement/990
9. How project's results will be evaluated or measured
10. Listing of board of directors, trustees, officers and other key people and their affiliations
11. Detailed description of project and amount of funding requested
12. Copy of current year's organizational budget and/or project budget

Deadlines: March 1, September 1 and November1

Dollar General Literacy Foundation

Headquarters

100 Mission Ridge
Goodlettsville, TN 37072-2170
Phone: 615-855-5208

www.dgliteracy.com/mission

Type of Grant Maker: Corporate Foundation

Description

Founded: 1993

Corporate Foundation Information: Supported by Dollar General

Financial Summary

Assets: $28,328,735
Total Giving: $11,951,784

Grants Information

GRANT TYPES

Literacy Programs

TYPICAL RECIPIENTS/SUBJECTS OF INTEREST

Grant-giving programs include:

Adult Literacy Grants: Awarding funding to nonprofit organizations that provide direct service to adults in need of literacy assistance. Organizations must provide help in one of the following instructional areas:

Adult Basic Education: General Education Diploma Preparation

English Language Acquisition: Applications available in January

Beyond Words: The Dollar General School Library Relief Program: Awarding grants to public school libraries that have sustained substantial damage or hardship due to a natural disaster (tornado, earthquake, hurricane, flood, avalanche, mudslide), fire or an act recognized by the federal government as terrorism. The goal is to provide funding for books, media, and/or library equipment that support learning in a school library environment. The impact can be through direct loss or through an increase in enrollment due to displaced/evacuee students. See website for details and application information.

Family Literacy Grants: Providing grants to family literacy service providers. The Foundation uses the federal government's definition of family literacy when reviewing grant applications.

Organizations applying for funding must have the following four components:

1. Adult Education Instruction
2. Children's Education
3. Parent and Child Together Time (PACT)
4. Parenting Classes

Applications available in January.

SUMMER READING GRANTS

Providing funding to local nonprofit organizations and libraries to help with the implementation or expansion of summer reading programs. Programs must target pre-K through 12th grade students who are new readers, below grade level readers or readers with learning disabilities. Applications available in January.

YOUTH LITERACY GRANTS

Providing funding to schools, public libraries, and nonprofit organizations to help students who are below grade level or experiencing difficulty reading. Grant funding is provided to assist in the following areas:

- Implementing new or expanding existing literacy programs
- Purchasing new technology or equipment to support literacy initiatives
- Purchasing books, materials or software for literacy programs

See website for application information

PAST GRANT RECIPIENTS

Library or School Related

Grants to schools and libraries are too numerous to list. Examples include:

- American Library Association, $200,000
- Ascension Parish Library, Gonzales (LA), $2,000
- Augusta Co. Library, Fishersville (GA), $3,000
- Carl Sandburg College, Galesburg (IL), $15,000
- Carol Co. Public Library, Carrolton (KY), $12,776
- Cotter High School, Cotter (AR), $5,000

REQUIREMENTS AND RESTRICTIONS

No support for political candidates or organizations, or private charities or foundations. No grants to individuals, or for endowments, capital campaigns, film or video projects, the purchase of vehicles, advertising, construction or building costs, general fund-raising events, or political causes or campaigns.

APPLICATION PROCEDURES

Online information available for each funding area. See website for details on each.

Deadlines: Vary

Donnelley, Gaylord and Dorothy Foundation

Headquarters

35 E. Wacker Dr., Ste. 2600
Chicago, IL 60601-2102
Phone: 312-977-2700
www.gddf.org

Contact: Susan Clark, Grants Mgr.

E-mail: info@gddf.org

Type of Grant Maker: Foundation

Description

Founded: 1952

Operating Locations/Geographic Preferences: Giving primarily in the Chicago, IL, area and in the low country area of SC

Financial Summary

Assets: $158,978,182
Total Giving: $5,928,801

Grants Information

GRANT TYPES

Program development, matching, general and operating support, investments and loans

TYPICAL RECIPIENTS/SUBJECTS OF INTEREST

Primary areas of interest include conservation and environment, and arts and culture

PAST GRANT RECIPIENTS

Library or School Related

- Chicago Film Archives, Chicago (IL), for Phase III of Core Collections, $60,000

General

- Field Museum of Natural History, Chicago (IL), for Calumet Environmental Education and Stewardship Expansion Project, $260,000
- Chicago Community Trust, Chicago (IL), for organizational development for Arts Work Fund, $180,000
- Chicago Cultural Alliance, Chicago (IL), to preserve history and diversity of Chicago ethnic communities, $112,900

REQUIREMENTS AND RESTRICTIONS

No support for religious purposes. No grants to individuals, or for pledges, endowments, capital campaigns, benefits, conferences, meetings, eradication of deficits, research, or studies, publications, films, videos or fund-raising events; no loans

APPLICATION PROCEDURES

Complete guidelines for each program are available on the website. Applicants should submit the following:

1. Results expected from proposed grant
2. Copy of most recent annual report/audited financial statement/990
3. How project's results will be evaluated or measured
4. Listing of board of directors, trustees, officers and other key people and their affiliations
5. Detailed description of project and amount of funding requested
6. Plans for cooperation with other organizations, if any
7. Copy of current year's organizational budget and/or project budget

Deadlines: Proposals are reviewed at the foundation's board meetings.

Dow Jones Foundation

Headquarters

PO Box 1802
Providence, RI 02901-1802
Contact: Thomas McGuirl

Fax: 212-852-3377

E-mail: tom.mcguirl@dowjones.com

Type of Grant Maker: Corporate Foundation
Applications not accepted. Contributes only to preselected organizations.

Dreyer's Grand Ice Cream Charitable Foundation

Headquarters

5929 College Ave.
Oakland, CA 94618-1325
Phone: 510-652-8187
Fax: 510-610-4400
www.nestleusa.com/Creating-Shared-Value/Community
Contact: Kelly M. Su'a, Secy.
Type of Grant Maker: Corporate Foundation

Description

Founded: 1987

Operating Locations/Geographic Preferences: Giving primarily in the East Bay, Oakland, and Pleasanton CA, area

Corporate Foundation Information: Supported by Dreyer's Grand Ice Cream, Inc.

Financial Summary

Assets: $8,048
Total Giving: $252,943
Number of Grants: 185
Grant Ranges: $20,000–$40

Grants Information

GRANT TYPES

Continuing, general and operating support, program development, Capital campaigns, equipment, donated products, employee volunteering

TYPICAL RECIPIENTS/SUBJECTS OF INTEREST

Programs that promote family, school, and community environments that build skills and foster talents in young people.

PAST GRANT RECIPIENTS

Library or School Related

- Fullerton Public Library, $100
- Maysville Public Library, $200

General
- New Leaders for New Schools, New York (NY), $40,000
- Oakland Museum of California, Oakland (CA), $7,500
- Reading Partners, Milpitas (CA), $5,000

REQUIREMENTS AND RESTRICTIONS

No support for religious organizations not of direct benefit to the entire community or political organizations or candidates. No grants to individuals, or for raffle tickets, one-time conventions or meetings, scholarships, athletic sponsorships, benefit advertising, field trips or tours, independent film or video productions, or endowment projects.

APPLICATION PROCEDURES

Letters of inquiry should be submitted using organization letterhead and should be no longer than 1 page. Telephone calls during the application process are not encouraged.

Deadlines: 8 weeks prior to need for small grants and product donations.

Duke Endowment

Headquarters

100 N. Tryon St., Ste. 3500
Charlotte, NC 28202-4012
Phone: 704-376-0291

www.dukeendowment.org

Contact: Eugene W. Cochrane, Jr., Pres.

E-mail: infotde@tde.org

Type of Grant Maker: Foundation

Description

Founded: 1924

Operating Locations/Geographic Preferences: Giving limited to NC and SC.

Financial Summary

Assets: $2,744,380,297
Total Giving: $110,499,816
Number of Grants: 385

Grants Information

GRANT TYPES

Program development, building and renovation, general, operating and continuing support, capital campaigns, endowments, equipment, seed money

TYPICAL RECIPIENTS/SUBJECTS OF INTEREST

Higher education, especially Duke, Furman, and Johnson C. Smith Universities and Davidson College, nonprofit health care and child care institutions in NC and SC, rural United Methodist churches in NC

PAST GRANT RECIPIENTS

- Johnson C. Smith University, Charlotte (NC), for capital campaign, $35,000,000
- Duke University, Durham (NC), for unrestricted operating support
- Duke University, Durham (NC), for rural United Methodists attending continuing education events at Duke University Divinity School, $250,000

General
- Children's Trust Fund of South Carolina, Columbia (SC), for Nurse Family Partnership sites in South Carolina, $4,000,000
- Beaufort Memorial Hospital, Beaufort (SC), to establish a community network of care for the low-income, uninsured in Beaufort and Jasper counties, $500,000

REQUIREMENTS AND RESTRICTIONS

No grants to individuals or for deficit financing or for loans

APPLICATION PROCEDURES

Applicants should submit:

1. Copy of IRS Determination Letter
2. Copy of most recent annual report/audited financial statement/990
3. Listing of board of directors, trustees, officers and other key people and their affiliations
4. Detailed description of project and amount of funding requested
5. Copy of current year's organizational budget and/or project budget
6. Listing of additional sources and amount of support
7. Additional materials/documentation

Deadlines: June 15 and December 15

DuPont, Jessie Ball Fund

Headquarters

1 Independent Dr., Ste. 1400
Jacksonville, FL 32202-5011
Phone: 800-252-3452

www.dupontfund.org

Contact: Sherry P. Magiel, Pres.

E-mail: contactus@dupontfund.org

Type of Grant Maker: Foundation

Description

Founded: 1976

Operating Locations/Geographic Preferences: Giving primarily in the South, especially DE, FL, and VA and only supports organizations that received gifts by the donor from 1960–1964. Included in this list are 17 independent schools and 42 small liberal arts colleges, among others.

Financial Summary

Assets: $261,313,532
Total Giving: $11,088,157
Number of Grants: 398
Feasibility grants: $5,000
Small College Grants and technical assistance grants of $10,000

Grants Information

GRANT TYPES

Program development, general and operating support, equipment, matching, investments and loans, seed money

TYPICAL RECIPIENTS/SUBJECTS OF INTEREST

Primary focus includes: organizational development, community responsiveness and access to financial assets, health care, quality education and job preparation, affordable housing and strong and safe communities and nonprofit strengthening.
   Program areas include:

- Competitive Grants for eligible organizations
- Feasibility Grants providing limited, short-term funding of up to $5,000
- Independent School Initiative helping the 17 private independent, pre-collegiate schools, with grants of $10,000
- Nonprofit Initiative giving funds to nonprofit organizations approved 16 hospitals and four foundations of $10,000
- Relief Grants
- Religion Initiative with grants to eligible religious institutions
- Small Liberal Arts Colleges Initiative to fund the 42 small private and public liberal arts college eligible
- Technical Assistance Grants providing grants of up to $5,000 to help support strategic planning, consultancies, staff and board professional development, or technology

PAST GRANT RECIPIENTS

Library or School Related

- Goucher College, Baltimore (MD), for Goucher College's Educational Opportunity Program to recruit and retain first-generation college students, $200,000
- Randolph College, Lynchburg (VA), for consultant to provide a full energy audit of the college campus, $100,000
- San Jose Episcopal Day School, Jacksonville (FL), for Independent School Discretionary Fund, $10,000

General

- Community Foundation, Jacksonville (FL), for a partnership between Community Foundation and Local Initiative Support Corporation (LISC) for Building Sustainable Communities Initiative, $750,000
- Wicomico United Methodist Church, Kilmarnock (VA), for repair and restoration grant, $50,000
- Lakewood United Methodist Church, Jacksonville (FL), for People in Need funds, $10,000

RESTRICTIONS AND REQUIREMENTS

Must be on pre-approved list of eligible organizations.
   No grants to individuals, or generally for capital campaigns or endowments.

APPLICATION PROCEDURES

Initial approach is by brief proposal or telephone call to program staff; must establish eligibility.
   Application form required. Applicants should submit:

1. Timetable for implementation and evaluation of project
2. Site description
3. Signature and title of chief executive officer
4. Qualifications of key personnel
5. Brief history of organization and description of its mission
6. Copy of most recent annual report/audited financial statement/990

7. How project's results will be evaluated or measured
8. Listing of board of directors, trustees, officers and other key people and their affiliations
9. Detailed description of project and amount of funding requested
10. Copy of current year's organizational budget and/or project budget
11. Additional materials/documentation

Deadlines: None

Dyson Foundation

Headquarters

25 Halcyon Rd.
Millbrook, NY 12545-6137
Phone: 845-677-0644
Fax: 845-677-0650

www.dysonfoundation.org

Contact: Diana M. Gurieva, Exec. V.P.

E-mail: info@dyson.org

Type of Grant Maker: Foundation

Description

Founded: 1957

Operating Locations/Geographic Preferences: Giving primarily in Dutchess County, NY, limited grants to other Mid-Hudson Valley counties (Columbia, Greene, Orange, Putnam and Ulster counties). National and other grants on a solicited basis.

Financial Summary

Assets: $270,602,092
Total Giving: $17,585,296
Number of Grants: 275
Grant Ranges: $1,500,000–$1,000

Grants Information

GRANT TYPES

Building and renovation, capital and annual campaigns, conferences, consulting, continuing, operating and general support, equipment, management development, matching, investments and loans, program development, seed money, technical assistance.

TYPICAL RECIPIENTS/SUBJECTS OF INTEREST

Basic needs such as food, housing, health care and other human services.

Giving areas include:

- Directors' Discretionary: Uninvited proposals or inquiries will not be considered.
- Legacy and Family Interest: Uninvited proposals or inquiries will not be considered.
- Management Assistance Program: All nonprofits based in the counties of Columbia, Dutchess, Greene, Orange, Putnam, and Ulster are eligible to apply.
- Grant amounts of up to $10,000 (covering no more than 80 percent of the project budget) are awarded on a competitive basis.
- Mid-Hudson Valley Nonprofit Strategic Restructuring Initiative: For organizations in the Mid-Hudson Valley that are engaging in strategic restructuring.

PAST GRANT RECIPIENTS

Library or School Related

- Marietta College, Marietta (OH), Construction of new library, $1,000,000
- Pierpont Morgan Library, New York (NY), renovation, $100,000
- Lagrange Association Library, Poughkeepsie (NY), Management Assistance Program, $5,000
- Millbrook Free Library, Millbrook (NY), General operating support, $5,000

General

- Mid-Hudson Children's Museum, Poughkeepsie (NY), for general operating support, $50,000
- Grace Smith House, Poughkeepsie (NY), for children's program at domestic violence shelter in Dutchess County (NY), $40,000

REQUIREMENTS AND RESTRICTIONS

No support for international organizations. No grants to individuals, or for debt reduction, direct mail campaign or fund-raising events.

APPLICATION PROCEDURES

See website for guidelines and online application.

Deadlines: None

Eccles, George S. and Dolores Dore Foundation

Headquarters

79 S. Main St., 14th Fl.
Salt Lake City, UT 84111
Phone: 801-246-5340

www.gsecclesfoundation.org

Contact: Lisa Eccles, Pres.

E-mail: gseg@gseccles.org

Type of Grant Maker: Foundation

Description

Founded: 1958

Operating Locations/Geographic Preferences: Giving primarily in the intermountain area, particularly UT.

Financial Summary

Assets: $395,439,032
Total giving: $23,731,582
Number of Grants: 383
Grant Ranges: $7,220,000–$800; average: $5,000–$250,000

Grants Information

GRANT TYPES

Program development, building and renovation, general and operating support, matching, capital campaigns

TYPICAL RECIPIENTS/SUBJECTS OF INTEREST

Education, preservation and conservation, arts and culture, social services, health care

PAST GRANT RECIPIENTS

Library or School Related

- Southern Utah University, Cedar City (UT), for Shakespearean Theatre, which will replace outdoor Thomas and Luella R. Adams Memorial Shakespearean Theatre, $1,000,000
- University of Utah, Salt Lake City (UT), for confidential gift, $7,200,000

General

- Utah's Hogle Zoo, Salt Lake City (UT), for architectural design and site testing for construction of new Arctic Exhibit, $1,000,000
- Visual Art Institute, Salt Lake City (UT), for program support, including outreach and low-income student scholarships, $18,500
- Ingles Para Latinos, Salt Lake City (UT), for general operating support of English as a Second Language programs and matching funds for AmeriCorps, $15,000

REQUIREMENTS AND RESTRICTIONS

No support for private foundations or conduit organizations. No grants to individuals, or for endowment funds, contingencies, deficits, debt reduction, conferences, seminars, or medical research.

APPLICATION PROCEDURES

Applicants should submit:

1. Name, address and phone number of organization
2. Copy of IRS Determination Letter
3. Brief history of organization and description of its mission
4. Copy of most recent annual report/audited financial statement/990
5. Listing of board of directors, trustees, officers and other key people and their affiliations
6. Detailed description of project and amount of funding requested
7. Contact person
8. Copy of current year's organizational budget and/or project budget
9. Additional materials/documentation

Deadlines: None

Educational Foundation of America

Headquarters

35 Church Ln.
Westport, CT 06880-3515
Contact: Diane M. Allison, Exec. Dir.

Fax: 203-227-0424

www.efaw.org

Type of Grant Maker: Foundation

Unsolicited requests for funds not accepted at this time. Proposals are by invitation only.

Edwards, Margaret Alexander Trust

Headquarters

600 Wyndhurst Ave., Ste. 246
Baltimore, MD 21210
Phone: 410-464-0100

www.carr.org/mae/trust.html

Contact: Julian Lapides, Esq.

Type of Grant Maker: Foundation

Description

Founded: 1989

Operating Locations/Geographic Preferences: Giving primarily in MD

Financial Summary

Assets: $819,354
Total Giving: $29,000
Number of Grants: 15
Grant Ranges: $6,000—$250

Grants Information

GRANT TYPES

General support, program development

TYPICAL RECIPIENTS/SUBJECTS OF INTEREST

Young adult librarians, programs to promote young adult reading

PAST GRANT RECIPIENTS

Library or School Related

- Traverse deSioux Library, Mankato (MN), $2,000
- Champlin Park High School, Camplin (MN), $2,500
- Hononegah High School, Rockton (IL), $500
- Uniondale Public Library, Uniondale (NY), $500

REQUIREMENTS AND RESTRICTIONS

Foundation issues grants only to promote reading among young adults

APPLICATION PROCEDURES

Complete online application (PDF file) and mail it to:

Julian L. Lapides, Esquire
Margaret Alexander Edwards Trust
600 Wyndhurst Ave, Suite 246
Baltimore, MD 21210

Deadlines: None

El Pomar Foundation

Headquarters

10 Lake Cir.
Colorado Springs, CO 80906-4201
Phone: 719-633-7733

www.elpomar.org

Contact: William J. Hybl, Chair.

Type of Grant Maker: Foundation

Description

Founded: 1937

Operating Locations/Geographic Preferences: Giving limited to CO

Financial Summary

Assets: $471,530,109
Total Giving: $12,235,962
Number of Grants: 1,076
Grant Ranges: $1,000,000–$120; average: $5,000–$200,000

Grants Information

GRANT TYPES

Program development, building and renovations, general, operating and continuing support, capital campaigns, matching, land acquisition

TYPICAL RECIPIENTS/SUBJECTS OF INTEREST

Public, educational, arts and humanities, health, and welfare purposes, including child welfare, the disadvantaged, and housing. Municipalities may request funds for specific projects.

Program areas include:

- American Council of Young Political Leaders
- Awards for Excellence

- El Pomar Fellowship
- El Pomar Internship Program
- El Pomar Youth in Community Service (EPYCS)
- Emerging Leaders Development Program
- Employee Matching Gifts
- Empty Stocking Fund
- Executive Leadership Program
- Forum for Civic Advancement
- Karl E. Eitel Fund
- Regional Councils
- Student Leadership Experience (SLE)
- Wildland Fire Fund

PAST GRANT RECIPIENTS

Library or School Related

- University of Denver, Denver (CO), for renovation of Penrose Library, $125,000
- Northglenn High School, Northglenn (CO), for Northglenn Key Club, $5,000
- Colorado College, Colorado Springs (CO), for capital improvements and hockey program, $1,000,000

General

- Foundation for Colorado Springs Future, Colorado Springs (CO), to purchase building for US Space Foundation, $385,000
- United Way, Pikes Peak, Colorado Springs (CO), to support campaign, $200,000
- Colorado Springs Philharmonic Orchestra, Colorado Springs (CO), for general operating support, $100,000

REQUIREMENTS AND RESTRICTIONS

No support for organizations that distribute funds to other grantees, religious or political organizations, primary or secondary education, or for camps or seasonal facilities. No grants to individuals, or for travel, film or other media projects, conferences, seminars, deficit financing, endowment funds, research.

APPLICATION INFORMATION

Applicants should submit:

1. How project will be sustained once grant-maker support is completed
2. Signature and title of chief executive officer
3. Results expected from proposed grant
4. Statement of problem project will address
5. Population served
6. Principal source of support for project in the past
7. Name, address and phone number of organization
8. Copy of IRS Determination Letter
9. Brief history of organization and description of its mission

10. Copy of most recent annual report/audited financial statement/990
11. How project's results will be evaluated or measured
12. Listing of board of directors, trustees, officers and other key people and their affiliations
13. Detailed description of project and amount of funding requested
14. Contact person
15. Copy of current year's organizational budget and/or project budget
16. Listing of additional sources and amount of support

Deadlines: One month before board meeting

Elsevier Foundation

Headquarters

2 Newton Pl., Ste. 350
Newton, MA 02458-1637
www.elsevierfoundation.org
Contact: John Regazzi, Chair
E-mail: foundation@elsevier.com
Type of Grant Maker: Corporate Foundation

Description

Founded: not available

Operating Locations/Geographic Preferences: United States and developing countries

Corporate Foundation Information: Supported by Elsevier, Inc.

Financial Summary

Assets: $26,405
Total Giving: $702,661
Number of Grants: 478
Grant Ranges: $200,000–$20

Grants Information

GRANT TYPES

Matching and general and operating support

TYPICAL RECIPIENTS/SUBJECTS OF INTEREST

Education, especially libraries in higher education for science, technology and medicine. Also health and human services

Innovative Libraries program supports projects in science, technology and medicine through training, education, infrastructure digitization and preservation of information.

Grants of $5,000–$100,000 are provided libraries in the developing countries and supporting organizations.

PAST GRANT RECIPIENTS

- University of Pennsylvania, for Health Information Delivery
- SEVA Foundation, for collaborative effort for resource sharing in eye care institutions.
- National University of Laos, Central Library, for Improving Library Resource Sharing

REQUIREMENTS AND RESTRICTIONS

Requests for hardware will only be considered if they are part of a comprehensive project approach integrating diverse elements such as training or research. Grants are awarded for specific projects rather than operating support.

APPLICATION PROCEDURES

A two-step application process. See website for online application and guidelines.

Deadlines: First-round applications will be accepted through June 24. In early July shortlisted candidates will be announced and invited to submit a full proposal in the second round.

Emerson Charitable Trust

Headquarters

8000 W. Florissant Ave.
PO Box 4100
St. Louis, MO 63136-8506
Phone: 314-553-2000

www.emerson.com/en-us/about/corporate-citizenship/
community-involvement/pages/charitable-giving.aspx

Contact: Robert M. Cox, Jr.

Type of Grant Maker: Corporate Foundation

Description

Operating Locations/Geographic Preferences: Giving primarily on a national basis in areas of company operations, with emphasis on St. Louis, MO

Corporation Foundation Information

Donors include:
- Emerson Electric Co.
- Daniel Industries, Inc
- Astec America Inc.
- Emerson Ventures.

Financial Summary

Assets: $25,799,093
Total Giving: $19,888,815
Number of Grants: 2,549
Grant Ranges: $1,300,000–$25

Grants Information

GRANT TYPES

Program development, employee matching and volunteering services, general and operating support

TYPICAL RECIPIENTS/SUBJECTS OF INTEREST

Education, arts and culture, health and human services, civic affairs, and youth arts and culture organizations including libraries, dance, music, and theater groups, educational television, public radio, museums, zoos, and science centers

PAST GRANT RECIPIENTS

Library or School Related
- Library Foundation for the Benefit of Saint Louis Public Library, Saint Louis (MO), for general support, $570,000
- Texas A & M Foundation, College Station (TX), for general support, $4,000

General
- American Red Cross, Saint Louis (MO), for general support, $250,000
- Interlochen Center for the Arts, Interlochen (MI), for general support, $250,000
- United Way of Greater Knoxville, Knoxville (TN), for general support, $10,000

REQUIREMENTS AND RESTRICTIONS

Not listed

APPLICATION PROCEDURES

Contact Foundation for details

Deadlines: None

ESA (Entertainment Software Association) Foundation

Headquarters

317 Madison Ave., 22nd Fl.
New York, NY 10017-5207
www.theesa.com/foundation
E-mail: esafinfo@theesa.com
Type of Grant Maker: Foundation

Description

Founded: 2000
Operating Locations/Geographic Preferences: Giving on national basis

Financial Summary

Not available

Grants Information

GRANT TYPES
Program development

TYPICAL RECIPIENTS/SUBJECTS OF INTEREST

Youth programs that improve their life, health and welfare.

Challenge Grants that implement innovative lesson plans.

Grant Program that supports programs that encourage youth to use technology and/or computer and video games to develop skills and personal development, improve health and welfare, reduce risk behavior, educate or promote multimedia arts and technology.

PAST GRANT RECIPIENTS

Library or School Related

Ball State University Department of History

Ball State University Department of History, for creation of training, materials and develops media projects for elementary school teachers and students

Brown University, for Bootstrap program to use games to teach urban middle-school students algebra and geometry concepts

REQUIREMENTS AND RESTRICTIONS

No grants for youth sports teams, religions organizations, political costs or campaigns. No endowments, indirect costs or research.

APPLICATION PROCEDURES

Form required. See website

Deadlines: April 6 for Challenge Grants; April 15 for Grants Program

Essick Foundation, Inc.

Headquarters

1379 La Solana Dr.
Altadena, CA 91001-2624
Type of Grant Maker: Foundation

Applications not accepted. Contributes only to preslected organizations.

Firestone, Harvey Jr. Foundation

Headquarters

2000 Brush St., Ste. 440
Detroit, MI 48226-2251
Phone: 313-961-0500
Contact: Christine Jaggi
Type of Grant Maker: Foundation

Description

Founded: 1983
Operating Locations/Geographic Preferences: Giving primarily in CT and MI; giving also in Washington, DC and NY.

Financial Summary

Assets: $19,671,050
Total Giving: $800,000

Grants Information

GRANT TYPES

General and operating support

TYPICAL RECIPIENTS/SUBJECTS OF INTEREST

Arts and humanities, civic, education, health, social services

PAST GRANT RECIPIENTS

Library or School Related

- Greenwich Library, Greenwich (CT), $2,500
- Redwood Library, Newport (RI), $500
- Darien Library, Darien (CT), $500
- Princeton University, Princeton (NJ), $35,000

General

- Leelanau Children's Center, Leland (MI), $5,000
- Historical Society of the Town of Greenwich, Cos Cob (CT), $2,000

REQUIREMENTS AND RESTRICTIONS

No grants to individuals.

APPLICATION PROCEDURES

Send letter.

Deadlines: None

Florida State Library and Archives, Division of Library and Information Services

Headquarters

500 S. Bronough St.
Tallahassee, FL 32399-0250
Phone: 850-245-6620

http://dlis.dos.state.fl.us/bld/grants/index.htm

Type of Grant Maker: Government

Grants Information

PUBLIC LIBRARY CONSTRUCTION GRANTS

Provides state funding to governments for the construction of public libraries. This includes the construction of new buildings and the acquisition, expansion or remodeling of existing buildings to be used for public library service.

However, no funds have been appropriated since 2008.

Grant Ranges: $10,000–$500,000

REQUIREMENTS AND RESTRICTIONS

The minimum allowable project size is 3,000 square feet.

Any eligible Florida governmental entity may apply for a Public Library Construction grant. This includes county governments, incorporated municipalities, special districts and special tax districts that establish or maintain a public library and provide free public library service.

APPLICATION PROCEDURES

Announcements about application availability are made through the Florida Administrative Weekly, and through announcements sent to libraries.

Application forms may be requested from the Grants Office, or they may be obtained from the Division's website: http://info.florida.gov/bld/grants/Construction/Construction.html

Deadlines: April 1

LIBRARY COOPERATIVE GRANTS

Provides state funding to multitype library cooperatives to assist them in meeting the educational and informational needs of Florida residents by encouraging and ensuring cooperation among libraries of all types for the development of library service.

Total Giving: $1,000,000 (2010–2011)

Grant Ranges: Up to $400,000

For the continual maintenance of the statewide database of library materials. Maintenance of this database involves bibliographic enhancement and related training for all Florida Library Information Network member libraries within each multitype library cooperative's geographic service area. Eligible multitype library cooperative organizations may apply for an annual grant of up to $400,000.

REQUIREMENTS AND RESTRICTIONS

Multitype library cooperatives are eligible to apply for grants under this program.

APPLICATION PROCEDURES

Announcements about application availability are made through the Florida Administrative Weekly, and through announcements sent to multitype library cooperatives.

Application forms may be requested from the Grants Office, or they may be obtained from the Division's Web site.

Deadlines: To be announced.

LIBRARY SERVICES AND TECHNOLOGY ACT GRANTS

State-based program with a broad mandate to use technology to bring information to people in innovative and effective ways, and to ensure that library service is accessible to all, especially those who have difficulty using the library.

Grant Ranges: Vary

REQUIREMENTS AND RESTRICTIONS

Florida libraries and nonprofit organizations primarily related to the provision or support of library services are eligible to apply for LSTA funds. Eligible entities include public libraries; public elementary, secondary, or charter school libraries; academic libraries; library consortia; and special libraries.

APPLICATION PROCEDURES

Announcements about application availability are made through the Florida Administrative Weekly, and through announcements sent to libraries.

Application information may be requested from the Grants Office, or they may be obtained from the Division's Web site: http://info.florida.gov/bld/grants/Lsta/LSTA .html

Deadlines: To be announced

STATE AID TO LIBRARIES

To encourage local governments to establish and continue development of free library service to all residents of Florida.

Grant ranges: Based on funding level. In 2011–2012, funding level was $21,300,000.

REQUIREMENTS AND RESTRICTIONS

A political subdivision that has been designated by a county or municipality as the single library administrative unit is eligible to receive an annual Operating grant of no more than 25 percent of all local funds centrally expended by the political subdivision during the second preceding fiscal year for the operation and maintenance of a library. At a minimum, the library manager must have a master's degree from a library education program accredited by the American Library Association and two subsequent years of full-time, paid professional experience; the library must be open at least 40 hours per week; and the library must provide free library service.

APPLICATION PROCEDURES

Announcements about application availability are made through the Florida Administrative Weekly, and through announcements sent to libraries.

Application forms may be requested from the Grants Office, or they may be obtained from the Division's Web site: http://info.florida.gov/bld/grants/StateAid/StateAid .html

Deadlines: October 1

COMMUNITY LIBRARIES IN CARING (CLIC)

To assist small, rural public libraries to improve library collections and services, improve adult and family literacy and develop the economic viability in targeted counties and communities. However, no funds have been appropriated since 2008.

REQUIREMENTS AND RESTRICTIONS

Public libraries in counties and communities with rural status, as defined in s. 288.0656(2) (b) Florida Statutes and subject to the provisions of s. 288.06561 Florida Statutes are eligible to participate in this program.

Ford Family Foundation

Headquarters

1600 N.W. Stewart Pkwy.
Roseburg, OR 97471-1957
Phone: 541-957-5574

www.tfff.org

Contact: Norman J. Smith, Pres.

E-mail: info@tfff.org

Type of Grant Maker: Foundation

Description

Founded: 1957

Operating Locations/Geographic Preferences: Giving primarily in rural OR, with special interest in Douglas and Coos counties; giving also in Siskiyou County, CA or for populations less than 30,000 not adjacent to or part of an urban area

Financial Summary

Assets: $745,185,712
Total Giving: $21,177,115
Number of Grants: 450
Grant Ranges: $3,300,000–$50

Grants Information

GRANT TYPES

Program development, general and operating support, building and renovations, capital campaigns, matching

TYPICAL RECIPIENTS/SUBJECTS OF INTEREST

Areas of giving include:

- Positive Youth Development
- Access to Health and Dental Services for Children
- Child Abuse and Intervention
- Public Convening Spaces
- Scholarship Program
- Ford Institute for Community Building

  Special Programs include:

- Public Convening Spaces: To encourage civic participation and collaboration through the development of places that bring the community together, have substantial and broad multi-users, are open to the public, and serve multiple populations.
- Artist-in-Residence
- Chalkboard Project: Focusing on effective teaching to raise student achievement
- Child Abuse Prevention and Intervention
- Ford Scholarships
- Hallie Ford Fellowships in the Visual Arts
- Health and Dental Services for Children
- Positive Youth Development
- Post-Secondary Education: To increase the number of rural students who are aware of, prepared for and enrolled in post-secondary education or training
- Technical Assistance: for community groups and leaders
- Unanticipated Opportunity Program: for visual artists
- Visual Arts Program

PAST GRANT RECIPIENTS

General

- Southern Oregon Child and Family Council, Central Point (OR), for Listo Family Literacy Program at White City, $40,000
- Ore-Cal Resource Conservation and Development Area Council, Dorris (CA), for Community Center and Recreational Park, Butte Valley, $330,000
- Oregon Arts Commission, Salem (OR), for Art Acquisition Fund, $300,000
- Boys and Girls Club of Lebanon, Lebanon (OR), for After School Program, $245,000

REQUIREMENTS AND RESTRICTIONS

No support for projects or programs that are indirectly funded through a fiscal agent, or for lobbying or propaganda. No grants to individuals (except for scholarships or fellowships), or for endowment/reserve funds, general fund drives, debt retirement, deficits, or for indirect or overhead expenses

APPLICATION PROCEDURES

Online application process required.

Deadlines: None

Ford Foundation

Headquarters

320 E. 43rd St.
New York, NY 10017-4801
Phone: 212-573-5000

www.fordfoundation.org

E-mail: office-secretary@fordfoundation.org

Type of Grant Maker: Foundation

Description

Founded: 1936

Operating Locations/Geographic Preferences: Giving in the United States, Africa, the Middle East, Asia, Latin America and the Caribbean.

Financial Summary

Assets: $10,344,933,000
Total Giving: $424,695,000

Grants Information

GRANT TYPES

Program development, continuing, general and operating support, management development, investments and loans

TYPICAL RECIPIENTS/SUBJECTS OF INTEREST

The foundation focuses on:

- Human Rights
- Democratic and Accountable Government
- Educational Opportunity and Scholarship
- Economic Fairness
- Metropolitan Opportunity
- Sustainable Development

- Freedom of Expression
- Sexuality and Reproductive Health and Rights
  Giving Programs include:
- Democratic and Accountable Government, including strengthening civil society
- Economic Fairness
- Educational Opportunity and Scholarship including:
  Transforming Secondary Education
  Advancing Higher Education Access and Success
  More and Better Learning Time
  Freedom of Expression, including Supporting Diverse Arts Spaces and media projects
- Human Rights
- Matching Gifts
- Metropolitan Opportunity, including housing, land use and environmental planning, public transportation, and workforce opportunity
- Sexuality and Reproductive Health
- Sustainability

PAST GRANT RECIPIENTS

General

- National Center on Time and Learning, Boston (MA), expanded learning time models in public schools of seven states and nationally, $1,000,000
- Non-Profit Incubator, Shanghai, China, to build the capacity of start-up and fast-growing NGOs and to promote the NPI Incubator Model and publish *Social Entrepreneur* magazine, $598,000
- Center for Land Reform, Flint (MI), to reuse vacant, abandoned and problem properties in American cities and towns, $1,100,000
- Center for Responsible Lending, Durham (NC), for general support for education and advocacy to protect homeownership and family wealth by eliminating abusive financial practices, $1,000,000
- Sundance Institute, Beverly Hills (CA), for production of social justice–themed documentaries worldwide through grants, workshops, research and public engagement, $1,000,000
- Nonprofit Finance Fund, New York (NY), for new public/private grant-making initiative to promote role of arts and culture in building livable, sustainable communities, $2,000,000

REQUIREMENTS AND RESTRICTIONS

No support for programs for which substantial support from government or other sources is readily available, or for religious sectarian activities. No grants for construction or maintenance of buildings, undergraduate scholarships, or for purely personal or local needs.

APPLICATION PROCEDURES

Carefully review the foundation's initiatives online. Review Grant Application Guide for additional details about the grant-review process at www.fordfoundation.org/pdfs/grants/grant-application-guide.pdf.

Deadlines: None

Ford Motor Company Fund

Headquarters

1 American Rd.
PO Box 1899
Dearborn, MI 48126-2798
Phone: 313-248-4745
Fax: 313-594-7001

www.corporate.ford.com/about-ford/community

E-mail: fordfund@ford.com

Type of Grant Maker: Corporate Foundation

Description

Founded: 1949

Operating Locations/Geographic Preferences: Giving primarily in areas of company operations, with emphasis on southeastern MI; giving also in Phoenix, AZ, San Diego, CA, Miami, FL, Chicago, IL, Detroit, MI, Nashville, TN, and San Antonio, TX.

Corporate Foundation Information: Supported by:
- Ford Motor Co.
- Ford Motor Credit Co.

Financial Summary

Assets: $49,885,020
Total Giving: $18,726,141
Number of Grants: 297
Grant Ranges: $1,862,461–$1,500

Grants Information

GRANT TYPES

Program development, annual and capital campaigns, building and renovation, continuing support, emergency funds, employee matching and volunteering, equipment, sponsorships

TYPICAL RECIPIENTS/SUBJECTS OF INTEREST

- Promoting innovation and education
- Community development and American heritage and diversity
- Auto-related safety education

    Giving areas include:

    - Alliance for Women in Media Scholarship Competition
    - Belt It Out Contest
    - Corazon de mi Vida
    - Driving Skills for Life
    - Ford Blue Oval Journalism Internship Program
    - Ford Blue Oval Scholars Program
    - Ford College Community Challenge
    - Ford Driving Dreams through Education
    - Ford Freedom Award
    - Ford Fund/Detroit Free Press Journalism Scholarship
    - Ford Partnerships for Advanced Studies
    - Heart Behind the Oval Scholarship Contest
    - See Me Safe
    - SME Ford PAS/Henry Ford Academy Scholarship
    - Smithsonian Latino Center Young Ambassadors Program

PAST GRANT RECIPIENTS

Library or School Related

- Regents of the University of Michigan Michigan Difference Campaign Pledge Payment, $800,000
- Wayne State University Capital Campaign, College of Engineering, $720,000
- Wayne State University Capital Campaign, School of Business Administration, $360,000
- Edison Institute, Inc., Support for Staff Presenters Fund, $175,000
- Edison Institute, Inc., Sponsorship Request, $175,000

General

- Michigan Opera Theatre Crowning Achievement Campaign, $600,000
- National Park Foundation Gettysburg National Military Park, $600,000
- Henry Ford Learning Institute Ford PAS, $484,095
- New Detroit, Inc., Support for New Detroit Educational Programs, $200,000
- Lorraine Civil Rights Museum Foundation Capital Campaign Grant, $400,000
- Smithsonian Institution Traveling Exhibition Service American Sabor Latinos in US Popular Music, $395,000

REQUIREMENTS AND RESTRICTIONS

No support for animal rights organizations, lobbying organizations, fraternal organizations, labor groups, political organizations, private K–12 schools, profit-making enterprises, religious organizations not of direct benefit to the entire community, species-specific organizations, or sports teams. No grants to individuals (except for scholarships), or for advocacy-directed programs, beauty or talent contests, general operating support, debt reduction, endowments, or sponsorships related to fund-raising activities; no loans for small businesses or program-related investments; no vehicle donations.

APPLICATION PROCEDURES

Complete online form.

Deadlines: See website

Freas Foundation, Inc.

Headquarters

11 Halstead Ln.
Branford, CT 06405-5508

Contact: David M. Trout, Mgr

Type of Grant Maker: Foundation

Applications not accepted. Contributes only to preslected organizations.

Fry, Lloyd A. Foundation

Headquarters

120 S. LaSalle St., Ste. 1950
Chicago, IL 60603-3419
Phone: 312-580-0310

www.fryfoundation.org

Contact: Unmi Song, Secy. and Exec. Dir.

E-mail: usong@fryfoundation.org

Type of Grant Maker: Foundation

Description

Founded: 1959

Operating Locations/Geographic Preferences: Giving generally limited to Chicago, IL

Financial Summary

Assets: $169,908,452
Total Giving: $7,607,236
Number of Grants: 300
Grant Ranges: $130,000–$250; average: $20,000–$50,000

Grants Information

GRANT TYPES

Program development, general, operating and continuing support

TYPICAL RECIPIENTS/SUBJECTS OF INTEREST

Addressing the problems of urban Chicago, with a focus on the following areas:

- Arts Education Program
- Education
- Employment Program–including employment-related literacy and English as a Second Language; pre-employment, job placement and job retention services; and vocational training connected to growing industries
- Health

PAST GRANT RECIPIENTS

Library or School Related

- University of Chicago, Chicago (IL), for general operating support for UTEP math and science teacher training survey, $250,000
- Namaste Charter School, Chicago (IL), for the Goal-Driven Coaching and Support Model, $50,000
- University of Illinois at Chicago, Chicago (IL), for High School Principals Network, $160,000

General

- Chicago Jobs Council, Chicago (IL), for City-Wide Workforce Development Advocacy, $70,000
- Doctors Without Borders USA, New York (NY), for Emergency Relief Fund, $50,000
- Free St. Programs, Chicago (IL), for Youth Performance Ensemble, $30,000

REQUIREMENTS AND RESTRICTIONS

No support for medical research, religious purposes, governmental bodies, or tax-supported educational institutions for services that fall within their responsibilities. No grants to individuals, or for general operating support for new grantees, annual campaigns, emergency funds, deficit financing, building funds, fund-raising benefits, land acquisition, renovation projects, or endowment funds; no loans

APPLICATION PROCEDURES

Applicants should submit:

1. Timetable for implementation and evaluation of project
2. Statement of problem project will address
3. Results expected from proposed grant
4. Qualifications of key personnel
5. Listing of board of directors, trustees, officers and other key people and their affiliations
6. Listing of additional sources and amount of support
7. How project's results will be evaluated or measured
8. Detailed description of project and amount of funding requested
9. Copy of most recent annual report/audited financial statement/990
10. Brief history of organization and description of its mission
11. Copy of current year's organizational budget and/or project budget

Deadlines: March 1, June 1, September 1, and December 1

Gates, Bill & Melinda Foundation

Headquarters

PO Box 23350
Seattle, WA 98102-0650
Phone: 206-709-3100
Fax: 206-709-3180

www.gatesfoundation.org

E-mail: info@gatesfoundation.org

Type of Grant Maker: Foundation

Description

Founded: 1994

In the United States, the Foundation does not accept unsolicited proposals for education and libraries.

Only unsolicited proposals are accepted for Pacific Northwest Community Grants. See website for details.

General Mills Foundation

Headquarters

1 General Mills Blvd.
MS CC-01
Minneapolis, MN 55426-1347
Fax: 763-764-4114

www.genmills.com/en/responsibility/community
_engagement/general_mills_foundation_2010.aspx

Contact: Ellen Luger, Exec. Dir.

E-mail: CommunityActionQA@genmills.com

Type of Grant Maker: Corporate Foundation

Description

Founded: 1954

Operating Locations/Geographic Preferences: Giving
primarily in areas of major company operations and
headquarters of Twin Cities, MN area; giving also in CA,
GA, IA, IL, IN, MA, MD, MI, MO, MT, NJ, NM, NY, OH, TN,
WA, and WI for the Community Action Councils Program;
limited giving in Malawi and Tanzania.

Corporate Foundation Information: Supported by
General Mills, Inc.

Financial Summary

Assets: $64,213,355
Total Giving: $25,401,047
Number of Grants: 735
Grant Ranges: $4,282,203–$700

Grants Information

GRANT TYPES

General and operating support program development,
capital campaigns, employee matching and volunteering

TYPICAL RECIPIENTS/SUBJECTS OF INTEREST

Hunger and nutrition wellness, education, family services,
and arts and culture.

PAST GRANT RECIPIENTS

Library or School Related

- Minneapolis Community College, Minneapolis (MN),
  Library Information Technology Center, $250,000

- Evart Public Library, Evart (MI), Restoration project,
  $20,000
- Vineland Public Library, Vineland (NJ), Computers,
  $8,500
- National Czech and Slovak Museum and Library, Cedar
  Rapids (IA), operating support, $5,000
- St. Luke's Lutheran School, Montgomery (IL), library
  books, $1,000
- Carlisle Public Library, Carlisle (IA), Summer Reading
  Program $1,500
- Minneapolis Public Library, Minneapolis (MN), Black
  History Month, $2,500
- Iowa City Public Library, Iowa City (IA), furniture $1,000
- Johnson City Public Library, Johnson City (TN), Summer
  Reading Program, $3,500

REQUIREMENTS AND RESTRICTIONS

No support for discriminatory organizations, religious,
political, social, labor, veterans', alumni, or fraternal
organizations, disease-specific organizations, or athletic
associations. No grants to individuals, or for endowments,
annual appeals, federated campaigns, fund drives,
recreational or sporting events, healthcare, research,
advertising, political causes, travel, emergency funding,
debt reduction or operating deficits, conferences,
seminars or workshops, publications, film, or television,
sponsorships, special events, or fund-raisers or loans.

APPLICATION PROCEDURES

Complete online letter of inquiry or online application, as
appropriate.

Deadlines: See website

George Foundation

Headquarters

PO Box 21609
Columbus, OH 43221-0609
Phone: 614-451-5468

Contact: Jack George, Pres.

Type of Grant Maker: Foundation

Description

Founded: 1982

Operating Locations/Geographic Preferences: Giving
primarily in Columbus, OH

Financial Summary

Assets: $6,423,001
Number of Grants: 88
Grant Ranges: $184,000–$50

Grants Information

GRANT TYPES

Program development, continuing and operating support

TYPICAL RECIPIENTS/SUBJECTS OF INTEREST

Arts, education, environment, museums, performing arts, orchestras

PAST GRANT RECIPIENTS

Library or School Related

- Ohio State University, Columbus (OH), $4,200

General

- Columbus Symphony Orchestra, Columbus (OH), $165,000
- Ballet Metropolitan, Columbus (OH), $23,000
- Columbus Museum of Art, Columbus (OH), $1,000
- Sierra Club Foundation, San Francisco (CA), $1,000

REQUIREMENTS AND RESTRICTIONS

Not listed

APPLICATION PROCEDURES

Application form not required.

Deadlines: None

Georgia Public Library Service

Headquarters

1800 Century Place, Suite 150
Atlanta, GA 30345-4304
Phone: 404-235-7200
Fax: 404-235-7201

www.georgialibraries.org

Type of Grant Maker: Government

Grants Information

PUBLIC LIBRARY STATE GRANTS

The Georgia Public Library Service (GPLS), a unit of the Board of Regents, University System of Georgia, is responsible for the administration and distribution of state grant funds to public libraries in Georgia.

Grants types include:

- State-Paid Public Library Position
- Public Library Materials Grants
- System Services Grants
- Sub-Regional Library for the Blind and Physically Handicapped Grants.

REQUIREMENTS AND RESTRICTIONS

In order to receive any state, federal or private library grant funds administered by GPLS and/or the benefits of any state administered program or service, a Library System must meet all of the requirements set forth at the website.

APPLICATION PROCEDURES AND DEADLINES

See website for details and deadlines: www.georgialibraries.org/lib/stategrants_accounting.

Georgia-Pacific Foundation, Inc.

Headquarters

133 Peachtree St. N.E., 39th FL
Atlanta, GA 30303-1808
Phone: 404-652-4581
Fax: 404-749-2754

www.gp.com/gpfoundation/index.html

Contact: Curley M. Dossman, Jr., Chair. and Pres.

Type of Grant Maker: Corporate Foundation

Description

Founded: 1958

Operating Locations/Geographic Preferences: Giving limited to areas of company operations in AL, AR, AZ, CA, Washington, DC, DE, FL, GA, IA, IL, IN, KS, KY, LA, MA, MI, MN, MO, MS, NH, NJ, NM, NV, NY, NC, OH, OK, OR, PA, SC, TN, VA, WA, WI, WV, WY, and Africa, Asia, Europe, and South America.

Corporate Foundation Information: Supported by Georgia-Pacific Corp.

Financial Summary

Assets: $478,326
Total Giving: $2,596,064
Number of Grants: 328
Grant Ranges: $384,211–$100

Grants Information

GRANT TYPES

Program development, annual and capital campaigns, building and renovation, continuing, general and operating support, employee volunteering, equipment, in-kind gifts, sponsorships

TYPICAL RECIPIENTS/SUBJECTS OF INTEREST

Education, environment, community enrichment, and entrepreneurship. Education focus includes: job training, literacy and school partnerships

PAST GRANT RECIPIENTS

Not available.

REQUIREMENTS AND RESTRICTIONS

* Applicants must have tax-exempt status.
* Foundation does not make grants to individuals.

APPLICATION PROCEDURES

Take the Eligibility Survey. If successful, complete Georgia-Pacific's Grant Application. Send the completed proposal to the name and address listed on the application

Deadlines: October 31

Getty, J. Paul Getty Trust

Headquarters

1200 Getty Ctr. Dr., Ste. 800
Los Angeles, CA 90049-1679
Phone: 310-440-7320
Fax: 310-440-7703

www.getty.edu

Contact: The Getty Foundation

E-mail: gettyfoundation@getty.edu

Type of Grant Maker: Foundation

Description

Founded: 1984

Operating Locations/Geographic Preferences: Giving on a national and international basis, with emphasis on Los Angeles and Southern CA.

Financial Summary

Assets: $9,584,879,219
Total Giving: $13,210,658
Number of Grants: 145
Grant Ranges: $1,000,000–$500

Grants Information

GRANT TYPES

Program development, matching

TYPICAL RECIPIENTS/SUBJECTS OF INTEREST

* Access to Museum and Archival Collections
* Art History as a Global Discipline
* Advancing Conservation Practice
* Leadership and Professional Development

Library research grants also available to individual scholars.

PAST GRANT RECIPIENTS

Library or School Related

* Henry Huntington Library, San Marino (CA), Art in LA, $150,000
* Henry Huntington Library, San Marino (CA), Multicultural Internship, $12,000
* Library of Los Angeles, Los Angeles (CA), Multicultural Internship, $4,000
* New York Public Library, Arts and Education, $15,000
* British Library (London), cataloging of manuscripts, $276,000
* Koc University (Istanbul), library acquisitions, $150,000
* University of Dublin, Conservation, $69,000

General

* Walker Art Center, Minneapolis (MN), for the implementation of online scholarly catalogue, $375,000
* Seattle Art Museum, Seattle (WA), for the implementation of online scholarly catalogue, $248,000

REQUIREMENTS AND RESTRICTIONS

No grants for operating or endowment purposes, start-up, construction or maintenance of buildings, or acquisition of works of art.

APPLICATION PROCEDURES

For application information, guidelines and updates, or to review current initiatives and programs in detail, please visit the foundation's website.

Deadlines: See website

Gould, Florence Foundation

Headquarters

c/o Cahill Gordon & Reindel LLP
80 Pine St., Ste. 1548
New York, NY 10005-1702
Phone: 212-701-3400

Contact: John R. Young, Pres.

Type of Grant Maker: Foundation

Description

Founded: 1957

Operating Locations/Geographic Preferences: Giving primarily in the United States and France.

Financial Summary

Assets: $74,028,098
Total Giving: $7,195,073
Number of Grants: 121
Grant Ranges: $347,950–$80

Grants Information

GRANT TYPES

General support, project development, endowments, exhibitions

TYPICAL RECIPIENTS/SUBJECTS OF INTEREST

Arts and the promotion of French-American amity and understanding

PAST GRANT RECIPIENTS

Library or School Related

- Morgan Library, Babar exhibition, $85,000
- Newberry Library, acquisition, $5,000
- Brown University, Haitian Library, $5,000
- Angers American Library, 10,000 Euros
- Nancy American Library, 10,000 Euros
- Ville D'Angers American Library, 15,000 Euros

General

- American Antiquarian Society, exhibition, $32,000
- New York City Opera, $50,000

REQUIREMENTS AND RESTRICTIONS

No grants to individuals

APPLICATION PROCEDURES

Submit letter or telephone inquiry.

Deadlines: None

Grable Foundation

Headquarters

650 Smithfield St., Ste. 240
Pittsburgh, PA 15222-3907
Phone: 412-471-4550
Fax: 412-471-2267

www.grable.org

Contact: Mary Anne Mistick, Grants Admin.

E-mail: grable@grable.org

Type of Grant Maker: Foundation

Description

Operating Locations/Geographic Preferences: Giving primarily in southwestern PA

Financial Summary

Assets: $240,362,928
Total Giving: $8,894,596
Number of Grants: 217
Grant Ranges: $675,000–$550; average: $1,000–$325,000

Grants Information

GRANT TYPES

Program development, continuing, general and operating support, consulting, seed money, technical assistance, investments and loans, matching

TYPICAL RECIPIENTS/SUBJECTS OF INTEREST

Projects that improve educational opportunities, strengthen families and support community efforts that create an environment in which children can succeed.

PAST GRANT RECIPIENTS

Library or School Related

- Jones Memorial Library, Aliquippa (PA), Outreach program, $17,500
- Monessen Public Library, Monessen (PA), Robotic program $36,500
- New Sun Rising, Milivate Community Library, Pittsburgh (PA), $35,000
- Carnegie Library, Philadelphia (PA), digital librarian, $50,000
- West Memorial Library, Pittsburgh (PA), library branch, $30,000

General

- Focus on Renewal, McKees Rocks (PA), Sio-Rox Children's Library, $50,000

APPLICATION PROCEDURES

Grable Grant Inquiry Sheet required and is available on website.

Deadlines: January 1, May 1, and September 1

Gund Foundation, George

Headquarters

1845 Guildhall Bldg.
45 Prospect Ave. W.
Cleveland, OH 44115-1018
Phone: 216-241-3114

www.gundfdn.org

Contact: David T. Abbott, Exec. Dir.; For Fellowships: Robert B. Jaquay, Assoc. Dir.

E-mail: info@gundfdn.org

Type of Grant Maker: Foundation

Description

Founded: 1952

Operating Locations/Geographic Preferences: Giving primarily in northeastern OH and the greater Cleveland, OH area

Financial Summary

Assets: $443,698,076
Total Giving: $19,981,673
Grant Ranges: $2,000,000–$200,000

Grants Information

GRANT TYPES

Program development, continuing, general and operating support, land acquisition, matching, investments and loans, seed money

TYPICAL RECIPIENTS/SUBJECTS OF INTEREST

Education, with emphasis on new concepts and methods of teaching and learning, and on increasing educational opportunities for the disadvantaged

Economic revitalization, job creation, ecology, environment, civic affairs, human services and the arts

Special Projects include Foundation Fellowship Program and Foundation Fighting Blindness

PAST GRANT RECIPIENTS

General

- Cleveland Restoration Society, Cleveland (OH), for preservation programs, $20,000
- Foundation Fighting Blindness, Columbia (MD), for retinal degenerative disease research, $2,000,000
- Cleveland Institute of Art, Cleveland (OH), for capital campaign, $1,500,000
- ParkWorks, Cleveland (OH), for LAND Studio operating and project support, $775,000
- Community Partnership for Arts and Culture, Cleveland (OH), for operating and project support, $260,000

REQUIREMENT AND RESTRICTIONS

No support for political groups, services for the physically, mentally or developmentally disabled, or the elderly. No grants to individuals, or for building or endowment funds, political campaigns, debt reduction, equipment, renovation projects, or to fund benefit events. No capital grants to projects that have not adopted green building principles.

APPLICATION PROCEDURES

Online proposal process. Mailed grant requests will not be considered. Application form required.

Deadlines: March 15, July 15, and November 15

H & R Block Foundation

Headquarters

1 H&R Block Way
Kansas City, MO 64105-1905
Phone: 816-854-4361

www.blockfoundation.org

Contact: David P. Miles, Pres.

E-mail: foundation@hrblock.com

Type of Grant Maker: Corporate Foundation

Description

Founded: 1974

Operating Locations/Geographic Preferences: Giving primarily in Johnson and Wyandotte, KS, and Clay, Jackson, Kansas City, and Platte, MO.

Corporate Foundation Information: Sponsored by H&R Block, Inc. and HRB Management, Inc.

Financial Information

Assets: $59,520,946
Total Giving: $2,605,947
Number of Grants: 357
Grant Ranges: $231,760–$100

Grants Information

GRANT TYPES

Program development, general, operating and continuing support, building and renovation, capital campaigns, matching and employee volunteering

TYPICAL RECIPIENTS/SUBJECTS OF INTEREST

Education, arts and culture, health, mental health, housing, youth development, human services, community development, and economically disadvantaged
  Major programs include:

- Education: for programs to promote early learning and adult literacy
- Arts and Culture
- Cash for Champions: for nonprofit organizations where H&R Block employees volunteer
- Community Development
- Health and Human Services

- Henry W. Bloch National Awards for Outstanding Community Service
- I. J. Mnookin Award: for Outstanding Community Service for a nonprofit organization selected by an employee
- Matching Gift Program

PAST GRANT RECIPIENTS

General

- Missouri Council on Economic Education, Kansas City (MO), for online personal finance course for teachers, $23,000
- Greater Kansas City Community Foundation, Kansas City (MO), for Neighborhood NOW initiative, $100,000
- Nelson Gallery Foundation, Kansas City (MO), for exhibition and to support educational programs and community outreach, $100,000
- Kansas City Ballet Association, Kansas City (MO), for ongoing programs and operations, $20,000

REQUIREMENTS AND RESTRICTIONS

No support for discriminatory organizations, businesses, or disease-specific organizations. No grants to individuals, publications, travel, conferences, telethons, dinners, advertising, fund-raising, animal-related causes, sports-programs, or historic preservation project.

APPLICATION PROCEDURES

Application form required.

Deadlines: February 2, April 26, July 26, and October 11

Haas, Walter and Elise Fund

Headquarters

1 Lombard St., Ste. 305
San Francisco, CA 94111-1130
Phone: 415-398-4474

www.haassr.org

Contact: Pamela H. David, Exec. Dir.

Type of Grant Maker: Foundation

Description

Founded: 1952

Operating Locations/Geographic Preferences: Giving primarily in San Francisco and Alameda County, CA

Financial Summary

Assets: $217,205,789
Total Giving: $13,210,708
Number of Grants: 170

Grants Information

GRANT TYPES

Program development, general, operating and continuing support, building and renovation, matching, investments and loans, seed money

TYPICAL RECIPIENTS/SUBJECTS OF INTEREST

Public education, the arts and culture, economic security, Jewish life

PAST GRANT RECIPIENTS

Library or School Related

- University of California, San Francisco (CA), 30,000
- Parents for Public Schools, San Francisco (CA), $100,000

General

- Jewish Community Federation of San Francisco, the Peninsula, Marin and Sonoma Counties, San Francisco (CA), $1,000,000
- Exploratorium, San Francisco (CA), $270,000

REQUIREMENTS AND RESTRICTIONS

No grants to individuals, or for general fund-raising, endowment campaigns, scholarships, fellowships, or for video or film production

APPLICATION PROCEDURES

Application form not required. Applicants should submit:

1. Copy of IRS Determination Letter
2. Brief history of organization and description of its mission
3. Copy of most recent annual report/audited financial statement/990
4. Detailed description of project and amount of funding requested
5. Copy of current year's organizational budget and/or project budget
6. Listing of additional sources and amount of support

Deadlines: None

Hartford Foundation for Public Giving

Headquarters

10 Columbus Blvd., 8th Fl.
Hartford, CT 06106-1976
Phone: 860-548-1888
www.hfpg.org

Contact: Virgil Blondet, Jr., V.P., Finance and Admin.

E-mail: hfpg@hfpg.org

Type of Grant Maker: Community Foundation

Description

Founded: 1925

Operating Locations/Geographic Preferences: Giving limited to the greater Hartford, CT area

Financial Summary

Assets: $762,222,900
Total Giving: $29,068,290

Grants Information

GRANT TYPES

Program development, continuing, general and operating support, building and renovation, matching, land acquisition, seed money, management development

TYPICAL RECIPIENTS/SUBJECTS OF INTEREST

Education, aging, arts, children, economic development, human services, health care

PAST GRANT RECIPIENTS

Library or School Related

- Tufts University, Medford (MA), $500,000
- University of Connecticut, Storrs (CT), for scholarship, $3,000

General

- Catholic Charities Archdiocese of Hartford, Hartford (CT), $500,000
- Greater Hartford Arts Council, Hartford (CT), $1,200,000
- Mutual Housing Association of Greater Hartford, Hartford (CT), $310,000

REQUIREMENTS AND RESTRICTIONS

No support for sectarian or religious activities, private foundations, tax-supported agencies, or activities primarily national or international in perspective. No grants to individuals or for recurring operating expenses, deficit financing, endowment funds, research, conferences, or support for one-time events.

APPLICATION PROCEDURES

See website for application information. If approved, application form required.

Deadlines: None

Hawaii Community Foundation

Headquarters

827 Fort St. Mall
Honolulu, HI 96813
Phone: 808-537-6333

www.hawaiicommunityfoundation.org

Contact: Kelvin H. Taketa, C.E.O.

E-mail: info@hcf-hawaii.org

Type of Grant Maker: Community Foundation

Description

Founded: 1916

Operating Locations/Geographic Preferences: Giving limited to HI

Financial Summary

Assets: $374,308,461
Total Giving: $24,959,075
Number of Grants: 400
Grant Ranges: highest $4,247,072, low range varies

Grants Information

GRANT TYPES

Program development, management development, capacity building

TYPICAL RECIPIENTS/SUBJECTS OF INTEREST

Giving programs include the following:

- Organizational Effectiveness Program: for nonprofit organizations
- PONO (Promoting Outstanding Nonprofit Organizations), leadership development for nonprofit organizations
- Scholarship Funds: including more than 85 different funds for higher education

PAST GRANT RECIPIENTS

Library or School Related

- University of Hawaii Foundation, Honolulu (HI), for University of Hawaii, Manoa Department of Art and Art History Visiting Artist Program, $7,500
- University of Hawaii, Honolulu (HI), for Kupuna Adult Care Home Project, $175,000

General

- Community Links Hawaii, Honolulu (HI), for Waianae digital media project, $172,000
- Teach for America Hawaii, Honolulu (HI), for unrestricted support, $150,000
- Dance Pioneers, Honolulu (HI), for From the Horse's Mouth Hawaii, $6,000

REQUIREMENTS AND RESTRICTIONS

No grants to individuals (except for scholarships), or for annual campaigns, emergency support, endowments, major capital projects, ongoing operating support, tuition aid programs, or deficit financing; no loans.

APPLICATION PROCEDURES

Application procedures vary for each grant-making programs. Visit website for application instructions, application forms, and specific deadlines

Deadlines: Vary

Hearst Foundation, Inc.

Headquarters

Hearst Twrs.
300 W. 57th St., 26th Fl.
New York, NY 10019-3741
Phone: 212-586-5404
Fax: 212-586-1917

www.hearstfdn.org

Contact: Paul I. Dinovitz, Exec. Dir.

Type of Grant Maker: Foundation

Description

Founded: 1945

Operating Locations/Geographic Preferences: Giving in the United States and its territories

Financial Summary

Assets: $263,657,505
Total Giving: $9,115,949
Number of Grants: 119
Grant Ranges: $250,000–$25,000

Grants Information

GRANT TYPES

Program development, capital campaigns, endowments, general and operating support, matching, technical assistance

TYPICAL RECIPIENTS/SUBJECTS OF INTEREST

Education, health, culture and social services

PAST GRANT RECIPIENTS

Library or School Related

- Pierpont Morgan Library, New York (NY), for the William Randolph Hearst Fund for Scholarly Curatorial Research and Exhibitions, toward an uncommitted goal of $1 million to be met by 2014, $350,000
- Sandusky Library, Sandusky (OH), $25,000

General

- Coalition for the Homeless, New York (NY), toward the First Step Job Training Program, $90,000
- New Alternatives for Children, New York (NY), to enhance services at NAC's medical clinic for children and families, $80,000

REQUIREMENTS AND RESTRICTIONS

No support for public policy, or public policy research, advocacy, or foreign countries. No grants to individuals, or for media or publishing projects, conferences, workshops, seminars, seed funding, multiyear grants, special events, tables, or advertising for fund-raising events; no loans or program-related investments.

APPLICATION PROCEDURES

All applications must be completed using the Hearst Foundations' Online Grant Application. Applications that are not submitted within six months of the date they were started will automatically be deleted from the database.

Deadlines: None

Henderson, A. D. Foundation, Inc.

Headquarters

PO Box 14096
Fort Lauderdale, FL 33302-4096
Phone: 954-764-2819

www.hendersonfdn.org

Contact: Karen Pfeiffer, Sr. Admin.

E-mail: staff@hendersonfdn.org

Type of Grant Maker: Foundation

Description

Founded: 1969

Operating Locations/Geographic Preferences: Giving primarily in Broward and Marion counties, FL, and VT.

Financial Summary

Assets: $50,585,515
Total Giving: $1,477,629
Number of Grants: 57
Grant Ranges: $86,250–$1,250

Grants Information

GRANT TYPES

Program development, continuing support, management development, seed money, technical assistance

TYPICAL RECIPIENTS/SUBJECTS OF INTEREST

Projects that:

1. Prepare children to be ready to learn when they enter school and become lifelong learners
2. Create and sustain accessible and effective childcare
3. Strengthen the bonds among communities, families, and children

4. Build organizational capacity and foster the use of technology by nonprofit organizations.

PAST GRANT RECIPIENTS

Library or School Related

- Broward Public Library, fort Lauderdale (FL), What's The Big Idea? Math & Science, $31,870

General

- VSA Arts Vermont, Inc., Winooski (VT), Start With The Arts Library Outreach, $20,000
- Pace Center for Girls, Wilton Manors (FL), $30,000
- Fairbanks Museum and Planetarium, Saint Johnsbury (VT), $25,000

REQUIREMENTS AND RESTRICTIONS

No support for private foundations or organizations lacking 501(c)(3) status, or for sectarian purposes. No grants to individuals, or for scholarships, annual campaigns, operating budgets, endowments, building or renovation, equipment (unless it is an integral part of an eligible project), capital campaigns, debt reduction, general operating support, or medical or clinical research or loans.

APPLICATION PROCEDURES

Applicants MUST contact a Foundation Program Director PRIOR to a formal submission to discuss their project idea. If the idea is a potential match with the Foundation's funding priorities, the applicant will be asked to submit an Application which includes a maximum of three pages for a Proposal, a project budget, an IRS tax exempt status letter no more than 5 years old and other documentation.

Deadlines: Quarterly

Hertog Foundation, Inc.

Headquarters

c/o Rampell and Rampell, P.A.
223 Sunset Ave., Ste. 200
Palm Beach, FL 33480-3855

Type of Grant Maker: Foundation

Description

Founded: N/A

Operating Locations/Geographic Preferences: Giving primarily in Washington, DC and New York, NY.

Financial Information

Assets: $36,414,759
Total Giving: $15,575,830
Number of Grants: 114
Grant Ranges: $2,682,550–$175

Grants Information

GRANT TYPES

Program support and research

TYPICAL RECIPIENTS/SUBJECTS OF INTEREST

Public libraries, higher education, historical preservation, Jewish organizations, medical research, public affairs

PAST GRANT RECIPIENTS

Library or School Related

- New York Public Library, New York (NY), $1,000,000
- New York University, New York (NY), payable over 1 year, $500,000
- Harvard University, Cambridge (MA), for Paul Peterson's Program on Education Policy and Governance, $50,000

General

- New York Historical Society, New York (NY), $2,680,000
- American Enterprise Institute for Public Policy Research, Washington, DC, $2,000,000

REQUIREMENTS AND RESTRICTIONS

Note: Applications not accepted as foundation contributes only to preslected organizations. However, this source is included because previous awards have been made to a library or libraries.

APPLICATION PROCEDURES AND DEADLINES

Contact Foundation

Hewlett, William and Flora Foundation

Headquarters

2121 Sand Hill Rd.
Menlo Park, CA 94025-6909
Phone: 650-234-4500
Fax: 650-234-4501
www.hewlett.org

Contact: Eric Brown, Dir., Comms.

Type of Grant Maker: Foundation

Description

Founded: 1966

Operating Locations/Geographic Preferences: Giving limited to the San Francisco Bay Area and Central Valley, CA for family and community development programs; performing arts primarily limited to the Bay Area.

Financial Summary

Assets: $7,377,220,546
Total Giving: $359,407,416
Number of Grants: 915
Grant Ranges: $15,000,000–$10,000

Grants Information

GRANT TYPES

Program development, continuing, general and operating support, matching

TYPICAL RECIPIENTS/SUBJECTS OF INTEREST

Education, the environment, global development, performing arts, philanthropy, and population, and grants to support disadvantaged communities in the San Francisco Bay Area

PAST GRANT RECIPIENTS

Library or School Related
- University of Iowa, Digital library, $55,000
- San Mateo Public Library Foundation, San Mateo (CA), matching gift $2,800

General
- Kaisahan Dance Company of San Jose, First Five Initiative library program, $20,000
- National Campaign to Prevent Teen and Unplanned Pregnancy, Washington (DC), for general operating support, $10,000,000
- Energy Foundation, San Francisco (CA), for China Sustainable Cities Initiative, $7,000,000

REQUIREMENTS AND RESTRICTIONS

Global Development and Population, Performing Arts, Philanthropy, and Special Projects are not accepting unsolicited requests for grants at this time.

No support for private foundations or organizations lacking 501(c)(3) status, or for sectarian purposes.

No grants to individuals, or for scholarships, annual campaigns, operating budgets, endowments, building or renovation, equipment (unless it is an integral part of an eligible project), capital campaigns, debt reduction, general operating support, or medical or clinical research or loans. No funds for individuals and generally the foundation does not fund scholarships, endowments, capital campaigns, building construction, for-profit organizations, or unincorporated associations or groups. In addition, the foundation's funds can be used only for purposes that are consistent with its status as a charitable organization.

APPLICATION PROCEDURES

Please read the information on our website about the Foundation's grant-making programs, goals and strategies, and geographic limitations. Only selected programs currently accept unsolicited Letters of Inquiry.

Deadlines: None

Hillcrest Foundation

Headquarters

c/o Bank of America, N.A.
901 Main St., 19th Fl., TX1-492-19-11
Dallas, TX 75283-1041

Phone: 214-209-1965

Contact: David T. Ross, Sr. V.P., Bank of America, N.A.

Type of Grant Maker: Foundation

Description

Founded: 1959

Operating Locations/Geographic Preferences: Giving limited to TX, with emphasis on Dallas County

Financial Summary

Assets: $124,363,401
Total Giving: $6,093,500
Number of Grants: 153
Grant Ranges: $400,000–$1,000

Grants Information

GRANT TYPES

Program development, building and renovation, land acquisition, matching, capital campaigns

TYPICAL RECIPIENTS/SUBJECTS OF INTEREST

Higher and other education, health and hospitals, social services, youth and child welfare, drug abuse, rehabilitation and housing

PAST GRANT RECIPIENTS

Library or School Related

- Dallas Baptist University, Dallas (TX), for funding for the construction of bookstore, resource center, and music practice rooms and classrooms, $250,000
- Graduate Institute of Applied Linguistics, Dallas (TX), for software, for student scholarships, to support Comprehensive Fund-raising Campaign, $150,000
- Fulton School, Heath (TX), for renovation of Lower School, new playground for Preschool and for campus infrastructure improvements, $20,000

General

- Parkland Foundation, Dallas (TX), for I Stand for Parkland capital campaign and new hospital, $200,000
- Happy Hill Farm Children's Home and Academy, Granbury (TX), for renovation and repair of residences, $100,000

APPLICATION PROCEDURES

Application form required. Applicants should submit:

1. Copy of IRS Determination Letter
2. Brief history of organization and description of its mission
3. Copy of most recent annual report/audited financial statement/990
4. Listing of board of directors, trustees, officers and other key people and their affiliations
5. Detailed description of project and amount of funding requested
6. Copy of current year's organizational budget and/or project budget

Deadlines: Rolling for proposals; Applications: February 28, July 31, and November 30

Home Depot Foundation

Headquarters

2455 Paces Ferry Road, C-17
Atlanta, GA 30339
Phone: 770-384-3889, 866-593-7019
Fax: 770-384-3908, 866-593-7027

http://homedepotfoundation.org/page/applying-for-a-grant
Type of Grant Maker: Corporate Foundation

Description

Founded: 2002
Operating Locations/Geographic Preferences: None

Financial Summary

Foundation has donated more than $22 million to 900 nonprofit organizations in Atlanta in the last five years

Grants Information

GRANT TYPES

Equipment, donated supplies, construction, general support

TYPICAL RECIPIENTS/SUBJECTS OF INTEREST

Community impact grants, up to $5,000, are available to registered 501(c)(3) nonprofit organizations, public schools, or tax-exempt public service agencies in the U.S. that are using the power of volunteers to improve the physical health of their community. Grants are given in the form of Home Depot gift cards for the purchase of tools, materials, or services.

PAST GRANT RECIPIENTS

See website for listing of all organizations that have received some form of support.

Library or School Related

- Morehouse College, for King historical papers to be stored in the Woodruff Library, $1,500,000

General

- National Center for Civil and Human Rights, construction, $1,000,000

REQUIREMENTS AND RESTRICTIONS

Proposals for the following community improvement activities will be considered:

- Repairs, refurbishments, and modifications to low-income and/or transitional veterans' housing, or community facilities (schools, community centers, senior centers, etc.)
- Weatherizing or increasing energy efficiency of low-income and/or transitional veterans' housing, or community facilities

- Planting trees or community gardens and/or landscaping community facilities that serve veterans
- Grants must support work completed by community volunteers in the U.S.
- Projects must be completed within six months following notification that the grant has been awarded, with reporting requirements due 30 days following the completion of the project.
- Grants are solely given in the form of Home Depot gift cards for the purchase of tools, materials, or services.
- Organizations who have received funding through The Home Depot Foundation's Community Impact Grant Program must wait 12 months after notification of award before applying for additional grants through this program. Each approved applicant must complete a Final Report before additional funding requests will be considered.

APPLICATION PROCEDURES

Online application required

Deadlines: August 13

Horncrest Foundation, Inc.

Headquarters

6 Sleator Dr.
Ossining, NY 10562-3918
Phone: 914-941-5533

Contact: Lawrence Blau, Pres.

Type of Grant Maker: Foundation

Description

Founded: 1960

Operating Locations/Geographic Preferences: Giving primarily St. Louis, MO and NY.

Financial Summary

Assets: $9,416,298
Total Giving: $14,428,167
Number of Grants: 91
Grant Ranges: $4,833,575–$1,000

Grants Information

GRANT TYPES

General and operating support, matching, seed money

TYPICAL RECIPIENTS/SUBJECTS OF INTEREST

Higher education and medical school education, housing, arts

PAST GRANT RECIPIENTS

Library or School Related

- Germantown Friends School, Philadelphia (PA), for endowment for community scholarship program, $1,800,000
- Sarah Lawrence College, Bronxville (NY), for endowment for Community Partnerships and Service Learning Program, $1,900,000

General

- Center of Creative Arts, Saint Louis (MO), for outreach to Saint Louis schools, $962,000
- Scholarship Foundation of Saint Louis, Saint Louis (MO), for Dee Dee Becker Fund, $1,950,000
- Beyond Housing-Neighborhood Housing Services, Saint Louis (MO), for building universal design house, $478,000

REQUIREMENTS AND RESTRICTIONS

No loans to individuals

APPLICATION PROCEDURES

Contact Foundation for application guidelines.

Deadlines: None

Houston Endowment Inc.

Headquarters

600 Travis, Ste. 6400
Houston, TX 77002-3003
Phone: (713) 238-8100
www.houstonendowment.org

E-mail: info@houstonendowment.org

Type of Grant Maker: Foundation

Description

Founded: 1937

Operating Locations/Geographic Preferences: Giving primarily in the greater Houston, TX area, with some funding throughout the state for projects central to TX history

Financial Summary

Assets: $1,527,022,391
Total Giving: $72,087,711
Number of Grants: 501
Grant Ranges: $5,000,000–$2,000

Grants Information

GRANT TYPES

Program development, building and renovation, continuing, general and operating support, land acquisition, capital campaigns

TYPICAL RECIPIENTS/SUBJECTS OF INTEREST

Education, the arts, community enhancement, health, human services, environment and neighborhood development

PAST GRANT RECIPIENTS

Library or School Related

- University of Texas, Austin (TX), for Regional College Access and Completion Initiative, $11,100,000
- Adult Reading Center, Pearland (TX), for general operating support, $150,000

General

- Houston Parks Board, Houston (TX), for Bayou Greenways Initiative and toward land acquisition and trail construction, $7,500,000
- Salvation Army of Houston, Houston (TX), for renovation and expansion of Sally's House, a transitional home for women exiting substance abuse, $2,000,000
- Mid-America Arts Alliance, Kansas City (MO), for capacity building program among small to mid-sized cultural institutions in greater Houston, $1,400,000
- Southwest Alternate Media Project, Houston (TX), for general operating support, $80,000
- Air Alliance Houston, Houston (TX), for Port Community Collaboration Project to address air quality, access to health care for residents of Galena Park, $200,000

REQUIREMENTS AND RESTRICTIONS

No support for religious organizations for religious purposes, or organizations that are the responsibility of the government. No grants to individuals, or fund-raising activities including galas, lobbying or for individual memorials or scholarships

APPLICATION PROCEDURES

Online process only. See website for details

Deadlines: None

Humana Foundation, Inc.

Headquarters

500 W. Main St., Ste. 208
Louisville, KY 40202-2946
Phone: 502-580-4140
Fax: 502-580-1256

www.humanafoundation.org

Contact: Barbara Wright; Virginia K. Judd, Exec. Dir.

E-mail: bwright@humana.com

Type of Grant Maker: Corporate Foundation

Description

Founded: 1981

Operating Locations/Geographic Preferences: Giving primarily in areas of company operations in Phoenix, AZ, San Diego and San Francisco, CA, Denver, CO, CT, FL, GA, Bloomington, Chicago, Peoria, and Rockford, IL, Indianapolis, IN, Louisville, KY, New Orleans, LA, Boston, MA, Baltimore, MD, Detroit, MI, Kansas City and St. Louis, MO, Charlotte, NC, NJ, Las Vegas, NV, NY, Cincinnati, OH, Philadelphia and Pittsburgh, PA, Columbia, SC, Nashville, TN, Austin, Dallas, and Houston, TX, Salt Lake City, UT, VA, and Green Bay and Milwaukee, WI.

Corporate Foundation Information: Supported by Humana, Inc.

Financial Summary

Assets: $102,957,802
Total Giving: $3,701,410
Number of Grants: 57
Grant Ranges: $774,920–$2,500

Grants Information

GRANT TYPES

Annual and capital campaigns, building and renovation, continuing, general and operating support, matching, program development, employee volunteering

TYPICAL RECIPIENTS/SUBJECTS OF INTEREST

Programs that promote healthy lives and healthy communities, with a focus on the needs of children, families, and seniors, with a special focus on promoting childhood health and education, health literacy, and active lifestyles and wellness.

PAST GRANT RECIPIENTS

Library or School Related

- National Society of Sons of the American Revolution, Louisville (KY), Library support, $10,000
- Jefferson County Public Education Foundation Louisville (KY), "Making Time for What Matters Most," $100,000

General

- Actors Theater of Louisville Louisville (KY), Humana Festival of New American Plays, $2,100,000
- Community Foundation of Louisville Louisville (KY), Degrees program, $150,000
- 21st Century Parks, Inc., Louisville (KY), Capital campaign, $200,000

REQUIREMENTS AND RESTRICTIONS

No support for social, labor, political, veterans', or fraternal organizations, lobbying efforts, or mission-focused activities. No grants for start-up needs or seed money, salary expenses or other administrative costs, general operating support for religious organizations, or for construction or renovation of sanctuaries.

APPLICATION PROCEDURES

All eligible applicants submit their grant application forms electronically.

See website for list of eligible locations and application deadlines

Deadlines: Vary

Hyde Family Foundations

Headquarters

17 W. Pontotoc Ave., Ste. 200
Memphis, TN 38103-3826
Phone: 901-685-3400
www.hydefoundation.org
Contact: Teresa Sloyan, Exec. Dir.
E-mail: info@hydefoundation.org
Type of Grant Maker: Foundation

Description

Founded: 1961
Operating Locations/Geographic Preferences: Giving primarily in Memphis, TN

Financial Summary

Assets: $117,971,247
Total Giving: $19,111,121
Number of Grants: 271
Grant Ranges: $1,000,000–$20

Grants Information

GRANT TYPES

Program development, general and operating, building and renovation, matching, seed money, capital campaigns

TYPICAL RECIPIENTS/SUBJECTS OF INTEREST

Foundation's areas of focus include:

Transforming Education: Including developing and rewarding teachers and school leaders, supporting all types of school and effective advocacy that meets the needs of kids and families

Positioning Authentic Assets: Including Arts and Culture, Civic Growth and Leadership, and Greening Initiatives

Strengthening Neighborhoods: to transform buildings, commerce, landscapes and lives of those in the community

PAST GRANT RECIPIENTS

Library or School Related

- Tennessee Charter Schools Association, Memphis (TN), for general operating support, $50,000

- University of North Carolina at Chapel Hill Arts and Sciences Foundation, Chapel Hill (NC), $665,000
- Catholic Memphis Urban Schools, Memphis (TN), for Jubilee Schools Endowment, $500,000
- Saint Mary's Episcopal School, Memphis (TN), for capital campaign, $750,000

General

- Shelby Farms Park Conservancy, Memphis (TN), for park improvements, $200,000
- Memphis Redbirds Baseball Foundation, Memphis (TN), $125,000

REQUIREMENTS AND RESTRICTIONS

No support for political organizations or individuals

APPLICATION PROCEDURES

Apply online, through e-mail or mail. Applicants should submit:

1. Timetable for implementation and evaluation of project
2. Results expected from proposed grant
3. Statement of problem project will address
4. Population served
5. Copy of most recent annual report/audited financial statement/990
6. How project's results will be evaluated or measured
7. What distinguishes project from others in its field
8. Listing of board of directors, trustees, officers and other key people and their affiliations
9. Detailed description of project and amount of funding requested
10. Plans for cooperation with other organizations, if any
11. Copy of current year's organizational budget and/or project budget

Deadlines: March 1, June 1, September 1 and December 1

Idaho Commission for Libraries

Headquarters

325 W State St.
Boise, ID 83702
Phone: 208-334-2150, 800-458-3271 (in-state toll free)
Fax: 208-334-4016

http://libraries.idaho.gov/landing/icfl-funding-libraries

Type of Grant Maker: Government

Grants Information

LSTA—LIBRARY SERVICES & TECHNOLOGY

Federal funds awarded to the Commission for Libraries from the Institute of Museum and Library Service (IMLS). The Commission for Libraries has temporarily suspended the Competitive and Just In Time grant programs due to decreased funding levels. Further information will be provided when these programs will be resumed.

CONTINUING EDUCATION GRANTS

Grant Ranges: $500–$5,000; $250–$1,000 per semester for formal course tuition and course material expenses
Program Description: Idaho libraries may apply for grants to support individual employee, or group continuing education (CE) activities. CE activities must be specific to library programs and/or services, address one or more of the priorities for LSTA and have a clear benefit identified for the library patron/end user.

APPLICATION PROCEDURES AND DEADLINES

Each type of CE grant project has an application form that can be found at http://libraries.idaho.gov/ce-grants. Applying library employees are required to contact the Commission for Libraries Continuing Education Consultant for specific information on the application process, timeline, and eligibility of the proposed project.

Illinois State Library

Headquarters

Services for Libraries
Library Development Group
Springfield Office
Gwendolyn Brooks Building
300 S. Second St.
Springfield, IL 62701
Phone: 217-524-8836 (grant programs)
www.cyberdriveillinois.com/departments/library/grants/home.html

Type of Grant Maker: Government

Grants Information

Grants for library and literacy services, programs and initiatives.

Grant programs provide access to ideas, resources and information through the efforts of Illinois' academic libraries, public libraries, school libraries, special libraries, regional library systems, literacy agencies and partnering workplaces.

Total Grant Giving: $94 million

Grant programs include:

- Adult Literacy Grants
- Blind and Physically Handicapped/Talking Book and Braille Service Grants
- Business and Libraries: Working Together
- Illinois Library and Information Science Training Grant Program
- Illinois Veterans' Home Libraries
- Library Services—Federal Library Services Fund
- Library Services and Technology Act (LSTA)
- Penny Severns Summer Family Literacy Grant
- Project Next Generation
- Public Library Per Capita and Equalization
- Public Library Construction
- School District Library Grant
- System Technology Grants

APPLICATION PROCEDURES

Most of the grant programs are competitive, unless announced otherwise. Each grant program has its own application processes, criteria and deadlines. See website for details.

Indiana State Library

Headquarters

315 West Ohio St.
Indianapolis, IN 46202
Phone: 317-232-3697

www.in.gov/library

Type of Grant Maker: Government

Grants Information

LSTA Digitization Grants

Grant Amount: up to $20,000

Indiana State Library will offer LSTA sub-grants to libraries in Indiana for the purpose of digitizing Indiana's historical records. The primary goal is to develop content for Indiana Memory, a digital library for Indiana residents (www.IndianaMemory.in.gov). Libraries should use these funds to digitize materials important to Indiana history and relevant to researchers today. Libraries should also be looking to establish partnerships with cultural institutions that house unique and important collections of Indiana history. The lead project director in these partnerships must be a library, and the library will be responsible for managing the project and acting as fiscal agent and grant administrator.

APPLICATION PROCEDURES

The grant application consists of:

1. An application form
2. A budget worksheet
3. Supplemental questions

Deadlines: Recommended prospectus form (optional) due in January; grant application materials due in February.

Technology Grants

Grant Amount: up to $450,000

Indiana State Library will offer LSTA sub-grants to help Indiana libraries provide their users with the new and improved technology necessary to meet their residents' ever-changing needs for library services and access to information. Libraries may use these sub-grants to better meet the technological needs of their community.

APPLICATION PROCEDURES

See online for application forms.

Deadlines: See deadlines posted online.

Institute of Museum and Library Services

Headquarters

1800 M St. NW, 9th Floor
Washington, DC 20036-5802
Phone: 202-653-IMLS (4657)
Fax: 202-653-4600

www.imls.gov/applicants/default.aspx

Type of Grant Maker: Government

LAURA BUSH 21ST CENTURY LIBRARIAN PROGRAM

Grant Amount: $50,000–$500,000
(subject to the availability of funds and IMLS discretion)
for up to three years, except for doctoral program projects,
which may be up to four years

Program Description: Supports projects to recruit and
educate the next generation of librarians, faculty, and
library leaders; and to support early career research. It
also assists in the professional development of librarians
and library staff. Project types include: Community
Engagement, formal Education, Informal Learning,
Partnerships, Professional Development/Continuing
Education, Research

APPLICATION PROCEDURES

See online forms.

CONTACTS

Mary Alice Ball, AMLS, PhD, Senior Library Program Officer
202-653-4730
mball@imls.gov

Kevin Cherry, MSLS, PhD, Senior Library Program Officer
202-653-4662
kcherry@imls.gov

Traci Stanley, Library Program Specialist
202-653-4689
tstanley@imls.gov

Deadline: September

LEARNING LABS IN LIBRARIES AND MUSEUMS

Grant Amount: up to $100,000 for 18 months

Program Description: Support the planning and designing
of up to 30 Learning Labs in libraries and museums
throughout the country. The Labs are intended to engage
middle- and high-school youth in mentor-led, interest-
based, youth-centered, collaborative learning using
digital and traditional media. Grantees will be required
to participate, in person and online, in a community of
practice that will provide technical assistance, networking,
and cross-project learning. Projects are expected to provide
prototypes for the field and be based on current research
about digital media and youth learning. Project types
include: Community Engagement, Informal Learning,
Partnerships.

APPLICATION PROCEDURES

See online forms.

CONTACTS

Amy Eshleman Program Leader for Education
Urban Libraries Council (ULC)
312-676-0958
aeshleman@urbanlibraries.org

Margaret Glass
Program Manager, Professional Development
Association of Science-Technology Centers (ASTC)
202-783-7200, x129
mglass@astc.org

Allison Boals, Program Specialist
Institute of Museum and Library Services (IMLS)
202-653-4702
aboals@imls.gov

Deadlines: vary

NATIONAL ARTS AND HUMANITIES YOUTH PROGRAM AWARDS

Program Description: Formerly Coming Up Taller, these
awards recognize and support outstanding community
arts and humanities programs that celebrate the creativity
of America's young people by providing them with
learning opportunities and chances to contribute to their
communities. These awards focus national attention on
exemplary programs currently fostering the creative and
intellectual development of America's youth through
education and practical experience in the arts and the
humanities.

   Project types include: Awards, Community
Engagement, Informal Learning, Public Programs

APPLICATION PROCEDURES

See www.nahyp.org.

Deadline: February

NATIONAL LEADERSHIP GRANTS FOR LIBRARIES

Grant Amount:
   Project Grants: $50,000–$500,000
   Planning Grants: up to $50,000
   Nat. Forum Grants: up to $100,000

Up to three years for Project Grants. Up to one year for
Planning Grants and National Forum Grants.

Program Description: National Leadership Grants support
projects that address challenges faced by the museum,
library, and/or archive fields and that have the potential to
advance practice in those fields. Successful proposals will
seek innovative responses to the challenge(s) identified in
the proposals, and will have national impact.

The National Leadership Grant program accepts applications under four main categories:

1. Advancing Digital Resources—Support the creation, use, presentation, and preservation of significant digital resources as well as the development of tools to enhance access, use, and management of digital assets.
2. Research—Support research that investigates key questions that are important to museum, library, and archival practice.
3. Demonstration—Support projects that produce a replicable model or practice that is usable, adaptable, or scalable by other institutions for improving services and performance.
4. Library Museum Collaboration Grants— Support collaborative projects (between museums and/or libraries and other community organizations) that address the educational, economic, cultural, or social needs of a community.

Applicants may choose to submit a Project Grant, Planning Grant, or National Forum Grant proposal in any of the above categories.

Project Grants support fully developed projects for which needs assessments, partnership development, feasibility analyses, prototyping, and other planning activities have been completed.

Project types include: Collections Management, Community Engagement, Demonstration, Digital Collections/Tools, formal Education, Informal Learning, Partnerships, Public Programs, Research

Planning Grants allow project teams to perform preliminary planning activities that could lead to a subsequent full project, such as needs and feasibility analyses, solidifying partnerships, developing project work plans, or developing prototypes or proofs of concept. Applications for Planning Grants must include at least one formal partner in addition to the lead applicant.

National Forum Grants provide the opportunity to convene qualified groups of experts and key stakeholders to consider issues or challenges that are important to libraries, museums, and/or archives across the nation. Grant-supported meetings are expected to produce widely disseminated reports with expert recommendations for action or research that address a key challenge identified in the proposal. The expert recommendations resulting from these meetings are intended to guide future proposals to the National Leadership Grant program.

REQUIREMENTS AND RESTRICTIONS

See program guidelines for special conditions of eligibility for this program.

APPLICATION PROCEDURES

See online forms.

CONTACTS

Anthony Donovan Smith, Senior Library Program Officer
202-653-4768
asmith@imls.gov

Charles "Chuck" Thomas, Senior Library Program Officer
202-653-4663
cthomas@imls.gov

Kathy Mitchell, Library Program Specialist
202-653-4687
kmitchell@imls.gov

SPARKS! IGNITION GRANTS FOR LIBRARIES AND MUSEUMS

Grant Amount: $10,000 to $25,000 for up to one year

Program Description: The Sparks! Ignition Grants for Libraries and Museums are a special funding opportunity within the IMLS National Leadership Grants program. These small grants encourage libraries, museums, and archives to test and evaluate specific innovations in the ways they operate and the services they provide. Sparks! Grants support the deployment, testing, and evaluation of promising and groundbreaking new tools, products, services, or organizational practices. You may propose activities or approaches that involve risk, as long as the risk is balanced by significant potential for improvement in the ways libraries and museums serve their communities.

Successful proposals will address problems, challenges, or needs of broad relevance to libraries, museums, and/ or archives. A proposed project should test a specific, innovative response to the identified problem and present a plan to make the findings widely and openly accessible.

To maximize the public benefit from federal investments in these grants, the Sparks! Grants will fund only projects with the following characteristics:

Broad Potential Impact—You should identify a specific problem or need that is relevant to many libraries, archives, and/or museums, and propose a testable and measurable solution. Proposals must demonstrate a thorough understanding of current issues and practices in the project's focus area and discuss its potential impact within libraries, archives, and/or museums. Proposed innovations should be widely adoptable or adaptable.

Significant Innovation—The proposed solution to the identified problem must offer strong potential for non-incremental, significant advancement in the operation of libraries, archives, and/or museums. You must explain how the proposed activity differs from current practices or takes advantage of an unexplored opportunity, and the potential benefit to be gained by this innovation.

APPLICATION PROCEDURES

See online forms.

CONTACTS

Helen Wechsler, Supervisory Grants Management Specialist
202-653-4779
hwechsler@imls.gov

Tim Carrigan, Museum Program Specialist
202-653-4639
tcarrigan@imls.gov

Anthony Donovan Smith, Senior Library Program Officer
202-653-4768
asmith@imls.gov

Charles "Chuck" Thomas, Senior Library Program Officer
202-653-4663
cthomas@imls.gov

Traci Stanley, Library Program Specialist
202-653-4689
tstanley@imls.gov

Deadline: February

International City/County Management Association (ICMA)

Headquarters

777 North Capitol St. NE, Suite 500
Washington, DC 20002-4201
Phone: 202 289-ICMA

www.icma.org

Type of Grant Maker: Nonprofit Organization

Grants Information

ICMA PUBLIC LIBRARY INNOVATION GRANTS

Grants awarded: $500,000

Number of Grants: 9

Program Description: The ICMA Public Library Innovation Grant program leverages the potential of public libraries to deliver services in such nontraditional areas as public safety, economic development, health, immigration, civic engagement, and sustainability. Recognizing the importance of the manager-librarian relationship to create and sustain change, the grants are anchored by a partnership between the office of the chief administrative officer (city, town, and county managers) and the public library. Program supports projects developed by local governments that utilize their public libraries in addressing local needs and providing new services with lasting benefits to their communities.

GRANT TYPES

Program development

PAST GRANT RECIPIENTS

Public libraries awarded grants include:

- Buena Vista (VA), for a Training and Call Center
- Dallas (TX), for Every Child Ready to Read @ Dallas Expansion
- Fairfax County (VA), for Changing Lives through Literature
- Fayetteville (AK), for Solar Test-Bed Library Project

APPLICATION PROCEDURES AND DEADLINES

See website.

International Federation of Library Associations and Institutions (IFLA)

Headquarters

Prins Willem-Alexanderhof 5
2595 BE The Hague
Netherlands

Postal Address
PO Box 95312
2509 CH The Hague
Netherlands

Phone: +31 70 3140884
Fax: +31 70 3834827

www.ifla.org/hq

E-mail: ifla@ifla.org

Type of Grant Maker: Library Organization

DR. SHAWKY SALEM CONFERENCE GRANT (SSCG)

Grant Amount: Up to $1,900 toward the cost of travel (economy class air transportation) to and from the host country of the conference, registration, hotel costs and a per diem allowance.

Program Description: Annual grant established by Dr. Shawky Salem and the International Federation of Library Associations and Institutions (IFLA). The aim of the grant is to enable one expert in library and information sciences from the Arab Countries (AC) to attend the Annual IFLA Conference.

REQUIREMENTS AND RESTRICTIONS

Candidates should not have attended an IFLA conference previously, be an Arab nationality, not exceed 45 years, have experience at least 5 years in LIS profession or teaching, have the approval of his or her organization.

APPLICATION PROCEDURES

See online form. Completed forms should be sent to:

Shawky Salem Conference Grant (SSCG)
IFLA Headquarters
POB. 95312
2509 CH The Hague
Netherlands
Fax: + 31 70 3834827
E-mail: ifla@ifla.org

Deadlines: February 1

Iowa, State Library of

Headquarters

1112 E. Grand Ave.
Des Moines, IA 50319-0233
Phone: 800 248-4483

www.statelibraryofiowa.org

Type of Grant Maker: Government

The State Library of Iowa works with libraries in the state to develop grants, but does not offer a competitive grant program to libraries.

Iowa West Foundation

Headquarters

25 Main Pl., Ste. 550
Council Bluffs, IA 51503-0700

Phone: 712-309-3000

www.iowawestfoundation.org

Contact: Debra Debbaut, Grants. Mgr.

E-mail: grantinfo@iowawest.com

Type of Grant Maker: Foundation

Description

Founded: 1992

Operating Locations/Geographic Preferences: Giving primarily in southwest IA, the Council Bluffs area, and Omaha, NE

Financial Summary

Assets: $320,693,002
Total Giving: $15,510,862
Number of Grants: 155
Grant Ranges: $1,361,038–$1,000; average:
$25,000–$500,000

Grants Information

GRANT TYPES

Program development, building and renovation, capital campaigns, general and operating support, management development, seed money, matching

TYPICAL RECIPIENTS/SUBJECTS OF INTEREST

- Education
- Community development and beautification
- Economic development
- Human and social needs

Focus includes assisting local schools to reduce the dropout rate, and to improve neighborhoods in Pottawattamie County, IA.

PAST GRANT RECIPIENTS

Library or School Related

- Council Bluffs Community School District, Council Bluffs (IA), for Phase Two Education Initiative, $5,200,000

General

- Applied Information Management Institute, Omaha (NE), for Iowa West Opportunity Scholarship program, $2,300,000
- Southwest Iowa Families, Clarinda (IA), for Stork's Nest, educational program for young families, $32,000
- Shelby, City of, Shelby (IA), to renovate city park with new playground equipment, $23,000

- Council Bluffs, City of, Council Bluffs (IA), for River's Edge Park, $5,450,000
- United Way of the Midlands, Omaha (NE), for community care fund to meet health and human service needs, $335,000
- Council Bluffs, City of, Council Bluffs (IA), for operating support for city arena, $300,000

REQUIREMENTS AND RESTRICTIONS

No support for medical research or church-affiliated organizations for religious purposes. No grants for fund-raising, benefit, and social events, capital requests, operating deficits or long-term operating support, publications, films, books, seminars, symposia or for conferences.

APPLICATION PROCEDURES

Begin with letter of inquiry. If requested, applicants are invited to complete an online proposal. Application form required, which will require:

1. Copy of IRS Determination Letter
2. Brief history of organization and description of its mission
3. Detailed description of project and amount of funding requested
4. Listing of additional sources and amount of support

Deadlines: For letter of inquiry: January 1, April 1, July 1, and October 1; for full proposal: January 15, April 15, July 15, and October 15

Irvine Foundation, James

Headquarters

575 Market St., Ste. 3400
San Francisco, CA 94105-2858
Phone: 415-777-2244

www.irvine.org

Contact: Kelly Martin, Dir., Grants Admin.

E-mail: grantsadmin@irvine.org

Type of Grant Maker: Foundation

Description

Founded: 1937

Operating Locations/Geographic Preferences: Giving limited to CA

Financial Summary

Assets: $1,589,353,533
Total Giving: $59,311,064
Number of Grants: 655
Grant Ranges: $5,437,500–$500

Grants Information

GRANT TYPES

Program development, matching, general and operating support, seed money

TYPICAL RECIPIENTS/SUBJECTS OF INTEREST

Foundation gives through the following programs:

Arts: including increasing engagement by low-income and/or ethnically diverse populations that have been traditionally underserved by arts nonprofits; expanding how people engage in the arts, such as through digital technology and advancing diverse, non-traditional spaces for arts engagement, especially in regions with few arts-specific venues

California Democracy: focusing on governance reform and civic engagement

Employee Matching Gifts

Exploring Engagement Fund: funding new approaches to help nonprofit arts organizations try new ways of engaging audiences and participants

Leadership Awards

Youth: to increase the number of low-income youth in California who complete high school on time and attain a postsecondary credential by the age of 25

PAST GRANT RECIPIENTS

Library or School Related

- Stanford University, Stanford (CA), for District Leadership Series of the California Linked Learning District Initiative, $1,200,000
- ConnectEd: The California Center for College and Career, Berkeley (CA), for California Linked Learning District Initiative, $8,800,000

General

- Nonprofit Finance Fund, New York (NY), for California-based projects of ArtPlace, public/private partnership to promote role of arts and culture in building livable, sustainable communities, $2,000,000
- Public Policy Institute of California, San Francisco (CA), for Californians and Their Government survey series, maintain online data site and conduct public and policymaker education activities, $2,000,000

- Youth UpRising, Oakland (CA), for program that advances college and career outcomes of out-of-school youth in health industry and/or digital media, arts and design pathways, $125,000

APPLICATION PROCEDURES

See website for application information. Application form required.

Deadlines: None. Accepted on a rolling basis

Jacksonville, Florida Community Foundation, Inc.

Headquarters

245 Riverside Ave., Ste. 310
Jacksonville, FL 32202
Phone: 904-356-4483

www.jaxcf.org

Contact: Cheryl Riddick, V.P., Grant-making Svcs. Or John Zell, V.P., Donor Svcs.

E-mail: info@jaxcf.org

Type of Grant Maker: Community Foundation

Description

Founded: 1979

Operating Locations/Geographic Preferences: Giving primarily in northeastern FL, including Baker, Clay, Duval, Nassau and St. Johns counties

Financial Summary

Assets: $141,766,473
Total Giving: $20,228,209
Number of Grants: 1,300
Grant Ranges: $681,687 and under

Grants Information

GRANT TYPES

Program development, matching, investments and loans, seed money, endowments

TYPICAL RECIPIENTS/SUBJECTS OF INTEREST

In addition to other areas of giving of education, community development and conservation, the foundation offers grants through the following areas:

Aging Adults: for projects that enable senior citizens to remain actively engaged in the community and living at home

Art Ventures: Individual Artists: supporting individual artists

Art Ventures: Small Arts Organizations: for the support of artistic and administrative development of small arts organizations.

Dr. JoAnn Crisp-Ellert Art Appreciation: for educating people about and bringing art to the people of St. Augustine.

PAST GRANT RECIPIENTS

Library or School Related

- Florida Memorial University, Miami (FL), for building renovation and expansion, $200,000
- University of North Florida Foundation, Jacksonville (FL), for fellowship tuition and books for Nurse Practitioner graduate student, $6,700

General

- Cummer Museum of Art and Gardens, Jacksonville (FL), for annual support and capital campaign, $245,000
- Everglades Foundation, Palmetto Bay (FL), for general operating support, $500,000
- Local Initiatives Support Corporation, Jacksonville, Jacksonville (FL), $250,000
- Creekside Ministries, Jacksonville (FL), for general operating support, $93,000
- American Red Cross, Jacksonville (FL), for emergency financial assistance grants to military personnel and their families, $230,000

REQUIREMENTS AND RESTRICTIONS

No support for food programs or religious instruction. No grants for general operating support, construction or renovation, equipment, or tickets for fund-raising activities.

APPLICATION PROCEDURES

See website for application form and guidelines. If requested to provide a full grant application, a form will be required.

Deadlines: March 1 for preliminary application; June 1 for final application

Johnson, Robert Wood Foundation

Headquarters

College Rd. E. and Rte. 1
PO Box 2316
Princeton, NJ 08543-2316
Phone: 877-843-7953

www.rwjf.org

E-mail: mail@rwjf.org

Type of Grant Maker: Foundation

Description

Founded: 1936

Financial Summary

Assets: $9,199,687,456
Total Giving: $359,172,005
Number of Grants: 1,949
Grant Ranges: $13,168,857–$5,000

Grants Information

GRANT TYPES

Program development, matching, investments and loans, seed money

TYPICAL RECIPIENTS/SUBJECTS OF INTEREST

Foundation focuses on public health, both improving the health of everyone in America and how health care is delivered, paid for, and how well it does for patients and their families. The foundation's program areas are: childhood obesity, coverage, human capital, pioneer, public health, quality/equality, and vulnerable populations.

PAST GRANT RECIPIENTS

Library or School Related

- Alliance for a Healthier Generation, Portland (OR), for Healthy Schools Program to help prevent epidemic of overweight and obesity among students, $23,000,000
- Yale University, New Haven (CT), for research to encourage industry and government action to reduce marketing unhealthy foods to children, $5,000,000

- University of Pennsylvania, Philadelphia (PA), for research toward building a database with the U.S. Army to assess the effects of health assets on illness, $4,000,000
- Robert Wood Johnson University Hospital Foundation, New Brunswick (NJ), for Community Care Coordination Initiative and Health Information Exchange Project, $4,000,000
- Rutgers, The State University of New Jersey, New Brunswick (NJ), for research to serve New Jersey in developing effective health policy, $3,000,000

General

- Project HOPE—The People-to-People Health Foundation, Millwood (VA), for grant to editorial office in Bethesda, MD to publish *Health Affairs,* $5,000,000

REQUIREMENTS AND RESTRICTIONS

Giving limited to the United States. No support for political organizations, international activities, programs or institutions concerned solely with a specific disease or basic biomedical research. No grants to individuals, or for ongoing general operating expenses, endowment funds, capital costs, including construction, renovation, or equipment, or research on unapproved drugs

APPLICATION PROCEDURES

Application Information: Open Calls for Proposals are periodically issues for all program areas. See website. Application forms required.

Deadlines: None

Jones, Dodge Foundation

Headquarters

PO Box 176
Abilene, TX 79604-0176
Phone: 325-673-6429

Contact: Lawrence E. Gill, V.P. and Grants Admin.

Type of Grant Maker: Foundation

Description

Founded: 1954

Operating Locations/Geographic Preferences: Giving primarily in Abilene, TX.

Financial Summary

Assets: $45,159,300
Total Giving: $12,756,250
Number of Grants: 166
Grant Ranges: $2,494,877–$500

Grants Information

GRANT TYPES

General and operating support, program development

TYPICAL RECIPIENTS/SUBJECTS OF INTEREST

Education, the arts, health, community funds, and youth programs.

PAST GRANT RECIPIENTS

Library or School Related

- Abilene Public Library, Abilene (TX), Book and Author Festival, $6,500
- Recording Library of West Texas, Midland (TX), Operating support, $5,000
- Abilene Independent School District, Abilene (TX), for Advanced Placement Incentive Program, $844,000
- Kenley School, Abilene (TX), for scholarship and capital campaign, $260,000
- Saint John's Episcopal School, Abilene (TX), for Learning for a Lifetime Fund, $75,000

General

- United Way of Abilene, Abilene (TX), for annual contribution, $50,000
- Community Foundation of Abilene, Abilene (TX), for scholarship program, $47,000

REQUIREMENTS AND RESTRICTIONS

No grants to individuals

APPLICATION PROCEDURES

Send letter and include:

1. Results expected from proposed grant
2. Statement of problem project will address
3. Detailed description of project and amount of funding requested

Deadlines: None

Jones, Helen Foundation, Inc.

Headquarters

PO Box 53665
Lubbock, TX 79453-3665

Contact: James C. Arnold, Pres.

Type of Grant Maker: Foundation

Description

Founded: 1984

Operating Locations/Geographic Preferences: Giving primarily in Lubbock, TX

Financial Summary

Assets: $140,621,435
Total Giving: $3,631,500
Number of Grants: 75
Grant Ranges: $500,000–$3,500

Grants Information

GRANT TYPES

General and operating support, equipment

TYPICAL RECIPIENTS/SUBJECTS OF INTEREST

Literary and educational purposes, charitable and scientific giving

PAST GRANT RECIPIENTS

Library or School Related

- Texas Tech University, Lubbock (TX), for art building, $600,000
- Lubbock Christian School, Lubbock (TX), for high school computer laboratory, $26,000

General

- American Cancer Society, Lubbock (TX), for Hope Lodge, $500,000
- Louise Hopkins Underwood Center for the Arts, Lubbock (TX), for Helen DeVitt Jones Endowment for Arts Education, $500,000
- YWCA of Lubbock, Lubbock (TX), for Downtown YWCA renovation, $180,000
- Texas Tech University, Lubbock (TX), for piano, $36,000

REQUIREMENTS AND RESTRICTIONS

No support for religious or political organizations. No grants to individuals.

APPLICATION PROCEDURES

Application form required. Applicants should submit:

1. Signature and title of chief executive officer
2. Name, address and phone number of organization
3. Copy of IRS Determination Letter
4. Detailed description of project and amount of funding requested
5. Contact person
6. Copy of current year's organizational budget and/or project budget
7. Copy of most recent annual report/audited financial statement/990

Deadlines: January 1 through April 30

Joyce Foundation

Headquarters

70 W. Madison St., Ste. 2750
Chicago, IL 60602-4344
Phone: 312-782-2464

www.joycefdn.org

Contact: Prog. Staff

E-mail: info@joycefdn.org

Type of Grant Maker: Foundation

Description

Founded: 1948

Operating Locations/Geographic Preferences: Giving primarily in the Great Lakes region, specifically the states of Illinois, Indiana, Michigan, Minnesota, Ohio, and Wisconsin. Some environment grants are made in Canada. Education grant making in K–12 focuses on Chicago, Indianapolis, and Minneapolis. The Employment Program will make some grants to support targeted metro-level progress in Chicago, Indianapolis, and Minneapolis/St. Paul. Culture grants are primarily focused on the Chicago metropolitan area, except for the Joyce Awards, which extend to other Midwest cities.

Financial Summary

Assets: $808,480,401
Total Giving: $33,882,337
Number of Grants: 324
Grant Ranges: $771,800–$1,000

Grants Information

GRANT TYPES

Program development, continuing, general and operating support, matching

TYPICAL RECIPIENTS/SUBJECTS OF INTEREST

Program giving areas include the following.

Culture: To serve Chicago's diverse populations

Education: To close gaps that separate low-income and minority children from their peers. Program priorities are:

1. Teacher Quality
2. Early Reading
3. Innovation Grants for charter schools in Chicago, Indianapolis, and Minneapolis.

Employment: To establish the Midwest as the leader of employment education and training. Priorities include:

1. Basic Foundational Skills
2. Industry Training Partnerships: Target metropolitan regions include Chicago, Indianapolis, and Minneapolis/St. Paul.

Environment: To protect and restore the Great Lakes

Gun Violence: To support local, state, regional, and national projects that:

1. Advance state-based policy advocacy
2. Improve public engagement in support of effective gun violence prevention policies
3. Build effective coalitions to secure support for gun violence prevention policy reform
4. Support Second Amendment legal strategies to uphold effective gun violence prevention
5. Encourage policy-oriented research and data collection

Matching Gifts

Money and Politics: To create political cultures in Illinois, Michigan, Minnesota, Ohio and Wisconsin for citizens to run for public office. Foundation supports organizations and coalitions in the Midwest.

President's Discretionary Fund

Special Opportunities: Providing some grants to projects outside its primary program areas. Preference is given to communications-oriented projects.

PAST GRANT RECIPIENTS

General

- American College of Preventive Medicine, Washington (DC), for education and advocacy campaign to expand National Violent Death Reporting System, $230,000
- Aspen Institute, Washington (DC), for employer community college survey, staffing building, and communications, $200,000
- Center on Budget and Policy Priorities, Washington (DC), for research on policies affecting low-income families, federally and in the Midwest, $200,000
- American Rivers, Washington (DC), for new federal stormwater rule to benefit water quality in the Great Lakes, $75,000
- League of Women Voters of Minnesota Education Fund, Saint Paul (MN), for State of Democracy Program, $75,000

REQUIREMENTS AND RESTRICTIONS

No support for religious activities, or for political organizations. No grants to individuals or for endowment campaigns, scholarships, direct service programs, commercial ventures, or capital proposals.

APPLICATION PROCEDURES

Applicants are encouraged to submit their proposals for the April or July meeting, since most grant funds will be distributed at those times. See website for information.

Deadlines: Letter of inquiry required at least 6 to 8 weeks before proposal deadlines. For formal proposals: December 11 (for April meeting); April 16 (for July meeting); August 15 (for December meeting)

Kansas City Community Foundation, Greater

Headquarters

1055 Broadway, Ste. 130
Kansas City, MO 64105-1595
Phone: 816-842-0944

www.gkccf.org

Contact: Laura McKnight, C.E.O.

E-mail: info@gkccf.org

Type of Grant Maker: Community Foundation

Description

Founded: 1978

Operating Locations/Geographic Preferences: Giving primarily in the bi-state greater Kansas City region

Financial Summary

Assets: $1,189,480,459
Total Giving: $251,886,514

Grants Information

GRANT TYPES

Program development, general and operating, capital campaigns and matching, seed money, investments and loans

TYPICAL RECIPIENTS/SUBJECTS OF INTEREST

Urban and community development, children and youth, arts, life sciences, civil rights, health

PAST GRANT RECIPIENTS

Library or School Related

- Kansas City Public Library, Kansas City (MO), $33,260,000
- Pembroke Hill School, Kansas City (MO), $2,000

General

- Kauffman Center for the Performing Arts, Kansas City (MO), $8,220,800
- Saint Luke's Hospital Foundation, Kansas City (MO), $5,000,000
- United Way of Greater Kansas City, Kansas City (MO), $5,200
- Kansas City Repertory Theater, Kansas City (MO), $3,500

REQUIREMENTS AND RESTRICTIONS

No grants to individuals or for deficit financing, endowments, or annual campaigns

APPLICATION PROCEDURES

See website for application guidelines. Application form required.

Deadlines: Vary

Kansas Health Foundation

Headquarters

309 E. Douglas
Wichita, KS 67202-3405

www.kansashealth.org

Contact: Valerie Black, Comms. Specialist; Chris Power, V.P., Comms.

E-mail: info@khf.org

Type of Grant Maker: Foundation

Description

Founded: 1978

Operating Locations/Geographic Preferences: Giving limited to KS

Financial Summary

Assets: $476,389,532
Total Giving: $16,968,871
Number of Grants: 158

Grants Information

GRANT TYPES

Program development, general, operating and continuing, matching, management development

TYPICAL RECIPIENTS/SUBJECTS OF INTEREST

Foundation gives to health issues as follows:

Promoting Healthy Behaviors

1. Promoting the healthy behaviors of Kansans
2. Strengthening the public health system
3. Improving access to health care for Kansas children
4. Growing community philanthropy
5. Providing health data and information to policymakers
6. Building civic leadership.

Foundational also awards Recognition Grants of up to $25,000 per organization for innovative work that improves the health of Kansans.

PAST GRANT RECIPIENTS

Library or School Related

- Kansas University Endowment Association, Lawrence (KS), to develop minimum of three additional courses offered in Wichita and Kansas City Masters of Public Health program, $622,600
- Kansas University Endowment Association, Lawrence (KS), to design the curriculum for a public health institute, $35,000

General

- Kansas Health Institute, Topeka (KS), for core support, $3,000,000
- Kansas Leadership Center, Wichita (KS), to expand the Leadership and Faith initiative, $546,000
- McPherson County Community Foundation, McPherson (KS), for a matching grant of endowment funds and annual operating funds, $17,500

REQUIREMENTS AND RESTRICTIONS

No support for political campaigns or political advocacy. No grants to individuals or for medical research, deficit or debt retirement, endowments, vehicles, construction projects, or mental or health services.

APPLICATION PROCEDURES

See website for online form.

Deadlines: March 15 and September 15 for Recognition Grants

Kansas Library Association

Headquarters

1020 SW Washburn
Topeka, KS 66604
Phone: 785-580-4518

http://kslibassoc.org/home/foundation-2/grants/

Type of Grant Maker: Library Organization

Grants Information

KLAEF CONTINUING EDUCATION GRANTS

Grant Amounts: $100 for KLA Conference grants, with additional funds available for other CE opportunities.

Number of Grants: 10 conference attendance grants

To provide continuing education grants for members of the Kansas Library Association.

APPLICATION PROCEDURES

See online form. E-mail, fax, or mail completed form to:

George Seamon, Treasurer of KLAEF
Director, Northwest Kansas Library System
#2 Washington Square
Norton, KS 67654
E-mail: nwklsdir@ruraltel.net
Fax: 785-877-5697

Deadlines: October

Kauffman, Ewing Marion Foundation

Headquarters

4801 Rockhill Rd.
Kansas City, MO 64110-2046
Phone: 816-932-1000

www.kauffman.org

Contact: Joy Torchia, Comms. Mgr.

E-mail: info@kauffman.org

Type of Grant Maker: Foundation

Description

Founded: 1966

Operating Locations/Geographic Preferences: Giving limited to the United States, with emphasis on the bi-state metropolitan Kansas City area (KS/MO) for K–12 education initiatives focused on math and science

Financial Summary

Assets: $1,881,375,000
Total Giving: $44,084,000

Grants Information

GRANT TYPES

Program development, general and operating support, matching, investments and loans

TYPICAL RECIPIENTS/SUBJECTS OF INTEREST

To encourage entrepreneurship across America and improve the education of children and youth.

Program areas include:

Advancing Innovation, Education: with an emphasis on delivering high-quality educational opportunities that prepare urban students for success in college and life beyond; and advancing student achievement in science, technology, engineering and math (STEM)

Entrepreneurship: Ewing Marion Kauffman Prize Medal for Distinguished Research in Entrepreneurship, for a scholar under 40 whose research has made a significant contribution to the literature in entrepreneurship

Ewing Marion Kauffman School: a new public charter school

Junior Faculty Fellowship in Entrepreneurship Research

Kauffman Dissertation Fellowship

Research and Policy: for research contributing to a broader and more in-depth understanding of what drives innovation and economic growth in an entrepreneurial world

PAST GRANT RECIPIENTS

Library or School Related

- Ewing Marion Kauffman School, Kansas City (MO), for Ewing Marion Kauffman School to develop, manage, and operate charter schools of excellence, $10,000,000
- George Washington University, for Financing Innovation Conference in Washington, DC, $35,000

General

- Public Forum Institute, Washington (DC), for Global Entrepreneurship Week series of activities, $3,300,000
- Urban Entrepreneur Partnership, Kansas City (MO), for Urban Entrepreneur Partnership, Inc.'s minority entrepreneurship efforts, $2,900,000
- Chamber of Commerce of Greater Kansas City, Kansas City (MO), for studies on teacher quality in Kansas City, Missouri, $12,000
- Boys and Girls Clubs of Greater Kansas City, Kansas City (MO), for 6th Annual Baseball benefit in Kansas City, Missouri, $4,700

REQUIREMENTS AND RESTRICTIONS

No support for international programs, political, social, fraternal, or arts organizations, and capital campaigns or construction projects. No grants for fund endowments, or for special events.

APPLICATION PROCEDURES

See website to request Guidelines for Grantseekers brochure. Applicants will be asked to submit:

1. Timetable for implementation and evaluation of project
2. Results expected from proposed grant
3. Statement of problem project will address

4. Explanation of why grant maker is considered an appropriate donor for project
5. Detailed description of project and amount of funding requested

Deadlines: None

Keats, Ezra Jack Foundation, Inc.

Headquarters

450 14th St.
Brooklyn, NY 11215-5702
www.ezra-jack-keats.org
Contact: Deborah Pope, V.P.
E-mail: foundation@ezra-jack-keats.org
Type of Grant Maker: Foundation

Description

Founded: 1964
Operating Locations/Geographic Preferences: National giving

Financial Summary

Assets: $0
Total Giving: $65,594

Grants Information

GRANT TYPES

Programs and events

TYPICAL RECIPIENTS/SUBJECTS OF INTEREST

Mini-grants of $500 are given to public schools and public libraries for projects that foster creative expression, working together and interaction with a diverse community.

PAST GRANT RECIPIENTS

N/A

REQUIREMENTS AND RESTRICTIONS

No grants to individuals.

APPLICATION PROCEDURES

Online form required for the mini-grant application. Applicants are invited to:

- Watch a video tutorial hosted by Executive Director Deborah Pope, with links to individual topics
- Read detailed instructions for following the application process
- Fill out the application form

Deadlines: September 15

Kellogg, W. K. Foundation

Headquarters

1 Michigan Ave. E.
Battle Creek, MI 49017-4005
Phone: 269-968-1611
www.wkkf.org
Type of Grant Maker: Foundation

Description

Founded: 1930
Operating Locations/Geographic Preferences: Giving primarily in the United States, with emphases on Michigan, Mississippi, New Mexico and New Orleans, LA. Also funds programs in Mexico, Haiti, northeast Brazil and southern Africa

Financial Summary

Assets: $7,696,627,040
Total Giving: $291,212,363

Grants Information

GRANT TYPES

Program development, matching, investments and loans, seed money

TYPICAL GRANT RECIPIENTS/ SUBJECTS OF INTEREST

Children, family and communities
   Three major goals include:

1. Educated kids: increasing the number of children who are reading-and-math proficient by third grade

2. Healthy Kids: increasing the number of children born at a healthy birth weight and who receive care and healthy food
3. Secure Families: increasing the number of children and families living at least 200 percent above the poverty level

Programs include:

- Community and Civic Engagement
- Education and Learning
- Employee Matching
- Family Economic Security
- Food, Health and Well-Being
- International
- Racial Equity

PAST GRANT RECIPIENTS

General

- Detroit Hispanic Development Corporation, Detroit (MI), to improve educational, financial and health outcomes for children in southwest Detroit by improving mothers' financial literacy and education, $238,000
- Hispanics in Philanthropy, San Francisco (CA), for general operating support, $1,400,000
- Pacific News Service, San Francisco (CA), to expand and develop culturally ethnic media's editorial collaboration, $400,000
- Albuquerque Partnership for Community Economic Development, Albuquerque (NM), for early learning and childhood development for New Mexican children, $300,000

REQUIREMENTS AND RESTRICTIONS

No support for religious purposes or for capital facilities. No grants to individuals, or for scholarships, endowment funds, development campaigns, films, equipment, publications, conferences, or radio and television programs, no grants for operating budgets

APPLICATION PROCEDURES

Online application required. See details online.

Deadlines: None

Kemper, William T. Foundation

Headquarters

c/o Commerce Bank
118 W. 47th St.
Kansas City, MO 64112-1692
Phone: 816-234-2568

Type of Grant Maker: Foundation

Description

Founded: 1989

Operating Locations/Geographic Preferences: Giving primarily in the Midwest with emphasis on MO and surrounding areas

Financial Summary

Assets: $239,273,880
Total Giving: $9,673,998
Number of Grants 262
Grant Ranges: $500,000–$500; average: $5,000–$100,000

Grants Information

GRANT TYPES

Program development, seed money, continuing, general and operating support, capital campaigns, building and renovations

TYPICAL RECIPIENTS/SUBJECTS OF INTEREST

Education, health, human services, civic improvements and the arts

PAST GRANT RECIPIENTS

Library or School Related

- Pembroke Hill School, Kansas City (MO), $1,000,000

General

- Nelson Gallery Foundation, Kansas City (MO), $1,000,000
- Missouri Botanical Garden, Saint Louis (MO), $450,000
- Salvation Army of Saint Louis, Saint Louis (MO), $150,000
- Mid-America Regional Council Community Services Corporation, Kansas City (MO), for arts and other programs, $12,000

- Wichita TOP Children's Fund, Wichita (KS), $15,000
- EnergyCare, Saint Louis (MO), $12,500

REQUIREMENTS AND RESTRICTIONS

No support for private foundations or for political purposes. No grants to individuals, or for tickets for dinners, benefits, exhibits, sports and other event activities, advertisements, endowment funds, or fund-raising activities

APPLICATION PROCEDURES

Application guidelines available upon request

Deadlines: Three weeks before board meetings

Kentucky Department for Libraries and Archives

Headquarters

PO Box 537
300 Coffee Tree Road
Frankfort, KY 40602-0537
Phone: 502-564-8300
http://kdla.ky.gov/librarians/funding/Pages/2012%20
    Library%20Grants.aspx

Type of Grant Maker: Government

Grants Information

SUMMER READING/SUMMER FOOD SERVICES PROGRAM

Program Description: To expand summer reading programs in conjunction with the Summer Food Service Program. These grant funds can be used to hire staff to manage the library's participation in the Summer Food Service Program as either a Sponsor or a Site, to extend and/or expand the duration of the Summer Reading Program (SRP), to expand the number of age-appropriate programs and ultimately to increase the number of children participating in SRP.

REQUIREMENTS AND RESTRICTIONS

Public libraries which meet the following requirements are eligible to submit an application.

- Have a legally established public library
- Have a library director who is properly certified by the Kentucky Board for Certification of Librarians
- Provide free countywide library services, without discrimination

APPLICATION PROCEDURES

See online forms.

Deadlines: April

KeyBank Foundation

Headquarters

800 Superior Ave., 1st Fl.
M.C. OH-01-02-0126
Cleveland, OH 44114-2601
Phone: 216-828-7349
www.key.com/html/A-12.html

Contact: Valerie Raines, Sr. Prog. Off.

E-mail: key_foundation@keybank.com

Type of Grant Maker: Corporate Foundation

Description

Founded: 1969

Operating Locations/Geographic Preferences: Giving primarily in areas of company operations in AK, CO, ID, IN, KY (ME), MI (NY) (OH), OR, UT, VT, and WA and national organizations

Corporate Foundation Information: Established by

- Society Corp
- Society Capital Corp.
- KeyBank N.A.
- KeyCorp

Financial Summary

Assets: $35,834,515
Total Giving: $12,792,969
Number of Grants: 1,876
Grant Ranges: $1,100,000–$250

Grants Information

GRANT TYPES

Program development, general, operating and continuing support, employee matching and volunteering, capital and annual campaigns

TYPICAL RECIPIENTS/SUBJECTS OF INTEREST

Arts and culture, education, health, human services, and civic affairs

Special emphasis on economic self-sufficiency through financial education, workforce development, and diversity

Giving programs include:

Community Leadership Grant Program

Diversity—with special emphasis on programs to provide vocational training and job placement for people with disabilities, and school-to-work readiness initiatives for underrepresented college students

Financial Education—with emphasis on educating people to access and manage financial resources effectively and foster savings and investments for low- and moderate-income people

Workforce Development—especially programs to foster career exploration, training, and placement and small business development

PAST GRANT RECIPIENTS

Library or School Related

- Ohio State University Foundation, Columbus (OH), for program support, $170,000
- University of Notre Dame, Notre Dame (IN), for operating support, $20,000

General

- Musical Arts Association, Cleveland (OH), for program support, $250,000
- Economic Growth Foundation, Cleveland (OH), $200,000
- YMCA of Greater Cleveland, Cleveland (OH), for program support, $50,000
- United Way of Greater Cleveland, Cleveland (OH), for program support, $15,000

REQUIREMENTS AND RESTRICTIONS

No support for lobbying or political organizations, veterans' or fraternal organizations, discriminatory organizations, professional organizations, or athletic teams. No grants to individuals, or for memberships or advertising.

APPLICATION PROCEDURES

See website for nearest company district office. Full proposals must include a proposal summary form.

Deadlines: None

Kids In Need Foundation

Headquarters

3055 Kettering Blvd., Suite 119

Dayton, OH 45439
825 Nicollet Mall, Suite 909
Minneapolis, MN 55402
Phone: 937-296-1230

www.kinf.org

E-mail: info@kinf.org

Type of Grant Maker: Foundation

Financial Summary

Number of Grants: 600
Grant Ranges: $500–$100

Grants Information

Teacher Grant awards are used to finance creative classroom projects. The number of grants awarded varies from year to year, depending on the amount of the funds being requested.

Sponsored by Jo-Ann Fabric and Craft Stores, Fred Meyer, and Via Credit Union. The program funds projects, not programs. Projects are usually not more than a few weeks long at the most and have a beginning, middle, and end.

REQUIREMENTS AND RESTRICTIONS

All certified K–12 teachers in the U.S. are eligible

APPLICATION PROCEDURES AND DEADLINES

Retail sponsors and designated education credit unions make the grant applications available at their outlets during the back-to-school season and online.

King, Carl B. and Florence E. Foundation

Headquarters

2301 Cedar Springs Rd., Ste. 330
Dallas, TX 75201-7886
Phone: 214-750-1884

www.kingfoundation.com

Contact: Michelle D. Monse, Pres.

E-mail: michellemonse@kingfoundation.com

Type of Grant Maker: Foundation

Description

Founded: 1966

Operating Locations/Geographic Preferences: Giving in eastern and southern AR and in the Dallas-Fort Worth, TX, area, and West TX

Financial Summary

Assets: $57,738,901
Total Giving: $2,120,509
Number of Grants: 94
Grant Ranges: $100,000–$1,750

Grants Information

GRANT TYPES

Program development, management development, building and renovation, capital campaigns

TYPICAL RECIPIENTS/SUBJECTS OF INTEREST

Education, aging, arts, culture, history, children and youth, economically disadvantaged and nonprofit organizational development

PAST GRANT RECIPIENTS

Library or School Related

- Jeff Davis County Library, Friends of the, fort Davis (TX), for Library Terrace Project, $20,000

General

- Southern Bancorp Capital Partners, Arkadelphia (AR), for strategic planning $250,000
- CitySquare, Dallas (TX), for the Community Health Services program for uninsured individuals, $36,000
- Southern Bancorp Capital Partners, Arkadelphia (AR), to develop educational content around Civil War Helena historic sites, $35,000
- Ronald McDonald House Charities of Lubbock, Lubbock (TX), for program support for the Ronald McDonald Care Mobile, $30,000
- Meals on Wheels of Tarrant County, fort Worth (TX), for program support, $25,000

REQUIREMENTS AND RESTRICTIONS

No support for religious organizations, or to nonexempt organizations. No grants to individuals directly, or for construction of churches or seminaries, or for religious programs or for ongoing operating expenses or funds to offset operating losses. No grants for loan financing; endowments; professional conferences or symposia; or balls, events, or for galas benefiting charitable organizations

APPLICATION PROCEDURES

Application information available on website. Submit letter of inquiry first. Contact foundation for requirements.

Deadlines: June 15 for letters of inquiry

King, Stephen and Tabitha Foundation, Inc.

Headquarters

PO Box 855
Bangor, ME 04402-0855
Phone: 207-990-2910

www.stkfoundation.org

Contact: Stephanie Leonard, Admin.

E-mail: info@stkfoundation.org

Type of Grant Maker: Foundation

Description

Founded: 1986

Operating Locations/Geographic Preferences: Giving limited to ME

Financial Summary

Assets: $1,639,152
Total Giving: $3,009,686
Number of Grants: 147
Grant Ranges: $150,000–$250

Grants Information

GRANT TYPES

Program development, seed money, building and renovation, general and operating support, land acquisition, matching, endowments

TYPICAL RECIPIENTS/SUBJECTS OF INTEREST

Giving primarily to education—including libraries, the arts, and human services

PAST GRANT RECIPIENTS

Library or School Related

- Bangor Public Library, Bangor (ME), $56,000
- Peninsula CSD School, Winter Harbor, $20,000

General

- American Red Cross, Bangor (ME), $150,000
- Penobscot Theater Company, Bangor (ME), $100,000
- Mabel Wadsworth Women's Health Center, Bangor (ME), $75,000
- Osborn Municipal Volunteer Fire Department, Osborn (ME), $50,000
- Lebanon Volunteer Rescue Department, Lebanon (ME), $30,000
- CARES, Winthrop (ME), $25,000

REQUIREMENTS AND RESTRICTIONS

Any renovations to historical society property must be connected to a library. No support for hospice programs, animal shelters/hospitals or rehabilitation centers. No grants to individuals or events, renovations to churches or other religious properties or institutions, or for film or video productions, transportation, book or publishing projects, conferences, meetings, exhibits, or workshops, no wheelchair vans. No organizations whose policies encourage discrimination. No research or loans.

APPLICATION PROCEDURES

See website for application guidelines.

Deadlines: December 31 and June 30

Kirby, F. M. Foundation, Inc.

Headquarters

17 DeHart St.
PO Box 151
Morristown, NJ 07963-0151
Phone: 973-538-4800

www.fmkirbyfoundation.org

Contact: William H. Byrnes, Jr., V.P., Grants

Type of Grant Maker: Foundation

Description

Founded: 1931

Operating Locations/Geographic Preferences: Giving primarily in the Raleigh/Durham, NC, area, the Morris County NJ, area, and eastern PA

Financial Summary

Assets: $434,823,954
Total Giving: $18,142,166
Number of Grants: 318
Grant Ranges: $770,000–$2,500

Grants Information

GRANT TYPES

Program development, building and renovations, capital and annual campaigns, continuing, general and operating support, endowments, land acquisition

TYPICAL RECIPIENTS/SUBJECTS OF INTEREST

Education organizations, community programs, the arts, historic preservation, social services, conservation, public policy and family planning

PAST GRANT RECIPIENTS

Library or School Related

- Lawrenceville School, Lawrenceville (NJ), to establish the Kirby Landscaping Endowment Fund, $350,000
- Wyoming Seminary, Kingston (PA), for creation and construction of the Allan P. and Marian Sutherland Kirby Center for Creative Arts, $250,000
- Peck School, Morristown (NJ), for the Annual Giving Fund, $25,000
- Albert Einstein College of Medicine of Yeshiva University, Bronx (NY), to establish the F.M. Kirby Chair in Neural Repair and Protection, $666,666
- New York University, New York (NY), for continued support of ischemic stroke research, $100,000

General

- Intercollegiate Studies Institute, Wilmington (DE), for Center for the Study of American Civic Literacy and general operating support, $180,000
- American Red Cross, Washington (NC), for Disaster Relief Fund, $500,000

REQUIREMENTS AND RESTRICTIONS

No support for churches other than ones attended by or used by members of the family. No grants to individuals, or for fund-raising benefits, dinners, theater, or sporting events; no loans or pledges

APPLICATION PROCEDURES

Begin requests with a letter of inquiry. Application form not required, but applicants should include:

1. Signature and title of chief executive officer
2. Copy of IRS Determination Letter
3. Copy of most recent annual report/audited financial statement/990

4. Listing of board of directors, trustees, officers and other key people and their affiliations

5. Detailed description of project and amount of funding requested

6. Copy of current year's organizational budget and/or project budget

Deadlines: None

Klingenstein, Esther A. & Joseph Fund, Inc.

Headquarters

787 7th Ave., 6th Fl.
New York, NY 10019-6016
Phone: 212-492-6181

www.klingfund.org

Contact: John Klingenstein, Pres.; Kathleen Pomerantz

E-mail: kathleen.pomerantz@klingenstein.com

Type of Grant Maker: Foundation

Description

Founded: 1945

Operating Locations/Geographic Preferences: Giving primarily in NY

Financial Summary

Assets: $73,237,833
Total Giving: $41,801,110
Number of Grants: 73
Grant Ranges: $36,286,920–$1,000

Grants Information

GRANT TYPES

Program development, general, operating and continuing support, seed money

TYPICAL RECIPIENTS/SUBJECTS OF INTEREST

Epilepsy neuroscientific research and independent school education. Some support also for the use of animals in biomedical research and church and state separation.

Foundation supports Klingenstein Fellowship Awards in the Neurosciences

PAST GRANT RECIPIENTS

Library or School Related

• New York Public Library, New York (NY), $500,000
• Teachers College Columbia University, New York (NY), $830,000
• Duke University Medical Center, Durham (NC), $55,000
• New York University, New York (NY), $50,000

General

• National Association of Independent Schools, Washington (DC), $73,000
• Mount Sinai Medical Center, New York (NY), for general support, $36,280,000
• Jewish Home Lifecare, New York (NY), $666,666

REQUIREMENTS OR RESTRICTIONS

No grants to individuals or for building or endowment funds

APPLICATION PROCEDURES

See website for applicant information.

Deadlines: None

Knapp Foundation, Inc.

Headquarters

PO Box O
St. Michaels, MD 21663-0450

Contact: Antoinette P. Vojvoda, Pres.

Type of Grant Maker: Foundation

Description

Founded: 1929

Operating Locations/Geographic Preferences: Giving limited to the United States, primarily in the eastern region, including CT, DE, FL, GA, MA, MD, ME, NC, NH, NJ, NY, PA, RI, SC, VA, and VT.

Financial Summary

Assets: $18,357,543
Total Giving: $253,195
Nubmer of Grants: 19
Grant Ranges: $56,380–$1,000

Grants Information

GRANT TYPES

Equipment and matching

TYPICAL RECIPIENTS/SUBJECTS OF INTEREST

Conservation and preservation of wildlife and wildfowl and assistance to college and university libraries in the purchasing of reading materials and equipment to improve education

PAST GRANT RECIPIENTS

Library or School Related

- New York University Libraries, New York (NY), Audio-visual materials, $24,642
- Framingham State College Library, Framingham (MA), Library acquisitions, 417,930
- Wilkes University Library, Wilkes-Barre (PA), Library acquisitions, $10,000
- Marlboro College Library, Marlboro (VT), Library acquisitions, $16,125
- New England College Library, Henniker (NH), Library acquisitions, $7,250
- Goldey-Beacom College Library, Wilmington (DE), Library acquisitions, $10,000

General

- Recording for Blind & Dyslexic Education, Princeton (NJ), Library materials, $10,000
- Amer. Foundation for the Blind, New York (NY), Library, $10,000

REQUIREMENTS AND RESTRICTIONS

No support for foreign projects or for political organizations, religious organizations or local area land trusts. No grants to individuals, or for endowment or building funds, operating budgets, or research.

APPLICATION PROCEDURES

Send detailed letter.

Deadlines: None

Knight, John S. and James L. Foundation

Headquarters

Wachovia Financial Ctr., Ste. 3300
200 S. Biscayne Blvd.
Miami, FL 33131-2349
Phone: 305-908-2600
Fax: 305-908-2698

www.knightfoundation.org

Contact: Grant Admin.

E-mail: web@knightfoundation.org

Type of Grant Maker: Foundation

Description

Founded: 1950

Operating Locations/Geographic Preferences: Giving limited to projects serving the 26 communities where the Knight brothers published newspapers for communities and local grants: Long Beach and San Jose, CA, Boulder, CO, Bradenton, Miami, Palm Beach County, and Tallahassee, FL, Columbus, Macon, and Milledgeville, GA, fort Wayne and Gary, IN, Wichita, KS, Lexington, KY, Detroit, MI, Duluth and St. Paul, MN, Biloxi, MS, Charlotte, NC, Grand Forks, ND, Akron, OH, Philadelphia and State College, PA, Columbia and Myrtle Beach, SC, and Aberdeen, SD; international giving for Journalism.

Financial Summary

Assets: $2,090,000,000
Total Giving: $97,289,233
Number of Grants: 497

Grants Information

GRANT TYPES

Program development, seed money, technical assistance, building and renovation, capital campaigns, matching, endowments, management development, investments and loans

TYPICAL RECIPIENTS/SUBJECTS OF INTEREST

Supports transformational ideas that promote quality journalism, advance media innovation, engage communities and foster the arts

PAST GRANT RECIPIENTS

Library or School Related

- Akron-Summit County Public Library, Akron (OH), for job training via mobile computer labs, $50,000
- Columbia Graduate School Low Library, New York (NY), for Journalism Studies Initiative, $140,000
- Muscogee County School District, Columbus (CA), for high-tech mobile information center, $285,400
- Stow-Munroe Falls Public Library, Stow (OH), for access to internet information, digital literacy training, $106,661
- Free Library of Philadelphia (PA), to expand access to broadband and digital literacy, $386,264
- Friends of the Saint Paul Public, St. Paul (MN), for access to job search assistance, $125,000

General

- Andreas H BechtlerArts Foundation, Carlotte (NC), for digital library of works in the Bechtler family, $107,500

REQUIREMENTS AND RESTRICTIONS

No support for organizations whose mission is to prevent, eradicate and/or alleviate the effects of a specific disease; hospitals, unless for community-wide capital campaigns; activities to propagate a religious faith or restricted to one religion or denomination; political candidates; international programs, except U.S.-based organizations supporting free press around the world; charities operated by service clubs; or activities that are the responsibility of government (the foundation will, in selective cases, join with units of government in supporting special projects). No grants to individuals, or for fund-raising events; second requests for previously funded capital campaigns; operating deficits; general operating support; films, videos, or television programs; honoraria for distinguished guest, except in initiatives of the foundation in all three cases; group travel; memorials; medical research; or conferences.

APPLICATION PROCEDURE AND DEADLINES

Start process online. Knight Foundation provides multiple opportunities to apply for funding. The most common process requires submitting an online letter of inquiry and proposal. These requests are reviewed throughout the year. In addition, Knight Foundation has other funding opportunities called challenges. Operated like contests, the challenges solicit applications within certain time frames. Please review the Funding Opportunities section for details. Knight Foundation awards the majority of its grants to tax-exempt public agencies, universities and public charities. In addition, a small percentage of grants go to individuals and for-profit organizations for work that is charitable or otherwise exempt under section 501(c)(3) of the federal internal revenue code. Knight Foundation does not fund scholarships, give support to start a for-profit business or to pay off debt expenses. In addition, the foundation does not support political activities or attempts to influence specific legislation.

Online Letter of Inquiry. The first step in submitting a funding request is to use our online letter of inquiry (LOI) system. We will send you an acknowledgment that your LOI was received, and will direct it to our appropriate program staff members for review. Keep in mind that you will not be able to save your work. We recommend that you edit your inquiry offline, then paste it in the form. You will have about 5,000 characters (~2 pages) to describe your project. Wait for feedback from program staff. We will notify you by e-mail if we are interested in your request or if we are not interested in funding. If we are interested in your LOI, you will be asked to submit a full proposal.

Submission of a full proposal. If we are interested in a full proposal we will contact you via e-mail with a link to the proposal form. Materials submitted in the proposal process become the property of Knight Foundation and won't be returned; they'll be used as the foundation deems appropriate. They are not subject to any right of confidentiality unless specifically agreed to in writing by Knight Foundation.

Proposal review and funding determination. The proposal review process includes review by program staff including program officers, directors, vice presidents, the President and Board of Trustees. The time frame varies depending on the size and scope of the proposal. Our program staff will be in contact with you during this process and will notify you of the final decision.

Knight Foundation is under no obligation to fund or otherwise have a future relationship with the applicant. If it does choose to have a relationship, Knight Foundation may suggest various kinds of relationships, including contracts, grants, loans, program-related investments, or other kinds of investments and relationships.

Koret Foundation

Headquarters

33 New Montgomery St., Ste. 1090
San Francisco, CA 94105-4526

www.koretfoundation.org

Contact: Susan Wolfe, Dir., Grant-making Progs. and Comms.

E-mail: info@koretfoundation.org

Type of Grant Maker: Foundation

Description

Founded: 1979

Operating Locations/Geographic Preferences: Giving limited to the Bay Area counties of San Francisco, Alameda, Contra Costa, Marin, Santa Clara, and San Mateo, CA; giving also in Israel and on a national basis for Jewish funding requests

Financial Summary

Assets: $444,724,401
Total Giving: $22,128,614
Number of Grants: 448
Grant Ranges: $2,250,000–$500; average: $10,000–$600,000

Grants Information

GRANT TYPES

Program development, general, operating and continuing support, matching, management development, annual campaigns

TYPICAL RECIPIENTS/SUBJECTS OF INTEREST

Arts/culture and civic institutions, K–12 education reform, Israel advocacy and Jewish community organizations.

Bay Area General Community giving focuses on development and support of K–12 education reform, higher education, arts, culture and civic institutions.
Education funding supports reform of K–12 public education through public policy change and support of programs that provide models of excellence.

Higher Education funds Jewish studies and public policy development.

PAST GRANT RECIPIENTS

Library or School Related

- Santa Clara University, Santa Clara (CA), for Capital Support, $500,000
- Jewish Theological Seminary of America, New York (NY), for Faculty Leadership Development Program, $20,000
- Stanford University, Stanford (CA), for Koret-Taube Task Force on National Security and Law, $525,000
- Stanford University, Stanford (CA), for Koret Task Force on K–12 Education, $525,000

General

- Jewish Family and Children's Services, San Francisco (CA), for Jewish Emergency Assistance Network, $1,000,000

- Contemporary Jewish Museum, San Francisco (CA), for General Operating Support, $500,000
- National Jewish Theater Foundation, Coral Gables (FL), for General Operating Support, $20,000

REQUIREMENTS AND RESTRICTIONS

No support for private foundations, or veterans', fraternal, military, religious, or sectarian organizations. No grants to individuals, or for endowment funds or deficit financing.

APPLICATION PROCEDURES

See foundation website for guidelines and letter of inquiry information.
  Applicants should submit:

1. Timetable for implementation and evaluation of project
2. Population served
3. Copy of IRS Determination Letter
4. Geographic area to be served
5. Copy of most recent annual report/audited financial statement/990
6. How project's results will be evaluated or measured
7. Descriptive literature about organization
8. Listing of board of directors, trustees, officers and other key people and their affiliations
9. Detailed description of project and amount of funding requested
10. Copy of current year's organizational budget and/or project budget

Deadlines: None

Kresge Foundation

Headquarters

3215 W. Big Beaver Rd.
Troy, MI 48084-2818
Phone: 248-643-9630

www.kresge.org

Contact: Rip Rapson, C.E.O. and Pres.

E-mail: info@kresge.org

Type of Grant Maker: Foundation

Description

Founded: 1924

Operating Locations/Geographic Preferences: Giving on a national basis with emphasis on Detroit, MI, as well as some international funding

Financial Summary

Assets: $3,293,222,730
Total Giving: $235,702,000

Grants Information

GRANT TYPES

Building and renovation, capital campaigns, matching, land acquisition, investments and loans

TYPICAL RECIPIENTS/SUBJECTS OF INTEREST

Grants are awarded to nonprofit organizations in education, health and long-term care, human services, arts and humanities, public affairs, and science, nature, and the environment.

Program giving areas include the following.

Arts and Culture

1. Institutional Capitalization
2. Artists' Support Services
3. Arts and Community Building—integrating arts and culture into effective community-building efforts by strengthening the role cultural organizations, artists and creative industries play in community revitalization.

See website for additional guidelines and eligibility requirements.

Challenge Grants

Community Development

Detroit Initiative

Education

1. Pathways for students
2. Strengthening institutions
3. Higher education productivity

Employee Matching Gifts

Environment

1. Energy
2. Renewable Energy
3. Adaptation to Climate Change
4. Special

Health

South Africa Initiative

PAST GRANT RECIPIENTS

Library or School Related

- Wayne State University, Detroit (MI), for Detroit Revitalization Fellows Program, $2,000,000
- Detroit Institute of Arts, Detroit (MI), for sustainability support, $4,000,000

General

- United Negro College Fund, Fairfax (VA), for Transforming Fund-raising at HBCUs: The HBCU Institutional Advancement Program, $1,400,000
- College for Creative Studies, Detroit (MI), for video documentation of project entitled Kresge Arts in Detroit, $150,000

REQUIREMENTS AND RESTRICTIONS

No support for religious organizations, private foundations, or elementary and secondary schools. No grants to individuals, or for debt retirement, projects that are already substantially completed, minor equipment purchases, or for constructing buildings for worship services.

APPLICATION PROCEDURES

See website for application information.

Deadlines: None

Kress, Samuel H. Foundation

Headquarters

174 E. 80th St.
New York, NY 10075-0439
Phone: 212-861-4993

www.kressfoundation.org

Contact: Wyman Meers, Prog. Admin.

E-mail: wyman.meers@kressfoundation.org

Type of Grant Maker: Foundation

Description

Founded: 1929

Operating Locations/Geographic Preferences: Giving primarily in the United States and Europe

Financial Summary

Assets: $79,955,372
Total Giving: $4,267,221
Number of Grants; 198
Grant Ranges: $250,000–$25

Grants Information

GRANT TYPES

Matching, internships, conferences

TYPICAL RECIPIENTS/SUBJECTS OF INTEREST

Art and art history and conservation, including the following programs.

1. fellowships for pre-doctoral research in art history
2. advanced training and research in conservation of works of art
3. development of scholarly resources in the fields of art history and conservation
4. conservation and restoration of monuments in Europe
5. related projects

Giving programs include:

Conservation Fellowships

Conservation Grants Program—providing grants to projects that create and disseminate specialized knowledge, including archival projects, development and dissemination of scholarly databases, documentation projects, exhibitions and publications focusing on art conservation, scholarly publications, and technical and scientific studies. See foundation website for complete guidelines.

Digital Resources—supporting the creation of important online resources in art history, including both textual and visual resources. Key interests include digitization of core art history photographic archives and primary textual sources. The program further supports efforts to integrate new technologies into the practice of art history, including classroom applications and online publishing.

History of Art Grants Program

Institutional Fellowships in the History of Art

Interpretive Fellowships at Art Museums

Responsive Fellowships

Travel Fellowships in the History of Art

PAST GRANT RECIPIENTS

Library or School Related

- University of Virginia, Charlottesville (VA), for Digital Resources Grant in the History of Art, $165,000
- New York University, New York (NY), for Conservation Fellowship, $145,000
- Smith College, Northampton (MA), for Interpretive Fellowship, $19,500

General

- National Gallery of Art, Washington (DC), for Digital Resources Grant in the History of Art, $150,000
- Smithsonian Institution, Washington (DC), for Digital Resources Grant in the History of Art, $100,000

REQUIREMENTS AND RESTRICTIONS

No support for art history programs below the pre-doctoral level, or the purchase of works of art. No grants for living artists, or for operating budgets, continuing support, annual campaigns, endowments, deficit financing, capital funds, exhibitions, or films or loans.

APPLICATION PROCEDURES

See website. Application form not required. Applicants should submit the following:

1. Copy of IRS Determination Letter
2. Detailed description of project and amount of funding requested
3. Copy of current year's organizational budget and/or project budget

Deadlines: Differ according to programs

Kroger Co. Foundation

Headquarters

1014 Vine St.
Cincinnati, OH 45202-1148
Phone: 513-762-4449, ext. 3
www.thekrogerco.com/community/kroger-foundation/
Contact: Lynn Marmer, Pres.
Type of Grant Maker: Corporate Foundation

Description

Founded: 1987

Operating Locations/Geographic Preferences: Giving primarily in areas of company operations in AL, AR, AZ, CA, CO, GA, IL, IN, KS, KY, MI, MS, NV, OH, OR, TN, TX, UT, VA, WA, and WV

Corporate Foundation Information: Foundation of the Kroger Co.

Financial Summary

Assets: $38,551,864
Total Giving: $8,625,093
Number of Grants: 1,409
Grant Ranges: $385,936–$100

Grants Information

GRANT TYPES

Program development, seed money, capital campaigns, employee volunteers

TYPICAL RECIPIENTS/SUBJECTS OF INTEREST

Education, women's health, breast cancer, hunger, minorities, and women

PAST GRANT RECIPIENTS

General

- American Red Cross National Headquarters, Washington (DC), $385,900
- Oregon Museum of Science and Industry, Portland (OR), $125,000
- Oregon Food Bank, Portland (OR), $94,000
- Homeboy Industries, Los Angeles (CA), $50,000
- Crayons to Computers, Cincinnati (OH), $3,888

REQUIREMENTS AND RESTRICTIONS

No support for national or international organizations, non-educational foundations, medical research organizations, or religious organizations or institutions not of direct benefit to the entire community. No grants to individuals, or for conventions or conferences, dinners or luncheons, endowments, general operating support, sports event sponsorships, program advertisements, or membership dues.

APPLICATION PROCEDURES

See website for company division addresses. Application form not required. Applicants should submit to the nearest company divisions:

1. Copy of IRS Determination Letter
2. Detailed description of project and amount of funding requested

Deadlines: None

Kronkosky, Albert & Bessie Mae Charitable Foundation

Headquarters

112 E. Pecan, Ste. 830
San Antonio, TX 78205-1574
Phone: 210- 475-9000
www.kronkosky.org
Contact: Palmer Moe, Managing Dir.
E-mail: kronfndn@kronkosky.org
Type of Grant Maker: Foundation

Description

Founded: 1991
Operating Locations/Geographic Preferences: Giving limited to Bandera, Bexar, Comal, and Kendall counties, TX

Financial Summary

Assets: $334,843,062
Total Giving: $9,461,291
Number of Grants: 138
Grant Ranges: $500,000–$1,750

Grants Information

GRANT TYPES

Program development, building and renovation, general, operating and continuing support, matching, seed money, land acquisition, management development

TYPICAL RECIPIENTS/SUBJECTS OF INTEREST

Culture

1. to foster meaningful cultural activities and broaden public participation
2. to expand or improve the public use of information and learning available through museums and libraries

Health and Human Services

Precious Minds, New Connections—to maximize children's early development

PAST GRANT RECIPIENTS

General

- Haven for Hope of Bexar County, San Antonio (TX), $500,000
- Autism Community Network, San Antonio (TX), for operating support, $400,000
- Christian Senior Services, San Antonio (TX), for Meals on Wheels, $300,000
- Jump Start Performance Company, San Antonio (TX), for Healing Arts, $50,000
- San Antonio Family Endeavors, San Antonio (TX), $50,000
- San Antonio Opera, San Antonio (TX), for Operations, $50,000

REQUIREMENTS AND RESTRICTIONS

No support for religious or political activities, private or public education, or for economic development. No grants to individuals, scholarships, capital grants annual funds, or for galas and other events.

APPLICATION INFORMATION

Nonprofit organizations must register with GuideStar Exchange Program Members, a free service of GuideStar (www.guidestar.org). See website for details and application forms

Deadlines: see website

Lannan Foundation

Headquarters

313 Read St.
Santa Fe, NM 87501-2628
Phone: 505-986-8160

www.lannan.org

Contact: Ruth Simms, Cont.

E-mail: info@lannan.org

Type of Grant Maker: Foundation

Description

Founded: 1960

Operating Locations/Geographic Preferences: Giving on a national basis

Financial Summary

Assets: $207,627,264
Total Giving: $5,524,602
Number of Grants: 151
Grant Ranges: $750,000–$50

Grants Information

GRANT TYPES

General and operating support, building and renovation, land acquisition, matching, investments and loans, endowment

TYPICAL RECIPIENTS/SUBJECTS OF INTEREST

Funding provided in the areas of contemporary visual art, literature, indigenous communities, and issues of cultural freedom
   Giving programs include:

Art Program—for contemporary art, including acquisitions and exhibition program

Cultural Freedom Program—Applications and nominations for cultural freedom awards or fellowships are not accepted.

Indigenous Communities Program—Applications are accepted only from new grant requests from United States Federally recognized tribes

Literary Program

Readings and Conversations Program

Residency Program—Unsolicited applications are not accepted

PAST GRANT RECIPIENTS

Library or School Related

- Texas State University, San Marcos (TX), for Etowah site excavation, $19,900
- Nizi Puh Wah Sin Schools, Browning (MT), for language immersion school, $100,000

General

- Los Angeles County Museum of Art, Los Angeles (CA), for construction costs, $1,350,000
- Democracy Now Productions, New York, (NY), for general operating support, $300,000
- Indian Law Resource Center, Helena, (MT), for general operating support, $250,000

REQUIREMENTS AND RESTRICTIONS

No grants to individuals

APPLICATION PROCEDURES

Letter of inquiry is required. Program staff will then contact selected organizations with an invitation to apply for funding.

Deadlines: None

Libri Foundation

Headquarters

PO Box 10246
Eugene, OR 97440-2246
Phone: 541-747-9655
Fax: 541-747-4348

www.librifoundation.org

Contact: Barbara J. McKillip, Pres. and Treas.

E-mail: libri@librifoundation.org

Type of Grant Maker: Foundation

Description

Founded: 1989

Operating Locations/Geographic Preferences: Giving on a national basis. Only libraries within the 50 states are eligible to apply. The Libri Foundation does not offer grants to libraries outside of the United States.

Financial Summary

Assets: $584,956

Grants Information

GRANT TYPES

Donates new, quality, hardcover children's books to small, rural public libraries in the United States. Minnesota libraries should contact the Foundation before applying.

TYPICAL RECIPIENTS/SUBJECTS OF INTEREST

Books for Children Program donates books to libraries that serve a population under 10,000 (usually under 5,000), have a very limited budget (generally less than $150,000), are in a rural area, and have an active children's department. Applications are accepted from independent libraries as well as those which are part of a county, regional, or cooperative library system. A library can receive up to $1,050 worth of new hardcover children's books.

PAST GRANT RECIPIENTS

Library or School Related

See website for grant recipients.

REQUIREMENTS AND RESTRICTIONS

See website for additional details about eligibility criteria for libraries and schools.

APPLICATION PROCEDURES

There are three ways to obtain a grant application from The Libri Foundation:

- Read the application instructions and fill out the form online. The form must be printed out, STAPLED, signed, and returned to The Libri Foundation via mail.
- Link to an Adobe Acrobat PDF version of the form to print out and complete by hand or using a typewriter.
- To receive a paper application in the mail, please e-mail your name and your library's name and mailing address to the Libri Foundation at libri@librifoundation.org. You may also request an application packet by mail, telephone, or fax at the address or phone numbers given on the Libri Foundation home page.

Deadlines: January 23 and May 15

Lilly Foundation

Headquarters

Lilly Corporate Ctr., D.C. 1627
Indianapolis, IN 46285-0001
Phone: 317-276-2000

www.lillyfoundation.org

Contact: Robert Lee Smith, Pres.

Type of Grant Maker: Corporate Foundation

Description

Founded: 1968

Operating Locations/Geographic Preferences: Giving on a national and international basis, with emphasis on areas of company operations, including Indianapolis, IN

Corporate Foundation Information: Sponsored by Eli Lilly and Co., Edmund A. Cyrol Trust

Financial Summary

Assets: $68,512,626
Total Giving: $30,345,734
Number of Grants: 436
Grant Ranges: $2,000,000–$250

Grants Information

GRANT TYPES

Continuing, general and operating support, matching, annual and capital campaign, employee matching and volunteer services

TYPICAL RECIPIENTS/SUBJECTS OF INTEREST

Arts and culture, K–12 education reform, mental health, disease, youth development, community development, diversity, and public policy research.
  Programs include:

- Community Development
- Culture
- Diversity
- Education and Youth Development
- Fencerow Neighborhood Groups to improve neighborhoods immediately surrounding major Eli Lilly facilities
- Health and Human Services Aligned with Major Therapeutic Interests
- Matching Gift Program
- Public Policy Research

PAST GRANT RECIPIENTS

Library or School Related

- Indiana University Foundation, Bloomington (IN), to recruit research talent, $1,500,000
- University of North Carolina, Chapel Hill (NC), for pre-doctoral fellowships, $25,000
- Stanford University, Stanford (CA), for General Operating Support, $10,000

General

- American Academy of Family Physicians Foundation, Leawood (KS), for Peers for Progress, global diabetes peer support program, $2,000,000
- Children's Museum of Indianapolis, Indianapolis (IN), for Global Perspectives Exhibit, $300,000

REQUIREMENTS AND RESTRICTIONS

No support for religious or sectarian organizations, fraternal, labor, athletic, or veterans' organizations or bands, or non-accredited educational organizations. No grants to individuals or for scholarships or travel, endowments, debt reduction, beauty or talent contests, fund-raising activities related to individual sponsorship, conferences or media production, or memorials. No loans or political contributions.

APPLICATION PROCEDURES

Applicants should submit:

1. Plans for acknowledgement
2. Listing of board of directors, trustees, officers and other key people and their affiliations
3. Listing of additional sources and amount of support
4. How project's results will be evaluated or measured
5. Detailed description of project and amount of funding requested
6. Copy of most recent annual report/audited financial statement/990
7. Copy of IRS Determination Letter
8. Copy of current year's organizational budget and/or project budget

Deadlines: None

Lincoln Financial Foundation

Headquarters

1300 S. Clinton St.
PO Box 7863
Fort Wayne, IN 46801-7863
www.lfg.com
Contact: Sandi Kemmish, Dir.
E-mail: sandi.kemmish@lfg.com
Type of Grant Maker: Corporate Foundation

Description

Founded: 1962

Operating Locations/Geographic Preferences: Giving limited to areas of company operations, with emphasis on Hartford, CT, Chicago, IL, fort Wayne, IN, Greensboro, NC, Omaha, NE, Concord, NH, and Philadelphia, PA

Corporate Foundation Information: Sponsored by Lincoln National Corp. and the Lincoln National Life Insurance Co.

Financial Summary

Assets: $6,937,030
Total Giving: $9,412,119

Number of Grants: 1,478
Grant Ranges: $280,000–$50

Grants Information

GRANT TYPES

Program development, building and renovation, matching, employee volunteer

TYPICAL RECIPIENTS/SUBJECTS OF INTEREST

Education, arts and culture, human service, and workforce and economic development

PAST GRANT RECIPIENTS

Library or School Related

• University of Mississippi Foundation, University (MS), $2,500

General

• Action Greensboro, Greensboro (NC), for Greensboro Downtown Greenway, $500,000
• Arts United of Greater Fort Wayne, fort Wayne (IN), for Annual Arts United Fund Drive and Nonprofit Arts Internship Initiative, $140,000
• Artlink, fort Wayne (IN), for 32nd Annual National Print Exhibition, $7,500

REQUIREMENTS AND RESTRICTIONS

No support for religious organizations, public or private elementary or secondary schools or school foundations, hospitals, hospital foundations, fraternal, political, or veterans' organizations, or sports organizations. No grants to individuals, or for endowments, continuing support, general operating support, capital campaigns, debt reduction, marketing programs, sporting events or tournaments, fund-raising for national organizations, sporting events, or national walks.

APPLICATION PROCEDURES

See website for nearest address. Application form required. Applicants should submit:

1. Copy of IRS Determination Letter
2. Copy of most recent annual report/audited financial statement/990
3. Listing of board of directors, trustees, officers and other key people and their affiliations
4. Copy of current year's organizational budget and/or project budget

Deadlines: Vary

Louisiana, State Library

Headquarters

701 North 4th St.
Baton Rouge, LA 70802
Phone: 225-342-4913
Fax: 225-219-4804

www.state.lib.la.us/public-libraries/grant-opportunities

Type of Grant Maker: Government

Currently, the state library grant process is being revisited. Grant applications and guidelines will be posted in the near future.

Lowe's Charitable and Educational Foundation

Headquarters

c/o Community Rels.
1000 Lowe's Blvd., NB3TA
Mooresville, NC 28117-8520
Phone: 704-758-2831
Fax: 704-757-4766

www.lowes.com/community

Contact: Cindy Williams
E-mail: cindy.l.williams@lowes.com
Type of Grant Maker: Corporate Foundation

Description

Founded: 1957

Operating Locations/Geographic Preferences: Giving on a national basis in areas of company operations;

Corporate Foundation Information: Supported by Lowe's Cos. Inc. and the Valspar Corp.

Financial Summary

Assets: $22,907,678
Total Giving: $23,280,020

Grants Information

GRANT TYPES

General and operating support, employee volunteering, equipment and renovation

TYPICAL RECIPIENTS/SUBJECTS OF INTEREST

Parks and playgrounds and organizations involved with K–12 education, environmental beautification, environmental education, home safety, and community development

PAST GRANT RECIPIENTS

Library or School Related

- Central Jr. High School, Springdale (AR), library expansion, $80,000
- Citizens for the Troutman Library, Troutman (NC), library landscaping, $10,500
- Garfield Elementary School, Danville (IL), library renovation, $80,000
- Glen Acres Elementary School, Lafayette (IN), library computer lab, $91,400
- Handley Reg. Library, Winchester (VA), outdoor garden, $13,500
- Kingston City School District, Kingston (NY), library restoration, $80,000

REQUIREMENTS AND RESTRICTIONS

No support for national health organizations or their local affiliates, religious organizations, political, labor, veterans', or fraternal organizations, civic clubs, or candidates, sports teams, animal rescue and support organizations, organizations not of direct benefit to the entire community, private schools, or local affiliates or chapters of Habitat for Humanity, the American Red Cross, the United Way, or the Home Safety Council; no support for schools established less than two years ago for Lowe's Toolbox for Education. No grants to individuals or families, or for academic or medical research, religious programs or events, special events, sponsorship of fund-raising events, advertising or marketing, athletic events or athletic programs, arts-based programs, travel-related events, book, film, video, or television program development or production, capital campaigns, endowments, or endowed chairs, continuing education for teachers and staff, institutional overhead and/or indirect costs, memorial campaigns, continuing support, international programs, or tickets to events; no grants for stipends, salaries, scholarships, or third-party funding.

APPLICATION PROCEDURES AND DEADLINES

Beginning in 2013, the foundation is moving to a cycle system for applications, with two cycles for education grants and two cycles for community improvement grants. See website for details and to review eligibility.

Luce, Henry Foundation, Inc.

Headquarters

51 Madison Ave., 30th Fl.
New York, NY 10010-1603
Phone: 212-489-7700
www.hluce.org
Contact: Michael Gilligan, Pres.
E-mail: hlf1@hluce.org
Type of Grant Maker: Foundation

Description

Founded: 1936

Operating Locations/Geographic Preferences: Giving on a national and international basis; international activities limited to East and Southeast Asia

Financial Summary

Assets: $762,603,542
Total Giving: $29,528,811
Number of Grants: 263
Highest Grant $1,000,000

Grants Information

GRANT TYPES

Program development, general and operating support, matching

TYPICAL RECIPIENTS/SUBJECTS OF INTEREST

Asian affairs, American art, public policy and the environment, theology, advancement of women in science and engineering, and higher education
  Program areas include:

- American Art
- Asia
- Clare Boothe Luce Program—exclusively for the thirteen institutions specifically designed by Mrs. Luce's will

- Employee Matching Gifts
- Environmental Initiative
- Henry R. Luce Initiative on Religion and International Affairs
- Higher Education
- Luce Scholars Program
- Public Policy
- Theology

PAST GRANT RECIPIENTS

Library or School Related

- Loyola University Maryland, Baltimore (MD), for Clare Boothe Luce Professorships, $500,000
  Union Theological Seminary, New York (NY), for Professor of Islamic Studies, $422,000
- Saint Paul School of Theology, Kansas City (MO), for faculty position in Native American Studies in Church and Society at Oklahoma City University campus, $240,000
- University of Pittsburgh, Pittsburgh (PA), for new faculty position, $415,000

General

- Asia Foundation, San Francisco (CA), for administration of Luce Scholars Program, $2,500,000
- Minnesota Public Radio, Saint Paul (MN), for coverage of religion and international affairs, $375,000

REQUIREMENTS AND RESTRICTIONS

No support for medical or health care projects. No grants to individuals or for endowments, domestic building campaigns, annual fund drives, or loans

APPLICATION PROCEDURES

Application form not required. Initial approach is letter of inquiry.

Deadlines: Vary

MacArthur, John D. and Catherine T. Foundation

Headquarters

140 S. Dearborn St., Ste. 1200
Chicago, IL 60603-5285
Phone: 312-726-8000
Fax: 312-920-6258

www.macfound.org

Contact: Richard J. Kaplan, Assoc. V.P., Institutional Research and Grants Mgmt.
E-mail: 4answers@macfound.org
Type of Grant Maker: Foundation

Description

Founded: 1970
Operating Locations/Geographic Preferences: Giving on a national and international basis

Financial Summary

Assets: $5,737,270,334
Total giving: $220,667,589
Number of Grants: 1,088
Grant Ranges: $5,000,000–$200

Grants Information

GRANT TYPES

Program development, general and operating support, matching, investments and loans

TYPICAL GRANT RECIPIENTS/
SUBJECTS OF INTEREST

Foundation supports creative people and effective institutions committed to building a more just, verdant, and peaceful world. In addition to selecting the MacArthur Fellows, the foundation works to defend human rights, advance global conservation and security, make cities better places, and understand how technology is affecting children and society.

PAST GRANT RECIPIENTS

Library or School Related

- Chicago Public Library Foundation, Chicago (IL), for YouMedia@CPL, $350,000 and $500,000
- Evanston Public Library, Evanston (IL), for matching gift, $600
- Columbia University, New York (NY), for the Research Network on an Aging Society, $3,625,000
- African Court on Human and Peoples' Rights, Arusha (TZ), to procure books, journals and other resources for library, $150,000
- Ahmadu Bello University, Zaria (NI), to strengthen technology and library information, $800,000

General

- Kids in Need of Defense, Washington (DC), for legal protection, research and advocacy on behalf of unaccompanied and separated migrant children, $300,000

- Center on Budget and Policy Priorities, Washington (DC), for general operations, $2,000,000

REQUIREMENTS AND RESTRICTIONS

No support for religious programs, political activities or campaigns. No grants for fund-raising appeals, institutional benefits, honorary functions or similar projects, tuition expenses, scholarships, or fellowships (other than those sponsored by the foundation).

APPLICATION PROCEDURES

Send letter of inquiry to the office of Grants Management via mail or by e-mail. Do not send fax. Direct applications for MacArthur Fellows programs not accepted. Grants increasingly initiated by the board.

Deadlines: None

Macy's Foundation

Headquarters

c/o Macy's Corp. Svcs., Inc.
7 W. 7th St.
Cincinnati, OH 45202-2424
Phone: 513-579-7000
www.federated-fds.com/community/

Contact: Dixie Barker, Mgr., Corp. Contribs.

E-mail: foundationapps@macys.com

Type of Grant Maker: Corporate Foundation

Description

Founded: 1995

Operating Locations/Geographic Preferences: Giving on a national basis in areas of company operations, with emphasis on CA, FL, GA, MO, NY, and OH

Corporate Foundation Information: Supported by:
- Federated Department Stores, Inc.
- The May Department Stores Foundation

Financial Summary

Assets: $6,214,362
Total Giving: $15,905,005
Number of Grants: 4,753
Grant Ranges: $1,500,000–$25

Grants Information

GRANT TYPES

Program development, general, operating and continuing support, annual and capital campaigns, seed money, matching

TYPICAL RECIPIENTS/SUBJECTS OF INTEREST

Education, arts and culture, the environment, HIV/AIDS, and women's issues and programs designed to assist minorities

PAST GRANT RECIPIENTS

Library or School Related

- Saint Benedict Day, New York (NY), for Literacy Program, $10,000

General

- United Way of Metropolitan Atlanta, Atlanta (GA), $1,110,000
- United Way of Greater Cincinnati, Cincinnati (OH), $450,000
- ArtsWave, Cincinnati (OH), for Campaign Gift, $439,000 Portland Opera Association, Portland (OR), for *Hansel and Gretel,* $10,000

REQUIREMENTS AND RESTRICTIONS

No support for private foundations, fraternal organizations, political or advocacy groups, religious organizations, or charities. No grants to individuals, or for event or program sponsorships, or salaries for nonprofit staffing.

APPLICATION PROCEDURES

Initial approach must be as an e-mailed letter of inquiry. Notification of an invitation to formally apply will follow if selected.

Deadlines: None

Maine Community Foundation, Inc.

Headquarters

245 Main St.
Ellsworth, ME 04605-1613
Phone: 207-667-9735
www.mainecf.org

E-mail: info@mainecf.org

Type of Grant Maker: Community Foundation

Description

Founded: 1983

Operating Locations/Geographic Preferences: Giving limited to ME

Financial Summary

Assets: $184,223,964
Total Giving: $15,685,713

Grants Information

GRANT TYPES

Program development, seed money, endowments, land acquisition, matching, investments and loans, management development

TYPICAL RECIPIENTS

Education, the arts, child welfare and youth, the disadvantaged, health, community development, and sustainable development.

Giving programs include:

Belvedere Historic Preservation Grant Program: to support the preservation of historic buildings in rural Maine communities

Community Building Grant Program: Programs must:

1. Use existing community resources
2. Strengthen community life; and
3. Be sustainable

PAST GRANT RECIPIENTS

Library or School Related

- Franklin County Community College Network, Farmington (ME), for programs and operations, $15,000
- Carrabassett Valley Academy, Carrabassett Valley (ME), for the Cummings Campus project, $25,000
- Ecology Education, Saco (ME), for Science and Ecology: Live and Unplugged, ecology education program K–5th grades, $5,000

General

- Healthy Community Coalition, Farmington (ME), for public education efforts, $75,000
- Maine Humanities Council, Portland (ME), for Let's Talk About It program, $4,000
- Nasson Center Redevelopment, Springvale (ME), for renovation of the Little Theatre, $4,000

REQUIREMENTS AND RESTRICTIONS

No support for religious organizations. No grants to individuals or for equipment, annual campaigns for regular operations, or for capital campaigns.

APPLICATION PROCEDURES

See website for application form and guidelines. Application form required. Applicants should submit:

1. How project will be sustained once grant-maker support is completed
2. Signature and title of chief executive officer
3. Results expected from proposed grant
4. Qualifications of key personnel
5. Statement of problem project will address
6. Name, address and phone number of organization
7. Copy of IRS Determination Letter
8. Brief history of organization and description of its mission
9. How project's results will be evaluated or measured
10. Listing of board of directors, trustees, officers and other key people and their affiliations
11. Detailed description of project and amount of funding requested
12. Plans for cooperation with other organizations, if any
13. Contact person
14. Copy of current year's organizational budget and/or project budget
15. Listing of additional sources and amount of support

Deadlines: February 15 for Community Building Prog.; Vary for others

Maine Health Access Foundation

Headquarters

150 Capitol St., Ste. 4
Augusta, ME 04330-6858
Phone: 207-620-8266

www.mehaf.org

Contact: Wendy J. Wolf M.D., M.P.H., C.E.O. and Pres.; Barbara A. Leonard M.P.H., V.P., Progs.

E-mail: cluce@mehaf.org

Type of Grant Maker: Foundation

Description

Founded: 2000

Financial Summary

Assets: $111,772,110
Total Giving: $3,354,069
Number of Grants: 76
Grant Ranges: $325,000–$500

Grants Information

GRANT TYPES

Program development, equipment

TYPICAL RECIPIENTS/SUBJECTS OF INTEREST

Health-related, including priorities of:
- Advancing health system reform
- Promoting patient-centered care
- Improving access to quality care
- Achieving better health in communities

PAST GRANT RECIPIENTS

Library or School Related
- University of Southern Maine, Portland (ME), for implementation of the hospital medication safety initiatives, $92,500
- University of New England, Biddeford (ME), for clinical site development and student recruitment for UNE's College of Dental Medicine, $82,000

General
- HealthInfoNet, Portland (ME), for statewide health information technology strategic plan, $10,000
- Aroostook County Action Program, Presque Isle (ME), to install a safe and accessible playground for low- to moderate-income children at the ACAP Child Care/Head Start Programs, $10,000

REQUIREMENTS AND RESTRICTIONS

No support for private foundations, political candidates, or lobbying. No grants to individuals or for endowments, debt retirement, annual appeals or membership campaigns, fund-raising or social events, or public relations campaigns.

APPLICATION PROCEDURES

See website for application guidelines and procedures. Application form required

Deadlines: Vary

Maine State Library

No grants provided to libraries at this time.

Marin Community Foundation

Headquarters

5 Hamilton Landing, Ste. 200
Novato, CA 94949-8263
Phone: 415-464-2500

www.marincf.org

Contact: Fred Silverman, V.P., Mktg. and Comms.

E-mail: info@marincf.org

Type of Grant Maker: Community Foundation

Description

Founded: 1986

Operating Locations/Geographic Preferences: Giving on a national and international basis with emphasis on the San Francisco Bay Area. Buck Trust giving limited to Marin County, CA

Financial Summary

Assets: $1,207,464,129
Total Giving: $57,484,094

Grants Information

GRANT TYPES

Program development, continuing, general and operating support, building and renovation, matching, land acquisition, seed money, capital campaigns, matching

TYPICAL RECIPIENTS/SUBJECTS OF INTEREST

Human needs, community development, education and training, religion, environment, and arts
Program areas include:

Affordable Housing

Climate Change

Education—especially programs that serve low-income children and children of color by investing in early learning experiences, parent involvement, and extended time spent learning

- Increase the number of low-income students and students of color who access post-secondary education
- Improve educational outcomes of low-income students and students of color

MCF Loan Fund

Poverty

PAST GRANT RECIPIENTS

Library or School Related

- Thacher School, Ojai (CA), $6,000

General

- Buck Institute for Age Research, Novato (CA), $5,900,000
- Marin County Housing Authority, San Rafael (CA), $140,000
- Foundation for AIDS Research, New York (NY), $5,000

REQUIREMENTS AND RESTRICTIONS

No grants to individuals, for planning initiatives, or capital projects

APPLICATION PROCEDURES

See website for grant applications, deadlines and guidelines. Application form required.
  Applicants should submit:

1. Signature and title of chief executive officer
2. Name, address and phone number of organization
3. Brief history of organization and description of its mission
4. Geographic area to be served
5. Detailed description of project and amount of funding requested
6. Contact person

Deadlines: Vary

MARPAT Foundation, Inc.

Headquarters

PO Box 1769
Silver Spring, MD 20915-1769

www.foundationcenter.org/grant-maker/marpat

Contact: Joan F. Koven, Secy.-Treas.

E-mail: jkoven@marpatfoundation.org

Type of Grant Maker: Foundation

Description

Founded: 1985

Operating Locations/Geographic Preferences: Giving primarily in the metropolitan Washington, DC, area

Financial Summary

Assets: $20,727,701
Total Giving: $3,568,000
Number of Grants: 151
Grant Ranges: $65,000–$500

Grants Information

GRANT TYPES

Program development, continuing, general and operating support, building and renovation, matching, land acquisition

TYPICAL RECIPIENTS/SUBJECTS OF INTEREST

- Museums
- Libraries
- Family planning or health care
- Natural and historical resource preservation
- History and cultural past
- Volunteer and citizen participation

PAST GRANT RECIPIENTS

General

- Jefferson Patterson Park and Museum, Saint Leonard (MD), for public archeology program, $65,000
- Bright Beginnings, Washington (DC), for general operating support and for the building campaign, $230,000
- DC Campaign to Prevent Teen Pregnancy, Washington (DC), for Youth Leadership Task Force, $30,000
- LifeSTARTS Youth and Family Services, Washington (DC), for general operating and program support, $30,000

REQUIREMENTS AND RESTRICTIONS

No support for projects or organizations for any weapons development, or for medical research. No support for social or youth services programs outside of Wards 7 and 8 in Washington, DC. No grants to individuals, or for endowment funds.

APPLICATION PROCEDURES

See website for application form and summary sheet. Full proposals by invitation only following initial inquiry.

Deadlines: May 26 for Stage One Summary; September 1 for applicants invited to submit Stage Two Application

Massachusetts Board of Library Commissioners

Headquarters

98 North Washington St., Suite 401
Boston, Massachusetts 02114
Phone: 617-725-1860, 800-952-7403
Fax: 617-725-0140

http://mblc.state.ma.us/grants/

Type of Grant Maker: Government

Grants Information

STATE AID TO PUBLIC LIBRARIES

Grant Amounts: Vary

Annual, voluntary program administered by the Massachusetts Board of Library Commissioners.
 The purpose is:
- to encourage municipalities to support and improve public library service
- to encourage reciprocal resource sharing among libraries across Massachusetts
- to compensate for disparities among municipal funding capacities
- to offset additional costs to municipalities whose libraries circulate materials to patrons from other certified Massachusetts municipalities

REQUIREMENTS AND RESTRICTIONS

A municipality and its library must be certified by the Massachusetts Board of Library Commissioners as meeting statutory and regulatory requirements to receive State Aid to Public Libraries.
 To be certified each fiscal year, a municipality and its library must:
- meet its Municipal Appropriation Requirement
- meet Minimum Standards of Free Public Library Service
- submit annual data and proof of compliance with requirements

APPLICATION PROCEDURES

See website for details.

Deadline: October

PUBLIC LIBRARY CONSTRUCTION PROGRAM

Helps build new library buildings and addition/renovation or conversion projects. The program also awards planning and design grants to support public libraries as they prepare to apply for a construction grant.

Grants & Green Incentive

Grant Amounts: Up to $40,000

Planning and Design Grants: Assist libraries in preparing to apply for MPLCP construction grants. Grant funds help with the preparation of library building programs, project management services, site investigations, soil studies, architectural design and engineering services for feasibility studies, schematic designs and site plans, and construction cost estimates.

Construction Grants: Assist libraries with major capital improvement projects that involve building new facilities, expanding and renovating an existing library building, or adapting and reusing another building for use as a library.

Green Library Incentives: Help offset the cost of incorporating environmentally friendly and energy-efficient systems and materials in library building projects.

REQUIREMENTS AND RESTRICTIONS

Applicant libraries must be certified by the MBLC as meeting minimum state standards for public library service and must have a long-range plan on file with the Board. Any project funded under the program must meet the 20-year needs of the applicant's municipality for library service. Proposals for new buildings and addition/renovations must be based on a library building program that has been written prior to retaining an architect. Applicants must have local approval to apply for, accept and expend grant funds as well as approval for the proposed preliminary design.

APPLICATION PROCEDURES

See website for more information.

Deadlines: See website.

LIBRARY SERVICES AND TECHNOLOGY ACT (LSTA)

Awarded as competitive direct grants to libraries of all types.
 Grant Amounts: Vary

APPLICATION PROCEDURES

See website when grant announcement is made in November. For information, contact:

Rachel Masse
Administrative Coordinator
Phone: 617-725-1860, x228
E-mail: rachel.masse@state.ma.us

Deadlines: See online calendar

Mathile Family Foundation

Headquarters

6450 Sand Lake Rd., Ste. 100
Dayton, OH 45414-2679
Phone: 937-264-4607

www.mathilefamilyfoundation.org

Contact: Angela Hayes, Grant Assoc.

E-mail: mffinfo@mathilefamilyfoundation.org

Type of Grant Maker: Foundation

Description

Founded: 1989

Operating Locations/Geographic Preferences: Giving primarily in the Dayton and Montgomery County, OH areas

Financial Summary

Assets: $275,708,048
Total Giving: $20,086,768

Grants Information

GRANT TYPES

Program development, general and operating support, building and renovation, matching, capital campaigns

TYPICAL RECIPIENTS/SUBJECTS OF INTEREST

Family, education and health

PAST GRANT RECIPIENTS

Library or School Related

- Chaminade Julienne High School, Dayton (OH), for development office capacity building and tuition assistance, $1,538,000

General

- Parents Advancing Choice in Education, Dayton (OH), $1,600,000
- Children's Medical Center, Dayton (OH), for child advocacy and mental health program, $600,000
- Ohio Association of Nonprofit Organizations, Columbus (OH), for general operating support and program support, $50,000
- Seedling Foundation, Dayton (OH), for Adjunct Staff at Stivers School for the Arts, $25,000

REQUIREMENTS AND RESTRICTIONS

No support for political organizations. No grants for sponsorships, endowment funds, or mass appeals for funding.

APPLICATION PROCEDURES

See website for more application information. Application form not required. Applicants should submit:

1. Timetable for implementation and evaluation of project
2. Site description
3. Results expected from proposed grant
4. Population served
5. Copy of IRS Determination Letter
6. Brief history of organization and description of its mission
7. Copy of most recent annual report/audited financial statement/990
8. How project's results will be evaluated or measured
9. Listing of board of directors, trustees, officers and other key people and their affiliations
10. Detailed description of project and amount of funding requested
11. Copy of current year's organizational budget and/or project budget
12. Listing of additional sources and amount of support

Deadlines: February 1, May 1, August 1, and November 1

McCormick, Robert R. Foundation

Headquarters

205 N. Michigan Ave., Ste. 4300
Chicago, IL 60601-5983
Phone: 312-445-5000
Fax: 312-445-5001

www.mccormickfoundation.org

Contact: Donald A. Cooke, Sr. V.P., Philanthropy

E-mail: info@mccormickfoundation.org

Type of Grant Maker: Foundation

Description

Founded: 1955

Operating Locations/Geographic Preferences: Giving primarily in the Chicago, IL region

Financial Summary

Assets: $1,176,585,115
Total Giving: $56,881,049

Grants Information

GRANT TYPES

Program development, building and renovation, conferences, continuing, general and operating support, matching, investments and loans, seed money, technical assistance

TYPICAL RECIPIENTS/SUBJECTS OF INTEREST

Through philanthropic programs, Cantigny Park and museums, the foundation helps develop citizen leaders and works to make life better in its communities.

Giving areas include:

- Civics
- Communities
- Education
- Journalism
- Veterans

PAST GRANT RECIPIENTS

Library or School Related

- Chicago Public Library, Chicago (IL), Summer Reading Program, $50,000, and $200,000 for computer tutoring program
- Denver Public Library, Denver (CO), Summer Reading Program, $10,000, and $20,000 for children's materials
- Long Beach Public Library, Long Beach (CA), for Family Learning Centers, $20,000
- SUNY Stony Brook, Stony Brook (NY), for Literacy Summit, $120,000
- Pritzker Military Library, Chicago (IL), for general support, $8,800

REQUIREMENTS AND RESTRICTIONS

Communities grants: Organizations must apply through one of the fund partners listed on the website.

Education grants: This program does not accept unsolicited applications or inquiries.

No grants to individuals, or for scholarships or endowment funds.

APPLICATION PROCEDURES

See website for application guidelines and procedures.

Deadlines: Vary

McGovern, John P. Foundation

Headquarters

2211 Norfolk St., Ste. 900
Houston, TX 77098-4044
Phone: 713-661-4808

Contact: Kathrine McGovern, Pres. and V.P.

Type of Grant Maker: Foundation

Description

Founded: 1961

Operating Locations/Geographic Preferences: Giving primarily in TX, with emphasis on Houston; giving also in the Southwest

Financial Summary

Assets: $177,756,070
Total Giving: $9,386,904
Number of Grants: 313
Grant Ranges: $1,000,000–$110; average: $5,000–$150,000

Grants Information

GRANT TYPES

Continuing, general and operating support, matching, building and renovation, endowments

TYPICAL RECIPIENTS/SUBJECTS OF INTEREST

Human welfare with special focus on children and family health education and promotion, treatment and disease prevention

PAST GRANT RECIPIENTS

Library or School Related

- University of Texas Health Science Center, Houston (TX), for Campus-Wide Ethics and Professionalism Program, $350,000
- McMaster University, Hamilton (Canada), for Special Fund, $10,000

General

- Houston Zoo, Houston (TX), for general support, $500,000
- Houston Downtown Park Conservancy, Houston (TX), for Discovery Green Downtown Park, $250,000
- Salvation Army of Houston, Houston (TX), $150,000
- Texas Children's Hospital, Houston (TX), for Project Medical Home, $100,000
- Gathering Place, Houston (TX), for spring luncheon, $10,000

REQUIREMENTS AND RESTRICTIONS

No grants to individuals.

APPLICATION PROCEDURES

Contact foundation for details.

Deadlines: None

McKnight Foundation

Headquarters

710 S. 2nd St., Ste. 400
Minneapolis, MN 55401-2290
Phone: 612-333-4220

www.mcknight.org

Contact: Kate Wolford, Pres.

E-mail: info@mcknight.org

Type of Grant Maker: Foundation

Description

Founded: 1953

Operating Locations/Geographic Preferences: Giving limited to organizations in MN, especially the seven-county Twin Cities, MN, area, except for programs in the environment which are made mainly in the 10 states bordering the Mississippi River and in the Twin Cities region, international aid, or research

Financial Summary

Assets: $2,014,523,000
Total Giving: $96,686,000

Grants Information

GRANT TYPES

Program development, general and operating support, building and renovation, capital campaigns, matching

TYPICAL RECIPIENTS/SUBJECTS OF INTEREST

Programs of giving include:

- Arts
- Education and Learning
- Employee Matching Gifts
- Environment: Climate Change
- Environment: Mississippi River
- International: East Africa
- International: Southeast Asia
- McKnight Distinguished Artist Award
- Multiservice—for organizations that:
    - Offer broad services that focus on the needs of families and individuals
    - Increase understanding of how to best support families in the context of their geographic/cultural communities
    - Are embedded in a neighborhood or neighborhoods
    - Engage and empower families in multiple ways
- Neuroscience
- Out-of-School Time
- Region and Communities—for programs that:
    - Manage regional growth to minimize sprawl and maximize opportunities
    - Create economically viable neighborhoods
    - Create affordable housing
    - Preserve, protect, and restore open spaces
    - Increase alternative transportation options
- Research: Collaborative Crop Research
- Virginia McKnight Binger Awards in Human Service

PAST GRANT RECIPIENTS

General

- Minnesota Early Learning Foundation, Minneapolis (MN), for Parent Aware quality rating and improvement system, $2,200,000
- Greater Metropolitan Housing Corporation-Twin Cities, Minneapolis (MN), for affordable housing development, $500,000
- Four-H Foundation, Minnesota, Minneapolis (MN), for Children and Youth Caucus, Youth Engagement Statewide Initiative, $310,000

- Lifetrack Resources, Saint Paul (MN), for early childhood and family programs, $50,000

REQUIREMENTS AND RESTRICTIONS

No support for religious organizations for religious purposes, or for medical health or health-related services. No grants to individuals or for basic research in academic disciplines, endowment funds, scholarships, fellowships, national fund-raising campaigns, ticket sales, travel or conferences.

APPLICATION PROCEDURES

See website for initial application instructions. The foundation will e-mail to decline requests or to provide additional instructions for submitting a full proposal online.

Deadlines: January 15, April 15, July 15, and October 15 for arts, and region and communities; February 1, May 1, August 1, November 1 for environment. See website for additional program deadlines

McLean Contributionship

Headquarters

945 Haverford Rd., Ste. A
Bryn Mawr, PA 19010-3814
Phone: 610-527-6330
Contact: Sandra L. McLean, Exec. Dir.

foundationcenter.org/grant-maker/mclean

Type of Grant Maker: Foundation

Description

Founded: 1951

Operating Locations/Geographic Preferences: Giving primarily in the greater Philadelphia, PA, area; some funding also in Nashua, NH, and Lake, Osceola and Pasco counties in FL

Financial Summary

Assets: $38,593,879
Total Giving: $2,114,120
Number of Grants: 102
Grant Ranges: $87,000–$1,000

Grants Information

GRANT TYPES

Program development, seed money, matching, building and renovation, capital campaigns and endowments, land acquisition

TYPICAL RECIPIENTS/SUBJECTS OF INTEREST

- Preservation of the environment
- Effective health care
- Improving the quality of life through capital and other projects

PAST GRANT RECIPIENTS

Library or School Related

- Easttown Library, Berwyn (PA), for redesign of the entrance from the lobby into the main area of the Library, allowing for the addition of shelving for the display of new materials, $30,000
- Mighty Writers, Philadelphia (PA), for renovations to second floor at the center's building, $25,000

General

- Nature Conservancy, Conshohocken (PA), for purchase of property, $33,600
- Friends of the Japanese House and Garden, Philadelphia (PA), for restoring, maintaining and preserving the hinoki bark roof, $25,000
- Metropolitan Area Neighborhood Nutrition Alliance, Philadelphia (PA), for new temperature-controlled delivery truck, $25,000

REQUIREMENTS AND RESTRICTIONS

Prefer special projects rather than continuing programs and focus on capital projects: bricks and mortar, endowment, or will provide seed money for purposes falling within the contributorship's guidelines. No grants to individuals.

APPLICATION PROCEDURES

See website for application guidelines and procedures. Application form not required. Applicants should submit:

1. Timetable for implementation and evaluation of project
2. Copy of IRS Determination Letter
3. Copy of most recent annual report/audited financial statement/990
4. Listing of board of directors, trustees, officers and other key people and their affiliations
5. Detailed description of project and amount of funding requested
6. Copy of current year's organizational budget and/or project budget

Deadlines: See website for meeting and deadline dates

MDU Resources Foundation

Headquarters

PO Box 5650
Bismarck, ND 58506-5650
Phone: 701-530-1087
Fax: 701-222-7607
www.mdu.com/CorporateResponsibility/Foundation/
    Pages/Overview.aspx

Contact: Rita O'Neill, Fdn. Mgr.

E-mail: rita.o'neill@MDUResources.com

Type of Grant Maker: Corporate Foundation

Description

Founded: 1983

Operating Locations/Geographic Preferences: Giving
primarily in areas of company operations

Corporate Foundation Information: Supported by:

- MDU Resources Group, Inc.
- WBI Holdings, Inc.
- Knife River Corp.
- Montana Dakota Utilities Co.
- Williston Basin Interstate Pipeline Co.

Financial Summary

Assets: $3,886,660
Total Giving: $1,981,190

Grants Information

GRANT TYPES

Annual and capital campaigns, building and renovation,
continuing, general and operating support, equipment,
matching, employee volunteering

PAST GRANT RECIPIENTS

Library or School Related

- A.H. Brown Library, Mobridge (SD), $6,000
- Penitas Public Library, Penitas (TX), $1,000
- Bismarck Public Library, Bismarck (ND), $5,000
- St. Cloud Public Library, St. Cloud (MN), $10,000
- Wray Public Library, Wray (CO), $5,000
- Marshall Lyon Public Library, Marshall (MN), $4,000

General

- ABLE, Inc., Dickinson (ND), $20,000
- Sheridan Heritage Center, Sheridan (WY), $20,000

REQUIREMENTS AND RESTRICTIONS

No support for athletic, labor, fraternal, veterans', political,
lobbying, social, or religious organizations or regional or
national organizations without local affiliation. No grants
to individuals or for endowments or economic development
or loans.

APPLICATION PROCEDURES

To be considered, all requests must include a completed
grant request form which is available to be downloaded
and printed from website.

Deadlines: October 1

Meadows Foundation, Inc.

Headquarters

Wilson Historic District
3003 Swiss Ave.
Dallas, TX 75204-6049
Phone: 214-826-9431
www.mfi.org

Contact: Bruce H. Esterline, V.P., Grants

E-mail: grants@mfi.org

Type of Grant Maker: Foundation

Description

Founded: 1948

Operating Locations/Geographic Preferences: Giving
limited to TX

Financial Summary

Assets: $720,435,662
Total Giving $21,662,218
Number of Grants: 1,983
Grant Ranges: $3,250,000–$500

Grants Information

GRANT TYPES

Program development, investments and loans, management development, general, operating and continuing support, building and renovation, matching, capital campaigns, seed money

TYPICAL RECIPIENTS/SUBJECTS OF INTEREST

Education, civic and cultural programs, arts, social services, community and rural development, health—including mental health

Historic preservation investment-related program

Other program areas include:

Charitable Schools Program—that supports projects that encourage and increase the number of young people who give back to their communities through volunteer service

Increase students' knowledge of their community

Develop leadership skills among students

Matching Grants Program

Wilson Historic District

PAST GRANT RECIPIENTS

Library or School Related

- MDC (Community College), Durham (NC), for Achieving the Dream Program, $500,000

General

- Dallas Arboretum and Botanical Society, Dallas (TX), for Children's Exploration Garden project, $1,200,000
- Dallas Society for the Prevention of Cruelty to Animals, Dallas (TX), for new animal shelter, $500,000
- Community Solutions of El Paso, El Paso (TX), for emergency operating support to continue programs, $85,000

REQUIREMENTS AND RESTRICTIONS

No grants to individuals, for annual campaigns, fund-raising events, professional conferences and symposia, travel expenses, construction of churches and seminaries, scholarships, or support of single artistic events or performances.

APPLICATION PROCEDURES

Online grant application form on website.

Deadlines: None

Medical Library Association

Headquarters

65 E. Wacker Pl.
Chicago, IL 60601-7298
Phone: 312-419-9094

http://hls.mlanet.org/wordpress/home/awards

Type of Grant Maker: Library Organization

Grants Information

HLS PROFESSIONAL DEVELOPMENT AWARD

Grant Amount: $500
Number of Grants: up to 4 per year

The purpose of the HLS Professional Development Award is to recognize those papers and/or posters at the MLA Annual Meeting that best represent hospital librarianship.

REQUIREMENTS AND RESTRICTIONS

The applicant must have a poster or paper accepted at the MLA Annual Meeting of the year in which the Award will be given. The applicant must be a current HLS member or institutional member.

APPLICATION PROCEDURES

Online form required.

Deadlines: March 1

Medtronic Foundation

Headquarters

710 Medtronic Pkwy., LC110
Minneapolis, MN 55432-5604
Phone: 763-505-2639

www.medtronic.com/foundation

Contact: Deb Anderson, Grants Admin.

E-mail: medtronicfoundation@medtronic.com

Type of Grant Maker: Corporate Foundation

Description

Founded: 1979

Operating Locations/Geographic Preferences: Giving primarily in areas of company operations, with emphasis on Maricopa County and Tempe, AZ, Santa Clarita, San Fernando, and Simi Valley regions, western Los Angeles, and Orange, Santa Barbara, Sonoma, Sunnyvale, and Ventura counties (CA), Denver metro area and Louisville, CO, Jacksonville, FL, Kosciusko County, IN, Beverly, Danvers, Middleton, North Shore, Peabody, and Salem, MA, Minneapolis, St. Paul, and Twin Cities-Seven County metro area MN, Humacao, Juncos, and Villalba, PR, Memphis, TN, fort Worth and San Antonio, TX, and King and Snohomish County, WA, and in Africa, Australia, Austria, Belgium, Brazil, Canada, Czech Republic, Shanghai, China, Denmark, Europe, France, Germany, Hungary, India, Ireland, Italy, Japan, Mexico, Netherlands, Poland, Russia, South Africa, Spain, Switzerland, and the United Kingdom.

Corporate Foundation Information: Supported by Medtronic, Inc.

Financial Summary

Assets: $54,187,794
Total Giving: $27,346,947
Number of Grants: 1,200
Grant Ranges: $2,239,222–$500

Grants Information

GRANT TYPES

Program development, continuing support, seed money, matching, employee volunteer services, management development, annual campaigns

TYPICAL RECIPIENTS/SUBJECTS OF INTEREST

Education, including primary and secondary science, math, and engineering initiatives and education reform

Health promotion, with focus on health systems in developing countries, chronic disease, patient advocacy and support, and sudden cardiac arrest

Community, through local human services and arts initiatives and disaster relief efforts

Programs include:

CommunityLink: Responding to community needs with emphasis on:

Health—to help people develop and maintain healthy lifestyles, with an emphasis on reducing disparities in health care

Education—supporting STEM education programs designed to promote public understanding of health and medical technology, and stimulate interest among young people. Special emphasis is directed on education projects at schools, science museums, and community centers; and programs designed to improve educational and career opportunities of underserved people

Arts, Civic, and Human Services—to reach out to the widest possible audiences

Education Reform: Supporting programs improve educational systems and close the gap between underserved and affluent school districts through education reform. Special emphasis on programs to improve administration and teacher quality in grades K–12.

Global Heroes

HeartRescue

Matching Gifts to Education

Medtronic Fellows

PatientLink—Empowering Patient Communities

PatientLink Leadership Development Awards

STEM Education: To support programs to encourage students' curiosity in science and technology and develop innovators through science and engineering scholarships and fellowships at selected post-secondary institutions. Special emphasis is directed toward programs designed to provide access to quality STEM (science, technology, engineering, and math) education for underrepresented students in primary (five years old) through post-secondary institutions.

Strengthening Health

Volunteer Grants

PAST GRANT RECIPIENTS

Library or School Related

- Deer Valley Unified School District No. 97, Phoenix (AZ), to link Science, Technology, Engineering and Mathematics (STEM) students from elementary through middle to high school and beyond in Step It Up program, $20,000
- University of Washington, Seattle (WA), for HeartRescue Flagship Premier Partner Program, $500,000

General

- Teach for America, New York (NY), for Teach for America Math And Science Initiative, $800,000
- Italian Multiple Sclerosis Society, Genoa (Italy), for Living Beyond MS, $39,000
- Volunteers in Medicine Jacksonville, Jacksonville (FL), for free health care clinic for the low-income working uninsured, A Project Dedicated to Young People, $15,000

REQUIREMENTS AND RESTRICTIONS

No support for lobbying, political, or fraternal organizations, fiscal agents, religious groups not of direct benefit to the entire community, or private foundations. No grants individuals, or for scholarships, capital campaigns, fund-raising events or activities, social events, goodwill advertising, general operating support, general support for educational institutions, long-term counseling or personal development, endowments or research.

APPLICATION PROCEDURES

Application form required. Applicants should submit:

1. Copy of most recent annual report/audited financial statement/990
2. How project's results will be evaluated or measured
3. Listing of board of directors, trustees, officers and other key people and their affiliations
4. Detailed description of project and amount of funding requested
5. Copy of current year's organizational budget and/or project budget
6. Listing of additional sources and amount of support

Deadlines: None

Mellon, Andrew W. Foundation

Headquarters

140 E. 62nd St.
New York, NY 10065-8124
Phone: 212-838-8400
Fax: 212-223-2778

www.mellon.org

Contact: Michele S. Warman, Genl. Counsel and Secy.

E-mail: inquiries@mellon.org

Type of Grant Maker: Foundation

Description

Founded: 1940

Operating Locations/Geographic Preferences: Giving on a national basis with some international giving, primarily focused on South Africa

Financial Summary

Assets: $5,490,877,291
Total Giving: $244,723,373
Number of Grants: 644
Grant Ranges: $7,091,000–$4,500

Grants Information

GRANT TYPES

Program development, continuing support, endowments, matching

TYPICAL RECIPIENTS/SUBJECTS OF INTEREST

Andrew W. Mellon Foundation supports grantees within five defined program areas:

1. Higher Education and Scholarship, which includes:
   Research Universities and Scholarship in the Humanities
   Liberal Arts Colleges Program
   Mellon Mays Undergraduate Fellowship Program, Historically Black Colleges and Universities, and Diversity Initiatives
   Special International Emphasis: South Africa
2. Scholarly Communications and Information Technology
3. Art History, Conservation, and Museums
4. Performing Arts
5. Conservation and the Environment

PAST GRANT RECIPIENTS

Library or School Related

- Indiana University Library, for shared technology services, $1,448,000
- Hamilton College, library collection, information technology and faculty development, $600,000
- Brown University, library fellowship, $199,075
- Gallaudet University, library video project, $500,000
- HBCU Library Alliance, history documentation project, $71,000
- Huntington Library, fellowship, $500,000
- Howard University Library, research center, $50,000

General

- Field Museum of Natural History, Chicago (IL), for Plants Initiative, $136,000
- Foundation of the American Institute for Conservation of Historic and Artistic Works, Washington (DC), for Photograph Conservation at the State Hermitage Museum, $3,460,000

REQUIREMENTS AND RESTRICTIONS

No support for primarily local organizations, no grants to individuals and no loans.

APPLICATION PROCEDURES

Because the Foundation is rarely able to respond positively to unsolicited requests, prospective applicants are encouraged to explore their ideas informally with program staff in a short e-mail describing their funding needs before submitting formal proposals. Letters of inquiry regarding ideas that fall within the program areas are welcome and reviewed throughout the year.

Please direct all inquiries to: Donald J. Waters, djw@mellon.org or Helen Cullyer, hc@mellon.org. Before writing, please review the Foundation's general requirements for grant proposals in the Grant Inquiries section online.

Deadlines: None

Mellon, Richard King Foundation

Headquarters

BNY Mellon Ctr.
500 Grant St., 41st Fl., Ste. 4106
Pittsburgh, PA 15219-2502

fdncenter.org/grant-maker/rkmellon

Contact: Scott Izzo, Dir.

Type of Grant Maker: Foundation

Description

Founded: 1947

Operating Locations/Geographic Preferences: Giving primarily in Southwestern PA

Financial Summary

Assets: $2,018,377,846
Total Giving: $85,869,711
Number of Grants: 254
Grant Ranges: $5,000,000–$2,500

Grants Information

GRANT TYPES

Program development, general, operating and continuing support, capital campaigns, matching, seed money, investments and loans, building and renovation

RECIPIENTS/SUBJECTS OF INTEREST

Conservation, education, families and youth, regional economic development

PAST GRANT RECIPIENTS

Library or School Related

- Catholic Diocese of Greensburg, Greensburg (PA), for capital improvements to Catholic schools, $4,000,000
- Point Park University, Pittsburgh (PA), to renovate YMCA building that will become University's Student and Convocation Center, $4,000,000

General

- Conservation Fund, Arlington (VA), for purchase of property located in McKean, Elk and Potter Counties, $4,100,000
- Innovation Works, Pittsburgh (PA), for operating support and Alpha Lab and for Energy Innovation Center, $2,400,000
- YMCA of Greater Pittsburgh, Pittsburgh (PA), to build full-service family YMCA in the Hill District, $2,000,000

REQUIREMENTS AND RESTRICTIONS

No grants to individuals, or for fellowships or scholarships, or conduit organizations.

APPLICATION PROCEDURES

Application form required. Applicants should submit:

1. Timetable for implementation and evaluation of project
2. How project will be sustained once grant-maker support is completed
3. Signature and title of chief executive officer
4. Results expected from proposed grant
5. Qualifications of key personnel
6. Copy of IRS Determination Letter
7. Brief history of organization and description of its mission
8. Copy of most recent annual report/audited financial statement/990
9. How project's results will be evaluated or measured
10. Listing of board of directors, trustees, officers and other key people and their affiliations

11. Copy of current year's organizational budget and/or project budget
12. Listing of additional sources and amount of support

Deadlines: None

Memphis (Greater) Community Foundation

Headquarters

1900 Union Ave.
Memphis, TN 38104-4029
Phone: 901-728-4600

www.cfgm.org

Contact: Robert M. Fockler, C.E.O.; Ashley Harper, Grants and Initiatives Off.

E-mail: rfockler@cfgm.org

Type of Grant Maker: Community Foundation

Description

Founded: 1969

Operating Locations/Geographic Preferences: Giving limited to Crittenden County, AR, DeSoto, Marshall, Tate, and Tunica counties, MS, and Fayette, Shelby, and Tipton Counties, TN

Financial Summary

Assets: $296,098,011
Total Giving: $26,322,914

Grants Information

GRANT TYPES

Program development, seed money, management development

TYPICAL RECIPIENTS/SUBJECTS OF INTEREST

Community Partnership Grants, including:

Intermediary grants—for agencies that provide support to other nonprofits

Capacity-Building grants—for nonprofits seeking to improve operations by pursuing activities identified through a comprehensive planning process involving board and staff

Bridge grants—for organizations that have historically played vital roles in the Memphis community but are facing temporary struggles.

Also offers scholarship funds

PAST GRANT RECIPIENTS

Library or School Related
- Presbyterian Day School, Memphis (TN), for Capital Campaign, $2,500

General
- Moving Image, New York (NY), for African Deep, $50,000
- Memphis Jewish Community Center, Memphis (TN), for MJCC Capital Campaign, $500,000
- Texas Presbyterian Foundation, Irving (TX), for general operating support, $295,000
- Women's Foundation for a Greater Memphis, Memphis (TN), for general operating support, $100,000
- Teach for America, Memphis (TN), for Teacher Sponsorships, $250,000

REQUIREMENTS AND RESTRICTIONS

No grants to individuals (except for scholarships), or for endowments, capital or building funds, annual campaigns, code enforcement, or core operating costs; no loans.

APPLICATION PROCEDURES

See website for grant application guidelines. Letter of Intent required as first step in Community Grants, after which applicants are notified whether or not they are invited to submit a full proposal. See website for details about mandatory pre-application workshops.

Deadlines: Vary

MetLife Foundation

Headquarters

1095 Ave. of the Americas, 40th Fl.
New York, NY 10036-6797
Phone: 212-578-6272

www.metlife.org

Contact: A. Dennis White, C.E.O. and Pres.

E-mail: metlifefoundation@metlife.com

Type of Grant Maker: Corporate Foundation

Description

Founded: 1976

Operating Locations/Geographic Preferences: Giving on a national and international basis, with emphasis in CA, CT, DC, FL, IL, MA, NY, PA, and TX

Corporate Foundation Information: Sponsored by Metropolitan Life Insurance Co.

Financial Summary

Assets: $126,119,057
Total Giving: $39,800,039
Number of Grants: 730
Grant Ranges: $1,200,000–$250

Grants Information

GRANT TYPES

Program development, general, operating and continuing support, investments and loans, matching

TYPICAL RECIPIENTS/SUBJECTS OF INTEREST

Food banks, arts and culture, education, health, Alzheimer's disease, housing, human services, community development, voluntarism promotion, civic affairs, senior citizens, and economically disadvantaged people. Special emphasis on strengthening communities, promoting good health and improving education.

Giving programs include:

Civic Affairs—with emphasis on:
Affordable housing and economic development
Financial literacy
After-school initiatives and mentoring
Volunteerism and civic engagement

Culture

Education—with emphasis on:
Promoting teachers and principal leadership
School community connections
Access to higher education, with emphasis on community colleges

Employee Matching Gifts

Employee Volunteer Programs

Employee-Related Scholarships

Health—with emphasis on:
Promoting Alzheimer's disease research
Healthy aging and caregiving
Health education and information

Social Investment Program

PAST GRANT RECIPIENTS

General

- National School Leaders Network, Hinsdale (MA), for School Leaders Network Expansion, $100,000
- World Trade Center Memorial Foundation, New York (NY), for Memorial and Museum, $1,000,000
- American Council on Education, Washington (DC). For D79 Accelerated Learning Pilot Project, $900,000
- Big Brothers Big Sisters of America, Philadelphia (PA), for Strengthening Educational Outcomes of Hispanic Youth, $500,000
- Afterschool Alliance, Washington (DC), for Afterschool Innovator Awards and Issue Brief Series, $300,000
- Boys and Girls Clubs of Las Vegas, Las Vegas (NV), for Smart Moves, $55,000
- Brooklyn Children's Museum, Brooklyn (NY), for The MetLife Early Learner Performance Series, $35,000

REQUIREMENTS AND RESTRICTIONS

No support for private foundations, religious, fraternal, athletic, political, or social organizations, hospitals, local chapters of national organizations, disease-specific organizations, labor groups, organizations primarily engaged in patient care or direct treatment, drug treatment centers, community health clinics, or elementary or secondary schools. No grants to individuals or for endowments, courtesy advertising, or festival participation.

APPLICATION PROCEDURES

Application form required. Applicants should submit:

1. Name, address and phone number of organization
2. Brief history of organization and description of its mission
3. Copy of most recent annual report/audited financial statement/990
4. Listing of board of directors, trustees, officers and other key people and their affiliations
5. Detailed description of project and amount of funding requested
6. Contact person
7. Copy of current year's organizational budget and/or project budget
8. Additional materials/documentation

Deadlines: None

Meyer Memorial Trust

Headquarters

425 N.W. 10th Ave., Ste. 400
Portland, OR 97209-3128
Phone: 503-228-5512

www.mmt.org

Contact: Doug Stamm, C.E.O.

E-mail: mmt@mmt.org

Type of Grant Maker: Foundation

Description

Founded: 1978

Operating Locations/Geographic Preferences: Giving primarily in OR and Clark County, WA

Financial Summary

Assets: $667,237,657
Total Giving: $23,971,891
Number of Grants: 422
Grant Ranges: $700,000–$500

Grants Information

GRANT TYPES

Program development, building and renovation, capital campaigns, general, operating support, matching, seed money, investments and loans

TYPICAL RECIPIENTS/SUBJECTS OF INTEREST

Giving programs include:

Grassroots Grants for grants of $1,000 to $25,000, limited to tax-exempt organizations operating in Oregon and Clark County, WA.

Matching Gifts

Program-Related Investments

Responsive Grants of $50,000–$300,000 for human services, health, affordable housing, community development, conservation and environment, public affairs, arts and culture and education.

PAST GRANT RECIPIENTS

Library or School Related

- Foundations for a Better Oregon, Portland (OR), for operating support for the Chalkboard Project, $440,000
- Oregon Children's Foundation, Portland (OR), for SMART reading program, $200,000
- Adelante Mujeres, forest Grove (OR), for operating support for education programs serving immigrant Latino families, $112,000

General

- Oregon Energy Services, Tualatin (OR), for organization's Oil Recycling Program, $97,125
- Peninsula Children's Center, Portland (OR), for comprehensive early childhood education services for low-income families, $75,000

REQUIREMENTS AND RESTRICTIONS

No support for sectarian or religious organizations for religious purposes, or for animal welfare organizations, projects that primarily benefit students of a single K–12 school (unless the school is an independent alternative school primarily serving low-income and/or special needs populations)

No grants to individuals or for endowment funds, annual campaigns, general fund drives, special events, sponsorships, direct replacement funding for activities previously supported by federal, state, or local public sources, deficit financing, acquisition of land for conservation purposes or hospital capital construction projects.

APPLICATION PROCEDURES

All applicants must apply online. Some programs use two-step process: Online Initial Inquiry with online Full Proposal if invited. Grassroots Grants program is a one-step online proposal process. See website for additional details.

Deadlines: None for Responsive Grants and PRIs; Grassroots Grants program: March 15, July 15, October 15

Michigan Center for the Book (MCF)

Headquarters

702 W. Kalamazoo St.
PO Box 30007
Lansing, MI 48909
Phone: 517-241-0021

www.michigan.gov/libraryofmichigan/0,2351,7-160-54574_36788_36790---,00.html

Type of Grant Maker: Government

Grants Information

Partially funds events or projects in Michigan that enhance or complement our mission to promote an awareness of books, reading, literacy, authors and Michigan's rich literary heritage.

Grant Amount: up to $3,000
Number of Grants: 11

APPLICATION PROCEDURES AND DEADLINES

Not available at this time.

Michigan Humanities Council

Headquarters

119 Pere Marquette Drive, Suite 3B
Lansing, MI 48912
Phone: 517-372-7770
Fax 517-372-0027

www.michiganhumanities.org/grants/index.php

Type of Grant Maker: Government

Grants Information

MAJOR GRANT PROGRAM

Grant Amount: Up to $15,000

Emphasizes collaboration among cultural, educational, and community-based organizations and institutions in order to serve Michigan's people with public humanities programming. Organizations are encouraged to explore and retrace our histories, roles in societies, advancements and changes, meaning in self-expression and fulfillment, commonalities and differences. Humanities disciplines include areas of study in comparative religion, ethics, philosophy, archaeology, classical and modern languages, linguistics, jurisprudence, history, literature, and criticism of the arts. Also included are social sciences that employ historical or philosophical approaches such as anthropology and geography, international relations, political science, or sociology.

REQUIREMENTS AND RESTRICTIONS

The applicant organization must be a nonprofit authorized to operate in the state of Michigan. The organization need not be incorporated and may be a public agency. Individuals are not eligible. Sponsoring organizations are encouraged to collaborate with other organizations.

APPLICATION PROCEDURES

See website. The Council strongly encourages applicants to submit DRAFT applications for staff review and assistance prior to submitting the final application.

Deadlines: Draft application deadline: February 27; final application deadline: March 15

QUICK & PLANNING GRANTS

Grant Amounts:
Up to $500, Quick Grants
Up to $1,000, Planning Grants

Provides support for public humanities programs that fall outside the design and deadline schedules of the major grants.

Funds can be used for:

1. Great Michigan Read
2. Planning
3. Guest Speakers
4. Reading/Discussion Programs

APPLICATION PROCEDURES

See website.

Deadlines: Four weeks prior to an event or planning session.

PRIME TIME FAMILY READING TIME® LIBRARY GRANTS

To implement or continue PRIME TIME Family Reading Time® programs.

Grant Amounts:
Up to $9,000 to selected libraries
Up to $2,000 for library systems that have previously implemented a program

REQUIREMENTS AND RESTRICTIONS

Any public library system in the state of Michigan is eligible to apply to host a six-week PRIME TIME® series. A library system must commit to hosting a minimum of three PRIME TIME® series over a two-year period.

APPLICATION PROCEDURES

See website.

Deadline: See website.

ARTS & HUMANITIES TOURING PROGRAM GRANTS

Grant Amounts: Up to 40% of expenses—$3,000 maximum

Provides nonprofit organizations a wide variety of cultural programming in the fields of dance, music, storytelling, theater, and traditional and visual arts.

APPLICATION PROCEDURES

See website.

Deadlines: None. Grants are first come-first served until funding is exhausted.

Middle Tennessee Community Foundation, Inc.

Headquarters

3833 Cleghorn Ave., No. 400
Nashville, TN 37215-2519
Phone: 615-321-4939

www.cfmt.org

Contact: Ellen E. Lehman, Pres.

E-mail: mail@cfmt.org

Type of Grant Maker: Community Foundation

Description

Founded: 1991

Operating Locations/Geographic Preferences: Giving limited to serving the 40 counties comprising the middle TN area

Financial Summary

Assets: $412,697,685
Total Giving: $44,664,210
Number of Grants: 528
Grant Ranges: $1,000,000 and under

Grants Information

GRANT TYPES

Program development

TYPICAL RECIPIENTS/SUBJECTS OF INTEREST

Discretionary Fund Grants—in the areas of the arts and humanities, conservation and preservation, environment, education, employment and training, health and human services, housing and economic and community development

Arts Build Communities (ABC) Grant Program—awarding matching grants for arts projects ranging from $500 to $2,000

Scholarship Program

PAST GRANT RECIPIENTS

Library or School Related

- Harding Academy, Nashville (TN), for annual fund, $5,000
- Ensworth School, Nashville (TN), $1,260,000

General

- Coastal Community Foundation of South Carolina, Charleston (SC), for Gaillard Renovation Fund, $1,000,000
- Nashville Symphony Association, Nashville (TN), in-kind forgiveness of interest on Symphony bonds, $750,000
- YMCA of Middle Tennessee, Nashville (TN), for General Fund, $300,000
- United Way of Metropolitan Nashville, Nashville (TN), $10,000

REQUIREMENTS AND RESTRICTIONS

No support for private foundations, religious or sectarian purposes, private schools, biomedical or clinical studies (other than those related to breast cancer), or fund-raising feasibility studies. No grants for fund-raising events, debt retirement, annual and capital campaigns, endowment campaigns, general operations, advertising, sponsorships, trips, conferences, computers or equipment.

APPLICATION PROCEDURES

See website for application forms and guidelines.
Application form required. Applicants should submit:

1. How project will be sustained once grant-maker support is completed
2. Signature and title of chief executive officer
3. Statement of problem project will address
4. Population served
5. Name, address and phone number of organization
6. Copy of IRS Determination Letter
7. Brief history of organization and description of its mission
8. Geographic area to be served
9. Copy of most recent annual report/audited financial statement/990

10. How project's results will be evaluated or measured
11. Listing of board of directors, trustees, officers and other key people and their affiliations
12. Detailed description of project and amount of funding requested
13. Plans for cooperation with other organizations, if any
14. Contact person
15. Listing of additional sources and amount of support

Deadlines: August 1

Milwaukee (Greater) Foundation

Headquarters

101 W. Pleasant St., Ste. 210
Milwaukee, WI 53212
Phone: 414-272-5805

www.greatermilwaukeefoundation.org

E-mail: info@greatermilwaukeefoundation.org

Type of Grant Maker: Community Foundation

Description

Founded: 1915

Operating Locations/Geographic Preferences: Giving primarily in Milwaukee, Ozaukee, Washington, and Waukesha, WI

Financial Summary

Assets: $429,446,000
Total Giving: $32,200,000

Gants Information

GRANT TYPES

Program development, building and renovation, capital campaigns, matching, seed money

TYPICAL RECIPIENTS/SUBJECTS OF INTEREST

Education, arts and cultural programs, community development, social services, health care, conservation and historic preservation.

Program giving areas include:

Arts and Culture funds projects that:
Strengthen the administrative and artistic capacity of arts and cultural organizations, particularly projects that enhance earned revenue
Improve access to the arts through community outreach and education.

Community Development funds projects that:
Improve the quality of life in Milwaukee neighborhoods through housing and economic development strategies
Strengthen the organizational capacity of community-based organizations and support their neighborhood revitalization efforts

Education funds projects that:
Promote collaborative initiatives and academic achievement in public and private schools, particularly for low-income and minority children
Support programs that enhance parental involvement in education, particularly for low-income and minority children.

Employment and Training funds project that:
Help at-risk individuals become self-supporting through job training, technical education, and job skills enhancement
Connect disadvantaged job seekers with meaningful employment.

Health and Human Services funds projects that:
Protect children and adults from abuse and neglect and provide support to victims of abuse
Foster independent living for the elderly and persons with special needs by providing alternatives to institutional care
Prevent disease and disabilities
Promote health education and advocacy to provide better access to health care for low-income and uninsured persons
Provide for basic human needs such as food and shelter.

Strengthening Children, Youth and Families funds projects that:
Develop support systems for children, youth and families
Nurture learning and growing in infants and young children
Promote positive youth development
Impact critical issues that negatively affect children, youth and family development.

PAST GRANT RECIPIENTS

Library or School Related

- Mount Mary College, Milwaukee (WI), for Urban Education Fellows—Cohort 8 Elementary Program, $200,000

- Milwaukee School of Engineering, Milwaukee (WI), for sustaining support, $4,000

General

- CORE-El Centro, Milwaukee (WI), for building renovation project, $150,000
- Land Stewardship Project, White Bear Lake (MN), for Farm Beginnings Program, $200,000
- North Point Lighthouse Friends, Milwaukee (WI), for the flag pole, $4,000
- Parenting Network, Milwaukee (WI), for marketing assistance, $4,000

REQUIREMENTS AND RESTRICTIONS

No support for the general use of churches or for sectarian religious purposes, or for specific medical or scientific projects, except from components of the foundation established for such purposes. No grants to individuals or for operating budgets, continuing support, annual campaigns, endowment funds, or deficit financing.

APPLICATION PROCEDURES

See website for online letter of inquiry and application guidelines. Selected applicants will be asked to submit full proposals based on letter of inquiry. Application form required.

Deadlines: Quarterly

Minneapolis Foundation

Headquarters

800 IDS Ctr.
80 S. Eighth St.
Minneapolis, MN 55402-2100
Phone: 612-672-3878

www.MinneapolisFoundation.org

Contact: Paul Verrette, Sr. Grants Admin.

E-mail: e-mail@mplsfoundation.org

Type of Grant Maker: Community Foundation

Description

Founded: 1915

Operating Locations/Geographic Preferences: Giving limited to MN, with emphasis on organizations in the Twin Cities metropolitan region

Financial Summary

Assets: $625,399,567
Total Giving: $45,193,056

Grants Information

GRANT TYPES

Program development, general, operating and continuing support, seed money, investments and loans, capital campaigns.

TYPICAL RECIPIENTS/SUBJECTS OF INTEREST

Giving programs include:

Build Social Capital

Program results:

Communities Speak and Act for Themselves—under-represented communities have the capacity to act on their own behalf

Organizations are Prepared to Work Effectively with Communities—institutions are prepared to work with underrepresented communities in new and more effective ways

Leaders Are Effective in Advancing a Shared Vision—leaders utilize community assets to advance their shared vision.

Promote Economic Vitality

Program results:

Stable Families—individuals and families have stable and affordable housing and are on the path to self-sufficiency

Prepared Workforce—a trained workforce exists to meet the demands of the economy

Community Wealth—job and small business creation is promoted.

Transform Education

Program results:

Student Success—children are ready to enter school, stay on grade, and graduate prepared to thrive in their post-secondary education/vocation

Effective Public Education—our public school systems ensure all children experience academic success

Community and Parent Engagement—parents, communities, and school systems work together toward shared goals.

PAST GRANT RECIPIENTS

Library or School Related

- Stanford University, Stanford (CA), for the School of Business Campus Sustainability Fund, $1,000,000

- University of Minnesota Foundation, Minneapolis (MN), for the HHH Civic Innovation Laboratory Fund, $2,000

General

- Minnesota Orchestral Association, Minneapolis (MN), for capital campaign, $3,000,000
- ServeMinnesota, Minneapolis (MN), for general operating support, $5,000
- Tubman, Minneapolis (MN), for general operating support, $2,000

REQUIREMENTS AND RESTRICTIONS

No support for national campaigns, direct religious activities, veterans' or fraternal organizations, or organizations within umbrella organizations. No grants to individuals, or for annual campaigns, deficit financing, building or endowment funds, scholarships, fellowships, conferences, courtesy advertising, direct fund-raising efforts, benefit tickets, telephone solicitations, or memberships.

APPLICATION PROCEDURES

See website for online application and guidelines. Application form required. Applicants should submit:

1. Results expected from proposed grant
2. Statement of problem project will address
3. Name, address and phone number of organization
4. Copy of IRS Determination Letter
5. Geographic area to be served
6. How project's results will be evaluated or measured
7. Detailed description of project and amount of funding requested
8. Contact person
9. Copy of current year's organizational budget and/or project budget

Deadlines: March 1 and September 1

Minnesota Department of Education State Library Services Division

Headquarters

1500 Highway 36 West
Roseville, MN 55113
Phone: 651-582-8805

www.education.state.mn.us/MDE/StuSuc/Lib/
StateLibServ/LSTA/index.html

Contact: James V. Wroblewski, LSTA Coordinator/Grant Administrator

E-mail: jym.wroblewski@state.mn.us

Type of Grant Maker: Government

Total Grants: $450,000

Grant Information

LSTA

Funds in the state grants program provide support for statewide library programs and seed money for projects that improve library services throughout the United States. In Minnesota funds are allocated based on the goals and programs in the five-year plan.

APPLICATION PROCEDURES

See website.

Deadlines: June 15

Mississippi Library Commission

Headquarters

3881 Eastwood Drive
Jackson, MS 39211
Phone: 800-647-7542, 800-446-0892

www.mlc.lib.ms.us/servicestolibraries/grants.html

Type of Grant Maker: Government

Grants Information

Grant Amounts: Vary according to program

Grant programs include:

- Library 2.0 Service
- Public Librarian Scholarship Program
- Public Library Programming
- Technology
- State Aid Sub-Grants

APPLICATION PROCEDURES

See online forms.

Deadlines: Vary

Missouri State Library

Headquarters

600 West Main St.
Jefferson City, MO 65101
Phone: 573-751-4936

www.sos.mo.gov/library/development/grants.asp

Type of Grant Maker: Government

Grants Information

STRENGTHEN SERVICE THROUGH TECHNOLOGY

Grant Ranges: $5,000–$35,000

Designed to help libraries move up the technology ladder to a higher level of service. Projects may be intricate in nature and/or require a longer time frame to provide solid evaluation measures

REQUIREMENTS AND RESTRICTIONS

Open to qualified public libraries needing financial assistance for technology hardware and software.

TECHNOLOGY MINI-GRANTS

Grant Ranges: $2,500–$15,000

For public libraries needing to replace, upgrade or add new equipment or software.

REQUIREMENTS AND RESTRICTIONS

Public libraries only

DIGITAL IMAGING GRANTS

Grant Ranges: $5,000–$75,000

For scanning, cataloging and web delivery of significant historic and cultural materials in Missouri and in Missouri history.

REQUIREMENTS AND RESTRICTIONS

All types of libraries are eligible, but grants are restricted to projects involving original source materials.

WEBSITE MAKEOVER

Grant Ranges: $2,500–$10,000

For public libraries to develop or redesign a website for more effective service delivery.

REQUIREMENTS AND RESTRICTIONS

Public libraries only, and they must be ADA compliant, contain a translation link, and link to state resources.

SHOW-ME STEPS TO CONTINUING EDUCATION

Grant Ranges: $1,000–$5,000

For library staff and trustees to participate in continuing education and training opportunities when local funds cannot finance the entire cost.

REQUIREMENTS AND RESTRICTIONS

All types of library are eligible, but continuing education events can be for individuals or groups, bust must be pertinent to the operational or service needs of the applicant's library.

SPOTLIGHT ON LITERACY

Grant Ranges: $2,500–$10,000

To provide libraries an opportunity to serve patrons through programs that support an educated and informed citizenry.

REQUIREMENTS AND RESTRICTIONS

All libraries except special libraries are eligible.

SUMMER READING PROGRAM

Grant Ranges: $2,500–$15,000

To expand opportunities for children, teens and adults to improve their reading skills enrich summer learning experiences and enhance opportunities to reach underserved summer populations.

REQUIREMENTS AND RESTRICTIONS

Only school and public libraries are eligible.

APPLICATION PROCEDURES

See website for online application procedures for each grant program

Deadlines: See website

Mitsubishi Electric American Foundation

Headquarters

1560 Wilson Blvd., Suite 1150
Arlington, VA 22209-2463
Phone: 703-276-8240
www.meaf.org/index.php

Contact: Kevin R. Webb, Exec. Dire.

E-mail: Kevin.webb@meus.mea.com

Type of Grant Maker: Corporate Foundation

Description

Founded: 1991

Operating Locations/Geographic Preferences: National giving, with emphasis on areas of company operations: CA, Washington, DC, GA, IL, KY, MA, MI, OH, PA, TN, VA

Corporate Foundation Information: Supported by Mitsubishi Electric Co.

Financial Summary

Assets: 17,422,791
Total Giving: $448,684
Number of Grants: 184
Grant Ranges: $50,000–$25

Grants Information

GRANT TYPES

Program development, general and operating support, seed money, employee volunteering

TYPICAL RECIPIENTS/SUBJECTS OF INTEREST

Young people with disabilities

Programs include:

Inclusion—to provide young people with disabilities full access to educational, vocational and recreational opportunities.

MOVE Award for volunteering

Matching Grants

National Grants

Starfish Matching Gifts for employees

PAST GRANT RECIPIENTS

Library or School Related

- University of California Los Angeles, for Students for the Advancement of Global Entrepreneurship (SAGE), $210,000

General

- Partners for Youth with Disabilities, for mentoring program for Big Brothers/Big Sisters, $60,000
- American Association of People with Disabilities, for Disability Mentoring Day Pipelines of Talent Program, $35,000

REQUIREMENTS AND RESTRICTIONS

No support for religious organizations, political or lobbying organizations, or individual schools or school districts. No grants to individuals or for endowments or capital campaigns.

APPLICATION PROCEDURES

See website for application information

Deadlines: June 1

Monell, Ambrose Foundation

Headquarters

c/o Fulton, Rowe, & Hart
1 Rockefeller Plz., Ste. 301
New York, NY 10020-2002
Phone: 212-586-0700
www.monellvetlesen.org

Contact: George Rowe, Jr., Pres.

E-mail: info@monellvetlesen.org

Type of Grant Maker: Foundation

Description

Founded: 1952

Operating Locations/Geographic Preferences: Giving primarily in NY

Financial Summary

Assets: $228,570,504
Total Giving: $9,063,333

Number of Grants: 155
Grant Ranges: $1,008,333–$2,500; average:
    $25,000–$100,000

Grants Information

GRANT TYPES

General, operating, and continuing support, annual
campaigns, building and renovation, matching

TYPICAL RECIPIENTS/SUBJECTS OF INTEREST

Hospitals and health services, scientific research, museums,
performing arts, and other cultural activities, and higher
and secondary education, social services, research in
political science, mental health, and aid to the handicapped

PAST GRANT RECIPIENTS

Library or School Related

- Harvard University, Cambridge (MA), for general
  purposes, $500,000
- Perkins School for the Blind, Watertown (MA), for
  general purposes, $25,000

General

- American Museum of Natural History, New York (NY),
  for general purposes, $300,000
- Carnegie Institution of Washington, Washington (DC), for
  general purposes, $100,000
- Museum of Arts and Design, New York (NY), for general
  purposes, $25,000
- Monell Chemical Senses Center, Philadelphia (PA), for
  general purposes, $625,000

REQUIREMENTS AND RESTRICTIONS

No grants to individuals.

APPLICATION PROCEDURES

See website for application information. Letter of inquiry
required as initial step. Full proposals by invitation only
based on letter review.

Deadlines: None

Montana Library Association

Headquarters

PO Box 1352
Three Forks, MT 59752
Phone: 406-579-3121

www.mtlib.org/contacts.asp

Contact: Debra Kramer, Administrative Director

Type of Grant Maker: Library Organization

Grants Information

MLA CONFERENCE GRANTS

Grant Amount: $150

REQUIREMENTS AND RESTRICTIONS

Applicant must be a current member of the Montana
Library Association. Up to five of the grants will be made
available to those members who are new to the profession
and to the Montana Library Association.

PROFESSIONAL DEVELOPMENT GRANTS

Grant Ranges: Not to exceed the actual amount associated
with program/event for which grant is requested.

REQUIREMENT AND RESTRICTIONS

Applicant must be a current member of the Montana
Library Association.

Professional Development Grants cannot be applied to
the MLA annual conference and are designated for regional
and national professional development opportunities.

LEADERSHIP INSTITUTE GRANTS

Grant Ranges: Grants will not exceed the actual amount
associated with the program/event for which the grant is
requested.

REQUIREMENTS AND RESTRICTIONS

Applicant must be a current member of the Montana
Library Association and must have been an MLA member
for at least the two (2) previous years.

ALA EMERGING LEADER GRANTS

Grant Ranges: N/A

REQUIREMENTS AND RESTRICTIONS

1. Applicant must be a current member of the Montana
   Library Association.
2. Applicant must meet Emerging Leaders application
   requirements and have been accepted to the program.
3. Applicant must be able to attend the two ALA
   conferences for the year of participation, and
4. Applicant must be willing to serve MLA for 2 years in a
   leadership position within the association. A leadership
   position will be defined as serving on an MLA committee
   or on the MLA Board.

5. Recipients will be required to either present a program at an MLA-sponsored retreat or conference and/or may be asked to serve as a mentor by the MLA mentor program.

APPLICATION PROCEDURES

See website for online procedures and forms.

Deadlines: See website.

Motorola Mobility Foundation

Headquarters

600 N. US Highway 45
Libertyville, Illinois 60048
Phone: 847-523-3597

http://responsibility.motorola.com

E-mail: giving@motorola.com

Type of Grant Maker: Corporate Foundation

Description

Founded: 1928

Operating Locations/Geographic Preferences: California, Illinois, Massachusetts, Florida, Oregon, Georgia, Texas or Pennsylvania

Corporate Foundation Information: Supported by Motorola Mobility, Inc.

Financial Summary

Total Giving: $500,000
Number of Grants: 51

Grants Information

GRANT TYPES

Capital, matching, general and continuing support, program development

TYPICAL RECIPIENTS/SUBJECTS OF INTEREST

Program areas include:

- Education
- Social cohesion
- Health and wellness
- Innovation
- Disaster relief
- Empowerment grants
- Employee engagements

PAST GRANT RECIPIENTS

Not available.

REQUIREMENTS AND RESTRICTIONS

Must be a U.S. registered or incorporated 501(c)(3) nonprofit organization or an NCES school or school district

Must serve communities in California, Illinois, Massachusetts, Florida, Oregon, Georgia, Texas or Pennsylvania; however can be an online or national program

Must be actively collaborating with at least one other nonprofit, social enterprise or community group

Must be aligned with funding priorities in education, health and wellness, community, or arts and culture

APPLICATION PROCEDURES

Guidelines and application process for different giving programs are posted online.

Deadlines: Vary

Motorola Solutions Foundation (*Formerly* Motorola Foundation)

Headquarters

c/o Motorola Solutions, Inc.
1303 East Algonquin Rd.
Schaumburg, IL 60196-4041
Phone: 847-538-7639
Fax: 847-538-1456

www.motorolasolutions.com/giving

Contact: Matt Blakely, Dir.

E-mail: foundation@motorolasolutions.com

Type of Grant Maker: Corporate Foundation

Description

Founded: 1953

Operating Locations/Geographic Preferences: Giving primarily on a national and international basis in areas of company operations, with emphasis on CA, Washington,

DC, FL, GA, IL, MA, MD, NJ, NY, TX, Argentina, Belgium, Brazil, China, England, France, Mexico, Poland, and Singapore.

Corporate Foundation Information: Supported by Motorola, Inc.

Financial Summary

Assets: $101,344,313
Total Giving: $17,890,729
Number of Grants: 428
Grant Ranges: $500,700–$55

Grants Information

GRANT TYPES

Program development, employee volunteering, general and operating support, equipment

TYPICAL RECIPIENTS/SUBJECTS OF INTEREST

Education: Supporting programs that encourage science, technology, engineering and math education in the U.S. and globally, preparing students for the workforce of tomorrow.

Public safety: For the safety of communities and to support the first responders who protect us around the world.

Disaster relief: Joining humanitarian organizations to address disasters when they strike, including donations of mission-critical equipment and money to provide infrastructure for emergency workers.

Employee volunteering

PAST GRANT RECIPIENTS

Library or School Related

- Chicago Public Library Foundation, ScienceConnections Science Mentors with hands-on STEM-focused drop-in sessions in libraries
- Chicago Public Schools, Student Science Fair
- Tallahassee Community College Foundation, Improving Student Science Achievement through Family Science and Teacher Development
- Florida International University Foundation, Inc., Motorola Summer PREP (Pre-college Enrichment and Preparation) Program

General

- Urban League of Broward County, Inc., Getting Ready For Opportunities With Technology
- Adler Planetarium, Summer Enrichment Programs

REQUIREMENTS AND RESTRICTIONS

No support for political or lobbying organizations, political candidates, or private foundations described under the U.S. IRS Code Section 509(a). No grants to individuals, or for endowments, sports sponsorships, or capital campaigns; no Motorola Solutions product or equipment donations.

APPLICATION PROCEDURES

Current funding opportunities and guidelines are available online, along with application forms.

Deadlines: Vary according to program

Mott, Charles Stewart Foundation

Headquarters

Mott Foundation Bldg.
503 S. Saginaw St., Ste. 1200
Flint, MI 48502-1851
Phone: 810-238-5651

www.mott.org

E-mail: info@mott.org

Type of Grant Maker: Foundation

Description

Founded: 1926

Operating Locations/Geographic Preferences: Giving nationally and to emerging countries in Central and Eastern Europe, Russia, and South Africa

Financial Summary

Assets: $2,130,000,000
Total Giving: $108,500,000
Number of Grants: 456
Grant Ranges: $3,100,000–$4,000

Grants Information

GRANT TYPES

Program development, general, operating and continuing support, matching investments and loans, seed money, management development

TYPICAL RECIPIENTS/SUBJECTS OF INTEREST

Giving programs include:

Civil Society:
> Central/Eastern Europe and Russia
> South Africa
> United States
> Global Philanthropy and Nonprofit Sector.

Environment:
> Conservation of Freshwater Ecosystems
> International Finance for Sustainability
> Special Initiatives

Exploratory and Special Projects:
> Includes Historically Black Colleges and Universities
> Arts, Culture and Education
> Economic Revitalization
> Strengthening Community
> Special Initiatives

Pathways Out of Poverty:
> Improving Community Education
> Expanding Economic Opportunity
> Building Organized Communities
> Special Initiatives

PAST GRANT RECIPIENTS

Library or School Related

- Genesee Area Focus Fund, Flint (MI), for operating support for YouthQuest After School Initiative, $3,100,000

General

- Collaborative Communications Group, Washington (DC), to support Statewide Afterschool Networks and Afterschool Technical Assistance Collaborative, $1,300,000
- American Association of Community Colleges, Washington (DC), for small business demonstration project, $995,000
- Flint Institute of Arts, Flint (MI), for operating support, $1,635,000
- Southern Education Foundation, Atlanta (GA), for Education Summer Youth Leadership Initiative, $140,000

REQUIREMENTS AND RESTRICTIONS

No support for religious activities or programs serving specific religious groups or denominations. Faith-based organizations may submit inquiries if the project falls within the foundation's guidelines and serves a broad segment of the population. No grants to individuals or for capital development (with the exception of the Flint area and legacy institutions). Grants for research, project replication or endowments are rarely funded. No support for local projects, except in the Flint area. No film or video projects, books, scholarships, loans

APPLICATION PROCEDURE

Application form not required. Applicants should submit:

1. Statement of problem project will address
2. Detailed description of project and amount of funding requested
3. Copy of current year's organizational budget and/or project budget

Deadlines: None

Murphy Foundation

Headquarters

200 N. Jefferson Ave.
El Dorado, AR 71730-5841
Phone: 870-862-4961

Contact: Brett Williamson, Secy.-Treas.

Type of Grant Maker: Foundation

Description

Founded: 1958

Operating Locations/Geographic Preferences: Giving primarily in Southern AR

Financial Summary

Assets: $71,258,377
Total Giving: $3,118,304
Number of Grants: 56
Grant Ranges: $600,189–$400

Grants Information

GRANT TYPES

General and operating support, annual campaigns, endowments

TYPICAL RECIPIENTS/SUBJECTS OF INTEREST

Higher education, arts and human services

PAST GRANT RECIPIENTS

Library or School Related

- Barton Library, El Dorado (AR), operating support, $25,000
- El Dorado School District, El Dorado (AR), operating support, $10,500
- South Arkansas Community College Foundation, El Dorado (AR), operating support, $10,000
- Hendrix College, Conway (AR), operating support, $1,000,000
- University of Arkansas for Medical Sciences, Little Rock (AR), operating support, $250,000
- George W. Bush Presidential Center, Dallas (TX), operating support, $200,000

REQUIREMENTS AND RESTRICTIONS

None, other than geographic preferences

APPLICATION PROCEDURES

Applicants should submit letter of inquiry with detailed description of project and amount of funding requested

Deadlines: None

Music Library Association (MLA)

Headquarters

8551 Research Way, Suite 180
Middleton, WI 53562
Phone: 608-836-5825
FAX: 608-831-8200

E-mail: mla@areditions.com

Grants Information

LENORE F. CORAL IAML TRAVEL GRANT

To help support travel and conference fees to attend an annual IAML meeting. The grant, a cash award, is usually offered biennially, in even numbered years, or more frequently at the discretion of the MLA Board of Directors.

REQUIREMENTS AND RESTRICTIONS

The grant is open to all MLA members who are also members of IAML, with priority given to members attending their first or second IAML conference who have not received this award in a previous year. Applicants for the travel award should have little or no support from their home institution or library.

KEVIN FREEMAN TRAVEL GRANT

To support travel and hotel expenses to attend the Music Library Association annual meeting.

Grant Ranges: Grant(s) include the conference registration fee and a cash award up to $750, subject to approval of the current year's budget by the MLA Board.

REQUIREMENTS AND RESTRICTIONS

The applicant must be a member of the Music Library Association and either be in the first three years of his/her professional career, a graduate library school student aspiring to become a music librarian, or a recent graduate (within one year of degree) of a graduate program in librarianship who is seeking a professional position as a music librarian. At least one grant will be awarded to a first-time attendee, if applicable.

APPLICATION PROCEDURES

See online for application procedures.

Deadlines: See website.

National Archives and Records Administration

Headquarters

National Historical Publications and Records Commission (NHPRC)
National Archives and Records Administration
700 Pennsylvania Avenue NW, Room 114
Washington, DC 20408-0001
Phone: 202-357-5101

www.archives.gov

Program website/request for proposal:
www.archives.gov/nhprc/announcement/access.html

Contact: Alexander Lorch, Archives Program officer

E-mail: alexander.lorch@nara.gov

Type of Grant Maker: Government

Grants Information

Number of Grants: 15
Grant Ranges: up to $200,000

Program Description: The National Historical Publications and Records Commission seeks proposals that promote the preservation and use of the nation's most valuable archival resources. Projects should expand our understanding of the American past by facilitating and enhancing access to primary source materials.

The Commission will support such activities as establishing archives programs, processing archival collections at the basic or detailed levels, surveying and accessioning archival records, and converting existing archival collection finding aids to new online formats. Applicants may submit proposals for one or any combination of the following four project categories.

CATEGORIES

1. Basic Processing

Proposals may be submitted for establishing archives and undertaking basic processing activities that promote the preservation and use of America's documentary heritage. Proposals must demonstrate how the applicant employs the best and most cost-effective archival methods.

For projects to establish new archives programs, a proposal may include the cost of a consultant to assess the need for an archives program. The assessment should identify the resources necessary for sustaining such a program and include a collection development plan, a plan for basic processing of unprocessed collections and new accessions in a timely manner, and a phased preservation plan. If the organization already has a detailed assessment, it may submit a proposal for costs associated with starting its archives program, as outlined in the assessment. Applicants may also submit proposals for records management projects with archival components. Applicants for start-up projects must provide convincing evidence of ongoing program support and must also demonstrate their commitment to creating equitable and timely access to their holdings.

For projects that process and reveal archival collections which researchers cannot easily discover through online search engines, proposals should demonstrate how repositories will process and catalog records at either the collection or the series level. Applicants will need to create collection- or series-level MARC catalog records in a national bibliographic utility. If finding aids are created, they should generally meet current Encoded Archival Description standards, and be made available to appropriate regional and national archival databases. Basic processing cannot include processing or description at the folder or item levels.

Institutions must develop or implement processing techniques to eliminate unprocessed backlogs of holdings at a level consistent with appropriate standards and at a reasonable rate. In addition, applicants must develop and establish adequate accessioning and processing techniques that will prevent future backlogs. Basic processing proposals should also include reappraisal of collections

and include a process for deaccessioning entire collections where appropriate.

Applicants must also include plans to promote the use of their collections after completing this processing.

Applications may request funds for limited preservation activities, such as preservation surveys of collections, the evaluation of environmental controls, and risk assessments. Although the NHPRC does not fund construction projects, applicants may include planning for necessary improvements to physical facilities. Impermissible activities include comprehensive reboxing and refoldering, the removal of staples and paper clips, and item-level repairs and conservation.

Reformatting, digitizing, and microfilming are also not permissible. Preservation copying of faded or damaged documents should be extremely limited.

2. Detailed Processing

For collections with proven high research demand or substantial preservation concerns, applicants may propose to conduct detailed processing and preservation reformatting of collections of national significance. For projects that focus entirely on detailed processing, the Commission will give preference to repositories that have virtually all of their collections processed sufficiently so that researchers can find them through online searches. In general, proposals should describe how the repository will process and create detailed descriptions at the series or file level. Projects should create or revise online descriptions and submit them to national library catalogs, national archival databases, and appropriate regional and institutional databases. Applicants must also create or revise detailed finding aids using Encoded Archival Description (EAD) unless other formats are more appropriate.

Applicants must explain whether any item-level processing or preservation treatment will be necessary, including refoldering, cleaning, flattening, copying, encapsulating, de-acidifying, and mending documents. If parts of collections deserve item-level processing, proposals must justify this detailed work and provide estimates of the percentage of collections to be processed to the item level.

Applicants may apply for grants in support of preservation reformatting. For collections containing unstable audio or video materials, applicants may propose preservation reformatting or migration to appropriate analog or digital formats. When appropriate, applicants should consider hybrid microfilm/digitization (using dual head cameras, or microfilm-to-digital or digital-to-microfilm techniques). For collections that include born digital files, applicants should include appropriate long-term digital preservation plans.

Applicants may propose limited digitization of series or items that have the most potential to benefit a broad public. Applications should detail the standards to be used in this process, itemize anticipated expenses, and estimate the percentage of the collections to be digitized. Applicants intending to submit projects that only digitize materials should see the Digitizing Historical Records announcement.

Applicants should also outline their publicity and outreach plans for promoting use of collections.

3. Documentary Heritage

Documentary heritage projects create more comprehensive documentation of US history and culture by supporting projects that identify, survey, collect, and make available nationally significant records relating to groups and topics traditionally underrepresented in the historical record. Eligible activities include arrangement and description projects, documentation surveys, archival needs assessments, or some combination of the three. The NHPRC does not support projects to create new documentation, except for oral history projects conducted by American Indian tribes and other indigenous peoples that rely on oral traditions to document their history and culture. Newspapers also are not considered historical records for the purposes of this announcement.

All projects that include collecting activities must show that the institution has developed, or will develop as a part of the project, initial processing techniques to gain basic physical and intellectual control over new accessions. If the repository has a large unprocessed backlog of holdings, collections development activities may only occur alongside basic processing activities. Projects that include elements of arrangement and description must not include item-level processing.

4. Retrospective Conversion of Descriptive Information

Proposals may be submitted for converting legacy finding aids and other sources of descriptive information into formats that provide improved online access to collections. Activities may include converting card catalogs and paper finding aids so that they may be made available electronically, or creating a comprehensive online database or finding aid from information only available in a variety of non-compatible formats. Applicants must use Encoded Archival Description (EAD) for finding aids unless other formats are more appropriate.

REQUIREMENTS AND RESTRICTIONS

Eligibility: Archives and other repositories of historical documents are eligible if they are part of:

- Nonprofit organizations
- Colleges, universities, and other academic institutions
- State or local government agencies
- Federally acknowledged or state-recognized Native American tribes or groups

REQUIREMENTS AND RESTRICTIONS

See comprehensive list of the Commission's limitations on funding available at What We Do and Do Not Fund.

APPLICATION PROCEDURES AND DEADLINES

See request for proposal

National Capital Region, Community Foundation for

Headquarters

1201 15th St. N.W., Ste. 420
Washington, DC 20005-2842
Phone: 202-955-5890

www.thecommunityfoundation.org

Contact: Terri Lee Freeman, President; for grant applications: Tracey Jarmon, Philanthropic Advisory Services Office

E-mail: tfreeman@cfncr.org

Type of Grant Maker: Community Foundation

Description

Founded: 1973

Operating Locations/Geographic Preferences: Giving limited to the Washington, DC, Prince George's and Montgomery counties, MD and northern VA

Financial Summary

Assets: $368,358,325
Total Giving: $62,969,894

Grants Information

GRANT TYPES

General and operating support, program development, management development, matching

TYPICAL RECIPIENTS/SUBJECTS OF INTEREST

Giving programs include:

Collaborative for Education Organizing: to double college-ready graduation rates in the District of Columbia.

Greater Washington Workforce Development Collaborative: to help low-income adults throughout the Greater Washington region obtain and retain jobs

Linowes Leadership Award

Neighbors in Need Fund

Scholarships

PAST GRANT RECIPIENTS

Library or School Related

- Saint Albans School for Boys, Washington (DC), $1,600,000

General

- Archdiocese of Washington, Hyattsville (MD), $1,000,000
- Fisher House Foundation, Rockville (MD), $800,000
- Fight for Children, Washington (DC), $25,000

REQUIREMENTS AND RESTRICTIONS

No grants to individuals or for annual campaigns, endowment funds, land acquisition or renovation projects

APPLICATION PROCEDURES

See website for application forms and guidelines.

Deadlines: Vary

National Center for Family Literacy, Inc.

Headquarters

c/o 325 W. Main St., Ste. 300
Louisville, KY 40202-2037

www.famlit.org

Type of Grant Maker: Foundation

Description

Founded: 1989

Operating Locations/Geographic Preferences: National giving

Financial Summary

Assets: $13,367,515
Total $1,343,450

Grants Information

GRANT TYPES

Program support

TYPICAL RECIPIENTS/SUBJECTS OF INTEREST

The improvements of literacy in adults and children through a family approach to education

Program giving areas include:

Toyota Family Literacy Program: TFLP serves English as Second Language (ESL) families with children in elementary school. Today, Toyota has funded 256 family literacy sites in 50 cities and 30 states that have impacted the lives of more than 1 million families. Established in 2003, TFLP addresses the growing needs of Hispanic and other immigrant families by increasing English language and literacy skills for adults while also supporting parents' involvement in their children's education.

Family and Child Education: The FACE program serves American Indian families with children from birth to grade three and is supported by the Bureau of Indian Education. Now operating in 44 American Indian schools, this program provides culturally responsive education, resources and support to American Indian parents and children. To date, the FACE program has reached more than 25,000 families.

The Family Literacy-Community College Initiative: This initiative is exploring the unique partnership between family literacy programs and community colleges in promoting a continuing education for adult learners. NCFL, with funding from the MetLife Foundation, is researching the latest best practices of community colleges in cultivating the enrollment and supporting the progress of former family literacy students.

Toyota Family Literacy Teacher of the Year: Each year, NCFL and Toyota recognize the outstanding efforts of a family literacy teacher with the Toyota Family Literacy Teacher of the Year (TOY) Award. NCFL awards this honor to a teacher who has made innovative and passionate contributions to improving the lives of adults and children through family literacy—whether through early childhood education, school-based programs, adult literacy and ESL programs, parenting education or a community literacy program.

Verizon Tech Savvy Award: These awards recognize outstanding educational programs that demystify technology for parents so that they may better support their children's academic and social growth in an increasingly complex 21st century. Established in 2007 by the Verizon Foundation, the National Center for

Family Literacy (NCFL) and Former First Lady of Iowa Christie Vilsack, the Verizon Tech Savvy Awards are the first national awards given to intergenerational digital learning programs.

Better World Books Community Book Drives: Better World Books has been a critical partner in NCFL's fight for a more literate nation, raising more than $330,000 for our mission to date and $5.2 million for literacy and education overall. With Better World Books' help, NCFL has been able to organize community support from libraries and college campuses all across the country. Better World Books has mobilized local book drives at more than 888 college campuses and libraries nationwide on behalf of NCFL.

McDonald's Family Mealtime Literacy Nights: Since October 2006, NCFL and the Southern California McDonald's Restaurants have teamed up for the highly successful Family Mealtime Literacy Nights program, designed to show parents of preschoolers how they can use simple household routines to teach literacy, math and science to their children. These fun and interactive workshops not only allow families special time to spend together, but they also improve school readiness for children and increase parents' excitement to support their children's learning.

Toys for Tots Literacy Program: NCFL, The UPS Store® and Mail Boxes Etc.® network, and the Marine Toys for Tots Foundation are placing books in the hands of children in communities nationwide. NCFL president and founder Sharon Darling was the official spokesperson for the 2009 Toys for Tots Literacy Program.

PAST GRANT RECIPIENTS

Library or School Related

- Columbus Metropolitan Library, Columbus (OH)
- Providence Public Library, Providence (RI)
- Salinas Public Library, Salinas (CA)
- Friends of the Dallas Public Library's Every Child Ready to Read@Dallas
- San Diego Library's READ/San Diego—Families for Literacy program
- Queens Library Family Literacy Program
- Vineland Public Library
- Mastics-Moriches-Shirley Community Library

REQUIREMENTS AND RESTRICTIONS

Application guidelines and online applications are available online as funding opportunities open.

Deadlines: Vary

National Endowment for the Humanities

Headquarters

Division of Education Programs
National Endowment for the Humanities
Room 302
1100 Pennsylvania Avenue, NW
Washington, DC 20506
Phone: 202-606-8380

www.neh.gov; www.neh.gov/grants/guidelines/
BridgingCulturesCCRFP.html (proposal website)

Type of Grant Maker: Government

Grants Information

Grant Ranges: up to $360,000

REQUIREMENTS AND RESTRICTIONS

Eligibility: State, County, City or Township, Special Districts, Public/State Higher Ed, Tribal Governments, Nonprofit.

　　Cooperative agreements may not be used for:

- creative or performing arts;
- empirical social scientific research;
- specific policy studies;
- educational or technical impact assessments;
- work undertaken in the pursuit of an academic degree;
- the preparation or publication of textbooks;
- projects that focus on pedagogical theory, research on educational methods, tests, or measurements;
- projects that seek to promote a particular political, religious, or ideological point of view; or
- projects that advocate a particular program of social action.

APPLICATION PROCEDURES AND DEADLINES

See request for proposal

AMERICA'S HISTORICAL AND CULTURAL ORGANIZATIONS

Division of Public Programs
National Endowment for the Humanities
Room 426
1100 Pennsylvania Avenue, NW
Washington, DC 20506

Phone: 202-606-8269

www.neh.gov/; www.neh.gov/grants/ahco
   (grant-specific website)

Description

America's Historical and Cultural Organizations grants provide support for museums, libraries, historic places, and other organizations that produce public programs in the humanities.

Program Description: America's Historical and Cultural Organizations grants provide support for museums, libraries, historic places, and other organizations that produce public programs in the humanities.

   Grants support the following formats:

- exhibitions at museums, libraries, and other venues
- interpretations of historic places, sites, or regions
- book/film discussion programs; living history presentations; and other face-to-face programs at libraries, community centers, and other public venues
- interpretive websites.

GRANT TYPES

Implementation grants support final scholarly research and consultation, design development, production, and installation of a project for presentation to the public.

GRANT VALUES

Grant Amounts: up to $1,000,000.

   In the last five competitions the America's Historical and Cultural Organizations: Implementation Grants program received an average of 56 applications. The program made an average of nine awards per competition, for a funding ratio of 16 percent.

REQUIREMENTS AND RESTRICTIONS

Eligible Institutions:

- State governments
- County governments
- City or township governments
- Special district governments
- Public and state controlled institutions of higher education
- Native American tribal governments (federally recognized)
- Nonprofits having a 501(c)(3) status with the IRS, other than institutions of higher education
- Private institutions of higher education

APPLICATION AND DEADLINES

See request for proposal

National Institutes of Health

Headquarters

Agency for Healthcare Research and Quality
540 Gaither Rd.
Rockville, MD 20850
Phone: 301-427-1444

www.hhs.gov

E-mail: cindy.brach@ahrq.hhs.gov

Type of Grant Maker: Government

Grants Information

UNDERSTANDING AND PROMOTING HEALTH LITERACY

Program Description: The ultimate goal of this program announcement is to encourage empirical research on health literacy concepts, theory and interventions as these relate to the US Department of Health and Human Services public health priorities that are outlined in its Healthier US and Healthy People initiative. Health literacy is defined as the degree to which individuals have the capacity to obtain, process, and understand basic health information and services needed to make appropriate health decisions.

   Researchers are encouraged to address health literacy as it pertains to prevention, healthy living, chronic disease management, patient-based health care, cultural competence, and health disparities. Research questions can focus on consumers, patients, clients, providers, educators, communities and organizations or systems.

   This Program Announcement invites applications to develop research on health literacy in general areas that include, but are not limited to, the following:

- Nature and Scope
- Lifespan and Cultural Differences
- Mediators and Moderators of Health Literacy: Protective and Risk Factors
- Education and Training
- Health Systems Interventions
- Methodology and Research Technology Development
- Examples of Research Topics

REQUIREMENTS AND RESTRICTIONS

Eligibility: State, County, City or Township, Special Districts, Independent School Districts, Public/State Higher Ed, Tribal Governments, Public/Indian Housing, Tribal Organizations (NonGovernments), NonProfit with 501(c)(3), NonProfit without 501(c)(3), Private Higher Ed, For-Profit Orgs (not small business), Small Businesses, Others.

Eligibility Notes: Other Eligible Applicants include the following: Alaska Native and Native Hawaiian-Serving Institutions; Eligible Agencies of the Federal Government; Faith-based or Community-based Organizations; Hispanic-serving Institutions; Historically Black Colleges and Universities (HBCUs); Non-domestic (non-U.S.) Entities (Foreign Organizations); Tribally Controlled Colleges and Universities (TCCUs).

Maximum Award: $200,000

APPLICATION PROCEDURES AND DEADLINES

See website for details and deadlines

National Library Medicine

Headquarters

8600 Rockville Pike
Bethesda, MD 20894
Phone: 888-346-3656

www.nlm.nih.gov

Type of Grant Maker: Government

Description

NATIONAL LIBRARY OF MEDICINE ADMINISTRATIVE SUPPLEMENTS FOR INFORMATIONIST SERVICES IN NIH-FUNDED RESEARCH PROJECTS (ADMIN SUPP)

Program Description: The National Library of Medicine, in conjunction with NIH Institutes and Centers provide administrative supplement funds to supported research and center grants to enhance the storage, organization, management and use of electronic research data through the involvement of informationists, also known as in-context information specialists.

The purposes of this administrative supplement program are (1) to enhance collaborative, multidisciplinary basic and clinical research by integrating an information specialist into the research team in order to improve the capture, storage, organization, management, integration, presentation and dissemination of biomedical research data and (2) to assess and document the value and impact of the informationist's participation.

Grants Information

Award amounts: $25,000 per year maximum, $50,000 over a two-year period
Eligible institutions include:

- Higher Education Institutions
- Public/State Controlled Institutions of Higher Education
- Private Institutions of Higher Education
- Hispanic-serving Institutions
- Historically Black Colleges and Universities (HBCUs)
- Tribally Controlled Colleges and Universities (TCCUs)
- Alaska Native and Native Hawaiian-Serving Institutions
- Nonprofits Other Than Institutions of Higher Education
    Nonprofits with 501(c)(3) IRS Status (Other than Institutions of Higher Education)
    Nonprofits without 501(c)(3) IRS Status (Other than Institutions of Higher Education)
- For-Profit Organizations

Guidelines and application information available at: http://grants.nih.gov/grants/guide/pa-files/PA-12-158.html

NLM Scientific Program Contact:

Valerie Florance, Ph.D.
Associate Director for Extramural Programs
National Library of Medicine
Phone: 301-496-4621
E-mail: florancev@mail.nih.gov

NLM INFORMATION RESOURCES GRANTS TO REDUCE HEALTH DISPARITIES

The National Library of Medicine (NLM) solicits resource grant applications for projects that will bring useful, usable health information to health disparity populations and the health care providers who care for those populations. Access to useful, usable, understandable health information is an important factor during health decisions. Proposed projects should exploit the capabilities of computer and information technology and health sciences libraries to bring health-related information to consumers and their health care providers. Preference will be given to applications that show strong involvement of health science libraries.

Link to Additional Information: http://grants.nih.gov/grants/guide/rfa-files/RFA-LM-12-001.html

Total Dollar Amount of Grants: NLM intends to fund up to 5 awards, for approximately $500,000.

GRANT VALUES

Budget up to $100,000 for one year, $200,000 over two years or $300,000 over 3 years, in direct costs, may be requested.

APPLICATION PROCEDURES

See guidelines at: http://grants.nih.gov/grants/guide/
rfa-files/RFA-LM-12-001.html#_Section_II._Award_1

CONTACT

Phone: 800-518-4726
E-mail: support@grants.gov

GRANTS INFO

Questions regarding application instructions and process, finding NIH grant resources

Phone: 301-435-0714

TTY: 301-451-5936

E-mail: GrantsInfo@nih.gov

SCIENTIFIC/RESEARCH CONTACT(S)

Dr. Alan VanBiervliet
NLM Extramural Programs
6705 Rockledge Drive
Rockledge 1, Suite 301
Bethesda, MD 20892-7968
Phone: 301-594-4882
Fax-301-402-2952

E-mail: alan.vanbiervliet@nih.gov

National Science Foundation

Headquarters

4201 Wilson Boulevard
Arlington, VA 22230

Contact: W. Carl Taylor, BRC Program Director, Directorate for Biological Sciences, Division of Biological Infrastructure

Phone: 703-292-8470

www.nsf.gov/; www.nsf.gov/publications/pub_summ.
jsp?ods_key=nsf06569 (grant website)

E-mail: dbibrc@nsf.gov

Contact: Anne M. Maglia

Phone: 703-292-8470

E-mail: amaglia@nsf.gov

Type of Grant Maker: Government

Grants Information

Est. Total Funding: $6,000,000
Expected Awards: 25
Grant Ranges: Up to $500,000 total for individual awards; up to $2,000,000 total for collaborative awards

BIOLOGICAL RESEARCH COLLECTIONS GRANTS

Program Description: The Improvements to Biological Research Collections Program provides funds for improvements to network, secure, and organize established natural history collections for sustained, accurate, and efficient accessibility of the collection to the biological research community.

The BRC program is encouraging collaborative proposals to network collections on regional and continental scales, especially collaborations that bring large and small collections together into networks. The BRC program also provides for enhancements to existing collections to improve collections, computerize specimen-related data, develop better methods of specimen curation and collection management through activities such as symposia and workshops.

Biological collections supported include those housing natural history specimens and jointly curated collections such as preserved tissues and other physical samples, e.g., DNA libraries and digital images. Such collections provide the materials necessary for research across broad areas of biological sciences.

REQUIREMENTS AND RESTRICTIONS

Proposals are accepted from US organizations, including colleges and universities that maintain research collections, natural history museums including herbaria, and other collections administered by independent organizations or by state, county, or local governments; non-federal and nonprofit research organizations that maintain collections; and field stations, marine laboratories, botanical gardens, zoological parks, and aquaria that maintain research collections that document biological diversity. The size of an organization is not a factor in determining eligibility.

APPLICATION PROCEDURES AND DEADLINES

See website

Nebraska Library Commission

Headquarters

The Atrium
1200 N St.
Suite 120
Lincoln, NE 68508-2023
Phone: 402-471-2045, 800-307-2665 (Nebraska only)

http://nlc.nebraska.gov

Type of Grant Maker: Government

Grants Information

CONTINUING EDUCATION AND TRAINING GRANTS

To assist Nebraska libraries in improving the library services provided to their communities through continuing education and training for their library personnel and supporters. Successful applications will show how the continuing education and/or training proposed will support the library's mission. Categories include:

- Reimbursement for tuition or registration fees for an online class.
- Reimbursement for expenses of attending a professional conference.
- Grant for a project or program.

Grant Ranges: N/A

INTERNSHIP GRANT PROGRAM

To enable Nebraska public libraries to hire one or more individuals (high school age and up) to serve as interns. Library grantees will recruit, select and hire their interns. Usually, interns are hired as contract workers and paid on a stipend rather than an hourly wage, but the terms of employment are determined by the library's governing body experiences.

Grant Ranges: $500–$1,000

REQUIREMENTS AND RESTRICTIONS

Only accredited Nebraska public libraries are eligible.

APPLICATION PROCEDURES AND DEADLINES

Contact:

Kathryn Brockmeier, Grant Program Manager
402-471-4002 or 800-307-2665

LIBRARY IMPROVEMENT GRANTS

Due to budget reductions, these grants may not be made.

Contact:
Richard Miller
Phone: 800-307-2665 for details.

YOUTH GRANTS FOR EXCELLENCE

For innovative projects for children and young adults in accredited public libraries and state-run institutional libraries in Nebraska. The program is designed to encourage creative thinking, risk-taking and new approaches to address problems and needs of children and young adults in your community. Grant awards enable youth librarians to begin needed programs and try projects which they have been unable to undertake. The grants also offer an opportunity to expand youth service capabilities in new and different directions. It is also expected that the funding will provide a foundation for ongoing rather than one-time services, which can be continued with community support or through a reallocation of library funds.

Grant Ranges: $250 and up

REQUIREMENTS AND RESTRICTIONS

Any children's librarian, young adult librarian, or adult librarian (in an accredited public library or a state-run institutional library) in charge of children's or young adult services and system administrators may apply. Schools, service agencies, and/or organizations may be involved through collaborative planning and programming, thus receiving benefit from this project.

APPLICATIONS PROCEDURES AND DEADLINES

See online information for forms and deadlines.

Nevada State Library and Archives

Headquarters

Development Services
100 North Stewart St.
Carson City, Nevada 89701-4285
Phone: 775-684-3407, 800-922-2880

http://nsla.nevadaculture.org/index.php?option=
com_content&view=article&id=537&Itemid=422

Type of Grant Maker: Government

: Ma

Grants Information

LIBRARY SERVICES AND TECHNOLOGY ACT (LSTA) MINI-GRANTS

To provide local assistance to eligible libraries in the areas of technology innovation, resource-sharing, and targeted services to people who are underserved, disadvantaged, geographically isolated, illiterate, etc.

Grant Ranges: N/A

REQUIREMENTS AND RESTRICTIONS

All types of libraries, including academic, public, school, governmental agency libraries and eligible information centers, and special libraries with public access may apply.

Applicants must certify that they meet the following criteria.

- Is supported by public revenues (51% or more) or is a nonprofit institution or agency;
- Makes the collection accessible to its primary clientele organized according to a nationally accepted classification system;
- Participates in resource sharing through the Information Nevada program;
- Serves its clientele free of charge;
- Has a fixed location with regular, published hours of operation;
- Has one or more paid library staff;
- Has an annual budget with funds reserved for library materials and services; and
- Has a current, written long-range or strategic plan that is available for review.

LIBRARY SERVICES AND TECHNOLOGY ACT (LSTA) GRANTS

Grants are awarded on a competitive basis from the funds available.

REQUIREMENTS AND RESTRICTIONS

All types of libraries, including academic, public, school, governmental agency libraries and eligible information centers, and special libraries with public access may apply. To be eligible to apply for LSTA funds, each applicant library and participant library must certify to NSLA that it meets all of the following eligibility criteria:

- Is supported by public revenues (51% or more) or is a nonprofit institution or agency;
- Makes the collection accessible to its primary clientele organized according to a nationally accepted classification system;
- Participates in resource sharing through the Information Nevada program;

- Serves its clientele free of charge;
- Has a fixed location with regular, published hours of operation;
- Has one or more paid library staff;
- Has an annual budget with funds reserved for library materials and services; and
- Has a current, written long-range or strategic plan that is available for review.

APPLICATION PROCEDURES AND DEADLINES

See online forms for procedures and deadlines. For assistance with the proposal, contact:

Library Planning and Development
Diane Baker
775-684-3407
dbaker@admin.nv.gov or

Karen Starr
(775) 684-3324
kstarr@admin.nv.gov

New Hampshire Charitable Foundation

Headquarters

37 Pleasant St.
Concord, NH 03301-4005
Phone: 603-225-6641
www.nhcf.org

Contact: Kate Merrow, V.P., Prog.

E-mail: info@nhcf.org

Type of Grant Maker: Community Foundation

Description

Founded: 1962

Operating Locations/Geographic Preferences: Giving in the Lakes, Manchester, Monadnock, Nashua, North Country, Piscataqua, and Upper Valley regions in NH

Financial Summary

Assets: $425,651,084
Total Giving: $28,331,165

Grants Information

GRANT TYPES

Program development, seed money, general and operating support, management development, investments and loans; emphasis on programs rather than capital needs

TYPICAL RECIPIENTS/SUBJECTS OF INTEREST

Arts, humanities, the environment and conservation, health, and social and community services

Giving programs include:

Community Impact Grants—for programmatic support, capacity building, and operating support.

Express Grants—for project support and capacity building of up to $5,000 on an expedited basis.

PAST GRANT RECIPIENTS

Library or School Related

- University of New Hampshire, Durham (NH), $216,000
- Plymouth State University, Plymouth (NH), $159,000 for Early Childhood provider network and degree program
- Radcliffe College, Cambridge (MA), $4,300
- New Hampshire Humanities Council, Concord (NH), $3,200

General

- Conservation International, Arlington (VA), $400,000
- Northern Human Services, Conway (NH), to expand and improve infant mental health services and referrals, $220,000
- Friends of the Music Hall, Portsmouth (NH), $100,000

REQUIREMENTS AND RESTRICTIONS

No support for sectarian or religious purposes. No grants to individuals; no grants for building funds, endowments, deficit financing, capital campaigns for acquisition of land or renovations to facilities, purchase of major equipment, academic research, travel, or to replace public funding or for purposes which are a public responsibility.

APPLICATION PROCEDURES

See website for application cover sheet and additional application guidelines.

Deadlines: March 1 and September 1 for Express grants (requests of $5,000 or less); April 1 and September 30 for Community Impact grants (requests over $5,000)

New Hampshire Library Association

Headquarters

53 Regional Drive, Suite 1
Concord, NH 03301
http://nhlibrarians.org/education/
Type of Grant Maker: Library Organization

Grants Information

NHLA CONTINUING EDUCATION COMMITTEE MINI-MONEY GRANT APPLICATION

Grants may be used for credit or non-credit courses, workshops, and seminars; State Library Education modules; online education classes; and classes offered by local educational institutions.

Grant Ranges: up to $200

REQUIREMENTS AND RESTRICTIONS

The funds may not be used for conference attendance.

APPLICATION PROCEDURES

Complete online form and send to:

Barbara Prince, Chair
Continuing Education Committee
Hanover Town Library
PO Box 207
Etna, NH 03750
Phone: 643-3116
E-mail: barbara.prince@hanovernh.org

New Jersey Council for the Humanities

Headquarters

28 West State St., 6th floor
Trenton, NJ 08608
Phone: 609-695-4838, 888-394-6524 (in-state)
Fax: 609-695-4929

www.njch.org/grants.html

E-mail: njch@njch.org

Type of Grant Maker: Government

Grants Information

NJCH GRANTS

These are provided to nonprofit organizations in New Jersey to support their public humanities projects. Projects offer ways to examine the meaning of the human experience. Especially interested in projects that address the theme of justice.

Grant Ranges:

Major grant: up to $20,000
Mini-grants up to $3,000

REQUIREMENTS AND RESTRICTIONS

Only NJ nonprofit organizations and government agencies within NJ are eligible to apply.

APPLICATION PROCEDURES AND DEADLINES

Vary according to type of grant. Contact the NJCH Grants Officer, Robert Apgar, at 1-888-394-6524 or grants@njch.org for more information

HUMANITIES FESTIVAL GRANTS

These grants are provided annually in celebration of National Arts and Humanities Month.

Grant Range: $500

APPLICATION PROCEDURES

See website for details.

Deadline: June 15

New Mexico Library Association

Headquarters

PO Box 26074
Albuquerque, NM 87125
Phone: 505-400-7309
Fax: 505-891-5171

http://nmla.org/scholarships-grants/

E-mail: admin@nmla.org

Type of Grant Maker: Library Organization

Grants Information

CONTINUING EDUCATION GRANTS

Grant Range: Up to $200

Program Description: Supports requests to attend workshops, conferences, and related activities. Awards are made on the basis of financial need.

REQUIREMENTS AND RESTRICTIONS

Apply in advance of the event. No reimbursements.

APPLICATION PROCEDURES

Online Continuing Education Grant Application required. Copy of the workshop brochure, conference agenda or registration form should accompany the completed application form.

Application should be sent via e-mail or US mail to:

Kevin Comerford
Assistant Professor, Digital Initiatives Librarian
University of New Mexico
Zimmerman Library 127G, MSC05 30201
University of New Mexico
Albuquerque NM 87131-0001
E-mail: kevco@unm.edu

Deadlines: None

New Mexico Library Foundation

Headquarters

PO Box 30572
Albuquerque, NM 87190-0572

www.nm-lf.org

E-mail: foundation@nm-lf.org

Type of Grant Maker: Library Organization

Grants Information

Program Description: Grants are available to libraries in New Mexico and/or related institutions in partnership with libraries for the improvement of information services. Grants will be provided to build and maintain collections, update information access technology, and enhance library programs.

Grant Range: Up to $1,000

REQUIREMENTS AND RESTRICTIONS

Any New Mexico library may apply (public, academic, school, special or private). Additionally, nonprofit groups that directly benefit NM libraries may apply.

APPLICATION PROCEDURES

Apply online.

Questions should be sent to: grants@nm-lf.org.

Deadlines: Grant applications accepted two times a year (in the spring and fall). See online Calendar of Events for deadlines.

New Mexico State Library

Headquarters

Division of the New Mexico Department of Cultural Affairs
1209 Camino Carlos Rey
Santa Fe, NM 87507
Phone: 505-476-9700

www.nmstatelibrary.org/services-for-nm-libraries/
funding-libraries

Type of Grant Maker: Government

Grants Information

TECHNOLOGY SUPPORT GRANTS

To help New Mexico public libraries gain technology support for computers and networks and provide affordable tech support, and encourage tech consultants to become familiar with libraries' unique tech needs.

Grant Range: Up to $15,000

REQUIREMENTS AND RESTRICTIONS

Open to public libraries that meet certain criteria. See guidelines for details.

APPLICATION PROCEDURES

See online application.
  For more information, contact:
    Patricia Moore, 505-476-9724 or 800-340-3890

Deadlines: November 5

E-AUDIO/E-BOOK GRANTS

To expand the availability of e-audio books and e-books to New Mexico residents.

Grant Range: Up to 80,000

REQUIREMENTS AND RESTRICTIONS

Only consortiums of New Mexico libraries are eligible.

APPLICATION PROCEDURES

See online for application.
  For more information, contact:
    Geri Hutchins 505-476-972 or geraldine.hutchins@state
    .nm.us

Deadlines: November 1

STATE GRANTS-IN-AID PROGRAM

To provide financial assistance that encourages and supports public library service by public libraries and developing public libraries. The library grants program is intended to supplement and encourage local effort in providing local library service. The library grants program consists of developing library grants and public library grants that may be used for: library collections; library staff salaries; library staff training; library equipment; or other operational expenditures associated with delivery of library services.

Grant Ranges: Eligible libraries receive a minimum grant of $1,500

APPLICATION PROCEDURES

See website for information.
  For more information, contact:
    Development Bureau 800-340-3890 or development@
    state.nm.us

Deadlines: See website.

TRIBAL LIBRARIES PROGRAM GRANTS

To provide financial assistance that encourages and supports tribal library services. The TLP Grant is intended to supplement and encourage local effort in providing local library service. The TLP Grant may be used for library collections, library programming, library staff salaries, library staff professional development, library equipment, or other operational expenditures associated with delivery of library services.
  Grant Ranges: Vary

REQUIREMENTS AND RESTRICTIONS

Open to all tribal libraries that currently meet the criteria for developing library, public library, or branch library as defined in 4.5.2 NMAC and receive a State Grants in Aid for Public Libraries grant.

APPLICATION PROCEDURES

See website for information.

New Orleans Foundation, Greater

Headquarters

1055 St. Charles Ave., Ste. 100
New Orleans, LA 70130-3981
Phone: 504-598-4663

www.gnof.org

Contact: Dr. G. Albert Ruesga, CEO; for grants: Ellen Lee, Sr. V.P., Programs.

E-mail: albert@gnof.org

Type of Grant Maker: Community Foundation

Description

Founded: 1924

Operating Locations/Geographic Preferences: Giving limited to southeastern LA, including the greater New Orleans area

Financial Summary

Assets: $236,519,327
Total Giving: $17,536,594
Number of Grants: 1,884
Grant Ranges: $1,150,000–$50

Grants Information

GRANT TYPES

Program development, matching, general and operating support, seed money, management development

TYPICAL RECIPIENTS/SUBJECTS OF INTEREST

1. Excellence in education
2. Economic expansion and job training
3. Affordable housing/neighborhood development
4. Race and equity
5. Sustaining and developing nonprofit capacity

PAST GRANT RECIPIENTS

Library or School Related

- Saint Georges Episcopal School, New Orleans (LA), for Early Childhood Expansion capital gift, $200,000
- Saint Alphonsus School, New Orleans (LA), $3,500

General

- America's Wetland Foundation, New Orleans (LA), for Senior Adviser and media outreach, $445,000
- New Orleans Botanical Garden Foundation, New Orleans (LA), $20,000

REQUIREMENTS AND RESTRICTIONS

No support for religious activities. No grants to individuals, or for annual fund campaigns, capital expenditures, sponsorship of special events, trips, continuing support, endowment funds, equipment, building funds, or deficit financing.

APPLICATION PROCEDURES

See website for application information. Each competitive fund has different priorities, criteria and guidelines.

Deadlines: Vary

New York Community Trust

Headquarters

909 3rd Ave., 22nd Fl.
New York, NY 10022-4752
Phone: 212-686-0010

www.nycommunitytrust.org

E-mail: aw@nyct-cfi.org

Type of Grant Maker: Community Foundation

Description

Founded: 1924

Operating Locations/Geographic Preferences: Giving limited to the metropolitan New York, NY area

Financial Summary

Assets: $1,877,885,562
Total Giving: $140,835,396

Grants Information

GRANT TYPES

Program development, matching, management development, seed money

TYPICAL RECIPIENTS/SUBJECTS OF INTEREST

Children, Youth, and Families—includes issues of hunger and homelessness, social services, substance abuse, youth development, girls and young women

Community Development and the Environment—includes civic affairs, community development, conservation, environment, and technical assistance

Education, Arts, and the Humanities—includes arts and culture, education, historic preservation, immigration, and human justice

Health and People With Special Needs—includes health services and policy, biomedical research, AIDS, visual handicaps, children and youth with disabilities, the elderly, and mental health and retardation

PAST GRANT RECIPIENTS

School or Library Related

- Harvard University, Cambridge (MA), for Postdoctoral Program in Economics, Politics and History, $3,000,000
- Saint Agatha School, Columbus (OH), for the Elizabeth Huffner Angel Fund, $2,500

General

- Council on Foreign Relations, New York (NY), for the Campaign for the Council, $4,000,000
- Brooklyn Museum, Brooklyn (NY), for general support, $1,400,000
- United Neighborhood Houses of New York, New York (NY), for settlement houses, $1,000,000
- New York Botanical Garden, Bronx (NY), for general support, $500,000
- Center for Investigative Reporting, Berkeley (CA), for Investigative Fund, $4,000

REQUIREMENTS AND RESTRICTIONS

No support for religious purposes. No grants to individuals or for deficit financing, emergency funds, building campaigns, films, endowment funds, capital projects or general operating support.

APPLICATION PROCEDURES

See website for application cover sheet and guidelines.

Deadlines: None

New York State Library

Headquarters

Cultural Education Center
222 Madison Avenue
Albany, NY 12230
www.nysl.nysed.gov/libdev/stateaid/index.html

Type of Grant Maker: Government

Grants Information

ADULT LITERACY LIBRARY SERVICES GRANT PROGRAM

To help library systems and libraries offer services to improve adult literacy on the job and in the home. The program theme is "Workforce Development at New York Libraries through Public Library Systems." Participating public library systems offer training and resources to help New York's workforce attain literacy levels as well as the skills and tools needed for successful careers. Workforce development includes literacy, GED (General Equivalency Diploma) preparation, citizenship information, as well as job and career information and assistance.

Grant Ranges: Grant funds will be allocated to public library systems based on a formula approved by the State Education Department

REQUIREMENTS AND RESTRICTIONS

Applicants must be public library systems.

APPLICATION PROCEDURES

Applications are submitted through the web-based application program.

Mail or deliver to:

Adult Literacy Library Services Grant Program
Attn: Lorraine Deitz, Education Program Assistant II
New York State Library, Division of Library Development
Room 10B41 CEC
Albany, New York 12230

Deadlines: January 31

FAMILY LITERACY SERVICES GRANTS PROGRAM

To help libraries and library systems provide family literacy services to children and their parents or caregivers.

Grant Ranges: Grant funds will be allocated to public library systems based on a formula approved by the State Education Department.

REQUIREMENTS AND RESTRICTIONS

Applicants must be public library systems.

APPLICATION PROCEDURES

Applications are submitted through the web-based application program.

Mail or deliver to:

Family Literacy Library Services Grant Program
Attn: Lorraine Deitz, Education Program Assistant II
New York State Library, Division of Library Development
Room 10B41 CEC
Albany, New York 12230

CONSERVATION/PRESERVATION PROGRAM

To encourage the proper care and accessibility of research materials in the State, to promote the use and development of guidelines and standards for conservation/preservation work, and to support the growth of local and cooperative preservation programs.

The discretionary grant program provides modest financial support for projects that contribute to the preservation of significant research materials in libraries, archives, historical societies and other agencies within the State of New York, whether by conducting surveys, improving collection storage environments, reformatting or treating collections or other preservation activities described in these guidelines.

REQUIREMENTS AND RESTRICTIONS

Public libraries, academic libraries, historical societies, archives, museum libraries, municipalities and other non-profit organizations are eligible.

APPLICATION PROCEDURES

Online application process required. In order to have access to this online grants system, institutions must first register for a user name and password.

Deadlines: December 2

LIBRARY SERVICES AND TECHNOLOGY ACT (LSTA)

Service Improvement Invitational Grant Program
Grant Ranges: $800,000 total grant giving
To assist library systems to help their member libraries improve library services for their customers and to implement New York State's 2007–2012 LSTA Five-Year Plan.

REQUIREMENTS AND RESTRICTIONS

Grants will be made to library systems only, based on a formula for each type of system. Each library system is eligible to submit only one application.

APPLICATION PROCEDURES

The application and all forms are on the State Library website at www.nysl.nysed.gov/libdev/lsta.

Deadline: March 7

LIBRARY SERVICES AND TECHNOLOGY ACT FEDERAL PROGRAM

SUMMER READING MINI-GRANTS PROGRAM

Noncompetitive grant program focused on assisting library systems help their member libraries support and carry out activities related to the New York State Library's statewide summer reading program: Summer Reading at New York Libraries.

Grant Ranges: Level of funding for eligible institutions vary

REQUIREMENTS AND RESTRICTIONS

Grants will be made to library systems only, using a formula based on summer reading participation statistics.

APPLICATION PROCEDURES

The application and all forms are on the State Library website at www.nysl.nysed.gov/libdev/lsta

Deadlines: January 18

Newhouse, Samuel I. Foundation, Inc.

Headquarters

c/o Paul Scherer & Co. LLP
1440 Broadway, 12th Fl.
New York, NY 10018
Phone: 212-588-2200

Contact: Steven Markovits

Type of Grant Maker: Foundation

Description

Founded: 1945

Operating Locations/Geographic Preferences: Giving primarily in New York City

Financial Summary

Assets: $85,053,406
Total Giving: $12,138,620
Number of Grants: 239
Grant Ranges: $1,500,000–$500; average: $1,500–$100,000

Grants Information

GRANT TYPES

Operating and general support, program development

TYPICAL RECIPIENTS/SUBJECTS OF INTEREST

Mass communication and media, education, children and youth, higher education, performing arts

PAST GRANT RECIPIENTS

Library or School Related

• Syracuse University, Syracuse (NY), $1,500,000

General

• Fund for Educational Advancement, Irvington (NJ), $50,000
• New York City Opera, New York (NY), $600,000
• National Parks of New York Harbor Conservancy, New York (NY), $30,000

REQUIREMENTS AND RESTRICTIONS

None

APPLICATION PROCEDURES

Approach with initial letter

Deadlines: None

Norris, Kenneth T. and Eileen L. Foundation

Headquarters

11 Golden Shore, Ste. 450
Long Beach, CA 90802-4274
Phone: 562-435-8444

www.ktn.org

Contact: Ronald R. Barnes, Exec. Dir.

E-mail: grants@ktn.org

Type of Grant Maker: Foundation

Description

Founded: 1963

Operating Locations/Geographic Preferences: Giving primarily in southern CA

Financial Summary

Assets: $148,074,715
Total Giving: $6,130,030
Number of Grants: 301
Grant Ranges: $2,000,000–$1,000; average: $10,000–$200,000

Grants Information

GRANT TYPES

Program development, general, continuing and operating support, building and renovation, annual campaigns and endowments, matching

TYPICAL RECIPIENTS/SUBJECTS OF INTEREST

Advancement of health and intellectual enlightenment through education

Cultivation of the arts, individual responsibility, freedom and dignity

Community

Culture

Youth

Medicine

Education/Science

PAST GRANT RECIPIENTS

Library or School Related

• Huntington Library, Art Collections and Botanical Gardens, San Marino (CA), for Desert Garden Master Plan, $200,000
• University of Southern California, Los Angeles (CA), for Norris Foundation Epigenome Center, $2,000,000
• Town and Gown of the University of Southern California, Los Alamitos (CA), for Eileen Norris Endowment Fund, $70,000

General

• Jeffrey Foundation, Los Angeles (CA), for after-school education and enrichment for special-needs children, $10,000
• Los Angeles Master Chorale Association, Los Angeles (CA), for Annual High School Choir Festival, $10,000

REQUIREMENTS AND RESTRICTIONS

No support for political organizations or campaigns. No grants to individuals, or for film or video projects or loans.

APPLICATION PROCEDURES

See website for application form. Applicants should submit:

1. Results expected from proposed grant
2. Copy of IRS Determination Letter
3. Brief history of organization and description of its mission
4. Copy of most recent annual report/audited financial statement/990
5. Descriptive literature about organization
6. Listing of board of directors, trustees, officers and other key people and their affiliations
7. Detailed description of project and amount of funding requested
8. Copy of current year's organizational budget and/or project budget
9. Listing of additional sources and amount of support
10. Additional materials/documentation

Deadlines

- Medicine: May 1–June 30
- Education/Science: May 1–June 30
- Youth: February 15–March 31
- Community/Cultural: December 1–January 31

North Carolina Community Foundation

Headquarters

4601 Six Forks Rd., Ste. 524
Raleigh, NC 27609-5286
Phone: 919-828-4387

www.nccommunityfoundation.org

Contact: Jennifer Tolle Whiteside, Pres.; for grants: Sally Migliore, Dir., Community Leadership

E-mail: smigliore@nccommunityfoundation.org

Type of Grant Maker: Community Foundation

Description

Founded: 1988

Operating Locations/Geographic Preferences: Giving primarily in NC

Financial Summary

Assets: $145,274,577
Total Giving: $6,812,508
Number of Grants: 1,042

Grants Information

GRANT TYPES

Program development, building and renovation, general, operating and continuing support, management development, endowments

TYPICAL RECIPIENTS/SUBJECTS OF INTEREST

Education, arts, humanities, animals/wildlife, environment, public affairs, religion, youth, health care

PAST GRANT RECIPIENTS

General

- Read and Feed, mobile classroom to improve reading, $45,000
- Urban Ministries, Helen Wright Center for Women, for homeless women, $50,000
- SAFEchild for Advocacy Center, $35,000

REQUIREMENTS AND RESTRICTIONS

Vary according to funding source.

APPLICATION PROCEDURES

See website for application information for each fund.
Online application form required.
Applicants should submit:

1. Population served
2. Listing of board of directors, trustees, officers and other key people and their affiliations
3. Detailed description of project and amount of funding requested
4. Copy of current year's organizational budget and/or project budget

Deadlines: Vary

North Carolina, State Library of

Headquarters

109 East Jones St.
Raleigh, NC

Phone: 919-807-7450

http://statelibrary.ncdcr.gov

Type of Grant Maker: Government

Grants Information

LIBRARY SERVICES AND TECHNOLOGY ACT (LSTA) GRANTS

EZ GRANTS

Grant Ranges: up to $50,000, no letter of intent required
Includes:

Collaboration & Innovation Grant
Literacy & Lifelong Learning Grants

PROJECT GRANTS

Grant Ranges: $50,000 or more, letter of intent required
Includes:

Access & Digitization Grants
Collaboration & Innovation Grants
Literacy & Lifelong Learning Grants

REQUIREMENTS AND RESTRICTIONS

The following libraries are eligible to apply for these grants:

- public libraries that meet the eligibility requirements for the Aid to Public Libraries Fund;
- community college libraries;
- libraries serving the constituent institutions of the University of North Carolina (which includes libraries serving the Area Health Education Centers); and
- libraries serving the member institutions of North Carolina Independent Colleges and Universities.

APPLICATION PROCEDURES

See State Library tip sheets that applicants should consider before developing their applications.

Application information online.

Deadlines: November 1 for letter of intent; February 28 for application

North Dakota Library Association

Headquarters

PO Box 1595
Bismarck ND 58502-1595

www.ndla.info/profdev.htm

Type of Grant Maker: Library Organization

Grants Information

NDLA PROFESSIONAL DEVELOPMENT GRANT

To further an individual's skills to benefit the North Dakota Library environment. Each year The Professional Development grant may be used for college or university classroom work, independent study, workshops, conferences, or participation in any activity that will benefit the library community in North Dakota.

RON RUDSER MEMORIAL CONTINUING EDUCATION GRANT

The Ron Rudser Memorial Continuing Education Grant may be used for credit courses, workshops, seminars or pre-conference programs that enhance the education of a practicing librarian in any type of library. Regular conference programs or conventions do not qualify.

M. VIVIAN HUBBARD MEMORIAL GRANT

To further interest in bookmobiles, the grant may be used for formal college or university classroom work, independent study, workshops, conferences, or participation in any other activity that will further the work of the bookmobile, including the purchase of books or other materials.

MIKE JAUGSTETTER LEADERSHIP MEMORIAL GRANT

The grant money may be used for library leadership institutes or programs.

REQUIREMENTS AND RESTRICTIONS

Professional Development & Rudser Grants

1. Applicants must:
    be ND residents or employed in North Dakota
    be current members of NDLA and must have been members for the past two years
    submit a detailed budget of expected expenses
    submit a narrative describing personal growth/career development expectations from the proposed program
    submit printed materials which describe the program
2. Applicants need not be currently employed in a library.
3. Applicants must submit an evaluative report to NDLA upon program completion for publication in *The Good Stuff.*

4. Grant money will be awarded after the evaluative report has been received by the NDLA President

5. No applicant may receive more than one grant per 18 months

6. A copy of CEU certificate or letter of recognition should accompany the report, if applicable

M. Vivian Hubbard Memorial Grant

1. Applicant must:

be a current member of NDLA

agree to submit an evaluative report of how the grant was used to the NDLA Executive Board and said report will be published in *The Good Stuff.*

Mike Jaugstetter Leadership Memorial Grant

1. Applicants must:

be current individual members of NDLA and must have been members for the past two years

submit a detailed budget of expected expenses

submit a narrative statement describing personal growth and career development expectations from the program they plan to attend

2. Applications should be accompanied with printed materials that describe the program

CONDITIONS

1. Applicants must:

be currently employed in a North Dakota library

agree to submit an evaluative report to the NDLA Executive Board upon completion of the program for publication in *The Good Stuff*

agree to participate in the leadership of the NDLA Executive Board for one year. Participation may include, but not be limited to, section chair, officer, committee chair or committee work appointed by the President of NDLA

present a leadership program at the NDLA conference following participation in the leadership program or institute

participate in the committee selection of the following year's recipient

2. No applicant may receive more than one grant per 24 months

3. Completed application forms must be submitted by August 1 of each year

4. A portion of expenses (dependent upon the NDLA budget) will be reimbursed upon completion of travel

5. A written contract between NDLA and the grant recipient will be entered into regarding completion of conditions

APPLICATION PROCEDURES

Forms available online. For more information, contact:

Lori K. West
Fargo Public Library

2801 32 Ave S
Fargo ND 58103
Phone: 701-476-5977
Fax: 701-476-5981
E-mail: lwest@cityoffargo.com

Deadlines: Completed application forms may be submitted at any time.

North Dakota State Library

Headquarters

604 East Boulevard Avenue
Bismarck, ND 58505-0800
Phone: 701-328-4622; or 800-472-2104 (within North Dakota)
Fax: 701-328-2040
www.library.nd.gov/librarian.html#tab_0
E-mail: statelib@nd.gov

Type of Grant Maker: Government

Grants Information

NORTH DAKOTA STATE LIBRARY TRAINING GRANT

To encourage North Dakotans to pursue a Master of Library and Information Science degree from an ALA accredited school (ALA/MLIS) and to work in North Dakota. Each year the program is for graduate activity that takes place beginning fall semester.

Grant Ranges: up to $8,500

REQUIREMENTS AND RESTRICTIONS

Must be a resident of North Dakota at the time she/he is beginning the MLIS graduate program and be employed by a North Dakota public grade, junior high, or high school library, a public library, or be an employee of the State Library. The applicant must be accepted into an ALA/MLIS program prior to the award. The applicant must successfully complete the program as outlined by the graduate program that they are enrolled in, and receive a minimum of a B for each course, or, if appropriate, a pass for pass/fail. If an applicant withdraws or is terminated from the program, she/he must return all grant money received from the State Library within one year of completion of the last class.

The applicant who receives a grant must work for 24 months in a full-time position in a North Dakota public school or public library after receiving her/his Master of

Library and Information Science degree. The successful applicant must be employed in a North Dakota library within three months of receiving the ALA/MLIS degree. If an applicant does not do so, she/he must pay back all of the money that has been paid to them from the State Library within one year from the three-month time period.

APPLICATION PROCEDURES

Mail signed guidelines and application to:

Cynthia Clairmont-Schmidt
North Dakota State Library
604 E. Boulevard Avenue
Bismarck, ND 58505-0800

For further information, please contact:

Cynthia Clairmont-Schmidt at the North Dakota State Library at 701-328-2492, 1-800-472-2104, or ccclairmont@nd.gov.

Deadlines: Applications are taken each year from March 1–May 30

INNOVATIVE PARTNERSHIP WITH A NON-LIBRARY ENTITY GRANT

For a new and innovative partnership program between a library and a non-library entity. The program will enhance library services in the local or statewide community. The program is to be an investment in the future (rather than sustaining the present) designed to provide a service that does not currently exist in the community. It needs to have a positive impact on the lives of people in the community by increasing usage of library and information services.

TECHNOLOGY TO PROVIDE ACCESS TO INFORMATION GRANT

To provide access to information for the community, patrons, and students, including access to the Online Library Resources, WorldCat, the Online Dakota Information Network (ODIN), and the wide array of information available electronically. The library will purchase technology to be owned by the library to meet the objectives of accessing Online Library Resources, WorldCat, ODIN, and other information available.

REQUIREMENTS AND RESTRICTIONS

The Library must meet the eligibility criteria in stated in guidelines.

PARTICIPATION IN THE STATEWIDE ONLINE CATALOG THROUGH WORLDCAT GRANT

To add libraries' bibliographic records to WorldCat. WorldCat serves as a powerful method to locate books and materials in the collections of North Dakota libraries, as well as libraries around the world, and allows for the common objectives agreed to in Library Vision 2014.

REQUIREMENTS AND RESTRICTIONS

1. A school library must have a qualified librarian (as defined by the Department of Public Instruction's standards) providing library services to students or faculty for a minimum of 15 hours per week.
2. A public library must be established according to NDCC 40-38-01 requirements, and must be open with paid staff providing library services for a minimum of 20 hours per week.

APPLICATION PROCEDURES

The completed original application form must be signed and sent Return-Receipt requested to:

North Dakota State Library
Attn: Cynthia Clairmont-Schmidt
604 East Boulevard Ave., Dept. 250
Bismarck, ND 58505-0800

For assistance, please call Cynthia Clairmont-Schmidt, 800-472-2104.

Deadlines: January 2.

Northwestern Mutual Foundation, Inc.

Headquarters

720 E. Wisconsin Ave.
Milwaukee, WI 53202-4703
Phone: 414-665-2200
www.nmfn.com/tn/aboutus--fd_intro
Contact: Deanna L. Tillisch, V.P.
E-mail: nmfoundation@northwesternmutual.com
Type of Grant Maker: Corporate Foundation

Description

Founded: 1992

Operating Locations/Geographic Preferences: Giving primarily in the southeastern, WI area, and also on a national basis

Corporate Foundation Information: Supported by The Northwestern Mutual Life Insurance Co and Lydell Inc.

Financial Summary

Assets: $93,218,903
Total Giving: $14,926,227
Number of Grants: 1,038
Grant Ranges: $1,500,600–$160

Grants Information

GRANT TYPES

General, operating and continuing support, building and renovation, capital campaigns, matching

TYPICAL RECIPIENTS/SUBJECTS OF INTEREST

Education, arts and culture, health, job training, hunger, nutrition, disaster relief, human services, community economic development, children, the disabled, and minorities

Program areas include:

Securing Future Generations
Special emphasis on:
Ensuring academic achievement through literacy
Wellness through healthy habits
Inspiration through arts education
Opportunities through innovative therapies for special needs.

Developing Our Local Economy
Special emphasis on:
Providing basic needs of food, shelter, dental, and medical care
Promoting self-sufficiency through job training and higher education for minority students
Enhancing quality of life through neighborhood revitalization and cultural development

Community Impact Awards

Community Service Award Program

Volunteer Support Program

PAST GRANT RECIPIENTS

Library or School Related

- Milwaukee Institute of Art and Design, Milwaukee (WI), $20,000

General

- United Way of Greater Milwaukee, Milwaukee (WI), $1,500,000
- United Performing Arts Fund, Milwaukee (WI), $647,000
- Boys and Girls Clubs of Greater Milwaukee, Milwaukee (WI), $425,000
- Skylight Opera Theater, Milwaukee (WI), $20,000

REQUIREMENTS AND RESTRICTIONS

No support to organizations with an operating budget under $300,000, groups or organizations that re-grant to other organizations or individuals, school teams, bands or choirs, or labor, religious, or fraternal groups.

No grants to individuals, or for debt reduction, capital or endowment campaigns unless approved by the foundation in advance, conferences, conventions, golf outings, school trips, concerts, or performances, athletic events, equipment, uniforms, travel, or any in-kind support of special events, or lobbying activities.

Food/Shelter, Medical/Dental, Higher Education, Job Training, Neighborhood Revitalization and Destination support is limited to the Developing Our Local Economy program in Milwaukee, Wisconsin.

Organizations applying for sponsorship support must have an ongoing funding relationship with the foundation or a Northwestern Mutual corporate employee must be a board member or volunteer with the organization.

APPLICATION PROCEDURES

Online eligibility and questionnaire required. Applicants should submit:

1. Copy of IRS Determination Letter
2. Copy of most recent annual report/audited financial statement/990
3. Explanation of why grant-maker is considered an appropriate donor for project
4. Listing of board of directors, trustees, officers and other key people and their affiliations
5. Detailed description of project and amount of funding requested
6. Copy of current year's organizational budget and/or project budget
7. Listing of additional sources and amount of support

Deadlines

60 days prior to need for sponsorships

January 31 for Food/Shelter

March 15 for Arts Education

March 31 for Special Needs and Medical/Dental

August 15 for Healthy Habits and Higher Education

August 31 for Job Training and Neighborhood Revitalization

September 30 for Literacy

November 12 for Destination

OCLC Online Computer Library Center, Inc.

Headquarters

6565 Kilgour Place
Dublin, Ohio 43017-3395 USA
Phone: 614-764-6000, 800-848-5878 (United States and Canada only)
Fax: 614-764-6096

www.oclc.org

E-mail: oclc@oclc.org

Type of Grant Maker: Library Organization

Grants Information

Library and Information Science Research Grant Program (LISRGP) for 2013

In recognition of the importance of research to the advancement of librarianship and information science, OCLC and ALISE promote independent research that helps integrate new technologies that offer innovative approaches and contributes to a better understanding of the information environment and user expectations and behaviors.

Research related (but not limited) to the following areas is encouraged:

- Impact of digital technology on libraries, museums, and archives
- Social media, learning, and information-seeking behavior
- New developments in knowledge organization (metadata, social tagging, linked data, etc.)

Grant Range: Up to $15,000

REQUIREMENTS AND RESTRICTIONS

Full-time academic faculty in schools of library and information science or related fields are eligible to apply. OCLC and ALISE encourage international proposals and collaborative projects under this program. To aid new researchers, priority will be given when possible to proposals from junior faculty and applicants who have not previously received LISRGP funds. Proposals must be signed by the principal investigator, by the dean/director (or equivalent) of the school, and by an authorized official of the university.

APPLICATION PROCEDURES

Submit proposals electronically via online form.

Deadlines: September 15

Ohio, State Library of

Headquarters

274 East 1st Avenue, Suite 100
Columbus, OH 43201-3692
Phone: 614-644-7061 or 800-686-1532 (Ohio only); Circulation Services: 614-644-6950; Research Services: 614-644-7051

www.library.ohio.gov

Type of Grant Maker: Government

Grants Information

TECHNOLOGICAL INNOVATION

Projects that incorporate the use of new technologies or use current technology in a different ways to improve access, services, or support to library customers.

AUTOMATION

To allow libraries that wish to automate to convert their card catalog and join a consortia and participate in statewide resource sharing.

TARGETED POPULATIONS

To provide services to targeted populations including, but not limited to, people of diverse geographic, cultural and socioeconomic backgrounds, individuals with disabilities, persons with limited functional literacy and information skills, and those individuals having difficulty using a library.

SERVICES TO YOUTH

To provide services to youth, ages birth through 18, with a particular emphasis on youth in poverty and those children from families with incomes below the poverty line.

TRAINING

To provide technology literacy training on all levels to the user public.

LIBRARY ENTREPRENEURSHIP

To develop new solutions or alternatives to library issues from which all libraries can learn and benefit and, if appropriate, replicate. Projects must meet the library users' needs in a fresh way, have the breadth to become a platform for related services, increase the library's value to the community, and offer an advantage over current services or processes.

REQUIREMENTS AND RESTRICTIONS

Eligible public, school, academic, research, or special libraries may initiate grant proposals.

Mini-grants

Grant Ranges: up to $24,000

Deadlines: late October

Full Grants

Grant Ranges: no limit

Full grants tend to be for larger, more broad-based projects with multiple partners.

Deadlines: early May

Special Grants

Grant Ranges: vary

Special grant cycles are initiated when a unique or specific need has been identified in the library community which can be addressed through LSTA dollars.

APPLICATION PROCEDURES

See website for information. Questions regarding LSTA should be addressed to:

Missy Lodge
Head
Library Programs and Development
800-686-1532, 614-644-6914 or
mlodge@library.ohio.gov

Oishei, John R. Foundation

Headquarters

1 HSBC Ctr., Ste. 3650
Buffalo, NY 14203-2805
Phone: 716-856-9490

www.oishei.org

Contact: Robert D. Gioia, Pres.

E-mail: info@oisheifdt.org

Type of Grant Maker: Foundation

Description

Founded: 1941

Operating Locations/Geographic Preferences: Giving limited to the Buffalo, NY area.

Financial Summary

Assets: $284,369,000
Total Giving: $13,766,000

Grants Information

GRANT TYPES

Program development, investments and loans, general and operating support, management development, seed money, matching

TYPICAL RECIPIENTS/SUBJECTS OF SUPPORT

Science and research, higher education, arts, community economic development, secondary schools

PAST GRANT RECIPIENTS

Library or School Related

- Read to Succeed Buffalo, Buffalo (NY), for community-wide literacy effort, The Resource Center, Inc., $252,500
- Buffalo Prep, Buffalo (NY), for Rising to Distinction Program support and expansion (two grants), $675,000
- Buffalo Independent Secondary School Network, Buffalo (NY), for scholarship program, $550,000

General

- Buffalo Philharmonic Orchestra, Buffalo (NY), for endowment campaign, $272,000
- Roswell Park Alliance Foundation, Buffalo (NY), for WNY Robotic Surgical Center, $700,000

REQUIREMENTS AND RESTRICTIONS

No support for religious organizations for sectarian or propagation of faith purposes. No grants to individuals, organizations which make grants to others, or lobbying or advocacy for specific political candidates or legislation.

APPLICATION PROCEDURES

See website for application guidelines. Application form not required. Applicants should submit:

1. Timetable for implementation and evaluation of project
2. How project will be sustained once grant-maker support is completed
3. Signature and title of chief executive officer
4. Statement of problem project will address
5. Population served
6. Copy of IRS Determination Letter
7. Brief history of organization and description of its mission
8. Copy of most recent annual report/audited financial statement/990

9. How project's results will be evaluated or measured
10. Listing of board of directors, trustees, officers and other key people and their affiliations
11. Detailed description of project and amount of funding requested
12. Plans for cooperation with other organizations, if any
13. Copy of current year's organizational budget and/or project budget
14. Listing of additional sources and amount of support
15. Additional materials/documentation

Deadlines: None

Oklahoma City Community Foundation, Inc.

Headquarters

PO Box 1146
Oklahoma City, OK 73101-1146
Phone: 405-235-5603

www.occf.org

Contact: Nancy B. Anthony, Exec. Dir.; Cathy Nestlen, Dir., Comms.

E-mail: info@occf.org

Type of Grant Maker: Community Foundation

Description

Founded: 1968

Operating Locations/Geographic Preferences: Giving primarily in the greater Oklahoma City, OK, area

Financial Summary

Assets: $465,792,526
Total Giving: $16,931,157

Grants Information

GRANT TYPES

Program development, continuing, general and operating support, management development, seed money

TYPICAL RECIPIENTS/SUBJECTS OF INTEREST

Education, arts, environment, health, human services

Programs include:

Agency Capacity Building—to support organizational capacity to provide services.

Clean and Beautiful Schools Program—to improve maintenance of public and private elementary school grounds and facilities in Oklahoma County.

PAST GRANT RECIPIENTS

Library or School Related

- Dale Rogers Training Center, Oklahoma City (OK), for general support, $5,000

General

- Kirkpatrick Science and Air Space Museum at Omniplex, Oklahoma City (OK), for operating support, $1,100,000
- Oklahoma Philharmonic Society, Oklahoma City (OK), for general support, $5,000

REQUIREMENTS AND RESTRICTIONS

No grants to individuals, or for endowment funds, deficit financing, debt reduction, capital campaigns, development or fund-raising campaigns, or academic research projects; no loans.

APPLICATION PROCEDURES

See website for application form and guidelines. Applicants should submit:

1. Timetable for implementation and evaluation of project
2. How project will be sustained once grant-maker support is completed
3. Signature and title of chief executive officer
4. Results expected from proposed grant
5. Qualifications of key personnel
6. Population served
7. Brief history of organization and description of its mission
8. Geographic area to be served
9. Copy of most recent annual report/audited financial statement/990
10. How project's results will be evaluated or measured
11. Listing of board of directors, trustees, officers and other key people and their affiliations
12. Detailed description of project and amount of funding requested
13. Plans for cooperation with other organizations, if any
14. Contact person
15. Copy of current year's organizational budget and/or project budget
16. Listing of additional sources and amount of support

Deadlines: Vary

Open Society Institute

Headquarters

400 W. 59th St.
New York, NY 10019-1105
Phone: 212-548-0600
Contact: Inquiry Mgr.

www.soros.org

Type of Grant Maker: Foundation

Description

Founded: 1993 (by George Soros)

Operating Locations/Geographic Preferences: Giving on a national and international basis

Financial Summary

Assets: $1,141,004,097
Total Giving: $60,670,957
Number of Grants: 280
Grant Ranges: $3,792,489–$2,500

Grants Information

GRANT TYPES

Program development, general, operating and continuing support, matching, investments and loans

TYPICAL RECIPIENTS/SUBJECTS OF INTEREST

Promoting democratic governance, human rights, and economic, legal, and social reform. On a local level, supporting the rule of law, education, public health, and independent media.

Programs include:

Baltimore Community Fellowships
Documentary Photography Project: Project requires a partnership between a photographer and an organization that combines expertise in documentary photography with experience working on the topic or community the project addresses. Five to eight grants of $5,000 to $30,000 are awarded.

Faculty Development Fellowship Program
Georgia Program for Education Professionals
International Pain Policy

Moving Walls: An exhibition series that features explorations of human rights and social issues.
Open Society Fellowships
Social Work Fellowship Program
Soros Fellowship
Supplementary Grant Program Asia

Undergraduate Exchange Program

Programs Administered from Budapest and New York Offices. New York Programs include:

- Open Society Justice Initiative
- The Public Health Program
- The Central Eurasia Project/Middle East and North Africa Initiative
- Burma Project/Southeast Asia Initiative, Scholarship Programs
- The International Women's Program
- The Open Society Fellowship
- U.S. Programs

PAST GRANT RECIPIENTS

Library or School Related

- Columbia University, New York (NY), to help the Government of Timor-Leste achieve sustainable development, $400,000

General

- Soros Economic Development Fund, New York (NY), for operating support, $11,200,000
- Save the Children Federation, Westport (CT), to provide immediate emergency care for disaster victims, $1,000,000
- Migration Policy Institute, Washington (DC), for the Mobility and Security Program, $50,000

REQUIREMENTS AND RESTRICTIONS

No support for political parties or organizations connected to political parties.

APPLICATION PROCEDURES

See website for application guidelines and deadlines and to determine eligibility. Application form not required.

Deadlines: see website

Orange County Community Foundation

Headquarters

4041 MacArthur Blvd., Ste. 510
Newport Beach, CA 92660-0000
Phone: 949-553-4202

www.oc-cf.org

Contact: Todd Hanson, V.P., Donor Rels. and Progs.

E-mail: thanson@oc-cf.org

Type of Grant Maker: Community Foundation

Description

Founded: 1989

Operating Locations/Geographic Preferences: Giving limited to Orange County, CA for most grants, but some national donor-designated funds

Financial Summary

Assets: $118,861,000
Total Giving: $22,392,000

Grants Information

GRANT TYPES

Program development, general, operating and continuing support, management development

TYPICAL RECIPIENTS/SUBJECTS OF INTEREST

Education, including early childhood education, arts, children and youth, race relations and civil rights, environment, health

PAST GRANT RECIPIENTS

Library or School Related

- Pomona College, Claremont (CA), $2,300,000
- Macalester College, Saint Paul (MN), $25,000

General

- Orange County Shared Spaces Foundation, Irvine (CA), $660,000
- Newport Harbor Nautical Museum, Newport Beach (CA), $645,000
- Southern California Public Radio, Pasadena (CA), $29,000

REQUIREMENTS AND RESTRICTIONS

None

APPLICATION PROCEDURES

See website for application information. Application form required.

Deadlines: Vary

Oregon Community Foundation

Headquarters

1221 S.W. Yamhill, Ste. 100
Portland, OR 97205-2108
Phone: 503-227-6846

www.oregoncf.org

Contact: Megan Schumaker, Prog. Off., Community Grants and Funds

E-mail: mschumaker@oregoncf.org

Type of Grant Maker: Community Foundation

Description

Founded: 1973

Operating Locations/Geographic Preferences: Giving limited to OR

Financial Summary

Assets: $1,040,106,343
Total Giving: $60,700,000

Grants Information

GRANT TYPES

Program development, general and operating support, building and renovation, land acquisition, matching, seed money, capital campaigns

TYPICAL RECIPIENTS/SUBJECTS OF INTEREST

Program areas include:

Community Grants: The average grant is $20,000–$22,000; larger awards are possible

Nike Employee Grant Fund: For aiding nonprofits in communities where local Nike employees live—Clackamas,

Columbia, Multnomah, Washington and Yamhill counties in Oregon and Clark County in Washington. Grants are $5,000 and $20,000.

Oregon Parks Foundation Fund Grants: grants generally range from $1,500 to $5,000

Land protection and restoration

Community outdoor recreation and education programs

Administrative expenses

Publications, conferences and seminars

Emergency funding

Student internships

Ready to Learn: Early Childhood Program

Early literacy and parenting programs

Scholarships for early childhood training and education

Initiatives to improve child care quality

Research on key early childhood issues and strategies

Forums for information sharing

Reed and Carolee Walker Fund Grants: Improving the Health and Wellbeing of Children in Poverty. Grants of $25,000 or more per year.

Children's dental health

Children's mental health

Substance abuse treatment for pregnant and parenting adults

Scholarship Funds: Grants of $25,000 or less. Funding also is available to schools, clubs and other organizations for enrichment programs for children in need. Preference is given to collaborative efforts, those that show a creative use of community resources, and those that make it easy for clients to receive assistance.

PAST GRANT RECIPIENTS

Library or School Related

- University of Oregon Foundation, Eugene (OR), for Alumni Center Capital Fund, $1,400,000
- University of Oregon, Eugene (OR), to train undergraduates and graduate students, $4,522

General

- Oregon Center for Career Development in Childhood Care and Education, Portland (OR), $217,000
- Liberty Youth Ranch, Bonita Springs (FL), for general support, $5,000

REQUIREMENTS AND RESTRICTIONS

No support for religious organizations for religious purposes or projects in individual schools. No grants to individuals or for annual fund appeals, sponsorship of one-time events or performances, emergency funding,

endowments, annual campaigns, deficit financing, scientific research, publications, films, or conferences.

APPLICATION PROCEDURES

See website for application forms, guidelines, and deadlines.

Applicants should submit:

1. Role played by volunteers
2. Timetable for implementation and evaluation of project
3. How project will be sustained once grant-maker support is completed
4. Results expected from proposed grant
5. Qualifications of key personnel
6. Statement of problem project will address
7. Population served
8. Principal source of support for project in the past
9. Name, address and phone number of organization
10. Copy of IRS Determination Letter
11. Brief history of organization and description of its mission
12. Geographic area to be served
13. Copy of most recent annual report/audited financial statement/990
14. How project's results will be evaluated or measured
15. Listing of board of directors, trustees, officers and other key people and their affiliations
16. Detailed description of project and amount of funding requested
17. Plans for cooperation with other organizations, if any
18. Contact person
19. Copy of current year's organizational budget and/or project budget
20. Additional materials/documentation

Deadlines: Vary

Oregon State Library

Headquarters

Library Development Services
250 Winter St. NE
Salem, OR 97301
Phone: 503-378-2525
Fax: 503-378-6439

www.oregon.gov/OSL/LD/Pages/grantmainalt.aspx

E-mail: ferol.weyand@state.or.us

Type of Grant Maker: Government

Grants Information

LSTA COMPETITIVE GRANTS

Grant Ranges: $700,000 total giving

Program Description: One of the main criteria in awarding a grant is that it supports the state's Five-Year Plan, or the purposes of the Library Services and Technology Act.

Grant projects can be small or large as the project scope demands, but smaller projects generally have a better chance of being funded. Projects may be funded for up to three years by a series of competitive one-year grants. Projects with a one- or two-year duration are viewed more favorably than a three-year project. The LSTA grant program won't replace personnel or other operating costs, fund-building projects, or purchase books or equipment without a strong programming component.

REQUIREMENTS AND RESTRICTIONS

Legally established libraries, or nonprofit entities serving libraries. Public, academic, and special libraries are eligible. School libraries are also eligible, but school library grants should be high-profile and coordinated with the Oregon Association of School Libraries.

APPLICATION PROCEDURES

Oregon has a two-step grant application process. The first step is a brief proposal that is due in mid-April. This document lays out the gist of the proposed project, and a fairly good estimate of the budget.

The second part of the process is a full grant proposal. The State Library sends a letter in June after the Board meeting inviting some projects to develop the full proposal, which is due in mid-August.

Deadlines: April 13 for brief proposals; August 10 for full proposals

EXTENDING LIBRARY SERVICE TO THE UNSERVED GRANT PROGRAM

Program Description: Currently 4% of the population of Oregon does not have tax-supported public library service. The State Library Board has made providing library service to the unserved a priority activity. This targeted grant opportunity is designed for those tax-supported public libraries that are adjacent to an unserved population and that are interested in developing creative methods for providing and sustaining library service to those Oregonians who currently do not have tax-supported public library service.

REQUIREMENTS AND RESTRICTIONS

Eligible public libraries are in: Clatsop, Columbia, Lane and Linn Counties and the City of Newberg.

APPLICATION PROCEDURES

See online packet contains information and forms that will be needed to apply. Prospective grantees are encouraged to contact:

MaryKay Dahlgreen
Library Development Program Manager
Phone: 503-378-5012
E-mail: marykay.dahlgreen@state.or.us

Deadlines: April 13

READY TO READ GRANTS

Program Description: To establish, develop or improve public library early literacy services for children from birth to five years of age and to provide the statewide summer reading program.

REQUIREMENTS AND RESTRICTIONS

All legally established public libraries in the state are eligible to apply for this noncompetitive form of state aid.

APPLICATION PROCEDURES

See the frequently asked questions, House Bill 2116, Revised State Statutes, and Administrative Rules governing the Ready to Read grant program or contact Katie Anderson, 503-378-2528.

Deadlines: August 31

Packard, David and Lucile Foundation

Headquarters

300 2nd St.
Los Altos, CA 94022-3632
Phone: 650-948-7658

www.packard.org

Contact: Communications Dept.

E-mail: communications@packard.org

Type of Grant Maker: Foundation

Description

Founded: 1968

Operating Locations/Geographic Preferences: Giving for national and international grants, with a special focus on the Northern CA counties of San Mateo, Santa Clara, Santa Cruz, Monterey, and San Benito, and Pueblo, Colorado

Financial Summary

Assets: $6,100,637,478
Total Giving: $262,445,606
Number of Grants: 1,052
Grant Ranges: $46,757,793–$1,314

Grants Information

GRANT TYPES

Program development, general, operating and continuing support, matching, land acquisition, management development, investments and loans

TYPICAL RECIPIENTS/SUBJECTS OF INTEREST

- Improving the lives of children
- Enabling the creative pursuit of science
- Advancing reproductive health
- Conserving and restoring the earth's natural systems

Giving programs include:

Children, Families, and Communities

Focus areas include:
Preschool for California's Children
Children's Health Insurance
After-School and Summer Enrichment

Conservation and Science

Focus areas include:
Harnessing market forces to drive changes in the management of the world's fisheries
Pioneering new approaches to the conservation of coastal systems in California, the Gulf of California, and the Western Pacific Ocean
Reversing the decline of marine bird populations
Enabling the creative pursuit of scientific research
Reducing the greenhouse gas emissions that cause climate change
Improving the environmental performance of agriculture and biofuels production
Protecting and restoring biologically important and iconic regions of western North America.

Local Grant-making

For the five California counties that surround the Foundation's headquarters in Los Altos, California: San Mateo, Santa Clara, Santa Cruz, Monterey, and San Benito, as well as Pueblo, Colorado

Fundamental issue areas:
Arts
Children and Youth
Conservation and Science
Food and Shelter
Population and Reproductive Health

Matching Gifts: Ranging from $35 to $10,000

Organizational Effectiveness and Philanthropy Funds: Unsolicited proposals are not accepted for the Philanthropy subprogram.

Population and Reproductive Health

Focus areas include:
Mobilizing policies, resources, and political will at the global, regional, and country levels to cultivate a climate that advances and protects family planning and reproductive health and rights
Expanding access to quality services by training providers in quality care, introducing new family planning methods, informing communities about reproductive health information (with an emphasis on young people), and expanding access to safe abortion and post-abortion care
Empowering women and girls to increase their ability to make informed family planning and reproductive health decisions

Packard Fellowships for Science and Engineering

PAST GRANT RECIPIENTS

Library or School Related

- Harvard University, Cambridge (MA), for 2011 Packard Fellowship for Alicia Soderberg, Department of Astronomy, $875,000

General

- ClimateWorks Foundation, San Francisco (CA), for general support, $66,100,000
- Monterey Bay Aquarium Research Institute, Moss Landing (CA), for operations, research projects and capital expenses, $36,700,000
- Community Initiatives, San Francisco (CA), for Preschool Project, $2,000,000
- Ventana Wildlife Society, Salinas (CA), for the outdoor youth and conservation internship programs, $160,000
- California State Parks Foundation, San Francisco (CA), for environmental and historic education, $109,000
- Third Sector New England, Boston (MA), for the Early Learning Challenge Collaborative, $100,000

REQUIREMENTS AND RESTRICTIONS

No support for religious or political organizations. No grants to individuals.

APPLICATION PROCEDURES

See website for program guidelines. Application form not required. Applicants should submit:

1. Timetable for implementation and evaluation of project
2. Signature and title of chief executive officer
3. Results expected from proposed grant
4. Qualifications of key personnel
5. Name, address and phone number of organization
6. Copy of IRS Determination Letter
7. Brief history of organization and description of its mission
8. Geographic area to be served
9. Copy of most recent annual report/audited financial statement/990
10. How project's results will be evaluated or measured
11. Listing of board of directors, trustees, officers and other key people and their affiliations
12. Detailed description of project and amount of funding requested
13. Contact person
14. Copy of current year's organizational budget and/or project budget
15. Listing of additional sources and amount of support
16. Additional materials/documentation

Deadlines: None

Park Foundation, Inc.

Headquarters

PO Box 550
Ithaca, NY 14851-0550
Phone: 607-272-9124

www.parkfoundation.org

Contact: Jon Jensen, Exec. Dir.

E-mail: info@parkfoundation.org

Type of Grant Maker: Foundation

Description

Founded: 1966

Operating Locations/Geographic Preferences: Giving limited to the eastern United States, primarily in central NY, Washington, DC, and NC

Financial Summary

Assets: $320,897,293
Total Giving: $17,719,762
Number of Grants: 394
Grant Ranges: $593,438–$10; average: $1,000–$500,000

Grants Information

GRANT TYPES

General, operating and continuing support, matching, investments and loans, program development, management development

TYPICAL RECIPIENTS/SUBJECTS OF INTEREST

Higher education, public affairs, and the environment
Programs include:

Animal Welfare

Employee Matching Gifts

Environment: Focusing on national or large regional organizations that work in multiple states in the Eastern U.S. Provides limited support for state advocacy and policy development, primarily in North Carolina and New York.

Higher Education: Scholarship programs are limited to Ithaca College and North Carolina State University

Media: Focusing on investigative journalism projects including public broadcasting and independent media. National media policy is a top priority.

Sustainable Ithaca: Focusing on Ithaca, NY Tompkins County, and the Cayuga Lake

Tompkins County New York: Focusing on organizations that serve low-income and underserved populations.

PAST GRANT RECIPIENTS

Library or School Related

- American University, Washington (DC), for Investigative Reporting Workshop, $175,000
- North Carolina State University, Raleigh (NC), for Park Scholarships and recruitment activities, $3,900,000

General

- Center for Public Integrity, Washington (DC), for general operating support, $250,000
- Food and Water Watch, Washington (DC), for National Water Campaign, $150,000

REQUIREMENT AND RESTRICTIONS

No grants to individuals

APPLICATION PROCEDURES

See website for application requirements. Application form required.

Deadlines: January 7, April 1, July 1, and September 30

Parsons, Ralph M. Foundation

Headquarters

888 W. 6th St., Ste. 700
Los Angeles, CA 90017
Phone: 213-362-7600

www.rmpf.org

Contact: Wendy Gren, C.E.O. and Pres.

Type of Grant Maker: Foundation

Description

Founded: 1961

Operating Locations/Geographic Preferences: Giving limited to Los Angeles County, CA

Financial Summary

Assets: $388,666,935
Total Giving: $17,713,425
Number of Grants: 255

Grants Information

GRANT TYPES

Program development, building and renovation, capital campaigns, matching, seed money

TYPICAL RECIPIENTS/SUBJECTS OF INTEREST

Civic and Cultural

Health

Higher Education: Strongly prefers to support colleges and universities in southern California.

Social Impact: Focusing on providing services to traditionally underserved and disadvantaged populations

PAST GRANT RECIPIENTS

Library or School Related

- ICEF Public Schools, Los Angeles (CA), for network of 15 high-performing charter schools serving low-income children, $1,000,000
- Marymount College, Rancho Palos Verdes (CA), for a partnership with the Boys and Girls Club of Los Angeles Harbor and the College's Center for Service Learning, $75,000

General

- Children's Institute, Los Angeles (CA), for agency's Youth Initiative, $600,000
- Ford Theater Foundation, Los Angeles (CA), for general support, $50,000

REQUIREMENTS AND RESTRICTIONS

No support for sectarian, religious, or fraternal purposes, or for political organizations. No grants to individuals, or for annual campaigns, fund-raising events, dinners, mass mailings, workshops, federated fund-raising appeals, seminars, conferences or generally for multiyear funding. No loans.

APPLICATION PROCEDURES

See website for application guidelines. Application form not required.

Applicants should submit:

1. Timetable for implementation and evaluation of project
2. Signature and title of chief executive officer
3. Results expected from proposed grant
4. Qualifications of key personnel
5. Statement of problem project will address
6. Copy of IRS Determination Letter
7. Brief history of organization and description of its mission
8. Copy of most recent annual report/audited financial statement/990
9. How project's results will be evaluated or measured
10. Explanation of why grant-maker is considered an appropriate donor for project
11. Listing of board of directors, trustees, officers and other key people and their affiliations
12. Detailed description of project and amount of funding requested
13. Contact person
14. Copy of current year's organizational budget and/or project budget
15. Listing of additional sources and amount of support
16. Additional materials/documentation

Deadlines: None

Penn, William Foundation

Headquarters

2 Logan Sq., 11th Fl.
100 N. 18th St.
Philadelphia, PA 19103-2757
Phone: 215-988-1830

www.williampennfoundation.org

Contact: Jeremy Nowak, Pres.

E-mail: moreinfo@williampennfoundation.org

Type of Grant Maker: Foundation

Description

Founded: 1945

Operating Locations/Geographic Preferences: Giving limited to the greater Philadelphia region, including Camden, NJ

Financial Summary

Assets: $3,987,087,217
Total Giving: $81,719,258
Number of Grants: 278

Grants Information

GRANT TYPES

Program development, building and renovation, capital campaigns, general and operating support, management development, matching

TYPICAL RECIPIENTS/SUBJECTS OF INTEREST

Giving areas include:

Arts and Culture: includes visual, media, collecting, and literary institutions; performing arts institutions; historically significant sites; arts education, community arts, and arts service organizations; and arts organizations that produce work for children and young audiences.

Children, Youth, and Families funds
Innovative pilot programs
Research and the development of quality data
Technical assistance and capacity building

Environment and Communities supports
Increased public and private resources for land
Advocacy for reforms

Collaborative regional initiatives, research and trend analysis
Advocacy for policies that facilitate sustainable redevelopment and improve fiscal health in Philadelphia and Camden

PAST GRANT RECIPIENTS

Library or School Related

- Center for Literacy, Philadelphia (PA), for support of the Integrated Literacy Model to address at scale the problem of low literacy among students in the School District of Philadelphia's comprehensive high schools, $190,000
- Mastery Charter Schools Foundation, Philadelphia (PA), for capacity building to support school expansion, $1,000,000
- OMG Center for Collaborative Learning, Philadelphia (PA), to develop arts education with the School District of Philadelphia, ArtsRising, and Philadelphia-area arts organizations, $160,000

General

- Bicycle Coalition of Greater Philadelphia, Philadelphia (PA), for communications and outreach, $82,000
- Fund for Philadelphia, Philadelphia (PA), for Citizens Planning Institute, $82,000

REQUIREMENTS AND RESTRICTIONS

No support for sectarian religious activities, recreational programs, political lobbying or legislative activities, nonpublic schools, pass-through organizations, mental health or retardation treatment programs, or programs focusing on a particular disease, disability, or treatment for addiction, or profit-making enterprises; no support for private foundations. No grants to individuals, or for debt reduction, hospital capital projects, medical research, programs that replace lost government support, housing construction or rehabilitation, scholarships, or fellowships. No loans.

APPLICATION PROCEDURES

Initial letter of inquiry required. If deemed a potential fit, applicants will be invited to submit a formal and complete proposal. Do not submit complete proposal until that date.
See website for details.

Deadlines: See website

Penney, J. C. Company Fund, Inc.

Headquarters

6501 Legacy Dr., MS 1205
Plano, TX 75024-3612
Phone: 972-431-1431
Fax: 972-431-1355

www.jcpenney.net/-Our-Company-aspx/Corporate-Social
-Responsibility.aspx

Contact: Jodi Gibson, Pres. and Exec. Dir.

Type of Grant Maker: Corporate Foundation

Description

Founded: 1984

Operating Locations/Geographic Preferences: Giving on a national basis in areas of company operations.

Corporate Foundation Information: Supported by: J. C. Penney Co., Inc.

Financial Summary

Assets: $15,336,115
Total Giving: $5,581,958
Number of Grants: 126
Grant Ranges: $1,500,000–$50

Grants Information

GRANT TYPES

Annual campaigns, employee volunteering, equipment, general and operating support, sponsorships

TYPICAL RECIPIENTS/SUBJECTS OF INTEREST

Arts and culture, education, health and welfare, cancer, disaster relief, youth development, human services, retail industry, and civic betterment.

PAST GRANT RECIPIENTS

Library or School Related
- Liberal Memorial Library, Liberal (KS), $1,000
- Snow Library, Snow (AR), $50

General
- Up Hog Wild, Iron Mountain (MI), $8,875

- YMCA of Metropolitan Dallas, Dallas (TX), $2,500
- United Negro College Fund, Dallas (TX), $20,000

REQUIREMENTS AND RESTRICTIONS

No support for individual K–12 schools lacking a community partnership with J. C. Penney, PTOs or PTAs, higher education institutions lacking a business or recruiting relationship with J. C. Penney, or membership, religious, political, labor, or fraternal organizations. No grants to individuals (except for disaster relief grants), or for door prizes, gift certificates, or other giveaways, fundraising or special events, proms or graduations, scholarships for colleges lacking a recruiting relationship with J. C. Penney, conferences or seminars, capital campaigns, multiyear or long-term support, or film or video projects or research projects; no merchandise donations; no employee matching gifts.

APPLICATION PROCEDURES

Send letter of inquiry.
Deadlines: None

Pennsylvania Department of Education, Bureau of Library Development

Headquarters

607 South Drive
Harrisburg, PA 17126-0333
Phone: 717-783-0565, 717-783-8445 (TTY)
Fax: 717-772-0044

www.portal.state.pa.us/portal/server.pt/community/
Library_Funding/8702, www.education.state.pa.us

E-mail: sedmunds@pa.gov

Type of Grant Maker: Government

Grants Information

STATE AID TO PUBLIC LIBRARIES

Public libraries that meet eligibility requirements can obtain State Aid to support their general operating budgets and to leverage local financial support, particularly local government funding.

For additional information, contact:

Eileen Kocher
State Aid Librarian

Pennsylvania Department of Education
Library Development
607 South Drive
Forum Building
Harrisburg, PA 17120-0600
Phone: 717-783-5743, 717-783-8445 (TTY)
Fax: 717-772-0044

E-mail: ekocher@pa.gov

www.education.state.pa.us

LIBRARY SERVICES AND TECHNOLOGY ACT (LSTA)

Academic, school, public and special libraries that meet eligibility requirements can apply through a competitive grant process for federal Library Services and Technology Act funds to support a special project.

For additional information, contact:

Constance Cardillo
Grants and Contracting Manager
Pennsylvania Department of Education—Grants & Subsidies
607 South Drive
Harrisburg, PA 17120-0600
Phone: 717-783-5746, 717-772-2863 (TTY)
Fax: 717-772-0044

E-mail: eccardillo@pa.gov

www.education.state.pa.us

KEYSTONE RECREATION, PARK AND CONSERVATION FUND LIBRARY

Municipalities can apply on behalf of eligible public libraries for Keystone Recreation, Park and Conservation Act Library Facilities grant funds to construct new library buildings renovate or rehabilitate existing facilities and make buildings accessible for persons with disabilities.

For additional information, contact:

Beth Bisbano
Advisor for Research & Statistics
Pennsylvania Department of Education
Library Development
607 South Drive
Forum Building
Harrisburg, PA 17120-0600
Phone: 717-783-5731, 717-783-8445 (TTY)
Fax: 717-772-0044

E-mail: bbisbano@pa.gov

www.education.state.pa.us

Peoples Bancorp Foundation, Inc.

Headquarters

138 Putnam St.
PO Box 738
Marietta, OH 45750-2923
Phone: 740-376-7128

www.peoplesbancorp.com

Contact: Kristi Close, Secy.

E-mail: kclose@peoplesbancorp.com

Type of Grant Maker: Corporate Foundation

Description

Founded: 2003

Corporate Foundation Information: Supported by Peoples Bank

Operating Locations/Geographic Preferences: Giving primarily in areas of company operations in Athens, Belmont, Fairfield, Franklin, Gallia, Guernsey, Meigs, Morgan, Noble, and Washington counties, OH, Boyd and Greenup counties, KY, and Cabell, Mason, Wetzel, and Wood counties, WV.

Financial Summary

Assets: $374,513
Total Giving: $151,450
Number of Grants: 55
Grant Ranges: $29,200–$500

Grants Information

GRANT TYPES

Program development, general and operating support

TYPICAL RECIPIENTS/SUBJECTS OF INTEREST

Community investment and economic development, youth and education, human services programs that improve the social needs of the low and moderate-income communities and families, and the arts and culture.

PAST GRANT RECIPIENTS

Library or School Related

- Franciscan University of Steubenville, $1,000

General

- Artsbridge, Parkersburg (WV), for general operating support, $4,000
- Paramount Arts Center, Ashland (KY), for general operating support, $5,000
- Ronald McDonald House Charities of the Tri-State, Huntington (WV), for general operating support, $5,000

REQUIREMENTS AND RESTRICTIONS

None

APPLICATION PROCEDURES

See website

Deadlines: None

Perdue, Arthur W. Foundation, Inc.

Headquarters

c/o Foundation Source
501 Silverside Rd., Ste. 123
Wilmington, DE 19809-1377

Type of Grant Maker: Foundation

Description

Founded: N/A

Operating Locations/Geographic Preferences: Giving primarily in CT, DE, KY (MD), TN, and VA.

Financial Summary

Assets: $24,686,949
Total Giving: $2,696,589
Number of Grants: 70
Grant Ranges: $2,000,000–$750

Grants Information

GRANT TYPES

General and operating support, building and renovation

TYPICAL RECIPIENTS/SUBJECTS OF INTEREST

Arts and humanities, civic, education, health, social services

PAST GRANT RECIPIENTS

Library or School Related

- Albemarle Reg. Library, Winton (NC), rebuilding library, $20,000
- Friends of Onancock School, Onancock (VA), general support, $5,000

General

- Junior Achievement of the Eastern Shore, Salisbury (MD), $15,000
- Maryland Food Bank, Baltimore (MD), $15,000

REQUIREMENTS AND RESTRICTIONS

No support for individual churches or religious denominations. No grants to individuals.

APPLICATION PROCEDURES

Use online website/application, www.perdue com/company/commitments/contributions/application.html.

Deadlines: At the end of each quarter.

Pfizer Foundation, Inc.

Headquarters

235 E. 42nd St.
New York, NY 10017-5703

www.pfizer.com/responsibility/grants_contributions/grants_and_contributions/

Type of Grant Maker: Corporate Foundation

Please note that Pfizer's Corporate Responsibility Department and The Pfizer Foundation do not accept unsolicited requests for support.

PG&E Corporation Foundation

Headquarters

Spear Tower
1 Market St., Ste. 400
San Francisco, CA 94105-1305

www.pge.com/giving

Contact: Carol Lee

E-mail: charitablecontributions@pge.com

Type of Grant Maker: Corporate Foundation

Description

Founded: 2000

Corporate Foundation Information: Supported by PG&E Gas Transmission and Texas Corp.

Financial Summary

Assets: $12,283,235
Total Giving: $10,822,795
Number of Grants: 532
Grant Ranges: $1,200,000–$100

Grants Information

GRANT TYPES

Program development building and renovation, matching, general and operating support

TYPICAL RECIPIENTS/SUBJECTS OF INTEREST

Education, energy preparedness, and workforce development.
Special emphasis on promoting sustainable communities, air quality, natural resources, climate change, renewable energy, and environmental education.
Environmental Education support programs designed to educate the public about environmental issues and education-related projects in schools.

PAST GRANT RECIPIENTS

General

- Habitat for Humanity International, Americus (GA), to install solar equipment on all newly built Habitat-built homes in PG&E service territory, $800,000
- United Negro College Fund, San Francisco (CA), for PG&E/UNCF Scholarship Program and Annual Walk for Education, $25,000
- Oakland Parks and Recreation, Oakland (CA), to implement Phase II of Greening of Oakland program, $20,000
- Chicana Foundation of Northern California, Burlingame (CA), for educational advancement and environmental education, $15,000

REQUIREMENTS AND RESTRICTIONS

No support for religious organizations not of direct benefit to the entire community, political or partisan organizations, or discriminatory organizations. No grants to individuals, or for tickets for contests, raffles, or other activities with prizes, endowments, filmmaking, debt-reduction campaigns, or political or partisan events.

APPLICATION PROCEDURES

Initial inquiry must be made to PG&E Public Affairs staff. Application form required. Applicants should submit:

1. Copy of IRS Determination Letter
2. Detailed description of project and amount of funding requested

Deadlines: Contact foundation

Philadelphia Foundation

Headquarters

1234 Market St., Ste. 1800
Philadelphia, PA 19107-3794
Phone: 215-563-6417

www.philafound.org

Contact: R. Andrew Swinney, Pres.; for grants: Alyson Miksitz, Prog. Asst., Philanthropic Svcs.

E-mail: almiksitz@philafound.org

Type of Grant Maker: Community Foundation

Description

Founded: 1918

Operating Locations/Geographic Preferences: Giving limited to Bucks, Chester, Delaware, Montgomery, and Philadelphia counties in southeastern PA

Financial Summary

Assets: $245,794,284
Total Giving: $19,107,632
Number of Grants: 1,600

Grants Information

GRANT TYPES

Program development, general, operating and continuing support, matching, seed money

TYPICAL RECIPIENTS/SUBJECTS OF INTEREST

Emphasis on:
- Education and cultural programs
- Capacity-building
- Empowerment of low-income persons
- Health and welfare

- Community activities
- Education and cultural programs

PAST GRANT RECIPIENTS

Library or School Related

- Harvard University, Cambridge (MA), for general support, $400,000
- KIPP Philadelphia Charter School, Philadelphia (PA), for Daisy program, $3,300

General

- Wilma Theater, Philadelphia (PA), for general support, $5,000
- Philadelphia Ranger Corps, Philadelphia (PA), for program support, $1,050,000

REQUIREMENTS AND RESTRICTIONS

No support for religious purposes; generally, low priority given to national organizations, government agencies, large budget agencies, public or private schools, or umbrella funding organizations. No grants to individuals or for annual or capital campaigns, building funds, land acquisition, endowment funds, research, publications, tours or trips, conferences, or deficit financing. No loans.

APPLICATION PROCEDURES

See website for application forms and guidelines. Contact the Grant-making Services Department before submitting an application. Application form required.

Deadlines: None

Pittsburgh Foundation

Headquarters

5 PPG Pl., Ste. 250
Pittsburgh, PA 15222-5414
Phone: 412-391-5122

www.pittsburghfoundation.org

Contact: For grant applications: Jeanne Pearlman, V.P., Prog. and Policy

E-mail: e-mail@pghfdn.org

Type of Grant Maker: Community Foundation

Description

Founded: 1945

Operating Locations/Geographic Preferences: Most funds limited to Pittsburgh and Allegheny County, PA

Financial Summary

Assets: $821,409,075
Total Giving: $41,545,328

Grants Information

GRANT TYPES

Program development, management development/capacity building, investments and loans, seed money

TYPICAL RECIPIENTS/SUBJECTS OF INTEREST

Healthy Communities: Ecological issues, safe communities, cultural and racial diversity, creative arts and civic design

Self-Sufficient Individuals and Families: Education, affordable housing, public transportation, health, children, and job development

Vibrant Democracy: Civic engagement, community issues, public policy

PAST GRANT RECIPIENTS

Library or School Related

- University of Pittsburgh, Pittsburgh (PA), for research project on youth and suicide and others, $200,000
- Carlow University, Pittsburgh (PA), for general operating support, $3,000

General

- Pittsburgh Trust for Cultural Resources, Pittsburgh (PA), for marketing campaign, $450,000
- FOCUS North America, Kansas City (MO), for general operating support, $80,000
- Alzheimer's Disease Research Foundation, Pittsburgh (PA), for general operating support, $15,000
- Pittsburgh Opera, Pittsburgh (PA), for general operating support, $3,000
- Saint Luke's Refugee Network, San Diego (CA), for general operating support, $3,000

REQUIREMENTS AND RESTRICTIONS

No support for sectarian purposes, private and parochial schools, or hospitals. No grants to individuals or for annual campaigns, endowment funds, travel, operating budgets, fellowships, internships, awards, special events or research of a highly technical or specialized nature.

APPLICATION PROCEDURES

See website for application form and guidelines. Organization will be contacted if additional information is required. Applicants should submit:

1. Results expected from proposed grant
2. Statement of problem project will address
3. Detailed description of project and amount of funding requested

Deadlines: None

PNC Foundation

Headquarters

1 PNC Plz.
249 5th Ave., 20th FL
Pittsburgh, PA 15222-1119
Phone: 412-762-2748

www.pncsites.com/pncfoundation/foundation_overview
.html

Contact: Eva Tansky Blum, Chair. and Pres

E-mail: eva.blum@pnc.com

Type of Grant Maker: Corporate Foundation

Description

Founded: 1970

Operating Locations/Geographic Preferences: Giving primarily in areas of company operations in Washington, DC, DE, FL, IL, IN, KY, MD, MI, MO, NJ, OH, TN, VA, and WI, with emphasis on PA

Corporate Foundation Information: Supported by:
- PNC Bank, N.A.
- PNC Financial Services Group, Inc.

Financial Summary

Assets: $129,211,775
Total Giving: $49,385,359

Grants Information

GRANT TYPES

Program development, building and renovation, capital campaigns, matching, investments and loans, general and operating support

TYPICAL RECIPIENTS/SUBJECTS OF INTEREST

Education, with emphasis on underserved pre-K children, community economic development
　　Giving programs include:

Affordable Housing

Arts and Culture

Community Development

Community Services: Including social services, job training, essential services, early learning, educational enrichment, low- and moderate-income community facilities

Economic Development

Education: Supporting educational programs for children and youth, teachers, and families, with emphasis on early education initiatives for low- and moderate-income children. Special emphasis on math, science, or the arts and providing direct services for children in their classroom or community; teacher development, family engagement, and PNC employee volunteering.

Green Building

Matching Gift Program: PNC Grow Up Great, to improve school readiness of children from birth to age five through grants to nonprofit organizations and early education centers involved with math, science, the arts, and financial education for young children.

Revitalization and Stabilization of Low-and Moderate-Income Areas: to improve low-and moderate-income communities, eliminate blight, and attract and retain businesses and residents.

PAST GRANT RECIPIENTS

Library or School Related
- Duquesne University, Pittsburgh (PA), for general support, $600,000
- Case Western Reserve University, Cleveland (OH), for general support, $10,000

General
- Sesame Workshop, New York (NY), to promote Math Is Everywhere, $2,660,000
- Carnegie Museum of Natural History, Pittsburgh (PA), for general support, $333,333

- YMCA of the U.S.A., Chicago (IL), for general support, $250,000
- South Jersey Cultural Alliance, Pleasantville (NJ), for general support, payable $20,000

REQUIREMENTS AND RESTRICTIONS

No support for discriminatory organizations, churches, religious organizations, advocacy groups, private foundations. No grants to individuals, or for endowments, conferences, seminars, tickets, or goodwill advertising, or annual campaigns for hospitals, colleges, or universities.

APPLICATION PROCEDURES

Contact nearest local representative about application. Application form not required.

Applicants should submit:

1. How project will be sustained once grant-maker support is completed
2. Qualifications of key personnel
3. Statement of problem project will address
4. Population served
5. Name, address and phone number of organization
6. Copy of IRS Determination Letter
7. Brief history of organization and description of its mission
8. Copy of most recent annual report/audited financial statement/990
9. How project's results will be evaluated or measured
10. Descriptive literature about organization
11. Listing of board of directors, trustees, officers and other key people and their affiliations
12. Detailed description of project and amount of funding requested
13. Copy of current year's organizational budget and/or project budget
14. Listing of additional sources and amount of support
15. Additional materials/documentation

Deadlines: None

Polk Bros. Foundation, Inc.

Headquarters

20 W. Kinzie St., Ste. 1110
Chicago, IL 60654
Phone: 312-527-4684

www.polkbrosfdn.org

Contact: Nikki W. Stein, Exec. Dir.; Suzanne Doornbos Kerbow, Assoc. Dir.

E-mail: info@polkbrosfdn.org

Type of Grant Maker: Foundation

Description

Founded: 1957

Operating Locations/Geographic Preferences: Giving primarily in Chicago, IL.

Financial Summary

Assets: $348,492,632
Total Giving: $22,412,230
Number of Grants: 502
Grant Ranges: $250,000–$100

Grants Information

GRANT TYPES

Program development, continuing support, matching, equipment

TYPICAL RECIPIENTS/SUBJECTS OF INTEREST

Poverty reduction, education, preventive health care, human services

Giving areas include:

Culture: Supporting Chicago public school students, with priority to teacher training, community-based instruction in music, art, dance and theater.

Education: Focusing on increasing student achievement and strengthening the skills of Chicago Public School principals, teachers and parents and adult literacy programs

Health

Matching Gifts

Small Grants: Grants of up to $25,000

Social Services: Focusing on workforce development, housing and legal services, youth and family support, strengthening families, community and economic development programs

PAST GRANT RECIPIENTS

Library or School Related

- Chicago High School for the Arts, Chicago (IL), for program support, $250,000
- Howard Area Community Center, Chicago (IL), for program support, $35,000

General

- Children's Memorial Foundation, Chicago (IL), for capital support, $150,000
- Old Town School of Folk Music, Chicago (IL), for capital support, $200,000
- Chicago Project for Violence Prevention, Chicago (IL), for program support, $175,000

REQUIREMENTS AND RESTRICTIONS

No support for political organizations or religious institutions seeking support for programs whose participants are restricted by religious affiliation, or for tax-generating entities (municipalities and school districts) for services within their normal responsibilities. No grants to individuals, or for medical, scientific or academic research, or purchase of dinner or raffle tickets.

APPLICATION PROCEDURES

Application form required. A new organization should review the foundation's program area guide before submitting a pre-application form. Applicants should submit:

1. Copy of IRS Determination Letter
2. Copy of most recent annual report/audited financial statement/990
3. Listing of board of directors, trustees, officers and other key people and their affiliations
4. Detailed description of project and amount of funding requested
5. Copy of current year's organizational budget and/or project budget
6. Listing of additional sources and amount of support

Deadlines: None

Prince Charitable Trusts

Headquarters

303 W. Madison St., Ste. 1900
Chicago, IL 60606-3394
Phone: 312-419-8700

www.fdncenter.org/grant-maker/prince

Contact: Benna Wilde, Managing Dir.

For Chicago and RI Proposals: Sharon Robison, Grants Mgr.

E-mail: srobison@prince-trusts.org

Type of Grant Maker: Foundation

Description

Founded: 1947

Operating Locations/Geographic Preferences: Giving limited to local groups in Washington, DC, Chicago, IL, and RI, with emphasis on Aquidneck Island

Financial Summary

Assets: $123,376,279
Total Giving: $5,549,454
Number of Grants: 361
Grant range: high: $250,000

Grants Information

GRANT TYPES

Program development, general, operating and continuing support, capital campaigns, matching, investments and loans, seed money

TYPICAL RECIPIENTS/SUBJECTS OF INTEREST

Cultural programs, youth organizations, social services, hospitals, hospital morale, rehabilitation, and environment

PAST GRANT RECIPIENTS

Library or School Related

- Maderia School, McLean (VA), for Cottages for Community capital campaign, $60,000

General

- Rhode Island Kids Count, Providence (RI), for general operating support, $40,000
- John G. Shedd Aquarium Society, Chicago (IL), for Oceanarium Revitalization Project, $250,000
- Chicago Theater Group, Chicago (IL), for Prince Prize for Commissioning Original Work, $75,000
- Voices for Illinois Children, Chicago (IL), for general operating support, $15,000

REQUIREMENTS AND RESTRICTIONS

No support for national organizations, or for religious or political organizations. No grants to individuals. Some funding areas for the Chicago office are via invitation only.

APPLICATION PROCEDURES

Check website prior to applying. Application form not required. Applicants should submit:

1. Copy of IRS Determination Letter
2. Brief history of organization and description of its mission

3. Copy of most recent annual report/audited financial statement/990
4. Listing of board of directors, trustees, officers and other key people and their affiliations
5. Detailed description of project and amount of funding requested
6. Copy of current year's organizational budget and/or project budget
7. Listing of additional sources and amount of support

Deadlines: January 13 for Social Services, May 1 for Health, June 1 for Arts/Culture

Prudential Foundation

Headquarters

Prudential Plz.
751 Broad St., 15th Fl.
Newark, NJ 07102-3777
Phone: 973-802-4791
www.prudential.com/view/page/public/12182

Contact: Shane Harris, V.P. and Secy.

E-mail: community.resources@prudential.com

Type of Grant Maker: Corporate Foundation

Description

Founded: 1977

Operating Locations/Geographic Preferences: Giving primarily in areas of company operations, with emphasis on Phoenix, AZ, Los Angeles, CA, Hartford, CT, Jacksonville, FL, Dubuque, IA, Chicago, IL, New Orleans, LA, Minneapolis, MN, Newark, NJ, New York, NY, Philadelphia and Scranton, PA, Dallas and Houston, TX, Brazil, India, Japan, Korea, Mexico, and Taiwan. Giving also to national organizations.

Corporate Financial Information: Supported by:
- Prudential Insurance Co. of America
- Prudential Equity Group, LLC.

Financial Summary

Assets: $89,063,341
Total Giving: $23,859,315
Number of Grants: 982
Grant Ranges: $668,000–$250

Grants Information

GRANT TYPES

Program development, general and operating support, capital campaigns, management development, investments and loans, seed money

TYPICAL RECIPIENTS/SUBJECTS OF INTEREST

Education, economic development, arts, and civic infrastructure.
  Programs include:
- Arts and Civic Infrastructure
- Economic Development
- Education—Educational Leadership
- Education—Youth Development
    Special emphasis on arts education opportunities and effective out-of-school-time programs for young people.
- Employee Matching Gifts
- Prudential CARES Volunteer Grants

PAST GRANT RECIPIENTS

Library or School Related
- Iowa State University Dubuque County Extension, Dubuque (IA), for youth development programs, $10,000
- Bank St. College of Education, New York (NY), for Newark Educators' Collaborative, $25,000

General
- New Jersey Performing Arts Center, Newark (NJ), for endowment support, $500,000
- Newark Now, Newark (NJ), for Super Summer Initiative, $25,000
- Pushcart Players, Verona (NJ), for Imagine Dream Discover performing arts education program for Newark elementary school students, $20,000

REQUIREMENTS AND RESTRICTIONS

No support for discriminatory organizations or veterans, labor, religious, fraternal, or athletic organizations, or single-disease health groups. No grants to individuals or for goodwill advertising.

APPLICATION PROCEDURES

Application form not required. Applicants should submit:
1. Results expected from proposed grant
2. Population served
3. Copy of IRS Determination Letter
4. Geographic area to be served
5. How project's results will be evaluated or measured
6. Detailed description of project and amount of funding requested

7. Contact person
8. Copy of current year's organizational budget and/or project budget
9. Listing of additional sources and amount of support

Deadlines: None

Puffin Foundation, Ltd.

Headquarters

20 Puffin Way
Teaneck, NJ 07666-4167

www.puffinfoundation.org

Contact: Gladys Miller-Rosenstein, Exec. Dir.

Type of Grant Maker: Foundation

Description

Founded: 1985

Operating Locations/Geographic Preferences:
United States

Financial Summary

Assets: $12,197,106
Total Giving: $1,079
Number of Grants: 496
Grant Ranges: $1,250–$2,500

Grants Information

GRANT TYPES

Funds individual artists and organizations

TYPICAL RECIPIENTS/SUBJECTS OF INTEREST

Arts and art projects, especially to encourage emerging artists in the fields of art, music, theater and literature whose works, due to their genre and/or social philosophy might have difficulty being aired.

PAST GRANT RECIPIENTS

Library or School Related

• Teaneck Public Library, for murals in reference library

General

• Ohio Craft Museum for "Transformation East" exhibition of fine craft using "repurposed" objects.

• Groundswell Community Mural Project for grass-roots groups and communities to create murals in underserved neighborhoods.

REQUIREMENTS AND RESTRICTIONS

No support for religious organizations. No grants for travel, general living expenses, continuing education, or publications.

APPLICATION PROCEDURES

To receive application packet, please send self-addressed stamped envelope to:

Puffin Foundation Ltd.
Application Request
20 Puffin Way
Teaneck, NJ 07666-4111

Deadline: December 7

Rasmuson Foundation

Headquarters

301 W. Northern Lights Blvd., Ste. 400
Anchorage, AK 99503-2648

www.rasmuson.org

Contact: Diane S. Kaplan, C.E.O. and Pres.

E-mail: rasmusonfdn@rasmuson.org

Type of Grant Maker: Foundation

Description

Founded: 1955

Operating Locations/Geographic Preferences: Limited to organizations based in and providing services to Alaska

Financial Summary

Assets: $430,526,658
Total Giving: $16,772,487
Number of Grants: 272
Grant Ranges: $1,000,000–$289

Grants Information

GRANT TYPES

Program development, management development, seed money, investments and loans, matching

TYPICAL RECIPIENTS/SUBJECT OF INTEREST

Education, arts and culture, health, social services, organizational capacity building, community development, and recreation.

Program areas include:

- Art Acquisition Fund
- Artist Fellowship
- Arts In Education
    Distinguished Artist
    Harper Arts Touring Fund
    Program-Related Investments
- Project Awards
- Sabbatical Program
- Pre-Development Program: assisting nonprofit organizations in planning for successful capital projects
- Tier 1 Awards: awarding grants of up to $25,000 for capital projects, technology updates, capacity building, program expansion, and creative works
- Tier 2 Awards: awarding grants over $25,000 for projects of demonstrable strategic importance or innovative nature

PAST GRANT RECIPIENTS

Library or School Related

- Ketchikan, City of, Ketchikan (AK), for construction of a new library, $500,000

General

- Alaska Community Foundation, Anchorage (AK), for Community Asset Building Initiative, $2,000,000
- Nonprofit Finance Fund, New York (NY), for ArtPlace Initiative, collaboration of foundations, the National Endowment for the Arts and various federal agencies, $2,000,000
- Alaska Children's Institute for the Performing Arts, Kenai (AK), to purchase and install new septic system, $14,000
- Volunteers of America Alaska, Anchorage (AK), for construction of low-income, multifamily housing, $350,000

REQUIREMENTS AND RESTRICTIONS

Only religious organization projects with a broad community impact are considered. Only government and tribe projects with a broad community impact beyond traditional government functions are considered. No giving for K–12 education. No support for organizations or foundations for redistribution of funds to entities of their own selection; or organizations that, as a major purpose, influence legislation or support candidates for public office, or organizations that discriminate by reason of race, religion, sex, or national origin, or other private foundation. No grants for general operations, administrative, indirect, or overhead costs, or for deficits or debt reduction, endowments, scholarships, fund-raising events or sponsorships, reimbursement for items already purchased, or for electronic health records and other emerging technologies.

APPLICATION PROCEDURES

See website for online forms.

Deadlines: Vary

Read, Charles L. Foundation

Headquarters

249 Millburn Ave.
PO Box 599
Millburn, NJ 07041-1735

Contact: Saul Eisenberg, Treas.

Type of Grant Maker: Foundation

Applications not accepted. Contributes only to preselected organizations.

Reese, Michael Health Trust

Headquarters

150 N. Wacker Dr., Ste. 2320
Chicago, IL 60606-1608
Phone: 312-726-1008
www.healthtrust.net

Contact: Gregory S. Gross, Pres. Or Jennifer M. Rosenkranz, Sr. Prog. Off., Responsive Grants

E-mail: wpalmer@healthtrust.net

Type of Grant Maker: Foundation

Description

Founded: 1995

Operating Locations/Geographic Preferences: Giving limited to the metropolitan Chicago, IL, area with emphasis on the city of Chicago

Financial Summary

Assets: $127,144,571
Total Giving: $6,890,592

Grants Information

GRANT TYPES

Program development, general and operating support

TYPICAL RECIPIENTS/SUBJECTS OF INTEREST

Improving health of Chicago's poor, children and youth, people with disabilities, the elderly, immigrants and refugees, and the uninsured

PAST GRANT RECIPIENTS

Library or School Related

- Chicago Public Schools, Student/Teacher Development in Health Sciences, $100,000
- DePaul College of Law, Human Trafficking Response, $27,500

General

- Girls in the Game, for after-school program, $25,000
- Chicago Community Trust, to expand community schools, $50,000

REQUIREMENTS AND RESTRICTIONS

No support for private foundations, or for durable medical equipment. No grants to individuals, or for capital campaigns, endowment funds, fund-raising events, debt reduction, or scholarships.

APPLICATION PROCEDURES

See website for online application process. Applicant will be informed if a full proposal will be invited. Applicant should submit:

1. Brief history of organization and description of its mission
2. Contact person
3. Copy of current year's organizational budget and/or project budget
4. Copy of IRS Determination Letter
5. Copy of most recent annual report/audited financial statement/990
6. Detailed description of project and amount of funding requested
7. Explanation of why grant-maker is considered an appropriate donor for project
8. Geographic area to be served
9. How project will be sustained once grant-maker support is completed
10. How project's results will be evaluated or measured
11. Listing of additional sources and amount of support
12. Listing of board of directors, trustees, officers and other key people and their affiliations
13. Name, address and phone number of organization
14. Population served
15. Qualifications of key personnel
16. Results expected from proposed grant
17. Statement of problem project will address
18. Timetable for implementation and evaluation of project
19. Additional materials/documentation

Deadlines: December 15 and June 15

Revson, Charles H. Foundation, Inc.

Headquarters

55 E. 59th St., 23rd Fl.
New York, NY 10022-1112
Phone: 212-935-3340

www.revsonfoundation.org

Contact: Julie A. Sandorf, Pres.

E-mail: info@revsonfoundation.org

Type of Grant Maker: Foundation

Description

Founded: 1956

Operating Locations/Geographic Preferences: Giving primarily in New York, NY and Israel

Financial Summary

Assets: $150,891,126
Total Giving: $5,625,130
Number of Grants: 58
Grant Ranges: $937,500–$3,000

Grants Information

GRANT TYPES

Program development, continuing support, investments and loans

TYPICAL RECIPIENTS/SUBJECTS OF INTEREST

Higher education, education, urban affairs, public policy—with a special emphasis on New York (NY), problems, as well as national policy issues

Biomedical research policy

Jewish philanthropy and education

PAST GRANT RECIPIENTS

Library or School Related

- American Library Association, Chicago (IL), for construction and touring of three exhibits to 75 libraries throughout the country, focusing on the cultural impact of prominent Jewish Americans, $40,000
- Rockefeller University, New York (NY), for fellow in Charles H. Revson Senior Fellowships in the Life Sciences Program, $183,000

General

- Public Interest Law Center, New York (NY), to continue support of Charles H. Revson Law Student Public Interest Fellowship Program, $1,296,000
- Poynter Institute for Media Studies, Saint Petersburg (FL), for educational programs in New York City schools, $600,000

REQUIREMENTS AND RESTRICTIONS

No support for local or national health appeals. No grants to individuals generally, or for film projects, endowments, capital or building campaigns or fund-raising dinner events.

APPLICATION PROCEDURES

See website for application information. Applicants should submit:

1. Timetable for implementation and evaluation of project
2. How project will be sustained once grant-maker support is completed
3. Results expected from proposed grant
4. Qualifications of key personnel
5. Statement of problem project will address
6. Copy of IRS Determination Letter
7. Brief history of organization and description of its mission
8. Copy of most recent annual report/audited financial statement/990
9. How project's results will be evaluated or measured
10. Listing of board of directors, trustees, officers and other key people and their affiliations
11. Detailed description of project and amount of funding requested
12. Copy of current year's organizational budget and/or project budget
13. Listing of additional sources and amount of support

Deadlines: None

Reynolds Foundation, Donald W.

Headquarters

1701 Village Center Cir.
Las Vegas, NV 89134-6303
Phone: 702-804-6000
www.dwreynolds.org
Contact: Karina Mayer, Grants Manager
E-mail: generalquestions@dwrf.org
Type of Grant Maker: Foundation

Description

Founded: 1954
Operating Locations/Geographic Preferences: Giving primarily in AR, NV, and OK.

Financial Summary

Assets: $536,212,682
Total Giving: $152,288,140
Number of Grants: 86
Grant Ranges: $30,000,000–$1,200

Grants Information

GRANT TYPES

Program development, building and renovation, matching

TYPICAL RECIPIENTS/SUBJECTS OF INTEREST

Improving local nonprofit organizations through improved facilities for their outstanding local nonprofit organizations

Accelerating the fight against atherosclerosis and atherosclerotic heart disease through research

Improving the quality of life of America's growing elderly population through better training of physicians in geriatrics

Enhancing the quality and integrity of journalism, focusing particularly on better training of journalists who serve smaller communities and on business journalism.

Program areas include:

Aging and Quality of Life Program

Charitable Food Distribution

Children's Discovery—creating statewide networks in Arkansas, Nevada and Oklahoma, each anchored by a hub museum, to foster discovery learning for children. Requests for proposals are initiated by the foundation.

Grant Programs for Capital Grant Recipients—The foundation is no longer accepting letters of inquiry or applications for this program

Journalism Program

Matching Gifts

Special Projects

PAST GRANT RECIPIENTS

Library or School Related

- University of Arkansas, Fayetteville (AR), to construct Steven L. Anderson Design Center, $10,000,000
- University of Missouri, Columbia (MO), for program support for Donald W. Reynolds Journalism Institute, $415,000

General

- Safenet Services, Claremore (OK), for Shelter/Program Facility, $4,200,000
- Kirkpatrick Science and Air Space Museum at Omniplex, Oklahoma City (OK), to establish Oklahoma Museum Network, $300,000

REQUIREMENTS AND RESTRICTIONS

No support for elementary or secondary education, or religious institutions or hospitals. No grants to individuals, or for continuing support, program or operating support, or endowment funds.

APPLICATION PROCEDURES

See website for guidelines before submitting proposal. Applicants are encouraged to discuss projects/requests with foundation staff by telephone or in writing.

Deadlines: Vary

Reynolds, Z. Smith Foundation, Inc.

Headquarters

147 S. Cherry St., Ste. 200
Winston-Salem, NC 27101-5287
Phone: 336-725-7541

www.zsr.org

E-mail: info@zsr.org

Type of Grant Maker: Foundation

Description

Founded: 1936

Operating Locations/Geographic Preferences: Giving limited to NC

Financial Summary

Assets: $15,186,713
Total Giving: $17,009,819
Number of Grants: 209
Grant Ranges: $2,250,000–$1,000; average: $10,000–$150,000

Grants Information

GRANT TYPES

Program development, continuing, general and operating support, matching, seed money

TYPICAL RECIPIENTS/SUBJECTS OF INTEREST

Community and economic development

Environment

Democracy and civic engagement

Precollegiate education

Social justice and equity (with an emphasis on women and families)

GRANT RECIPIENTS

Library or School Related

- Wake Forest University, Winston-Salem (NC), for general support, faculty development, and scholarships, $1,200,000

General

- Teach for America, Durham (NC), for general operating support, $150,000
- North Carolina Center for Voter Education, Raleigh (NC), $225,000
- Neuse River Foundation, New Bern (NC), for general operating support, $35,000

REQUIREMENTS AND RESTRICTIONS

No support for athletic teams, civic clubs, day care centers, fraternal groups, parent/teachers associations, private K–12 schools, single-site public schools, volunteer fire departments, or emergency medical service organizations, art organizations, historic preservation organizations, homeless shelters, or health care.

No grants to individuals or for endowment funds, equipment purchases, research, athletic events, building projects or renovations, capital campaigns, computer hardware or software purchases, conferences, seminars, symposiums, fund-raising events, initiatives promoting religious education or doctrine, land purchases, payment of debts, salaries for personnel or other general operating expenses in public schools, or after-school programs.

APPLICATION PROCEDURES

See website for application form. Applicants should submit:

1. Copy of IRS Determination Letter
2. Brief history of organization and description of its mission
3. How project's results will be evaluated or measured
4. Listing of board of directors, trustees, officers and other key people and their affiliations
5. Detailed description of project and amount of funding requested
6. Copy of current year's organizational budget and/or project budget
7. Listing of additional sources and amount of support
8. Additional materials/documentation

Deadlines: February 1 and August 1

RGK Foundation

Headquarters

1301 W. 25th St., Ste. 300
Austin, TX 78705-4236
Phone: 512-474-9298
Fax: 512-474-7281

www.rgkfoundation.org

Contact: Suzanne Haffey, Grants Assoc.

Type of Grant Maker: Foundation

Description

Founded: 1966

Operating Locations/Geographic Preferences: Giving on a national basis.

Financial Summary

Assets: $136,138,498
Total Giving: $6,702,310
Number of Grants: 131
Grant Ranges: $5,000,000–$1,000; average: $10,000–$100,000

Grants Information

GRANT TYPES

Program development, management development, matching, conferences

TYPICAL RECIPIENTS/SUBJECTS OF INTEREST

Community: Supporting a broad range of human services, community improvement, abuse prevention, and youth development programs

Education: Primary interests include K–12 education (particularly mathematics, science, and reading), literacy, teacher development, and higher education.

Medicine/Health: Promoting health and well-being of children and families, access to health services, and foundation-initiated support for ALS.

PAST GRANT RECIPIENTS

Library or School Related

- Library Foundation of Los Angeles, Los Angeles (CA), for Read to Me LA early literacy initiative across all Los Angeles public library branches, $150,000.
- Reading Partners, Oakland (CA), for literacy tutoring for Los Angeles School children, K–5, $25,000
- Mainspring School, Austin (TX), for early childhood education, $25,000

General

- Reach Out and Read, Boston (MA), to provide specialized books and reading programs to children on military bases, $20,000

REQUIREMENTS AND RESTRICTIONS

No support for:

- Annual funds, galas, or other special-event fund-raising activities
- Capital campaigns/renovation projects
- Debt reduction
- Emergency or disaster relief efforts
- Dissertations or student research projects
- Indirect/administrative costs
- Sectarian religious activities, political lobbying, or legislative activities

- Institutions that discriminate on the basis of race, creed, gender, or sexual orientation in policy or in practice
- Loans, scholarships, fellowships, or grants to individuals
- Unsolicited requests for international organizations or programs
- Unsolicited requests for ALS research projects

APPLICATION PROCEDURES

Submit an electronic Letter of Inquiry.

Deadlines: None

Rhode Island Foundation

Headquarters

1 Union Station
Providence, RI 02903-1746
Phone: 401-274-4564

www.rifoundation.org

Contact: Carol Golden, Exec. V.P.

E-mail: cgolden@rifoundation.org

Type of Grant Maker: Community Foundation

Description

Founded: 1916

Operating Locations/Geographic Preferences: Giving limited to RI

Financial Summary

Assets: $573,440,744
Total Giving: $26,110,615

Grants Information

GRANT TYPES

Program development, building and renovation, capital campaigns, matching, management development, general and operating support, land acquisition, investments and loans, seed money

TYPICAL RECIPIENTS/SUBJECTS OF INTEREST

Arts and Culture, targeting programs that:
  Foster artistic and operational collaboration within the sector and result in efficiencies
  Deepen, expand, and diversify audiences for artistic and cultural presentations
  Support art making with youth in public schools and community settings

Community and Economic Development, targeting programs that:
  Increase the availability of affordable housing, providing ample rental and homeownership units
  Focus on job training and readiness that address the workforce needs of employers and employees

Education, targeting programs that:
  Focus on middle school and high school retention
  Invest in charter schools and specialty schools where best practices can be learned and shared with larger schools and districts
  Address professional development and peer support for educational leaders

Health, targeting programs that:
  Integrate oral health and mental health with primary care
  Improve primary care management of chronic conditions
  Positively change the way the system pays for primary care

Human Services, targeting programs that:
  Use evidence-based practices tailored to meet the needs of target populations
  Develop systems, policies and advocacy to improve the overall well-being of and outcomes for children

Scholarships

PAST GRANT RECIPIENTS

Library or School Related

- Tiverton Library Services, Tiverton (RI), for Marketing Plan for New Tiverton Public Library, $9,400
- Deerfield Academy, Deerfield (MA), for Outdoor Experience Project, $80,000
- College of the Atlantic, Bar Harbor (ME), for Richard J. Borden Chair in the Humanities/David Hales Director of Sustainability, $1,000,000

General

- Teach for America, New York (NY), $1,000,000
- Rhode Island Philharmonic Orchestra, East Providence (RI), for Internal Organization Assessment, $7,300
- Youth Pride, Providence (RI), for Gay/Straight Alliance Activities, $5,000

REQUIREMENTS AND RESTRICTIONS

No support for religious organizations for sectarian purposes.

No grants for endowment funds, research, hospital equipment, capital needs of health organizations, annual campaigns, deficit financing, or educational institutions for general operating expenses.

APPLICATION PROCEDURES

See website for application guidelines. Application form required.

Applicants should submit:

1. Statement of problem project will address
2. Population served
3. Copy of IRS Determination Letter
4. Copy of most recent annual report/audited financial statement/990
5. Detailed description of project and amount of funding requested
6. Copy of current year's organizational budget and/or project budget

Deadlines: Vary

Rhode Island (State of), Office of Library and Information Services

Headquarters

RI Department of Administration
One Capitol Hill, 4th Floor
Providence, Rhode Island 02908-5803
Phone: 401-574-9300
Fax: 401-574-9320

www.olis.ri.gov/grants/

E-mail: webmaster@olis.ri.gov

Type of Grant Maker: Government

Grants Information

LORI GRANTS

The purposes of the LORI Grant program are analogous to the overall LSTA purposes. In addition to the prerequisites set forth by the LSTA, OLIS is interested in funding some particular areas of library endeavor.

OLIS will give priority attention to proposals:

From groups of libraries and other nonprofit partners to create an infrastructure that would enable them to provide library services or programs for, to, or among the partners that could not be provided as well by a single partner alone

That enhance and expand the functionality of LORI, by the addition of member libraries or by creating access to previously unavailable resources

That enhance library capacity or performance in order for the library to comply with LORI Standards and join LORI

That develop and integrate social media into library collections and services

That increase library collections with materials that can also be loaned as part of the statewide interlibrary network

REQUIREMENTS AND RESTRICTION

Capital; expenditures are not eligible for LORI Grants.

APPLICATION PROCEDURES AND DEADLINES

See the online LORI Grant application which provides comprehensive information about funding priorities, the application process and the grant schedule.

PUBLIC LIBRARY CONSTRUCTION REIMBURSEMENT GRANTS

Provides grant-in-aid for the construction and capital improvement of any free public library in the state to provide better free library services to the public. Up to 50% of the eligible costs of public library construction and capital improvement projects may be reimbursed through this program.

REQUIREMENTS AND RESTRICTIONS

In order to be considered for reimbursement funding, applicants must meet the requirements of the program as specified in regulations promulgated by the Library Board of Rhode Island and OLIS. These regulations include library requirements, project requirements, application procedures, allowable costs, and contractor requirements. When a project application meets these requirements, funding approval is requested from the Director of the Department of Administration.

APPLICATION PROCEDURES AND DEADLINES

Construction Reimbursement Regulations and Application available online.

Direct inquiries regarding Public Library Construction Reimbursement to:

Karen Mellor
401-574-9304
Rhode Island Department of Administration
Office of Library and Information Services
One Capitol Hill
Providence, RI 02908
E-mail: Karen.Mellor@olis.ri.gov

Rochester Area Community Foundation

Headquarters

500 East Ave.
Rochester, NY 14607-1912
Phone: 585-271-4100

www.racf.org

Contact: Edward Doherty, V.P., Community Progs.; for grants: Mairead Hartmann, Prog. Off.

E-mail: edoherty@racf.org

Type of Grant Maker: Community Foundation

Description

Founded: 1972

Operating Locations/Geographic Preferences: Giving limited to Genesee, Livingston, Monroe, Ontario, Orleans, and Wayne counties, NY

Financial Summary

Assets: $208,498,147
Total Giving: $17,084,058

Grants Information

GRANT TYPES

Program development, building and renovation, management development, general and operating support, seed money

TYPICAL RECIPIENTS/SUBJECTS OF INTEREST

Primary interests include early childhood education, community development, leadership programs for young people, after-school program quality, civic engagement, and strengthening families and children.

PAST GRANT RECIPIENTS

Library or School Related

- Rochester Institute of Technology, Rochester (NY), for Carlson Center for Imaging Science, $100,000
- Saint John Fisher College, Rochester (NY), for annual fund and 2020 vision campaign, $2,000

General

- Metropolitan Opera Association, New York (NY), for general support, $500,000
- Genesee Country Museum, Mumford (NY), for general support, $2,000
- Catholic Charities of Wayne County, Newark (NY), for Early Intervention Program, $93,000

REQUIREMENTS AND RESTRICTIONS

No support for religious projects.

No grants to individuals or for capital or annual campaigns, debt reduction, special events, land acquisition, or endowment or emergency funds.

APPLICATION PROCEDURES

See website for forms and guidelines.

Deadlines: Vary

Rockefeller Brothers Fund, Inc.

Headquarters

475 Riverside Dr., Ste. 900
New York, NY 10115
Phone: 212-812-4200

www.rbf.org

Contact: Hope Lyons, Dir., Grants Mgmt.

E-mail: grantsmgmt@rbf.org

Type of Grant Maker: Foundation

Description

Founded: 1940

Operating Locations/Geographic Preferences: Giving primarily in the United States and internationally, with an emphasis on three pivotal places: New York City, Southern China and the Western Balkans

Financial Summary

Assets: $789,378,035
Total giving: $28,004,330

Grants Information

GRANT TYPES

Program development, general and operating support, matching, seed money, investments and loans

TYPICAL RECIPIENTS/SUBJECTS OF INTEREST

Democratic Practice—to strengthen the vitality of democracy in the United States and in global governance.

Peacebuilding

Pivotal Place:

New York City—encourage immigrant civic and political participation, support individual achievement and artistic expression, and generate prosperity; arts and culture are central.

Southern China

Western Balkans

Sustainable Development

PAST GRANT RECIPIENTS

Library or School Related

- New York Public Library, Astor, Lenox and Tilden Foundations, New York (NY), for endowment at Jerome Robbins Dance Division of New York Public Library, $250,000
- Tufts University, Medford (MA), for Global Development and Environment Institute, $200,000

General

- Architecture 2030, Santa Fe (NM), for general support, $400,000
- Health Care Without Harm, Reston (VA), for climate and energy initiative, $100,000

REQUIREMENTS AND RESTRICTIONS

No grants to individuals, or for land acquisitions or building funds.

APPLICATION PROCEDURES

See website for application guidelines and preliminary grant compatibility quiz

Deadlines: See website

Rockefeller Foundation

Headquarters

420 5th Ave.
New York, NY 10018-2702
Phone: 212-869-8500

www.rockefellerfoundation.org

Type of Grant Maker: Foundation

Description

Founded: 1913

Operating Locations/Geographic Preferences: Giving primarily in New York City, Africa, North America, and Southeast Asia.

Financial Summary

Assets: $3,593,289,629
Total Giving: $139,408,226
Number of Grants: 596
Grant Ranges: $6,000,000–$340

Grants Information

GRANT TYPES

Program development, continuing, general and operating support, matching, investments and loans, seed money

TYPICAL RECIPIENTS/SUBJECTS OF INTEREST

Advancing Innovation Processes to Solve Social Problems:

Testing the value and applicability of commercial innovation models for addressing social problems

Scaling up or replicating existing socially focused or not-for-profit innovation models

Influencing providers of innovation platforms and techniques to sustainably and systematically provide their services to the social sector

Encouraging NGOs, researchers, funders, and entrepreneurs focused on pro-poor innovation to use open-innovation models.

Bellagio Center Residency Programs

Bellagio Creative Arts Fellowships

Climate Change Resilience

Helping Build an Impact Investing Industry:

> Catalyzing platforms for collective action that enable leading impact investors and intermediaries to coordinate efforts, such as disseminating standards and sharing information

> Supporting the development of scaled intermediation vehicles that help absorb impact investments at a scale necessary to attract the institutional investors who control the lion's share of global capital

> Building industry-wide infrastructure that enables broader and more effective participation in the impact investing industry

> Supporting research and advocacy efforts that promote an analytical understanding of the impact-investing industry and take necessary steps to facilitate its maturation.

Linking Global Disease Surveillance

New York City Opportunities Fund:

> Supporting creativity and the arts, with an emphasis on innovation. Grants range from $50,000 to $250,000

> The Jane Jacobs Medal

> Opportunity NYC providing payment to low-income families and individuals to increase participation

Promoting Equitable, Sustainable Transportation Policies: To advance equitable, sustainable and economically beneficial transportation policies

Protecting American Workers' Economic Security: Campaign for American Workers

Strengthening Food Security: Alliance for Green Revolution in Africa

Transforming Health Systems

PAST GRANT RECIPIENTS

General

- Smart Growth America, Washington (DC), for initiative to strengthen capacity of US states to implement equitable and sustainable transportation policies, $1,250,000
- Teneo Strategy Consulting, New York (NY), to build capacity, create new coalitions, strengthen existing networks, and advance public policy, $3,400,000

REQUIREMENTS AND RESTRICTIONS

No grants to individuals or for endowment funds or building or operating funds.

APPLICATION PROCEDURES

See website and contact staff for proposals that fit guidelines. Do not submit proposal unless invited to do so.

Deadlines: None

Rose Community Foundation

Headquarters

600 S. Cherry St., Ste. 1200
Denver, CO 80246
Phone: 303-398-7400

www.rcfdenver.org

Contact: For grants: Cheryl McDonald, Grants Mgr.

E-mail: grantsmanager@rcfdenver.org

Type of Grant Maker: Foundation

Description

Founded: 1995

Operating Locations/Geographic Preferences: Giving limited to the greater Denver, CO, area.

Financial Summary

Assets: $219,097,000
Total Giving: $10,933,000
Number of Grants: 887

Grants Information

GRANT TYPES

Program development, building and renovation, capital campaigns, matching, general and operating support

TYPICAL RECIPIENTS/SUBJECTS OF INTEREST

- Aging
- Child and Family Development
- Education
- Health
- Jewish Life

PAST GRANT RECIPIENTS

General

- Colorado Legacy Foundation, Denver (CO), for initiatives focused on educator effectiveness in Colorado as part of Colorado Educator Effectiveness Initiative, $421,000
- Relationship Roots Children's Center, Lakewood (CO), for professional development training for child care center staff, $30,000
- Jewish Community Centers of Denver, Denver (CO), for start-up costs for new Jewish campus in southern metropolitan area, $800,000

REQUIREMENTS AND RESTRICTIONS

No support for political candidates or pass-through organizations.

No grants to individuals, or for endowments, annual appeals, membership drives, or fund-raising events.

APPLICATION PROCEDURES

See website for application guidelines and form. Applicants should submit:

1. Timetable for implementation and evaluation of project
2. Qualifications of key personnel
3. Copy of IRS Determination Letter
4. Brief history of organization and description of its mission
5. Copy of most recent annual report/audited financial statement/990
6. How project's results will be evaluated or measured
7. Listing of board of directors, trustees, officers and other key people and their affiliations
8. Detailed description of project and amount of funding requested
9. Contact person
10. Copy of current year's organizational budget and/or project budget
11. Listing of additional sources and amount of support

Deadlines: None

Rubin, Cele H. & William B. Family Fund, Inc.

Headquarters

32 Monadnock Rd.
Wellesley Hills, MA 02481-1338
Phone: 781-235-1075

Contact: Ellen R. Gordon, Pres.

Type of Grant Maker: Foundation

Description

Founded: 1943

Operating Locations/Geographic Preferences: Giving primarily in IL, MA, and NY.

Financial Summary

Assets: $70,890,165
Total Giving: $2,987,413

Number of Grants: 78
Grant Ranges: $2,114,000–$50

Grants Information

GRANT TYPES

General support

TYPICAL RECIPIENTS/SUBJECTS OF INTEREST

Arts and humanities, civic, education, environment, health, religion, science, social services

PAST GRANT RECIPIENTS

Library or School Related

- Wellesley Free Library, Wellesley (MA), $3,000
- Wellesley College, Wellesley (MA), $10,000
- University of Chicago Medical Center, Chicago (IL), $515,000
- Dartmouth College, Hanover (NH), $15,000
- Duke University, Durham (NC), $2,000

General

- Our Bodies Ourselves, Cambridge (MA), $7,500
- Partners In Health, Boston (MA), $5,000
- Suam Lakes Natural Science Center, Holderness (NH), $3,500

REQUIREMENTS AND RESTRICTIONS

No grants to individuals. Giving primarily to a donor advised fund, as well as for colleges and universities.

APPLICATION PROCEDURES

Call or send letter of inquiry

Deadlines: None

S & T Bancorp Charitable Foundation

Headquarters

c/o S&T Bank, Trust Dept.
PO Box 220
Indiana, PA 15701-0220
Phone: 724-465-1443

Contact: Todd B. Price, Pres.

Type of Grant Maker: Corporate Foundation

Description

Founded: 1993

Operating Locations/Geographic Preferences: Giving limited to areas of company operations in Indiana, PA

Corporate Foundation Information: Supported by S&T Bancorp, Inc. and S&B Bank

Financial Summary

Assets: $112,309
Total Giving: $490,693
Number of Grants: 135
Grant Ranges: $100,000–$100

Grants Information

GRANT TYPES

Annual and capital campaigns, building and renovation, general and operating support, program development, sponsorships

TYPICAL RECEIPTS/SUBJECTS OF INTEREST

Arts and culture, education, health, athletics, human services, community development, and economically disadvantaged people.

PAST GRANT RECIPIENTS

Library or School Related

- Indiana Free Library, Indiana (PA), general support $1,000
- Mengle Memorial Library, capital campaign, $2,000
- Monroeville Public Library, Monroeville (PA), general support, $1,000
- Plum Borough Community Library, Plum (PA), general support, $1,000

General

- United Way, Du Bois Area, Du Bois (PA), for general support, $12,000
- Jefferson County Area Agency on Aging, Brookville (PA), for capital campaign, $6,000

REQUIREMENTS AND RESTRICTIONS

Awards will be restricted to within the marketing area of the bank.

APPLICATION PROCEDURES

Send letter of inquiry with amount and purpose.

Deadline: None

Sage Foundation

Headquarters

PO Box 1919
Brighton, MI 48116-5719
Contact: Melissa Sage Fadim, Chair.
Type of Grant Maker: Foundation

Description

Founded: 1954

Operating Locations/Geographic Preferences: Giving primarily in IL and MI.

Financial Summary

Assets: $53,305,150
Total Giving: $2,524,500
Number of Grants: 116
Grant Ranges: $200,000–$1,000

Grants Information

GRANT TYPES

Annual and capital campaigns, building and renovation, continuing, general and operating support, equipment, endowments

TYPICAL RECIPIENTS/SUBJECTS OF INTEREST

Arts, education, health organizations, social services, and Roman Catholic churches and agencies

PAST GRANT RECIPIENTS

Library or School Related

- Lenawee Community Tecumseh Carnegie Preservation, Tecumseh (MI), renovation of Carnegie Library, $100,000
- Tecumseh Area Communities in School, Tecumseh (MI), general, charitable, and educational, $10,000

General

- Art Institute of Chicago, Chicago (IL), Scholarships and endowment, $235,000
- Kartemquin Educational Films General, charitable and educational contribution, $100,000

REQUIREMENTS AND RESTRICTIONS

Applicants must have tax-exempt status.

APPLICATION PROCEDURES

Send letter.

Deadlines: None

Saint Louis Community Foundation, Greater

Headquarters

319 N. 4th St., Ste. 300
Saint Louis, MO 63102-1906
Phone: 314-588-8200

www.stlouisgives.org

Contact: Dwight D. Canning, C.E.O.

E-mail: info@stlouisgives.org

Type of Grant Maker: Community Foundation

Description

Founded: 1915

Operating Locations/Geographic Preferences: Giving primarily in the metropolitan St. Louis, MO, area, including IL

Financial Summary

Assets: $170,208,904
Total Giving: $27,013,704
Number of Grants: 1,795
Grant Ranges: $1,000,000–$50

Grants Information

GRANT TYPES

Program development, general and operating support, management development, matching, seed money

TYPICAL RECIPIENTS/SUBJECTS OF INTEREST

Education, arts and culture, community building, environment, health, and human services

PAST GRANT RECIPIENTS

Library or School Related

- Saint Louis Mercantile Library Association, Saint Louis (MO), for general support, $20,670
- Colorado International School, Denver (CO), for general support, $59,600

General

- Saint Louis Art Museum Foundation, Saint Louis (MO), for capital campaign, $25,000
- Humane Society of Missouri, Saint Louis (MO), for general support, $343,000
- Annie Malone Children and Family Service Center, Saint Louis (MO), for general support, $10,700

REQUIREMENTS AND RESTRICTIONS

No grants to individuals or for deficit financing, or endowment or building funds.

APPLICATION PROCEDURES

See website for guidelines and special grant initiative guidelines. Application form required.

Deadlines: None

San Diego Foundation

Headquarters

2508 Historic Decatur Rd., Ste. 200
San Diego, CA 92106-6138
Phone: 619-235-2300

www.sdfoundation.org

Contact: Robert A. Kelly, C.E.O.

E-mail: info@sdfoundation.org

Type of Grant Maker: Community Foundation

Description

Founded: 1975

Operating Locations/Geographic Preferences: Giving primarily in the greater San Diego, CA region

Financial Summary

Assets: $560,136,000
Total Giving: $38,004,000

Grants Information

GRANT TYPES

Program development, matching, general and operating support, land

TYPICAL RECIPIENTS/SUBJECTS OF INTEREST

Education, arts and culture, asset building, civil society, environment/animal welfare, scholarship, human/social services, and health

PAST GRANT RECIPIENTS

Library or School Related

- Escondido Public Library, Escondido (CA), for general support, $150,000
- University of San Diego, San Diego (CA), for the men's basketball program, $2,500

General

- Challenged Athletes Foundation, San Diego (CA), for completion of the new building, $530,000
- San Diego Symphony Orchestra, San Diego (CA), for general support, $239,700
- San Diego Dance Theater, San Diego (CA), for general support, $5,000

REQUIREMENTS AND RESTRICTIONS

No support for religious organizations. No grants to individuals or for annual or capital fund campaigns, endowment funds, conferences, travel, or to underwrite fund-raising events and performances.

APPLICATION PROCEDURES

See website for grant application and guidelines. Application form required.

Applicants should submit:

1. Timetable for implementation and evaluation of project
2. Results expected from proposed grant
3. Qualifications of key personnel
4. Statement of problem project will address
5. Population served
6. Name, address and phone number of organization
7. Brief history of organization and description of its mission
8. Geographic area to be served
9. How project's results will be evaluated or measured
10. Listing of board of directors, trustees, officers and other key people and their affiliations
11. Detailed description of project and amount of funding requested
12. Plans for cooperation with other organizations, if any
13. Contact person
14. Copy of current year's organizational budget and/or project budget
15. Listing of additional sources and amount of support

Deadlines: Vary

San Francisco Foundation

Headquarters

225 Bush St., Ste. 500
San Francisco, CA 94104-4224
Phone: 415-733-8500

www.sff.org

Contact: Sandra R. Hernandez M.D., C.E.O.

E-mail: info@sff.org

Type of Grant Maker: Community Foundation

Description

Founded: 1948

Operating Locations/Geographic Preferences: Giving limited to the San Francisco Bay Area, CA, counties of Alameda, Contra Costa, Marin, San Francisco, and San Mateo

Financial Summary

Assets: $1,101,069,000
Total Giving: $82,473,000

Grants Information

GRANT TYPES

Program development, general and operating, investments and loans, matching

TYPICAL RECIPIENTS/SUBJECTS OF INTEREST

Education, arts and culture, community health, environment, neighborhood and community development, and social justice.

Giving programs include:

Art Awards

Arts and Culture

Areas of special emphasis:

1. Culturally diverse organizations

2. Programs that promote the direct participation of Bay Area residents in cultural activities, often under the auspices of festivals, workshops, parades, amateur associations, or fairs
3. Cultural programs that inspire positive development of children and youth
4. Capacity-building of elementary and secondary schools, to enhance the creative and critical reasoning skills of youth
5. Support organizations that promote the development of audiences.

Bay Area Documentary Fund

Community Health

Community Leadership Awards

Education: Funding priorities include school improvement, youth development, early childhood education, and family support.

Areas of special emphasis:

1. Programs that address the developmental and academic needs of the whole child, especially those from low-income and culturally and linguistically diverse families
2. Strategies that strengthen parental participation in children's development and education
3. Programs emphasizing respectful, engaging, and personalized relationships between adults, children, and youth and that promote a sense of belonging
4. Programs that address equity and access to a quality education for underserved children, and culturally responsive approaches that promote intra- and inter-cultural understanding
5. Innovative approaches that can be replicated and influence public policy
6. Strategies that promote inter-agency collaboration and multidisciplinary approaches

Environment

JD Phelan, J&G Murphy, EA&AB Cadogan Fellowships in the Fine Arts

Koshland Civic Unity Awards

Koshland Organizational Grants

Literary Awards
Note: winning manuscripts will be permanently housed in UC Berkeley's Bancroft Library

Multicultural Fellowship Program
Social Justice

PAST GRANT RECIPIENTS

Library or School Related

- San Pablo Library, Arts and cultural programs, $3,000
- Urban University, Early childhood education, $20,000
- San Mateo Co. Office of Education, Professional development for teachers of English learners, $18,000
- Raising a Reader, Early Literacy, $18,500
- Metro ECE Academy, to enhance technology, $25,000

REQUIREMENTS AND RESTRICTIONS

No support for religious purposes, or medical, academic, or scientific research. No grants to individuals or for conferences or one-time events.

APPLICATION PROCEDURES

See website for online application, application guidelines and specific deadlines. Application form required.
Deadline: November

Sarkeys Foundation

Headquarters

530 E. Main St.
Norman, OK 73071-5823
Phone: 405-364-3703
Fax: 405-364-8191
www.sarkeys.org
Contact: Susan C. Frantz, Sr. Prog. Off.
E-mail: sarkeys@sarkeys.org
Type of Grant Maker: Foundation

Description

Founded: 1962
Operating Locations/Geographic Preferences: Giving limited to OK

Financial Summary

Assets: $87,958,706
Total Giving: $3,400,464
Number of Grants: 119
Grant Ranges: $500,000–$100

Grants Information

GRANT TYPES

Free conference facilities, nonprofit grants, board retreat grants, building and renovation, capital campaigns, matching, program development, technical assistance, equipment, endowment, management development

TYPICAL RECIPIENTS/SUBJECTS OF INTEREST

Education, social service and human service needs cultural and humanitarian programs of regional significance

PAST GRANT RECIPIENTS

Library or School Related

- University of Oklahoma Foundation, Norman (OK), for Museum of Art addition to house the Weitzenhoffer Collection and to purchase band uniforms, $250,000
- Oklahoma Partnership for School Readiness Foundation, Oklahoma City (OK), to expand public engagement campaign and implement the Strengthening Families program, $200,000
- University of Oklahoma Foundation, Norman (OK), toward construction of an indoor tennis arena and establishment scholarship, $200,000

General

- Little Dixie CAA Early Head Start Program, Hugo (OK), $20,000
- Oklahoma City Museum of Art, Oklahoma City (OK), to increase the corpus of the Sarkeys Foundation Arts Endowment, $125,000

REQUIREMENTS AND RESTRICTIONS

Needs normally outside the range of support by the Sarkeys Foundation:

1. Local programs appropriately financed within the community
2. Direct-mail solicitations and annual campaigns
3. Out of state institutions
4. Hospitals
5. Operating expenses
6. Purchase of vehicles
7. Grants to individuals
8. Responsibility for permanent financing of a program
9. Programs whose ultimate intent is to be profit making
10. Start-up funding for new organizations
11. Feasibility studies
12. Grants which trigger expenditure responsibility by Sarkeys Foundation
13. Direct support to government agencies
14. Individual public or private elementary or secondary schools, unless they are serving the needs of a special population which are not being met elsewhere

APPLICATION PROCEDURES

The Trustees invite proposals and applications from qualified charitable institutions. A careful evaluation of each such request will be made. Applicants are required to participate in a pre-grant interview with a program officer at which time they will receive an access code for the online application. Nonprofit representatives are urged not to wait until the final deadline.

Deadlines: August 1

Scott & Fetzer Foundation

Headquarters

c/o The Scott Fetzer Co.
28800 Clemens Rd.
Westlake, OH 44145-1134
Phone: 440-892-3000

Contact: Angela Stacey

Type of Grant Maker: Corporate Foundation

Description

Founded: 1967

Operating Locations/Geographic Preferences: Giving primarily in OH, with emphasis on Cleveland

Corporate Foundation Information: Supported by The Scott Fetzer Co.

Financial Summary

Assets: $138,817
Total Giving: $81,000
Number of Grants: 9
Grant Ranges: $17,500–$500

GRANT TYPES

General and operating support

TYPICAL RECIPIENTS/SUBJECTS OF INTEREST

Education, health, heart disease, human services, and community economic development

PAST GRANT RECIPIENTS

Library or School Related

- Cuyahoga Community College, Cleveland (OH), $1,000

General

- United Way of Greater Cleveland, Cleveland (OH), $17,500
- Hospice of Cincinnati, Cincinnati (OH), $1,000
- Cleveland Clinic Children's Hospital, Cleveland (OH), $1,000
- Home Depot Foundation, Atlanta (GA), $4,250
- CopsRide LLC, Westlake (OH), $5,000

REQUIREMENTS AND RESTRICTIONS

No grants to individuals.

APPLICATION PROCEDURES

Send letter with federal tax ID number.

Deadlines: None

Seattle Foundation

Headquarters

1200 5th Ave., Ste. 1300
Seattle, WA 98101-3151
Phone: 206-622-2294

www.seattlefoundation.org

Contact: Ceil Erickson, Dir., Grant-making

E-mail: info@seattlefoundation.org

Type of Grant Maker: Community Foundation

Description

Founded: 1946

Operating Locations/Geographic Preferences: Giving limited to King County, WA

Financial Summary

Assets: $663,201,900
Total Giving: $52,117,881

Grants Information

GRANT TYPES

Building and renovation, capital campaigns, general and operating, investments and loans, program development

TYPICAL RECIPIENTS/SUBJECTS OF INTEREST

Education: including, but not limited to support for school children, early learning, caregiver support, job training, continuing education, distance learning, libraries, public radio and television, ESL, after-school programs and youth development

Arts and Culture: including, but not limited to music, art and literature, drama, dance, cultural heritage and historical societies, community celebrations, public art, and film

Basic Needs

Economy

Environment

Global Giving

Health and Wellness

Neighborhoods and Communities

Scholarship Funds

PAST GRANT RECIPIENTS

Library or School Related

- Gage Academy of Art, Seattle (WA), for general support, $3,000
- Seattle University, Seattle (WA), for general support, $3,000

General

- Seattle Opera Association, Seattle (WA), for general support, $333,333
- League of Education Voters Foundation, Seattle (WA), for general support, $250,000
- MCA of Tacoma-Pierce County, Tacoma (WA), for capital campaign, $250,000

REQUIREMENTS AND RESTRICTIONS

No support for religious purposes. No grants for endowment funds, debt reduction, fund-raising events, fund-raising feasibility projects, conferences or seminars, film or video production, publications, first-year organizations, or operating expenses for public or private elementary and secondary schools, colleges, and universities.

APPLICATION PROCEDURES

See website for application form and guidelines. Applicants should submit:

1. How project will be sustained once grant-maker support is completed
2. Results expected from proposed grant
3. Name, address and phone number of organization
4. Copy of IRS Determination Letter
5. Brief history of organization and description of its mission

6. Copy of most recent annual report/audited financial statement/990
7. How project's results will be evaluated or measured
8. Listing of board of directors, trustees, officers and other key people and their affiliations
9. Detailed description of project and amount of funding requested
10. Contact person
11. Copy of current year's organizational budget and/or project budget
12. Listing of additional sources and amount of support

Deadlines: Vary

Sherwood Foundation

Headquarters

3555 Farnam St.
Omaha, NE 68131-3302
Phone: 402-341-1717

www.sherwoodfoundation.org

Type of Grant Maker: Foundation

Description

Founded: 1999

Operating Locations/Geographic Preferences: Giving primarily in Omaha, NE

Financial Summary

Assets: $161,103,598
Total Giving: $82,016,449
Number of Grants: 357
Grant Ranges: $10,100,478–$150

GRANT TYPES

General and operating support, program development, capital campaigns

TYPICAL RECIPIENTS/SUBJECTS OF INTEREST

Public education, human services and social justice

PAST GRANT RECIPIENTS

- Omaha Schools Foundation, Omaha (NE), for Read Right Phase III, $534,000
- Omaha Schools Foundation, Omaha (NE), for Nathan Hale Middle School, $28,000
- University of Nebraska Foundation, Lincoln (NE), for Faculty at Eppley Cancer Center Facility, $2,000,000

General

- Buffett Early Childhood Fund, Omaha (NE), for operating support, $5,000,000
- William J. Clinton Presidential Foundation, Little Rock (AR), for operating support, $500,000
- Women's Fund of Greater Omaha, Omaha (NE), for Excellence Award, $25,000

REQUIREMENTS AND RESTRICTIONS

No support for political candidates, campaigns or organizations, or for organizations that discriminate in hiring staff and/or providing services on the basis of race, religion, gender, sexual orientation, age or disability. No grants to individuals.

APPLICATION PROCEDURES

Letter of inquiry will determine the eligibility of organizations. See website for information. For full proposal, applicants should submit:

1. Results expected from proposed grant
2. Statement of problem project will address
3. Population served
4. Name, address and phone number of organization
5. Copy of IRS Determination Letter
6. Brief history of organization and description of its mission
7. Detailed description of project and amount of funding requested
8. Contact person
9. Copy of current year's organizational budget and/or project budget

Deadlines: For letter of inquiry: February 15 and August 15

Silicon Valley Community Foundation

Headquarters

2440 W. El Camino Real, Ste. 300
Mountain View, CA 94040-1498
Phone: 650-450-5400

www.siliconvalleycf.org

Contact: Vera Bennett, C.F.O.

E-mail: info@siliconvalleycf.org

Type of Grant Maker: Community Foundation

Description

Founded: 2007

Operating Locations/Geographic Preferences: Giving limited to efforts that benefit the San Mateo and Santa Clara counties in CA

Financial Summary

Assets: $1,749,109,000
Total Giving: $154,255,000
Number of Grants: 304

Grants Information

GRANT TYPES

Program development, continuing, general and operating support, investments and loans, seed money, management development

TYPICAL RECIPIENTS/SUBJECTS OF INTEREST

Community Opportunity Fund: Providing essential safety-net needs, such as access to food, shelter, homeless prevention services and emergency assistance for low-income and vulnerable individuals, families and seniors.

Economic Security, including:
    Foreclosure Prevention Counseling
    Combining Financial Education with Asset Building
    Anti-Payday Lending Policy Advocacy

Education: Closing the middle-school achievement gap in mathematics that separates low-income students and students of color from others in preparing for college and future success. Supports in-school strategies and out-of-school strategies, which seek to increase the number and effectiveness of extended learning opportunities.

Immigration Integration: Including
    Bridging the Cultural Gap
    Strengthening the Legal Services Infrastructure
    Adult English Language Acquisition

Regional Planning: Supporting
    Technical assistance
    Community outreach and convening
    Education of community-based organization staff
        and/or of community members
    Advocacy
    Communications training
  Scholarship Programs

PAST GRANT RECIPIENTS

Library or School Related

- New Teacher Center, Santa Cruz (CA), for Collaborating for Academic Success in Algebra, $100,000

General

- Asian Americans for Community Involvement, San Jose (CA), for Asian American Voices project, $90,000

REQUIREMENTS AND RESTRICTIONS

No support for religious purposes or private nonoperating foundations.

APPLICATION PROCEDURES

See website for request for proposal forms, application and guidelines.

Deadlines: See website

Skoll Foundation

Headquarters

250 University Ave., Ste. 200
Palo Alto, CA 94301-1738
Phone: 650-331-1031
www.skollfoundation.org
E-mail: grants@skollfoundation.org
Type of Grant Maker: Foundation

Description

Founded: 2002

Operating Locations/Geographic Preferences: None stated

Financial Summary

Assets: $463,297,672
Total Giving: $33,383,519
Number of Grants: 81
Grant Ranges: $10,000,000–$3,374

Grants Information

GRANT TYPES

General and operating support, investments and loans

TYPICAL RECIPIENTS/SUBJECTS OF INTEREST

Skoll Awards for Social Entrepreneurship supports large-scale efforts of social entrepreneurs whose work has the potential for large-scale influence on environmental sustainability, health, tolerance and human rights, institutional responsibility, social and economic equality, peace and security.

PAST GRANT RECIPIENTS

General

- Ashoka: Innovators for the Public, Arlington (VA), for core support and Collaborative Action and Tropical Forests Initiative, $1,500,000
- Free the Children USA, Hartford (CT), for core support, $750,000
- YouthBuild USA, Somerville (MA), for YouthBuild expansion, $750,000
- Manchester Bidwell Corporation, Pittsburgh (PA), for National Center for Arts and Technology, $600,000
- Global Footprint Network, Oakland (CA), for core support, $250,000

REQUIREMENTS AND RESTRICTIONS

No support for organizations' new or early-stage business plans or ideas, schools and school districts, or programs promoting religious doctrine. No grants to individuals, or for scholarships, endowments, deficit reduction or land acquisition.

APPLICATION PROCEDURES

See website for eligibility quiz and application information.

Deadlines: See website

Sloan, Alfred P. Foundation

Headquarters

630 5th Ave., Ste. 2550
New York, NY 10111-0242
Phone: 212-649-1649

www.sloan.org

Contact: Paul L. Joskow, Pres.

Type of Grant Maker: Foundation

Description

Founded: 1934

Operating Locations/Geographic Preferences: Giving primarily focused on United States

Financial Summary

Assets: $1,703,820,396
Total Giving: $73,270,482
Number of Grants: 281
Grant Ranges: $2,138,785–$5,000

Grants Information

GRANT TYPES

Program development, evaluation, research

TYPICAL RECIPIENTS/SUBJECTS OF INTEREST

Basic Research: Focusing on research in science, technology, engineering, and mathematics

Civic Initiatives: Focusing on opportunities to benefit the New York City metro area to advance science, technology, engineering, mathematics and economics

Digital Information Technology and the Dissemination of Knowledge
Focusing on:
Data and computational research
Scholarly communication
Universal access to knowledge

Economic Performance and Quality of Life

Postsecondary STEM Education: Promoting access to the scientific enterprise at the postsecondary level and encouraging improvements to and innovations in scientific instruction and training

Public Understanding of Science: Supporting the use of books, film, radio, television, theater, and other efforts to reach a wide general audience.

Sloan Research Fellowships

PAST GRANT RECIPIENTS

Library or School Related

- University of Michigan, Ann Arbor (MI), to create and analyze datasets that combine the Health and Retirement Study (HRS) with data from the Census Bureau, $4,400,000
- Polytechnic University, Brooklyn (NY), for a pilot project for a cyber security lecture series, $125,000
- Princeton University, Princeton (NJ), for Alfred P. Sloan Research Fellowship in Computer Science, $50,000

General

- Goudreau Museum of Mathematics in Art and Science, New Hyde Park (NY), for science festival and activities, $400,000
- Wikimedia Foundation, San Francisco (CA), to help Wikipedia develop and sustain its educational mission, $3,000,000
- WGBH Educational Foundation, Boston (MA), for documentaries on the role of science and technology, $2,500,000

REQUIREMENTS AND RESTRICTIONS

No support for nonprofit institutions, or for creative or performing arts (except for those that educate the public about science), humanities, religion, or primary or secondary education, or for projects aimed at precollege students. No grants to individuals or for endowment or building funds, medical research, or equipment. No loans.

APPLICATION PROCEDURES

See website for application procedures.

Deadlines: Rolling deadlines

Smart Family Foundation, Inc.

Headquarters

74 Pin Oak Road
Wilton, CT 06897-1329
Phone: 203-834-0400

Contact: Raymond L. Smart, Pres.

Type of Grant Maker: Foundation

Description

Founded: 1951

Operating Locations/Geographic Preferences: Giving primarily in CT, IL, NJ and NY

Financial Summary

Assets: $143,942,173
Total giving: $5,721,001
Number of Grants: 100
Grant Ranges: $883,286–$5,000

Grants Information

GRANT TYPES

General and operating, seed money, investments and loans

TYPICAL RECIPIENTS/SUBJECTS OF INTEREST

Education, especially projects that affect primary and secondary school children

PAST GRANT RECIPIENTS

Library or School Related

- University of Chicago, Chicago (IL), to fund current operating expenses, $274,000

General

- David and Alfred Smart Museum of Art, Chicago (IL), to fund current operating expenses, $140,000
- Hope for Vision, New York (NY), to fund current operating expenses, $292,000
- Center for Jewish History, New York (NY), to fund current operating expenses, $40,000
- Chicago Children's Choir, Chicago (IL), to fund current operating expenses, $25,000

REQUIREMENTS AND RESTRICTIONS

No grants to individuals.

APPLICATION PROCEDURES

Unsolicited applications are discouraged; however, applicants that wish to apply should send a one-page letter describing the project and cost.

Deadlines: None

Snapdragon Book Foundation

Headquarters

2133 Bering Drive
Houston, TX 77057-3711

www.snapdragonbookfoundation.org/index.html

Contact: Stacy Birdsell, Grant Off.

E-mail: info@snapdragonbookfoundation.org

Type of Grant Maker: Foundation

Description

Founded: 2008

Operating Locations/Geographic Preferences: Giving on a national basis

Financial Summary

Assets: $488,106
Total Giving: $25,038

Grants Information

GRANT TYPES

Library collections and improvement

TYPICAL RECIPIENTS/SUBJECTS OF INTEREST

To provide funds to improve school libraries for disadvantaged children.

PAST GRANT RECIPIENTS

Library or School Related

Grants ranging from $800 to $20,000 were awarded to the schools below for their exemplary proposals and innovative programs:

- Mackay Junior-Senior High School, Mackay (ID), funding was provided to increase the fiction and nonfiction options for students in a district with many cutbacks.
- Herff Elementary, San Antonio (TX), funding was provided to update a 20-year-old collection with a focus on increasing the love of reading through programs run by the librarian and social worker.
- W.W. White Elementary School, San Antonio (TX), funding was provided to increase the variety of popular authors, genres and award-winning books to encourage students to read for pleasure more regularly.
- Kayenta Unified School District #27, Kayenta (AZ), funding was provided to launch a Language Arts Wilderness course focused on providing high-interest texts to this 99% Navajo student population. Funds will also be used to add books for a newly split school so there are enough books to serve the students.
- Southeast Middle School, Baton Rouge (LA), funding was provided to launch a school-wide differentiated book club with separate sections for advanced readers and struggling readers.
- Whittier Elementary School, West Valley City (UT), funding was provided to create a board book library for students with special needs for whom typical books present physical challenges.

- Dixon Middle School, Provo (UT), funding was provided to increase the diversity of the fiction and nonfiction collections through books that feature multiple perspectives on a topic or multicultural protagonists.

REQUIREMENTS AND RESTRICTIONS

Grants limited to school libraries.

APPLICATION PROCEDURES

Online application required. Open-ended questions on the online application are designed to encourage extended answers. See website.

Deadlines: April 15

Snow, John Ben Foundation, Inc.

Headquarters

50 Presidential Plz., Ste. 106
Syracuse, NY 13202-2279
www.johnbensnow.com/jbsf

Contact: Jonathan L. Snow, Pres.

E-mail: johnbensnow@verizon.net

Type of Grant Maker: Foundation

Description

Founded: 1948

Operating Locations/Geographic Preferences: Giving limited to central NY, with emphasis on Onondaga and Oswego counties

Financial Summary

Assets: $8,036,684
Total Giving: $279,075
Number of Grants: 31
Grant Ranges: $25,000–$800

Grants Information

GRANT TYPES

Program development, building and renovation, equipment, matching, seed money

TYPICAL RECIPIENTS/SUBJECTS OF INTEREST

Arts and culture, community, education, journalism, disabilities, and the environment

PAST GRANT RECIPIENTS

Library or School Related

- Waterloo Library and Historical Society, Waterloo (NY), accessible front door and handrails, $5,000

General

- Central New York Jazz Arts Foundation, Inc., Syracuse (NY), scholarships, $1,500
- Frederic Remington Art Museum, Ogdensburg (NY), air conditioning, $5,000
- Imagine Syracuse, Syracuse (NY), arts program, $5,000
- YMCA of Oswego, Oswego (NY), stair glides, $11,185

REQUIREMENTS AND RESTRICTIONS

No support for religious organizations or for-profit groups. No grants to individuals, endowment funds, or contingency financing.

APPLICATION PROCEDURES

All grant applications must be submitted using the Foundation grant application form. The following information must also be included with the formal grant application:

1. Executive summary (not to exceed one page)
2. Detailed project budget including itemized expenses and sources of income
3. Listing of the Board of Directors including names and board positions held
4. A copy of the organization's 501(c)(3) determination letter from the IRS
5. Most recent audited financial statement
6. Organization budget

Deadlines: April 1

Society of American Archivists

Headquarters

17 North State St.
Suite 1425
Chicago, IL 60602-4061
Phone: 312-606-0722, 866-722-7858
Fax: 312-606-0728

www.archivist.org

Type of Grant Maker: Library Organization
Organization does not offer grants, but does offer several awards.

APPLICATION PROCEDURES AND DEADLINES

The deadline for nominations is February 28 (except for the Theodore Calvin Pease Award, for which the deadline is May 31).

Send nomination/application forms and supporting documentation to:

Name of Award Subcommittee (located on the nomination/application form)
Society of American Archivists
17 North State St., Suite 1425
Chicago, IL 60602-3315

South Arts

Headquarters

1800 Peachtree St. N.W., Ste. 808
Atlanta, GA 30309-7603
Phone: 404-874-7244
Fax: 404-873-2148

www.southarts.org

Contact: Gerri Combs, Exec. Dir.

E-mail: saf@southarts.org

Type of Grant Maker: Foundation

Description

Founded: 1975

Operating Locations/Geographic Preferences: South Arts' nine-state region (AL, FL, GA, KY, LA, MS, NC, SC, TN)

Financial Summary

Assets: $1,437,195
Total Giving: $995,911

Grants Information

GRANT TYPES

Program development, consulting service, management development, matching, technical assistance

TYPICAL RECIPIENTS/SUBJECTS OF INTEREST

Federation promotes and supports arts regionally, nationally, and internationally; enhances the artistic excellence and professionalism of Southern arts organizations and artists.

Giving programs include:

- Regional Touring
- Block-Booked Tours
- Literary Arts
- Southern Fast Track Touring
- Presenter Assistance

PAST GRANT RECIPIENTS

Library or School Related

- Friends of Hoover Public Library, Hoover (AL), Library Theatre public performance, $5,625
- Georgia State University, Atlanta (GA), public performance, $7,500

General

- Georgia Tech Center for the Arts, Atlanta, Public performance, $6,375
- Germantown Performing Arts, Germantown (TN), Public Performance, $5,625

REQUIREMENTS AND RESTRICTIONS

Eligible projects must take place in South Arts' nine-state region (AL, FL, GA, KY, LA, MS, NC, SC, TN). Projects must include a public performance or reading and an educational component. A presenter cannot request funding for an artist/company/writer who resides in the presenter's state.

APPLICATION PROCEDURES

New applicants are strongly encouraged to contact:

Nikki Estes, 404-874-7244, x16, prior to submitting an application.

Review the FAQs and Glossary pages available online

Deadlines: Vary based on the grant program. The deadlines for Regional Touring and Block-Booked Tour applications are in March. The deadline for Literary Arts applications is in May. The deadline for Southern Fast Track Touring applications is 60 days prior to the project start date. The deadline for Presenter Assistance applications is two months prior to the activities.

South Carolina State Library

Headquarters

PO Box 11469
Columbia, South Carolina 29211
Phone: 803-734-8666 (Reception Desk); 803-734-8026
(Information Desk)

www.statelibrary.sc.gov

E-mail: reference@statelibrary.sc.gov

Type of Grant Maker: Government

Grants Information

CONFERENCE ATTENDANCE GRANTS

For library staff wishing to expand their professional knowledge by attending a professional conference such as SCLA, PLA, or ALA. Reimbursement of related expenses is available for conference attendance that allows librarians to develop, expand, deliver, or promote services and programs that are related to the six federal purposes.

Grant Amounts: $1,000 for out-of-state conferences, to defray rising costs of travel. $750 maximum for Conference Attendance Grants for in-state (South Carolina) conferences.

APPLICATION PROCEDURES

Applications for conference attendance may be submitted August through May for conferences occurring between October 1 and July 31. Conferences falling into the interim period (August 1 through September 30) are difficult to fund and therefore will be considered on a case-by-case basis.

LIBRARY SERVICE AND TECHNOLOGY ACT (LSTA) PLANNING GRANTS

Funds can be used for professional assistance in research or professional consultation, or can be used to free up staff who will conduct the research or allow staff to spend time devoted to the research and planning process.

The Planning Grant project must result in a document or a presentation (such as a PowerPoint demonstration or a professionally mounted poster session or other graphical illustration) that shows a clear foundation for a project to be implemented. (The resulting document could also be a report that demonstrates why the project is not feasible.) The document or a one-page summary thereof will be submitted to the State Library in lieu of an evaluation/final.

Can be used for consultant services, to perform community needs assessment, to perform project-based strategic planning, or other preparatory planning or research in support of a future library project such as a building project or a major outreach program mounted by the library. The knowledge gained from the planning process will improve the likelihood of successful outcomes for the later project.

Grant Amounts: Up to $2,500

APPLICATION PROCEDURES

Notify the Federal Grants Coordinator at the State Library of your intention to apply:

Kathy Sheppard
Phone: 803-734-8653
E-mail: ksheppard@statelibrary.sc.gov

Online application required

LSTA Tuition Assistance Grants

Grants of Library Services and Technology Act (LSTA) funds are available in for reimbursement of tuition paid by a County Library for a Library employee's coursework completed in pursuit of the Masters Degree in Library and Information Science.

REQUIREMENTS AND RESTRICTIONS

Full-time Library staff only may receive assistance under this program. "Full time" means that the employee holds a paid permanent position at the library and works the number of hours defined as a full week by the county.

The employee must be enrolled in a Masters program at an accredited, ALA-approved school of librarianship.

Only coursework in preparation for the MLIS is reimbursable under this grant (no Ph.D., B.S., or certificate programs are eligible for reimbursement.)

Participant must have successfully completed at least nine (9) hours of prior coursework in library and information studies before applying for this award.

Assistance can only be given for coursework that meets at least one of the six Federal purposes for LSTA as stated in the SCSL 2008–2012 Five-Year Plan. Courses which are general introductions to librarianship do not meet these specific goals, and are not eligible for assistance. Students are advised to take introductory courses as the first nine hours of their program of study. Most subsequent coursework will likely correspond to the LSTA purposes.

APPLICATION PROCEDURES AND DEADLINES

Refer to these guidelines and directions for completing and submitting an application for Tuition Assistance grants and requests for reimbursement.

South Dakota Library Association

Headquarters

28363 472nd Ave
Worthing, SD 57077
Phone: 605-372-0235
www.sdlibraryassociation.org/displaycommon.cfm?an=5

Contact: Jan Brue Enright, President, Augustana College, Sioux Falls, SD

Contact: jenright@augie.edu

Contact: Laura Olson, Executive Secretary/Treasurer

Contact: sdlaest@gmail.com

Type of Grant Maker: Library Organization

Grants Information

To develop and improve library services in South Dakota by helping individuals expand and continue their education and background and to improve their expertise in the area of librarianship. Association members are encouraged to apply for these funds which may be used for the following: formal coursework at a college or university; an independent study program; or attendance at workshops, institutes, seminars and conferences.

Two Professional Development Grants of up to $450 each are available to assist South Dakota Library Association members with the costs of attending conferences, workshops, or other professional learning opportunities. These grants are designed for those who are already established in the area of librarianship.

Two Scholarships of up to $500 each are available to assist SDLA members with the costs of professional education in the field of librarianship.

Two SDLA Conference Grants are available to defray costs of registration, travel and hotel expenses, plus costs of a substitute at the home library if needed. Grants of up to $400 may be awarded. Recipients must be members of SDLA.

REQUIREMENTS AND RESTRICTIONS

1. The applicant must be a resident of South Dakota or be employed in a South Dakota library.
2. The applicant must be a current member of SDLA.
3. The applicant must submit a completed application that includes a budget of expected expenses and a brief narrative statement describing personal growth and career development expected from the program.

4. Scholarship applicants must be accepted by an American Library Association accredited graduate school of library/information science, OR an undergraduate library media program that meets the ALA/AASL curriculum guidelines within a unit accredited by the National Council for the Accreditation of Teacher Education.
5. The application should be accompanied, whenever possible, by printed materials which describe the program.
6. Current Professional Development Grants Committee members are eligible for grants or scholarships; however, they may not vote on their own applications.

APPLICATION PROCEDURES

An indication of interest and a request for an application may be made to the committee chairperson or the SDLA president. Applications are also available on the SDLA website.

Completed applications may be submitted to the Professional Development Grants Committee at any time during the year.

Deadlines: May 15 for scholarships; March 15, September 15 for professional development grants

Southeast Michigan Community Foundation

Headquarters

333 W. Fort St., Ste. 2010
Detroit, MI 48226-3134
Phone: 313-961-6675
www.cfsem.org

Contact: M. C. Noland, Pres.

E-mail: cfsem@cfsem.org

Type of Grant Maker: Community Foundation

Description

Founded: 1984

Operating Locations/Geographic Preferences: Giving limited to Livingston, Macomb, Monroe, Oakland, St. Clair, Washtenaw, and Wayne counties, MI

Financial Summary

Assets: $600,483,119
Total Giving: $55,208,050

Grants Information

GRANT TYPES

Program development, seed money

TYPICAL RECIPIENTS/SUBJECTS OF INTEREST

Education, civic affairs, social services, arts and culture, health, environment and land use, neighborhood and regional economic development and workforce development.
Giving programs include:

- Access to Recreation
- Childhood Obesity
- Detroit Neighborhood Fund
- GreenWays Initiative
- Mariam C. Nolan Award for Nonprofit Leadership
- New Economy Initiative
- Scholarships
- Senior Engagement Program

PAST GRANT RECIPIENTS

Library or School Related

- College for Creative Studies, Detroit (MI), for development of Argonaut Building as education, research and creative enterprise incubation center, $3,000,000
- Detroit Waldorf School, Detroit (MI), for planning efforts for community outreach and curriculum enhancement initiatives, $62,700
- Oakland University, Rochester (MI), for Riverview Center for Excellence in Clinical Education, $500,000

General

- Urban Entrepreneur Partnership Detroit, Detroit (MI), for economic development program, $3,000,000
- New Detroit, Detroit (MI), for general operations, $150,000

REQUIREMENTS AND RESTRICTIONS

No support for sectarian religious programs. No grants to individuals or for capital projects, endowments, annual campaigns, general operating support, conferences, computers and computer systems, fund-raising, annual meetings, buildings, or equipment.

APPLICATION PROCEDURES

See website for general application guidelines and separate guidelines for targeted grant-making projects. Applicants should submit:

1. Timetable for implementation and evaluation of project
2. How project will be sustained once grant-maker support is completed

3. Signature and title of chief executive officer
4. Results expected from proposed grant
5. Qualifications of key personnel
6. Population served
7. Name, address and phone number of organization
8. Copy of IRS Determination Letter
9. Brief history of organization and description of its mission
10. Geographic area to be served
11. Copy of most recent annual report/audited financial statement/990
12. How project's results will be evaluated or measured
13. Listing of board of directors, trustees, officers and other key people and their affiliations
14. Detailed description of project and amount of funding requested
15. Plans for cooperation with other organizations, if any
16. Contact person
17. Copy of current year's organizational budget and/or project budget.

Deadlines: February 15, May 15, August 15, and November 15

Sprague, Seth Educational and Charitable Foundation

Headquarters

c/o Bank of America, N.A.
1 Bryant Park NY1-100-28-05
New York, NY 10036-6715
Phone: 646-855-1011

Contact: Christine O'Donnell, Bank of America

Type of Grant Maker: Foundation

Description

Founded: 1939

Operating Locations/Geographic Preferences: Giving primarily in NY, Boston and Cape Cod, MA, ME and San Diego, CA

Financial Summary

Assets: $64,922,983
Total Giving: $2,502,000
Number of Grants: 235
Grant Ranges: $60,000–$1,000

Grants Information

GRANT TYPES

General and operating support, matching, program development

TYPICAL RECIPIENTS/SUBJECTS OF INTEREST

Public school education, arts, housing and basic needs, health and human services

PAST GRANT RECIPIENTS

- William A. Farnsworth Library, $20,000
- Library Association of La Jolla, $2,000

General

- Ocean Classroom Foundation, Boothbay Harbor (ME), $40,000
- Coalition for the Homeless, New York (NY), $25,000
- City Harvest, New York (NY), $20,000
- Manomet Center for Conservation Sciences, Plymouth (MA), $15,000

REQUIREMENTS AND RESTRICTIONS

No grants to individuals or for building funds loans.

APPLICATION PROCEDURES

Applicants are urged to contact the foundation office for the most updated guidelines.

Deadlines: April 1 and September 1

Starr Foundation

Headquarters

399 Park Ave., 17th Fl.
New York, NY 10022-4614
Phone: 212-909-3600
Fax: 212-750-3536

www.starrfoundation.org

Type of Grant Maker: Foundation

The Foundation no longer accepts unsolicited proposals. Please DO NOT send unsolicited materials to the Foundation.

Steelcase Foundation

Headquarters

PO Box 1967, GH-4E
Grand Rapids, MI 49501-1967

www.steelcase.com/en/company/who/steelcase_foundation

Contact: Susan Broman, Pres.

E-mail: sbroman@steelcase.com

Type of Grant Maker: Corporate Foundation

Description

Founded: 1951

Operating Locations/Geographic Preferences: Giving limited to areas of company operations, with emphasis on Athens, AL, City of Industry, CA, Grand Rapids, MI, and Markham, Canada

Corporate Foundation Information: Supported by Steelcase Inc.

Financial Summary

Assets: $84,824,026
Total Giving: $3,897,074
Number of Grants: 59
Grant Ranges: $250,000–$900

Grants Information

GRANT TYPES

Program development, building and renovation, management development, matching, seed money, general and operating support, land acquisition, capital campaigns

TYPICAL RECIPIENTS/SUBJECT OF INTEREST

Education, arts and culture, environment, health, human services, and community development. Special emphasis on youth, the elderly, disabled people, and economically disadvantaged.

PAST GRANT RECIPIENTS

Library or School Related

- Grand Valley State University, Grand Rapids (MI), for Mary Idema Pew Library Learning and Information Commons, $100,000

- Kent Intermediate School District, Grand Rapids (MI), for Kent School Services Network, $75,000
- Michigan State University, East Lansing (MI), for MSU West Michigan Medical School, $200,000

General

- Urban Institute for Contemporary Arts, Grand Rapids (MI), for "Where Art Happens" capital campaign, $200,000
- Grand Rapids Art Museum, Grand Rapids (MI), for Centennial Year—Art—Legacy—Vision, $150,000
- Grand Action Foundation, Grand Rapids (MI), for Grand Rapids Urban Market, $75,000

REQUIREMENTS AND RESTRICTIONS

No support for churches or religious organizations not of direct benefit to the entire community or discriminatory organizations. No grants to individuals or for endowments or conferences or seminars.

APPLICATION PROCEDURES

Initially, send letter of inquiry. Full proposal may be requested at a later date.

Deadlines: Quarterly

Steele-Reese Foundation

Headquarters

32 Washington Sq. W.
New York, NY 10011-9156
Phone: 212-505-2696

www.steele-reese.org

Contact: William T. Buice

Type of Grant Maker: Foundation

Description

Founded: 1955

Operating Locations/Geographic Preferences: Giving primarily in ID, MT, and the Appalachian Mountain region of KY, NC, and TN

Financial Summary

Assets: $31,246,133
Total Giving: $2,099,500

Number of Grants: 75
Grant Ranges: $75,000–$6,000

Grants Information

GRANT TYPES

Endowments, equipment, general and operating support, matching, management development, land acquisition

TYPICAL RECIPIENTS/SUBJECTS OF INTEREST

Education (primarily elementary and secondary), health and hospices, welfare (including programs for drug abuse and youth), conservation, and the humanities, with a strong preference for rural projects

PAST GRANT RECIPIENTS

Library or School Related

- Great Falls Public Library, Great Falls (MT), $35,000
- Friends of the Joliet Public Library, Joliet (MT), $6,000
- Idaho State University, Pocatello (ID), $50,000

General

- Florence Prever Rosten Foundation for the Media Arts, Darby (MT), $30,000
- Montana Wilderness Association, Helena (MT), $30,000

APPLICATION PROCEDURES

The Foundation requires that all applicants submit their proposal materials electronically via the Foundation's secure web application portal. Please see the online information for instructions on how to apply, and please do not hesitate to contact the Foundation with any questions about navigating the application process.

Applicants are encouraged to reach out to the Foundation's two regional directors with any questions about your organization's request for support or about the online application process. The directors may be reached as follows:

In the case of Kentucky organizations, please contact:

Judy Owens
Appalachian Director
The Steele-Reese Foundation
2613 Clubside Court
Lexington, KY 40513
Phone and Fax: 859-313-5225

E-mail: jkowensjd@aol.com

In the case of Idaho and Montana organizations, please contact:

Linda Tracy
Western Director

The Steele-Reese Foundation
PO Box 8311
Missoula, MT 59807-8311
Phone: 406-207-7984
Fax: 207-470-3872
E-mail: linda@steele-reese.org

Deadline: March 1

Stuart Foundation

Headquarters

500 Washington St., 8th Fl.
San Francisco, CA 94111-4735
Phone: 415-393-1551

www.stuartfoundation.org

Contact: Anne Campbell Washington, Dir., Opers. and Special Projects

E-mail: awashington@stuartfoundation.org

Type of Grant Maker: Foundation

Description

Founded: 1937

Operating Locations/Geographic Preferences: Giving primarily in CA and WA

Financial Summary

Assets: $354,011,604
Total Giving: $16,024,548
Number of Grants: 226
Grant Ranges: $475,000–$100

Grants Information

GRANT TYPES

Program development, continuing, general and operating support, seed money

TYPICAL RECIPIENTS/SUBJECTS OF INTEREST

Child Welfare

Education
  Targeted on:
    Informing public policy through nonpartisan, independent research and analysis

Supporting and disseminating identified successful, exemplary practice from districts and systems of schools

Supporting dynamic education leadership from the role of the principal as instructional leader through the importance of central offices, the superintendent, and district-wide governance

Teaching and learning by improving teaching performance assessment and evaluation systems, and addressing the critical issue of ensuring the most qualified teachers serve the students with the greatest need

Employee Matching Gifts

PAST GRANT RECIPIENTS

Library or School Related

- Center for the Future of Teaching and Learning, Santa Cruz (CA), to provide educators, school administrators and policymakers with information about educational experiences and outcomes of California's K–12 students in foster care, $300,000
- Emery Ed Fund, Emeryville (CA), to improve student engagement and achievement in Emery Unified School District, $530,000
- Highline Public Schools, Burien (WA), to implement community school partnerships, $500,000
- Aspire Public Schools, Oakland (CA), for general support to operate schools in Los Angeles and the Central Valley, $430,000
- University of California, Berkeley (CA), for core support for California Child Welfare Performance Indicators Project, $800,000
- Green Dot Education Project, Los Angeles (CA), for general support to implement school transformation, $430,000

REQUIREMENTS AND RESTRICTIONS

Submit letter of inquiry. Following review, selected applicants will be invited to submit full proposal.

Deadlines: None

Surdna Foundation, Inc.

Headquarters

330 Madison Ave., 30th Fl.
New York, NY 10017-5001
Phone: 212-557-0010

www.surdna.org

Contact: Phillip Henderson, Pres.
E-mail: questions@surdna.org
Type of Grant Maker: Foundation

Description

Founded: 1917

Operating Locations/Geographic Preferences: Giving primarily in CA, Washington, DC, and NY

Financial Summary

Assets: $754,986,525
Total Giving: $34,033,993

Grants Information

GRANT TYPES

Program development, general, continuing and operating support

TYPICAL RECIPIENTS/SUBJECTS OF INTEREST

1. Sustainable Environments
2. Strong Local Economies
3. Thriving Cultures

Giving programs include:

Organizational Capacity Building: Grants of up to $15,000 to address important management and governance issues for nonprofit organizations

Strong Local Economies, focusing on:
Connecting People to Opportunities
Creating Economic Opportunities
Surdna Arts Teachers Fellowships

Sustainable Environments, focusing on:
Climate Change
Green Economy
Transportation and Smart Growth

Thriving Cultures
Focusing on:

Weaving a Community's Fabric: including institutions that play an anchoring role with respect to cultural life and identity within communities such as arts schools, cultural awareness centers and community gardens; development of cultural drivers—individuals and groups engaging in culture-based actions aimed at protecting and promoting just and sustainable communities, and cultural education

Building Capacity for Weaving

PAST GRANT RECIPIENTS

Library or School Related

- University of Southern Maine, Portland (ME), to establish sustainable Healing Circles, $112,000

General

- Living Cities: The National Community Development Initiative, New York (NY), for Living Cities' efforts, $1,000,000
- Blue Green Alliance Foundation, Minneapolis (MN), for general operations of the Blue Green Alliance and partner organizations, $600,000
- NOCCA Institute, New Orleans (LA), to strengthen artistic learning for student and faculty/artist mentors, $300,000
- Make the Road New York, Brooklyn (NY), to connect youth and immigrant adults with expanded economic opportunity, $100,000

REQUIREMENTS AND RESTRICTIONS

No support for international projects, or programs addressing toxics, hazardous waste, environmental education, sustainable agriculture, food production and distribution.

No grants for individuals or for endowments or land acquisition, capital campaigns or for building construction.

APPLICATION PROCEDURES

See website for online application information. Applicant should submit:

1. Results expected from proposed grant
2. Qualifications of key personnel
3. Copy of IRS Determination Letter
4. Brief history of organization and description of its mission
5. Copy of most recent annual report/audited financial statement/990
6. Listing of board of directors, trustees, officers and other key people and their affiliations
7. Detailed description of project and amount of funding requested
8. Contact person
9. Copy of current year's organizational budget and/or project budget
10. Listing of additional sources and amount of support

Deadlines: None

Taper, S. Mark Foundation

Headquarters

12011 San Vicente Blvd., Ste. 400
Los Angeles, CA 90049-4946
Phone: 310-476-5413
Fax: 310-471-4993
www.smtfoundation.org
Contact: Raymond F. Reisler, Exec. Dir.
E-mail: questions@smtfoundation.org
Type of Grant Maker: Foundation

Description

Founded: 1989
Operating Locations/Geographic Preferences: Giving primarily in Los Angeles County, CA

Financial Summary

Assets: $108,056,312
Total giving: $4,049,150
Number of Grants: 77
Grant Ranges: High: $400,000

Grants Information

GRANT TYPES

Program development, annual and capital campaigns, building and renovation, conferences, general and operating support, equipment, matching, seed money, investments and loans

TYPICAL RECIPIENTS/SUBJECTS OF INTEREST

Children and youth, health care, social services, employment, education, and the environment

PAST GRANT RECIPIENTS

Library or School Related

- School Calabasas High School Parent/Faculty Club, Calabasas (CA), $40,000

General

- California Institute of the Arts, Valencia (CA), $200,000
- California Wildlife Center, Malibu (CA), $5,000
- Center for Nonprofit Management, Los Angeles (CA), $80,000

- Center for Nonviolent Education and Parenting, Los Angeles (CA), $40,000
- Center for the Arts, Eagle Rock, Los Angeles (CA), $25,000

REQUIREMENTS AND RESTRICTIONS

No support for religious organizations, specific diseases or grants to individuals.

APPLICATION PROCEDURES

The first step in applying for a grant from the S. Mark Taper Foundation is to send a Letter of Inquiry. Please see Grant Guidelines for guidance in preparing a Letter of Inquiry. Once all of the Letters of Inquiry have been received and reviewed by the Foundation, some organizations will proceed to the next step.

Deadlines: Letters of Inquiry (LOIs) are accepted from December 1 through February 29

Target Corp.

Headquarters

1000 Nicollet Mall, TPN1144
Minneapolis, MN 55403-2467
Phone: 800-388-6740
Fax: 612-696-4706

http://sites.target.com/site/en/company/page.jsp
  ?contentId = WCMP04-031767

Contact: Jeanne Kavanaugh, Sr. Specialist

E-mail: community.relations@target.com

Type of Grant Maker: Corporation

Description

Founded: 1902

Operating Locations/Geographic Preference: Nationwide giving

Financial Summary

(of Target Foundation)
Assets: $28,325,004
Total giving: $9,750,000
Number of Grants: 175
Grant Ranges: $1,225,000–$3,000

Grants Information

GRANT TYPES

Continuing, general and operating support, program development

TYPICAL RECIPIENTS/SUBJECTS OF INTEREST

Education, environment, well-being and safety and preparedness
  Grant Giving programs include:

Field Trip Grants: Providing the opportunity to enhance their studies in the arts, math, science and social studies. As part of the program, each Target store will award three Target Field Trip Grants to K–12 schools nationwide—enabling one in 25 schools throughout the U.S. to send a classroom on a field trip. Each grant is valued up to $700. Application cycle opens August 1.

Early Childhood Reading Grants: Target awards grants to schools, libraries and nonprofit organizations to support programs such as after-school reading events and weekend book clubs.

Early Childhood Reading Grants are $2,000: Grant applications are typically accepted between March 1 and April 30 each year, with grant notifications delivered at the end of August.

Arts Grants: Through these grants, Target helps schools bring more arts and culture into the classroom, enabling them to expand their creativity . . . and their horizons.

Art, Culture + Design in Schools Grants are $2,000: Grant applications are typically accepted between March 1 and April 30 each year, with grant notifications delivered in September.

  In addition, the Target Foundation offers grants to organizations based in the Minneapolis-St. Paul area in the areas of arts and social services.

Other programs include/have included:

Focus on Reading: Target School Library Makeovers, which has transformed school libraries, including 42 library make-overs in 2011. These libraries underwent a tremendous transformation—featuring 2,000 new books; larger spaces with new carpet, furniture and technology; and seven new books for each student to take home and call their own.

REQUIREMENTS AND RESTRICTIONS

Organizations must be a federally tax-exempt, section 501(c)(3) charitable organization, a school, a library, or a public agency.

  Please review the funding guidelines available on Target.com/grants for a complete list of eligibility criteria.

Target does not make grants to:

- Individuals
- Programs located outside Target communities
- Educational institutions for regular instructional programs
- Religious organizations for religious purposes
- Treatment programs such as substance or alcohol abuse
- Athletic teams or events
- Fund-raiser or gala events
- Advocacy or research groups
- Capital or building construction projects
- Endowment campaigns

APPLICATION PROCEDURES AND DEADLINES

Target store grant applications are accepted at two different times per year:

Arts and Culture in Schools and Early Childhood Reading: March 1 through April 30

Field Trips: August 1 through September 30

Target Foundation grant applications are accepted at two different times per year:

Arts: January 1 through February 1

Social Services: April 1 through May 1

When the application process opens, you will be able to print a copy as you are filling out the online application form. Click on the Printer Friendly Version link located in the top right-hand corner of each application page.

Tauck Foundation

Headquarters

PO Box 5020
Norwalk, CT 06856
Phone: 203-899-6742
Fax: 203-286-1340
www.tauckfoundation.org
Contact: Eden Werring, Executive Director
E-mail: eden@tauckfoundation.org
Type of Grant Maker: Foundation

Foundation is currently developing a new mission and strategy, which will be announced in the fall of 2012.

At this time, Foundation is not accepting any unsolicited letters of inquiry or new proposals, and will not be making grants to any organizations that are not currently funded by the Tauck Foundation.

TE Foundation (*Formerly ADC Foundation*)

Headquarters

c/o TE Corporation
PO Box 3608 MS 140-10
Harrisburg, PA 17105-3608
Phone: 717-592-4869
www.te.com/en/about-te/responsibility/community.html
Contact: Mary Rakoczy
E-mail: TEfoundation@te.com
Type of Grant Maker: Corporate Foundation

Description

Operating Locations/Geographic Preferences: Worldwide. Giving limited to organizations in geographic areas where TE has employees.

Corporate Foundation Information: Supported by TE Connectivity, formerly ADC Telecommunications of Eden Prairie, MN

Financial Summary

Total Giving: $4,000,000
Number of Grants: 1,400

Grants Information

GRANT TYPES
Program development

TYPICAL RECIPIENTS/SUBJECTS OF INTEREST
Energy and the environment, community development, education, with emphasis on math, science, and engineering

PAST GRANT RECIPIENTS
Library or School Related

- Junior Engineering Technical Society, for high school students to discover applications of science, technology, engineering, and mathematics (STEM)
- MATHCOUNTS Foundation, program to combine volunteers, educators, industry partners, government, and the technology community to promote mathematics excellence among middle school students

General

- JobTrain, for launching new careers to combat homelessness, drugs, crime, and incarceration.

REQUIREMENTS AND RESTRICTIONS

No support for:

- Organizations in geographic areas where TE has few or no employees.
- Individuals, private foundations, national organizations, service clubs, fraternal, social and labor or trade organizations.
- Organizations that discriminate on the basis of race, religion, color, national origin, physical or mental conditions, veteran or marital status, age or sex.
- Churches or religious organizations, with the exception of nondenominational programs sponsored by a church or religious group such as a food bank, youth center or nonsectarian education programs.
- Political campaigns.
- Loans or investments, or programs that pose a potential conflict of interest.

APPLICATION PROCEDURES

Submit the following:

- Organization Name
- Address
- Phone
- E-mail Address
- Organization Contact Name
- Description of the organization and its purposes
- List of governing board members
- Current operating budget and sources of income for the organization
- Audited financial statement and most recent IRS Form 990
- Copy of IRS determination evidencing Section 501(c)(3) status

Deadlines: See website

Temple, T. L. L. Foundation

Headquarters

204 Champions Dr.
Lufkin, TX 75901-7321
Phone: 936-634-3900

Contact: M.F. "Buddy" Zeagler, Cont. and Deputy Exec. Dir.

Type of Grant Maker: Foundation

Description

Founded: 1962

Operating Locations/Geographic Preferences: Giving primarily in counties in TX constituting the East Texas Pine Timber Belt

Financial Summary

Assets: $304,749,686
Total Giving: $16,468,240
Number of Grants: 195
Grant Ranges: $6,602,200 and under

Grants Information

GRANT TYPES

Program development, building and renovation, general and operating support, matching, capital campaigns, investments and loans

TYPICAL RECIPIENTS/SUBJECTS OF INTEREST

Education, health, community and social services, civic affairs, cultural programs

PAST GRANT RECIPIENTS

Library or School Related

- T. L. L. Temple Memorial Library and Archives, Diboll (TX), for Customary Matching Grant for General Support, $584,000
- West Sabine Independent School District, Pineland (TX), for New Secondary School, $2,000,000
- Angelina College, Lufkin (TX), for Matching Grant and Customary Grant for Undergraduate Scholarships, $67,000

General

- Pineland, City of, Pineland (TX), for Customary Grant for General Support, $169,000
- Alcohol and Drug Abuse Council of Deep East Texas, Lufkin (TX), for utilities and PARTY Program, $122,000

REQUIREMENTS AND RESTRICTIONS

No support for private foundations. No grants to individuals, or for deficit financing.

APPLICATION PROCEDURES

Application form required. Applicants should submit:

1. Results expected from proposed grant
2. Population served
3. Name, address and phone number of organization
4. Copy of IRS Determination Letter

5. Brief history of organization and description of its mission
6. Geographic area to be served
7. Copy of most recent annual report/audited financial statement/990
8. Listing of board of directors, trustees, officers and other key people and their affiliations
9. Detailed description of project and amount of funding requested
10. Copy of current year's organizational budget and/or project budget

Deadlines: None

Temple-Inland Foundation

Headquarters

1300 S. Mopac Expwy., FL 3N
Austin, TX 78746-6907
Phone: 512-434-3160
Fax: 512-434-2566

www.templeinland.com/ourmission/corporatecitizenship

Contact: Karen Newton Lee, Secy.-Treas.

E-mail: karenlee@templeinland.com

Type of Grant Maker: Corporate Foundation

Description

Founded: 1985

Operating Locations/Geographic Preferences: Giving primarily in areas of company operations, with emphasis on Texas

Corporate Foundation Information: Supported by:

- Temple-Inland Inc.
- Temple-Inland Forest Products Corp.

Financial Summary

Assets: $27,730
Total Giving: $1,889,858
Number of Grants: 875
Grant Ranges: $51,000–$25

Grants Information

GRANT TYPES

General and operating support, matching

TYPICAL RECIPIENTS/SUBJECTS OF INTEREST

Arts and culture, education, health, youth development, and human services

PAST GRANT RECIPIENTS

- T. L. L. Temple Memorial Library, Dibell (TX), $40,000
- Buena Park Library, Buena Park (CA), $1,000
- Carmel Clay Public Library Fdn, Carmel Clay (IN), $100
- Humphreys County Public Library, Waverly (TN), $500
- Lakeview Elementary School and Library, New Johnsonville (TN), $850 and $75

General

- United Way of Metropolitan Dallas, Dallas (TX), $200,000
- Ronald McDonald House Charities of Austin (TX), $200,000

APPLICATION PROCEDURES

Call to request application information.

Deadlines: None

Tennessee State Library and Archives

Headquarters

403 7th Avenue North
Nashville, TN 37243
Phone: 615-741-2764

www.tennessee.gov/tsla/index.htm

E-mail: reference.tsla@tn.gov

Type of Grant Maker: Government

Grants Information

COMPETITIVE TECHNOLOGY GRANTS

Available to eligible public libraries that can provide an equal amount of local funding for purchase of computer hardware, software, fax machines, and other library technology.

APPLICATION PROCEDURES

See website for application forms. Applications must be submitted to the Tennessee State Library and Archives

Deadlines: November 18

COMPETITIVE DIRECT SERVICE GRANTS FOR LIBRARY SERVICES TO THE DISADVANTAGED

Available biennially to eligible public libraries.

APPLICATION PROCEDURES

See website for application forms. Applications must be submitted to the Tennessee State Library and Archives. Applicants must attend one of the Grant-Writing Workshops.

Deadlines: February 2

Terra Foundation for American Art

Headquarters

980 N. Michigan Ave., Ste. 1315
Chicago, IL 60611-4501
Phone: 312-664-3939

www.terraamericanart.org

Contact: Amy Zinck, V.P.

E-mail: grants@terraamericanart.org

Type of Grant Maker: Foundation

Description

Founded: 1981

Operating Locations/Geographic Preferences: Giving in the United States, with emphasis on Chicago, Illinois, and internationally

Financial Summary

Assets: $444,761,954
Total Giving: $4,973,248
Number of Grants: 44
Grant Ranges: $350,000–$1,758

Grants Information

GRANT TYPES

Program development

TYPICAL RECIPIENTS/SUBJECTS OF INTEREST

American art, especially innovative exhibitions, research, and educational programs
    Focus includes:

- Exhibitions
- Chicago Art Exhibitions
- Academic and Public Programs
- Chicago K–12 Education
- Publications

PAST GRANT RECIPIENTS

Library or School Related

- Pierpont Morgan Library, New York (NY), for catalogue and exhibition, Roy Lichtenstein: The Black-and-White Drawings, 1961–1968, $225,000
- Stanford University, Stanford (CA), for catalog and exhibition Rodin and America: Influence and Adaptation 1876–1930, $300,000

General

- Art Institute of Chicago, Chicago (IL), for exhibition, John Marin's Watercolors: A Medium for Modernism, $50,000
- Terra Foundation for American Art, Chicago (IL), for pilot Research and Development grants for International Curatorial Travel, $252,000

REQUIREMENTS AND RESTRICTIONS

No support for artwork conservation. No grants to individuals.

APPLICATION PROCEDURES

See website for application guidelines. Letter of inquiry required as initial step.

Deadlines: None

Texas State Library and Archives Commission

Headquarters

Lorenzo de Zavala State Archives and Library Building
Physical address:
1201 Brazos St.
Austin, TX 78701

Mailing address:
PO Box 12927
Austin, TX 78711-2927

Phone: 512-463-5455

www.tsl.state.tx.us/landing/libfunds.html

E-mail: info@tsl.state.tx.us

Type of Grant Maker: Government

Grants Information

IMPACT GRANTS

Focused on broad community needs for economic recovery, early childhood literacy, and electronic access to information, Impact Grants are designed to distribute funding as broadly as possible to impact lives all across Texas.

The purpose of this grant is to encourage libraries to create or expand their programming and services in innovative ways that directly impact the lives of Texans. The grant provides seed funding for new library programming or services, or to improve existing programming and services that support best practices in the field.

The programming must be new to the library's community, or improve existing services, and must be sustainable after the first year of grant funding with other or local resources. Libraries or library systems will not be awarded more than one grant in a single grant cycle; nor will they be awarded a grant for the same type of program in two consecutive grant cycles.

Applications will be accepted in three focus areas:

1. Skills for Economic Recovery
2. Family and Early Childhood Literacy
3. Electronic Information Technology

SPECIAL PROJECTS AND LIBRARY COOPERATION GRANTS

This grant program provides funds for programs that expand library services to all members of the library's community. It enables libraries to develop programs for populations with special needs. Programs involving collaboration are encouraged. Programs must emphasize improved services by the library to its customers.

Programs may be in one of the following categories:

1. Target library services to individuals of diverse geographic, cultural, or socioeconomic backgrounds, to individuals with disabilities, and to individuals with limited functional literacy or information skills.
2. Target library and information services to persons having difficulty using a library and to underserved urban and rural communities, including children from families below the poverty line.

GRANT AMOUNT

Applications of all sizes are encouraged. While the request may be part of a larger program, awards will not exceed $75,000.

REQUIREMENTS AND RESTRICTIONS

Through their governing authority, major resource library systems, regional library systems, and libraries that are members of the TexShare Library Consortium or Texas Library System are eligible to apply for funds. These funds are awarded to major resource or regional library systems, or TexShare member libraries or Texas Library System members but may be used with all types of libraries as specified in the grant guidelines and application. Applicants must be members of the TexShare Library Consortium or the Texas Library System at the time of application and for the period of grant funding. Nonprofit organizations may be awarded funds for projects that involve a number of TexShare or Texas Library System member libraries, as well as other types of libraries or organizations. Public school libraries that are not members of the Texas Library System may participate as partners in grants lead by eligible entities.

Successful applicants are eligible to apply for grant funds for the two years following the initial grant year. The second and third application will be evaluated with the same criteria as new applications. No applicant will be eligible for a fourth year of funding for the same project.

COOPERATION GRANTS

Provide funds for programs that promote cooperative services for learning and access to information. Projects involving collaboration are encouraged. Programs must emphasize improved services by the library to its customers. Programs must involve a substantive level of cooperation with at least one other library that is a member of the TexShare Library Consortium or the Texas Library System.

Programs may be in the following categories:

1. Expand services for learning and access to information and educational resources in a variety of formats
2. Develop library services that provide all users access to information through local, state, regional, national and international electronic networks
3. Provide electronic and other linkages between and among all types of libraries
4. Develop public and private partnerships with other agencies and community-based organizations

The purpose is not for collection development, or other activities primarily focused on the acquisition of library materials or resources.

GRANT AMOUNT

Applications of all sizes are encouraged. While the request may be part of a larger program, awards will not exceed $75,000.

REQUIREMENTS AND RESTRICTIONS

Through their governing authority, major resource library systems, regional library systems, and libraries that are members of the TexShare Library Consortium or Texas Library System are eligible to apply for funds. These funds are awarded to major resource or regional library systems, or TexShare member libraries or Texas Library System members but may be used with all types of libraries as specified in the grant guidelines and application. Applicants must be members of the TexShare Library Consortium or the Texas Library System at the time of application and for the period of grant funding. Nonprofit organizations may be awarded funds for projects that involve a number of TexShare or Texas Library System member libraries, as well as other types of libraries or organizations. Public school libraries that are not members of the Texas Library System may participate as partners in grants lead by eligible entities.

Successful applicants are eligible to apply for grant funds for the two years following the initial grant year. The second and third application will be evaluated with the same criteria as new applications.

TEXAS READS GRANTS

Funds public library programs to promote reading and literacy within local communities.

Programs may be targeted to the entire community or to a segment of the community. Programs involving collaboration with other community organizations are encouraged. The agency may designate specific funding priorities for each grant cycle in response to identified needs.

Reading promotion programs are those that actively encourage people to read and to develop a lifelong love of reading. One goal of reading promotion programs is to develop a more literate community. Typically, this involves presenting or hosting programs that will involve people in reading activities and that will generate enthusiasm for reading.

Libraries may also coordinate programs in basic literacy, family literacy, and the ability to read, write and speak English and to compute and solve problems at levels of proficiency necessary to function on the job and in society.

GRANT AMOUNT

$3,000 maximum

REQUIREMENTS AND RESTRICTIONS

Public libraries and local public library systems, through their governing authority (city, county, corporation, or district) are eligible to apply for grants. To receive a grant, applicants must be accredited for the fiscal year the grant contracts are issued. Libraries or library systems will not be awarded more than one grant in a single grant cycle. Libraries or library systems will not be awarded a grant in two consecutive grant cycles.

TEXTREASURES

Designed to help libraries make their special collections more accessible for the people of Texas and beyond. Activities considered for possible funding include digitization, microfilming, and cataloging.

The TexTreasures grant program provides assistance and encouragement to libraries to provide access to their special or unique holdings and to make information about these holdings available to library users across the state. Applicants may propose projects designed to increase accessibility through a wide range of activities such as organizing, cataloging, indexing, or digitizing local materials.

GRANT AMOUNT

$20,000 for a single institution and $25,000 for collaborative grant projects.

REQUIREMENTS AND RESTRICTIONS

Libraries that are members of the TexShare Library Consortium, or nonprofit organizations that are applying on behalf of TexShare members, are eligible to apply for funds through their governing authority. These funds are awarded to eligible applicants, but may be used with all types of libraries or with nonprofit organizations that participate as partners in the grant project.

APPLICATION PROCEDURES

TSLAC recommends that potential applicants view and/or attend the appropriate webinars.

For help in determining the appropriate grant program for your library project, contact Erica A. McCormick, TSLAC Grants Administrator, via e-mail at emccormick@tsl.state.tx.us or phone at 512-463-5527.

Deadlines: February 27

Texas, Communities Foundation of, Inc.

Headquarters

5500 Caruth Haven Ln.
Dallas, TX 75225-8146
Phone: 214-750-4222
www.cftexas.org
E-mail: info@cftexas.org
Type of Grant Maker: Community Foundation

Description

Founded: 1953
Operating Locations/Geographic Preferences: Giving primarily in the Dallas, TX, area

Financial Summary

Assets: $769,107,000
Total Giving: $55,784,000

Grants Information

GRANT TYPES

Program development, building and renovation, land acquisition, matching, capital campaigns, seed money

TYPICAL RECIPIENTS/SUBJECTS OF INTEREST

Applications accepted for all grant categories: education, animals, arts, elderly, environment, health, social services, youth and miscellaneous.
   Also administers scholarship programs.

PAST GRANT RECIPIENTS

Library or School Related

- University of Texas at Dallas, Richardson (TX), for program support, $2,000,000

General

- Dallas Center for the Performing Arts Foundation, Dallas (TX), for general support, $1,255,555
- Salvation Army of Dallas, Dallas (TX), for Dallas Forth Worth Metroplex Command's long-range plan implementation, $300,000

- Educational Foundation for the Fashion Industries, New York (NY), $7,500
- Dallas Opera, Dallas (TX), $5,000

REQUIREMENTS AND RESTRICTIONS

No support for religious purposes from general fund or organizations which redistribute funds to other organizations. No grants to individuals or for continuing support, media projects or publications, deficit financing, endowment funds, fellowships, salaries, annual campaigns, or operational expenses of well-established organizations.

APPLICATION PROCEDURES

See website for application information. Application form not required
Deadline: May 27 for letter of inquiry

Timken Foundation of Canton

Headquarters

200 Market Ave. N., Ste. 210
Canton, OH 44702-1437
Phone: 330-452-1144
Contact: Nancy Knudsen, Secy.-Treas.
Type of Grant Maker: Foundation
Unsolicited requests for funds not accepted.

Tisch Foundation, Inc.

Headquarters

655 Madison Ave., 19th Fl.
New York, NY 10065-8043
Phone: 212-521-2930
Contact: Mark J. Krinsky, V.P.
Type of Grant Maker: Foundation
Contributes only to preselected organizations.

Titus, C. W. Foundation

Headquarters

427 S. Boston Ave., Ste. 950
Tulsa, OK 74103-4114
Phone: 918-582-8095

Contact: Timothy Reynolds, Tr.

Type of Grant Maker: Foundation

Description

Founded: 1968

Operating Locations/Geographic Preferences: Giving primarily in MO and OK

Financial Summary

Assets: $31,050,570
Total Giving: $1,591,800
Number of Grants: 54
Grant Ranges: $250,000—$1,000

Grants Information

GRANT TYPES

General and operating support, building and renovation

TYPICAL RECIPIENTS/SUBJECTS OF INTEREST

Health, children and social services, arts and cultural programs

PAST GRANT RECIPIENTS

Library or School Related

- Drury University, Springfield (MO), scholarships, $20,000
- Crosstown Learning Center, Tulsa (OK), Classroom Supplies $10,000

General

- Gilcrease Museum, Tulsa (OK), Charles Russell Exhibit, $50,000
- Girl Scouts of Eastern Oklahoma, Tulsa (OK), $10,000
- Philbrook Museum of Art, Tulsa (OK), $40,000
- Humane Society of Joplin, Joplin (MO), $100,000

REQUIREMENTS AND RESTRICTIONS

No grants to individuals.

APPLICATION PROCEDURES

Send letter and copy of IRS determination letter.

Deadlines: None

Tourism Cares, Inc.

Headquarters

275 Turnpike St., Ste. 307
Canton, MA 02021-3013
Phone: 781-821-5990, ext. 208
www.tourismcares.org

Contact: Carolyn Viles, Dir., Grants and Scholarship Progs.

E-mail: carolynv@tourismcares.org

Type of Grant Maker: Foundation

Description

Founded: 2005

Operating Locations/Geographic Preferences: Worldwide

Financial Summary

Assets: $2,800,000
Total Giving: $1,270,520

Grants Information

GRANT TYPES

Program development, building and renovation

TYPICAL RECIPIENTS/SUBJECTS OF INTEREST

Organizations for conservation, preservation, restoration, or education at tourism-related sites of exceptional cultural, historic, or natural significance around the world
    Giving programs include:

- Worldwide Grants
- Special Grants (with corporate partners)
- Save Our Sites

PAST GRANT RECIPIENTS

Library or School Related

- Library of Alexandria Antiquities Museum, Egypt, in 2011. To add exhibit showcases and security cameras, $10,000

- City University of New York—Kingsborough Community College's Tourism Research Center, Brooklyn (NY)
- Beauvoir, the Jefferson Davis Home and Presidential Library, Biloxi (MS)

General

- Back St. Cultural Museum, New Orleans (LA)
- Baltimore & Ohio Railroad Museum, Baltimore (MD)

REQUIREMENTS AND RESTRICTIONS

No grants for capital campaigns, general or operating support, or management development or capacity building.

APPLICATION PROCEDURES

Step one of process is completion of an online application. See website.

Deadlines: March 1 and July 2

Toyota TAPESTRY Grants for Science Teachers

Headquarters

Cosponsored by National Science Teachers Association
National Science Teachers Association
1840 Wilson Boulevard
Arlington, VA 22201
Phone: 703-243-7100

www.nsta.org

E-mail: tapestry@nsta.org

Type of Grant Maker: Company (and nonprofit collaboration)

Description

Operating Locations/Geographic Preferences: None. TAPESTRY grants funded in all 50 states, the District of Columbia, The Marianas Islands, Puerto Rico, and the U.S. Virgin Islands.

Financial Summary

Number of Grants: 197 grants, over 21 years
Total Giving: $9.7 million
Grant Ranges: Up to $10,000

Grants Information

Grant program designed to implement innovative, community-based science projects in environmental science, physical science, and integrating literacy and science. A large number of these projects expanded to include multiple schools and communities.

PAST GRANT RECIPIENTS

Library or School Related

- Lincoln Junior High School, Curious George Teaches Science
- Leslie J. Steele Elementary School, My First (Grade) Science Yearbook

APPLICATION PROCEDURES AND DEADLINES

See website.

Travelers Foundation

Headquarters

385 Washington St.
St. Paul, MN 55102-1309
Phone: 651-310-7757

www.travelers.com/about-us/community/

Contact: Marlene Ibsen, Pres. and C.E.O.

E-mail: lcolanin@travelers.com

Type of Grant Maker: Corporate Foundation

Description

Founded: 1998

Operating Locations/Geographic Preferences: Primarily gives to education initiatives in key cities of St. Paul/Minneapolis, MN, and Hartford, CT and select cities nationally

Corporate Foundation Information: Supported by:

- The St. Paul Companies, Inc.
- The St. Paul Travelers Companies, Inc.
- The Travelers Companies, Inc.

Financial Summary

Assets: $142,398
Total Giving: $10,827,276

Number of Grants: 429
Grant Ranges: $1,500,000–$500

Grants Information

GRANT TYPES

Program development, capital campaigns, general and operating support, matching

TYPICAL RECIPIENTS/SUBJECTS OF INTEREST

Education, Community Development, Arts and Culture

PAST GRANT RECIPIENTS

Library or School Related

- Hartford Public Schools, Hartford (CT), for program support for academic year including High School Inc., Principal Leadership Academy and Asian Studies Academy, $622,000
- University of Connecticut, Storrs (CT), for program support for EDGE (Empowering Dreams for Graduation and Employment) Initiative and for M-CUBED program for students gifted in math, $621,000
- Achieve Hartford, Hartford (CT), to establish and implement local education foundation, $151,000

General

- Habitat for Humanity International, Americus (GA), to eliminate poverty housing and homelessness in cities across the country, $595,000

REQUIREMENTS AND RESTRICTIONS

Limited number of proposals for Community Development and Arts and Culture accepted.

No support for discriminatory organizations, sectarian religious organizations, political, lobbying, veterans', or fraternal organizations, health or disease-specific organizations, or hospitals or other health services organizations generally supported by third-party reimbursement mechanisms, or environmental programs. No grants to individuals, or for scholarships, benefits, fund-raisers, walk-a-thons, telethons, galas or other revenue-generating events, advertising, medical research, medical equipment, hospital capital or operating funds, replacement of government funding, human services such as counseling, chemical abuse treatment or family programs, or special events.

APPLICATION PROCEDURES

See website for grant guidelines and application information.

Deadlines: See guidelines

Treakle, J. Edwin Foundation, Inc.

Headquarters

PO Box 1157
Gloucester, VA 23061-1157
Phone: 804-693-0881

Contact: John Warren Cooke, Pres. and Genl. Mgr.

Type of Grant Maker: Foundation

Description

Founded: 1963

Operating Locations/Geographic Preferences: Giving primarily in VA

Financial Summary

Assets: $6,969,625
Total Giving: $320,000
Number of Grants: 60
Grant Ranges: $48,000–$500

Grants Information

GRANT TYPES

Annual and capital campaigns, building and renovation, continuing, general and operating support, equipment

TYPICAL RECIPIENTS/SUBJECTS OF INTEREST

Local and educational organizations.

PAST GRANT RECIPIENTS

Library or School Related

- Gloucester Library, Gloucester (VA), for books and library materials, $19,500
- Mathews Memorial Library, Mathews (VA), for books, periodicals, etc., $19,500
- Ware Academy, Gloucester (VA), for library materials and technology, $1,000
- Middlesex County Public Library, Urbanna (VA), for after-school program, $500
- Rappahannock Community College, Warsaw (VA), $7,000

General

- Gloucester Housing Partnership, Hayes (VA), $14,000
- Hands Across Mathews Interfaith Service Council, Mathews (VA), $14,000

REQUIREMENTS AND RESTRICTIONS

No grants to individuals.

APPLICATION PROCEDURES

Send letter or call to request application form

Deadlines: Submit between January 1 and April 30

Triangle Community Foundation

Headquarters

324 Blackwell St., Ste. 1220
Durham, NC 27701-3690
Phone: 919-474-8370

www.trianglecf.org

Contact: For grants: Robyn Ferhman, Community Prog. Off.; For Scholarships: Libby Long, Scholarship, Special Proj. Coord.

E-mail: info@trianglecf.org

Type of Grant Maker: Community Foundation

Description

Founded: 1983

Operating Locations/Geographic Preferences: Giving limited to Chatham, Durham, Orange, and Wake counties, NC.

Financial Summary

Assets: $122,492,712
Total Giving: $11,738,053
Number of Grants: 1,500

Grants Information

GRANT TYPES

Program development, annual and capital campaigns, continuing support, matching, management development, seed money, investments and loans

TYPICAL RECIPIENTS/SUBJECTS OF INTEREST

Giving programs include:

Borchardt Fund Grants: Supporting education through international exchanges in the field of technology as it applies to education.

Community Grant-making Program: Grants from $10,000–$15,000 to promote civic engagement and youth development.

GlaxoSmithKline Impact Awards: For community-based healthcare nonprofits.

Raising Voices: A Youth Choral Program: For grants of $4,000–$5,000 for choral music and choral music education.

Scholarship Funds

Tomorrow Fund for Hispanic Students Grants: Grants of up to $15,000 for NC institutions of higher education supporting Hispanic students

PAST GRANT RECIPIENTS

Library or School Related

- Hopkins School, New Haven (CT), $200,000
- Duke University, Durham (NC), $57,000

General

- North Carolina Museum of History Associates, Raleigh (NC), for Chronology exhibit, $100,000
- Project HOPE—The People-to-People Health Foundation, Millwood (VA), $2,500
- Child Care Services Association, Chapel Hill (NC), for annual gift, $50,000

REQUIREMENTS AND RESTRICTIONS

No grants for budget deficits.

APPLICATION PROCEDURES

See website for application form and guidelines. Application form required.

Deadlines: February 15 and August 15

TriMix Foundation

Headquarters

c/o Rex Capital Advisors, LLC
50 Park Row West, Ste. 113
Providence, RI 02903-1114

Contact: Gail S. Mixer, Pres.

Type of Grant Maker: Foundation

Description

Founded: 1997

Operating Locations/Geographic Preferences: Giving primarily in MA, RI, and FL

Financial Summary

Assets: $11,228,460
Total Giving: $455,186

Grants Information

GRANT TYPES

Program development, continuing, general and operating support, annual campaigns, seed money, technical assistance

TYPICAL RECIPIENTS/SUBJECTS OF INTEREST

Improve the lives of children, build cohesive neighborhoods and communities, and improve animal welfare

PAST GRANT RECIPIENTS

Library or School Related

- San Miguel School, $20,000
- Urban Collaborative Accelerated Program, Beyond School Program, $25,000

General

- City Year Miami, $25,000
- Crossroads Rhode Island, $10,000
- Amos House, $1,000

REQUIREMENTS AND RESTRICTIONS

No grants to individuals

APPLICATION PROCEDURES

Send letter on organization letterhead.

Deadlines: None

U.S. Airways

Headquarters

111 W. Rio Salado Parkway
Tempe, AZ 85281
Phone: 480-693-0800

www.usairways.com/en-US/aboutus/corporategiving/default.html

Operating Mailing address:
4000 E. Sky Harbor Blvd.
Phoenix, AZ 85034

Type of Grant Maker: Corporation

Description

Locations/Geographic Preferences: Major metropolitan areas around Charlotte, Philadelphia, Phoenix and Washington, DC.

Financial Summary

Not available

Grants Information

TYPICAL RECIPIENTS/SUBJECTS OF INTEREST

Corporate Giving Program: Focuses on 501(C)(3) nonprofit arts, human services, and education organizations that focus on sustainable change and building healthy, vibrant communities.

Arts: Partners with major arts organizations that provide access to the arts for all and encourage the overall development and economic prosperity of our communities. Invests in programs that provide basic needs (food, clothing and shelter) to develop economic self-reliance and create pipelines to employment.

Education: Supports literacy and STEM (science, technology, engineering and math) education to drive academic achievement.

PAST GRANT RECIPIENTS

General

- Philabundance in Philadelphia to build a new community food center in Chester (PA), $150,000
- United Family Services of Charlotte to expand the Shelter for Battered Women, $45,000

- Charlotte Rescue Mission to expand the Dove's Nest residential recovery programs for homeless and at risk women, $75,000
- Ballet Arizona to renovate a 45,000-square-foot warehouse, $25,000

REQUIREMENTS AND RESTRICTIONS

Substantial restrictions and limitations for each funding category above. See website for information.

APPLICATION PROCEDURES

Online application required. See website.

Deadlines: Vary

U.S. Bancorp Foundation, Inc.

Headquarters

BC-MN-H21B
800 Nicollet Mall, 21st Fl.
Minneapolis, MN 55402
Phone: 612-303-4000

www.usbank.com/community/charitable-giving.html

Contact: John Pacheco, Grants Coord.

E-mail: USBancorp@Easymatch.com

Type of Grant Maker: Corporate Foundation

Description

Founded: 1979

Operating Locations/Geographic Preferences: Giving primarily in AR, AZ, CA, CO, ID, IA, IL, IN, KS, KY, MN, MO, MT, ND, NE, NV, OH, OR, SD, TN, UT, WA, WI, and WY

Corporate Foundation Information: Donors include:

- First Bank System, Inc.
- U.S. Bancorp
- U.S. Bank, N.A.

Financial Summary

Assets: $14,332,927
Total Giving: $19,968,742

Grants Information

GRANT TYPES

Program development, capital campaigns, general and operating support, in-kind contributions

TYPICAL RECIPIENTS/SUBJECTS OF INTEREST

Education, arts and culture, employment, housing, youth development, human services, and community development Giving programs include:

Affordable Housing

Cultural and Artistic Enrichment: Focusing on programs that build audiences for the arts, especially among underserved population, rural communities, along with arts in education.

Economic Development

Education: Supporting help for low-income and at-risk students to succeed in school and prepare for post-secondary education. Financial literacy training and mentoring supported. Special emphasis on reaching broad number of students, bringing together community resources and supporting curriculum innovation.

Employee Matching Gifts

Self-Sufficiency: Focusing on work-entry programs, specific skills training, employment retention, and personal financial management training.

PAST GRANT RECIPIENTS

Library or School Related

- Team Read, Seattle (WA), for general operating support, $5,000
- Saint Louis University, Saint Louis (MO), for capital support, $150,000

General

- Greenlining Institute, Berkeley (CA), for general operating support, $100,000
- Minnesota Orchestral Association, Minneapolis (MN), for capital support, $200,000
- Saint Louis ArtWorks, Saint Louis, (MO), for program/project support, $4,000

REQUIREMENTS AND RESTRICTIONS

No support for fraternal organizations, merchant associations, or 501(c)(4) or (6) organizations, 509(a)(3) supporting organizations, pass-through organizations or private foundations, religious organizations, political organizations or lobbying organizations, United Way–supported organizations, or child care providers.

No grants to individuals, or for fund-raising events or sponsorships, travel, endowments, debt reduction, or chamber memberships or programs.

APPLICATION PROCEDURES

See website for state charitable giving contacts and application deadlines. Application form required. Applicants should submit:

1. Copy of IRS Determination Letter
2. Copy of most recent annual report/audited financial statement/990
3. Listing of board of directors, trustees, officers and other key people and their affiliations
4. Detailed description of project and amount of funding requested
5. Copy of current year's organizational budget and/or project budget
6. Listing of additional sources and amount of support
7. Additional materials/documentation

Deadlines: Vary

U.S. Department of Commerce

Headquarters

Oceanic and Atmospheric Research (OAR)
National Oceanic Atmospheric Administration (NOAA)
National Oceanic and Atmospheric Administration
1401 Constitution Avenue, NW
Room 5128
Washington, DC 20230
Phone: 301-734-1076

www.noaa.gov (agency website); www.grants.gov/
search/announce.do;jsessionid = lTR1P44Qw3Bfy5y654J
rDQLS7wHZGBmQZStRR4ppFGs24sgkmQdh!760517813
(grant website)

Contact: Ms. Amy Painter, NOAA R/SG

E-mail: oar.hq.nsgo.competitions@noaa.gov

Mailing address:
National Sea Grant Office
1315 East West Highway
Silver Spring, MD 20910-3283

Grants Information

Number of Grants: 1
Grant Amount: $235,000

NATIONAL SEA GRANT LIBRARY

NOAA's Office of Oceanic and Atmospheric Research (OAR), National Sea Grant College Program, invites applications to establish or continue a National Sea Grant Library. Applicants should provide a two-year grant proposal for a National Sea Grant Library that will be part of the larger National Sea Grant network, a partnership between the federal government and universities to conduct integrated research, education and outreach in fields related to ocean, coastal and Great Lakes resources.

Program Objective: The National Sea Grant College Program plays a leading role in the sustainable development of the Nation's marine resources. It accomplishes this through an extensive program of research, education, and outreach. Sea Grant meets national needs by providing information to citizens pertaining to a diverse set of concerns ranging from how best to educate K–12 children on coastal issues to advanced scientific research. However, as the development of various marine resources evolves, matures, and receives greater attention nationally and worldwide, it becomes increasingly important to ensure that Sea Grant research and outreach information is accessible to the public. Efforts to disseminate information about ocean and coastal research, outreach and policy, and to provide the Sea Grant College Programs and coastal citizens with access to books, papers, proceedings and other publications must be pursued in order to ensure that this information broadly available to these audiences.

All Sea Grant Programs publish information about research, education and outreach investments and the results of this work for their coastal constituents. However, it was felt that the work of individual Programs should be coordinated, communicated among Programs, and made available to a broader constituency.

These needs gave rise to the concept of a Sea Grant Library–a centralized resource that could coordinate and make available to the public Sea Grant's publications in research, education and outreach related to coastal and ocean issues.

Now, the National Sea Grant College Program would like to use this Federal Funding Opportunity announcement to establish a formal long-term partnership with a grantee to maintain a National Sea Grant Library, so that subsequent awards for continuing the Library may be made on a noncompetitive "institutional" basis, as long as certain conditions of performance are met.

REQUIREMENTS AND RESTRICTIONS

Eligibility: Institutions of higher education, nonprofit organizations, commercial organizations, State and local and Indian tribal governments are eligible.

APPLICATION PROCEDURES AND DEADLINES

See website

U.S. Department of Education

Headquarters

U.S. Department of Education
400 Maryland Avenue, SW.
Washington, DC 20202
Phone: 202-260-2514, 800-872-5327 (toll-free)
Fax: 202-260-8969

www.ed.gov (agency website); www2.ed.gov/programs/lsl/ (grant website)

Contact: Peter Eldridge, Team Leader

E-mail: Peter.Eldridge@ed.gov

Mailing Address:
U.S. Department of Education, OESE
Academic Improvement and Teacher Quality Programs
400 Maryland Ave. S.W., Rm. 3E246
LBJ Federal Office Building
Washington, DC 20202-6200

Grants Information

Number of Grants: 50
Grant Ranges: $100,000–$371,000

IMPROVING LITERACY THROUGH SCHOOL LIBRARIES

The purpose of this program is to improve student reading skills and academic achievement by providing students with increased access to up-to-date school library materials; well-equipped, technologically advanced school library media centers; and well-trained, professionally certified school library media specialists.

Districts may use funds for the following activities:

- Purchase up-to-date school library media resources, including books
- Acquire and use advanced technology that is integrated into the curricula to develop and enhance the information literacy, information retrieval, and critical-thinking skills of students
- Facilitate Internet links and other resource-sharing networks

- Provide professional development for school library media specialists of PK–3 students and provide activities that foster increased collaboration among library specialists, teachers, and administrators of PK–12 students
- Provide students with access to school libraries during nonschool hours, weekends, and summer vacations.

REQUIREMENTS AND RESTRICTIONS

Eligibility: Local education agencies (LEAs) in which at least 20 percent of students served are from families with incomes below the poverty line may apply. Outlying areas (American Samoa, Guam, the Northern Mariana Islands, and the U.S. Virgin Islands) and the Bureau of Indian Affairs are eligible for funds under a set-aside.

APPLICATION PROCEDURES AND DEADLINES

See website

U.S. Department of Labor

Headquarters

U.S. Department of Labor
200 Constitution Ave., NW
Washington, DC 20210
Phone: 202-693-2606

www.dol.gov (agency website); www.doleta.gov/youth_services/YouthBuild.cfm (program website/request for proposal)

Contact: Kia Mason, Grants Management Specialist

Type of Grant Maker: Government

Grants Information

Number of Grants: 75
Grant Ranges: $700,000–$1,100,000

YOUTHBUILD GRANTS

YouthBuild is a youth and community development program that simultaneously addresses several core issues facing low-income communities: affordable housing, education, employment, crime prevention, and leadership development. The YouthBuild model balances in-school learning that leads to the achievement of a high school diploma or passing the General Education Development (GED) test and occupational skills training that prepares youth for career placement. The in-school component is an alternative education program that assists youth who are often significantly behind in basic skills to obtain a high school diploma or GED credential. The target populations for YouthBuild are high school dropouts who may also be adjudicated youth, youth aging out of foster care, youth with disabilities, and other at-risk youth populations.

REQUIREMENTS AND RESTRICTIONS

Eligible applicants for these grants are public or private nonprofit agencies or organizations including rural, urban or Native American agencies, but not limited to:

Faith-based and community organizations

An entity carrying out activities under Workforce Investment Act (WIA), such as a local workforce investment board, One-Stop Career Center, or local school board

A community action agency

A state or local housing development agency

An Indian tribe or other agency primarily serving American Indians

A community development corporation

A state or local youth service conservation corps

A consortium of such agencies or organizations with a designated lead applicant

Any other public or private nonprofit entity that is eligible to provide education or employment training under a Federal program

APPLICATION PROCEDURES AND DEADLINES

See request for proposal

Unilever United States Foundation, Inc.

Headquarters

c/o Unilever United States, Inc.
800 Sylvan Ave.
Englewood Cliffs, NJ 07632-3113
Phone: 416-415-3164

Contact: Catherine McVitty

E-mail: catherine.mcvitty@unilever.com

Type of Grant Maker: Corporate Foundation

Description

Founded: 1952

Operating Locations/Geographic Preferences: Giving primarily in areas of company operations, with emphasis on Washington, DC, IL, NJ, and NY

Corporate Foundation Information: Supported by:

- Unilever United States, Inc.
- Lever Bros. Co.
- Van den Bergh Foods Co.
- Unilever Research

Financial Summary

Assets: $1,782,097
Total giving: $3,524,916
Number of Grants: 214
Grant Ranges: $250,000–$100

Grants Information

GRANT TYPES

Program development, matching, general and operating support

TYPICAL RECIPIENTS/SUBJECTS OF INTEREST

Building healthier lifestyles for families and children with a focus on good nutrition, active healthy lifestyles, self-esteem, and hunger relief, climate change, water conservation, waste and packaging, and environmental preservation.

PAST GRANT RECIPIENTS

Library or School Related

- Leonia Public Library, $500
- Wilton Library Association Incorporated, $200
- Killingworth Library Association Inc, $100
- Perrot Memorial Library Association of Old Greenwich Incorporated, $100
- Korean War Veterans National Museum and Library, $75
- Norwood Library Association, Inc., Norwood Public Library, $25
- Town of Roxbury - Roxbury Public Library, $275
- New York Public Library Astor Lenox and Tilden Foundations, $60
- Friends of the Brown County Library Inc, $50
- Friends of the Closter NJ Public Library Inc, $25

General

- Friends of the World Food Program, Washington (DC), $500,000
- National Park Foundation, Washington (DC), $500,000

REQUIREMENTS AND RESTRICTIONS

No support for religious, labor, political, or veterans' organizations, grants to individuals, for goodwill advertising, fund-raising events or testimonial dinners, or capital campaigns or loans.

APPLICATION PROCEDURES

Send proposal and letter of IRS determination.

Deadlines: None

Urban Libraries Council

Headquarters

125 S. Wacker Drive, Suite 1050
Chicago IL, 60606
Phone: 312-676-0999

www.urbanlibraries.org

Type of Grant Maker: Library Organization

Organization does not provide grants, but does provide several award programs. See website for details.

Utah State Library Division

Headquarters

250 North, 1950 West, Suite A
Salt Lake City, UT 84116-7901
Phone: 801-715-6777 (State Library); 801-715-6789
   (Library for the Blind); 800-662-9150 (in-state toll free)
Fax: 801-715-6767

http://library.utah.gov/grants/index.html

Type of Grant Maker: Government

Grants Information

CAPITAL FACILITIES GRANT

Provides for an annual capital grant request program. By definition, capital facilities grants shall include new construction, preservation, restoration, or renovation.
   Prioritization will be based on the following criteria:

1. Goals of application
2. Public benefit of project
3. Strategic value of partnerships

APPLICATION PROCEDURES

All applications must be submitted electronically via the Department of Community and Culture (DCC) and its division web portals.
   For more information or assistance contact: Steve Matthews, 800-662-9150, x722 (Utah toll-free) or 801-715-6722, smatthews@utah.gov.

Deadline: June 1

COMMUNITY LIBRARY ENHANCEMENT FUND (CLEF) GRANTS

Grants are calculated for all qualified and certified public libraries following the State Legislature session and are awarded at the beginning of the next calendar year. CLEF payments are based on a formula which takes into account the population the library serves, the wealth of the community, and the financial effort the local government is making to support library services.
   Community Library Enhancement Funds may be used for the following three areas:

Collection Development (such as children's materials, video materials, online resources, materials in another language, special new collections, enhanced current collections)

Technology that Directly Affects the Public (such as public access computing, library catalogs, online resources, technology training, wifi)

Community Outreach (such as services for seniors, teens, migrants, head starts, outreach to those who don't use the library)

APPLICATION PROCEDURES AND DEADLINES

Contact: Cheryl Mansen, 801-715-6747

E-mail: cmansen@utah.gov

ASSOCIATION FOR RURAL AND SMALL LIBRARIES (ARSL) GRANT

Pays for conference attendance. See more about the conference on the ARSL Website.

Deadline: July 17

UPLIFT ORGANIZATION RESOURCE GRANT

Available to formal library organizations for specialized library training. It allows organizations to upgrade the skills of library staff, trustees, and their supporters by addressing local needs.

APPLICATION PROCEDURES

Contact: Colleen Eggett, Training Coordinator

Phone: 800-662-9150, x776 (Utah toll-free) or
   801-715-6776

E-mail: ceggett@utah.gov

Deadlines: February 15, June 15, October 15

LIBRARY SERVICES AND TECHNOLOGY ACT (LSTA)

LSTA funds are used to promote improvements in services to all types of libraries; to facilitate access to, and sharing of, resources; and to achieve economical and effective delivery of service for the purpose of cultivating an educated and informed citizenry.

In addition, LSTA funds are targeted for statewide library services and support a wide array of programs from literacy to providing broad access to databases. This program develops the role of libraries as information brokers, helping to make resources and services, which are often prohibitively expensive, more readily available. LSTA also supports efforts to educate the current and future library workforce in Utah.

In 2012–2013, the Utah State Library awarded grants tied to three library service areas:

Technology, Collections, and Digitization

Grant Amount: Total giving: $600,000

APPLICATION PROCEDURES

See online forms

Deadline: August 1

LENDER SUPPORT PROGRAM (INCLUDING THE OCLC AND RESOURCE SHARING GRANT)

To encourage resource sharing among Utah's libraries by providing funds to help defray the costs of providing materials to other libraries.

The Lender Support program consists of two components: The Lender Support Grant, the OCLC Support Grant.

The Lender Support Grant is based upon the percentage of lending to other libraries in the state by the grantee. The following procedure is utilized to determine the amount of the grant: Qualified loans from Utah libraries are totaled for the period (one year). (Qualified Loans are defined as materials loaned or otherwise provided without charge to other Utah libraries not affiliated with for-profit organizations and which provide access to the public, and shall include traditional loans of printed and multimedia materials, and photocopies or otherwise electronically reproduced materials from the lending library's collection. Loans made from one entity to another, within one parent institution are not qualified loans.) Loans from libraries whose total qualified lending does not exceed 1 percent of the total will not receive the Lender Support Grant,

but may be eligible for the OCLC Support Grant. The library will receive a dollar grant equal to its percentage of qualified lending multiplied by the total funds allocated to the program. (For example, a library with 10% of the qualified lending will receive 10% of the allocated funds.)

GRANT AMOUNT:

Grant funds are allocated to each library on a stepped scale based on the amount of qualified lending:

Up to 1, $2,250
1% to 5%, $3,750
5% to 10%, $5,250
10% and over, $7,500

REQUIREMENTS AND RESTRICTIONS

This program is open to all lending libraries in Utah. The OCLC Support Grant is available only to those libraries who utilize OCLC.

APPLICATION PROCEDURES AND DEADLINES

Contact: Craig Neilson

E-mail: cneilson@utah.gov

Valley, Wayne & Gladys Foundation

Headquarters

1939 Harrison St., Ste. 510
Oakland, CA 94612-3532
Phone: 510-466-6060
Fax: 510-466-6067

www.foundationcenter.org/Grant Maker/wgvalley

Contact: Michael D. Desler, Exec. Dir.

E-mail: info@wgvalley.org

Type of Grant Maker: Foundation

Description

Founded: 1977

Operating Locations/Geographic Preferences: Giving primarily in Alameda and Contra Costa counties, CA

Financial Summary

Assets: $506,478,375
Total Giving: $40,897,055

Number of Grants: 73
Grant Ranges: $3,750,000–$13,000

Grants Information

GRANT TYPES

Program development, building and renovation, capital campaigns, general and operating support, matching

TYPICAL RECIPIENTS/SUBJECTS OF INTEREST

Higher, secondary, and other education, medical research, health care, youth, local parks and recreational facilities and local Catholic organizations

PAST GRANT RECIPIENTS

Library or School Related

- Santa Clara University, Santa Clara (CA), Construction of the Harrington Learning Commons, Sobrato Technology Center and the Orradre Library, $3,000,000
- Samuel Merritt University, Oakland (CA), Renovation and expansion of the John A. Graziano Memorial Library, $172,000
- St. James Academy, Solana Beach (CA), Purchase of Smartboards and related items for K–8 classrooms and science library, $68,461
- Berkeley Public Library Foundation, Berkeley (CA), Neighborhood Libraries Campaign, $300,000

General

- Oakland Museum of California Foundation, Oakland (CA), for renovation of galleries and building, $1,875,000
- YMCA, Berkeley-Albany, Berkeley (CA), for construction of new Berkeley-Albany YMCA Teen Center, $500,000

REQUIREMENTS AND RESTRICTIONS

No support for veterans, fraternal, labor, service club, military, or similar organizations. No grants to individuals, or for fund-raising events, dinners, advertising, private operating foundations, or generally for endowments.

APPLICATION PROCEDURES

The Foundation does not encourage lengthy application letters. The application letter should be concise and include the following:

1. Description and very brief history of the applicant organization. A short narrative on the success of the organization, including overall financial stability.
2. Description of the project.
3. Statement of the purpose and goals of the project.
4. Number of people that will benefit from the project.
5. References to outside sources, materials and research, if any, that have demonstrated a need for the proposed project.
6. Time frame in which the project will be undertaken and proof of a well-thought out business plan.
7. Documentation of the planning process of the project for which funds are sought.
8. Amount of funds requested from the Foundation.
9. The total cost of the project.
10. Other sources of funds for the project, including the current status of other funding requests.
11. Name(s) of person(s) in direct charge of project with brief biographical information. Include comments on qualifications and commitment of personnel.
12. How progress and success of the project will be measured.

The following attachments should be included with the application:

1. An income and expense budget for the project, to include projected sources of revenues.
2. A list of the Board of Directors and their business or professional affiliations.
3. IRS Letter of Determination of 501(c)(3) and public charity status, State of California Exemption Letter from the Franchise Tax Board, and letter from chief financial officer of the applicant stating that tax exempt and public charity status has not been revoked or modified.
4. A copy of the most recent audited financial statement of the applicant. If the applicant ended with an operating deficit in any of the last four fiscal years, an explanation of the reason and corrective action taken to remedy the loss.
5. A copy of the most recent fiscal year's entire filed IRS Form 990 of the applicant, including all schedules. (The Foundation may request prior fiscal years, if needed.)

If, after the initial screening, the Foundation determines that it has sufficient interest to warrant further consideration, the applicant will be so advised and additional information may be sought. In most cases, site visits will then be scheduled.

Unless initiated by a Foundation Board Director, personal communication with individual Foundation Directors by representatives of the applicant is not encouraged.

All grant applications and other correspondence should be directed in writing as follows:

Michael D. Desler, Executive Director
Wayne and Gladys Valley Foundation
1939 Harrison Street, Suite 510
Oakland, CA 94612-3532

Deadlines: None

Verizon Foundation

Headquarters

1 Verizon Way
Basking Ridge, NJ 07920-1025
Phone: 866-247-2687
Fax: 908-630-2660

www.foundation.verizon.com

E-mail: verizon.foundation@verizon.com

Type of Grant Maker: Corporate Foundation

Description

Founded: 1985

Operating Locations/Geographic Preferences: Giving on a national basis, with emphasis on CA, Washington DC. Giving also in Argentina, Australia, Brazil, Hong Kong, India, and Singapore.

Corporate Foundation Information—supported by:

- NYNEX Corp.
- Bell Atlantic Corp.
- Verizon Communications Inc.

Financial Summary

Assets: $201,527,537
Total Giving: $59,365,756

Grants Information

GRANT TYPES

Program development, general and operating support, building and renovation, matching, employee volunteering, equipment, sponsorships, technical assistance

TYPICAL RECIPIENTS/SUBJECTS OF INTEREST

Verizon Foundation is dedicated to improving lives and giving back to communities, specifically focusing on:

- Education
- Health Care
- Sustainability

Education giving focuses on increasing student interest and achievement in Science, Technology, Engineering and Math.

Verizon Innovative Learning Schools: Improves student achievement in Science, Technology, Engineering and Math by providing free online content, mobile applications and technology-focused teacher and administrator training.

Verizon Innovative Learning Community: Free online community gives educators the opportunity to collaborate, connect, and share resources and best practices.

Free Digital Content: Thinkfinity resources offer free lesson plans and educational online activities, games, videos, podcasts and more.

PAST GRANT RECIPIENTS

Library or School Related

- American Library Association, $222,553
- Altoona Area Public Library, Altoona (PA), $15,000
- Anne Arundel Public Library, Annapolis (MD), $10,000
- Brooklyn Public Library, Brooklyn (NY), $25,000
- Carnegie Library, Pittsburgh (PA), $15,000
- Dauphin County Library System, Harrisburg (PA), $12,500
- Richmond Public Library, Richmond (VA), $10,000
- African Library Project, Portola Valley (CA), $150

General

- National Council of Teachers of English, Urbana (IL), $651,000
- John F. Kennedy Center for the Performing Arts, Washington (DC), $625,000
- Prince Georges Child Resource Center, Largo (MD), $9,200

REQUIREMENTS AND RESTRICTIONS

Applicants must be:

Classified by the Internal Revenue Service as a tax-exempt charity under section 501(c)(3) of the Internal Revenue Code and are further classified as a public charity under section 509(a)(1)-509(a)(3) of the Internal Revenue Code, as follows:

Section 509(a)(1)—Organizations described in section 170(b)(1)(A) clauses (i)–(vi):

170(b)(1)(A)(i)—Church, provided that the grant will benefit a large portion of a community without regard to religious affiliation and does not duplicate the work of other agencies in the community.

170(b)(1)(A)(ii)—School.

170(b)(1)(A)(iii)—Hospital or medical research organization.

170(b)(1)(A)(iv)—Organization that operates for benefit of college or university and is owned or operated by a governmental unit.

170(b)(1)(A)(v)— Governmental unit.

170(b)(1)(A)(vi)—Organization which receives a

substantial part of its support from a governmental unit or the general public.

Section 509(a)(2)—Organizations that normally receives no more than one-third of its support from gross investment income and unrelated business income and at the same time more than one-third of its support from contributions, fees, and gross receipts related to exempt purposes.

Section 509(a)(3)—Organizations operated solely for the benefit of and in conjunction with organizations described in the previous items.

An elementary or secondary school (public or private) registered with the National Center for Education Statistics (NCES), providing that the grant is not for the sponsorship of a field trip.

APPLICATION PROCEDURES

Applicants must first see if they are eligible by taking an online quiz.

If the organization is the right match, applicants can set up an online account, then fill out the application form and submit it through the website.

Deadlines: Unsolicited online proposals are reviewed on a continuous calendar-year basis from January 1 through October 14

Virginia, The Library of

Headquarters

800 East Broad Street
Richmond, VA 23219
Phone: 804 692-3500

http://www.lva.virginia.gov/lib-edu/LDND/state-aid/

Type of Grant Maker: Government

Grants Information

STATE AID GRANT

A formula-based grant that encourages the formation of library systems at the regional, county, and city level. Approximately 76 percent of State Aid is used for books and library materials. For many systems, State Aid is the only funding source for materials. Nine percent is used for salaries for professional librarians. The remaining 12 percent is used for equipment (including computers), furniture, automation systems, etc.

REQUIREMENTS AND RESTRICTIONS

To be eligible for a state aid grant, a library must comply with the Requirements of The Library Board (last amended in 1991). The major change affected requirement number 3, the "50% of the median local operating expenditure per capita" replaced a requirement of expenditures of at least $2 per capita.

APPLICATION PROCEDURES

Contact agency for details.

Deadline: June 1

Volunteer USA Foundation, Inc.

Headquarters

516 N. Adams St.
Tallahassee, FL 32301-1112
Phone: 850-562-5300
Fax: 850-224-6532

www.volunteerusafoundation.org

Type of Grant Maker: Foundation

Description

Founded: 2007

Operating Locations/Geographic Preferences: Giving limited to the southeastern U.S., primarily to FL, GA, LA, and TN.

Financial Summary

Assets: $1,836,207
Total Giving: $471,276

Grants Information

GRANT TYPES

Literacy, mentoring services

TYPICAL RECIPIENTS/SUBJECTS OF INTEREST

To help all people achieve their educational goals

PAST GRANT RECIPIENTS

- Calhoun Co. Public Library, Blountstown (FL), $27,559
- Pinellas Public Library Cooperative, $28,686

General

- Family Literacy Academy, Babson Park (FL), $87,500
- Gilford County Reading Connection, Greensboro (NC), $65,000

REQUIREMENTS AND RESTRICTIONS

Programs requesting grants must be in the southern U.S. Programs must have nonprofit tax-exempt status.

APPLICATION PROCEDURES

Contact foundation for application guidelines

Deadline: October 1 for Family Literacy Grants

Wallace Foundation

Headquarters

5 Penn Plz., 7th Fl.
New York, NY 10001-1837
Phone: 212-251-9700
Fax: 212-679-6990

www.wallacefoundation.org

Contact: Genl. Mgmt.

E-mail: info@wallacefoundation.org

Type of Grant Maker: Foundation

Wallace Foundation rarely funds unsolicited proposals.

Rather, the Foundation approach is to fund selected organizations to test promising new ideas, to conduct independent research about their efforts and related matters, and to share what we learn. In most cases, the Foundation identifies prospective grantees and invites them, through "requests for proposals" or other careful screening, to submit applications for grants.

Nevertheless, you may submit an inquiry by e-mail, briefly describing your project, your organization, the estimated total cost of the project and the portion requiring funding to: The Wallace Foundation, grantrequest@ wallacefoundation.org.

Wallace, George R. Foundation

Headquarters

c/o Goodwin Procter LLP
1 Exchange Pl.
Boston, MA 02109-2881

Contact: Lucia B. Thompson, Clerk

E-mail: lthompson@goodwinprocter.com

Type of Grant Maker: Foundation

Description

Founded: 1963

Operating Locations/Geographic Preferences: Giving primarily in the Fitchburg and Leominster, MA, area

Financial Summary

Assets: $6,927,029
Total Giving: $295,714
Number of Grants: 10
Grant Ranges: $100,000–$10,000

Grants Information

GRANT TYPES

General and operating support, annual campaigns, building and renovation, capital campaigns, matching, seed money, endowments, equipment

TYPICAL RECIPIENTS/SUBJECTS OF INTEREST

Education (particularly for programs that benefit low-income students), and museums and libraries

PAST GRANT RECIPIENTS

- Leominster Public Library, Leominster (MA), $20,000
- Fitchburg State College Foundation, Fitchburg (MA), $100,000

General

- Fitchburg Historical Society, Fitchburg (MA), $50,000
- Children's Aid and Family Services, Fitchburg (MA), $25,000

REQUIREMENTS AND RESTRICTIONS

No support for religious organizations, except for grants to support the education of disadvantaged and/or disabled children. No grants to individuals, or for scholarships, fellowships or loans.

APPLICATION PROCEDURES

Inquire by mail, telephone, or e-mail.

Deadlines: None

Walmart Foundation, Inc.

Headquarters

702 S.W. 8th St., Dept. 8687, No. 0555
Bentonville, AR 72716-0555
Phone: 800-530-9925
Fax: 479-273-6850
www.walmartfoundation.org

Contact: Julie Gehrki, Sr. Dir., Business Integration

Type of Grant Maker: Corporate Foundation

Description

Founded: 1979

Operating Locations/Geographic Preferences: Giving on a national basis in areas of company operations, with emphasis on AR, Washington, DC, IL, NY, TN, UT, and VA

Corporate Foundation Information: Supported by Wal-Mart Stores, Inc.

Financial Summary

Assets: $34,535,274
Total Giving: $164,588,396
Number of Grants: 13,523
Grant Ranges: $9,659,762–$140

Grants Information

GRANT TYPES

Program development, emergency funds, matching, employee volunteering, management development, sponsorships

TYPICAL RECIPIENTS/SUBJECTS OF INTEREST

Education, workforce development and economic opportunity, health and wellness, and environmental sustainability, hunger relief, disaster relief, women, military and veterans, the disabled, and economically disadvantaged people.

Giving programs include:

Facility Giving Programs: Local Community Contribution and Hunger Outreach Grant programs, Walmart Stores, Sam's Clubs, and Logistics Facilities can recommend grants beginning at $250 to local nonprofit organizations.

National Giving Program: Organizations that are considered for funding through the Walmart Foundation's National Giving Program implement programs in multiple sites across the country or have innovative initiatives that are ready for replication nationally.

State Giving Program: The State Giving Program awards grants starting at $25,000 to nonprofit organizations that serve a particular state or region.

Volunteerism Always Pays: The Walmart Foundation encourages Walmart associates to get involved in charitable organizations that matter to their families and the communities where they live and work.

Walmart Foundation Scholarship Programs

PAST GRANT RECIPIENTS

Library or School Related

- White County Public Library, Searcy (AR), $2,000

General

$1 Million and Above

- Alliance for Equity in Higher Education
- America's Promise Alliance
- American Council on Education
- American Association of Community Colleges
- Communities in Schools
- Council of Independent Colleges
- Excelencia in Education
- Gateway to College Network
- Goodwill Industries International
- Hispanic Scholarship Fund
- Institute for Higher Education Policy
- Jobs for the Future
- League for Innovation in the Community College
- Meals on Wheels Association of America
- National 4-H Council
- National CASA
- National Center on Family Homelessness
- National Council of La Raza
- National Energy Education Development, NEED
- National Recreation and Park Association
- National Urban League

$500,000–$999,999

- Clinton Global Initiative
- Congressional Black Caucus Foundation Inc.
- Count Me In
- Food Research and Action Center
- Foundation for Independent Higher Education
- Jobs for America's Graduates
- NAACP
- National Assoc. of Elementary School Principals
- National Disability Institute
- National Education Association Health Information Network
- National Public Radio
- School Nutrition Foundation

$250,000–$499,999

- Business and Professional Women's Foundation
- Hispanic Association of Colleges and Universities
- Network for Teaching Entrepreneurship
- Students in Free Enterprise

APPLICATION PROCEDURES

Different application procedures apply to each giving area. See website for details on applying and deadlines.

Deadlines: Vary according to giving program

Walton Family Foundation, Inc.

Headquarters

PO Box 2030
Bentonville, AR 72712-2030
Phone: 479-464-1570

www.waltonfamilyfoundation.org

Contact: Buddy D. Philpot, Exec. Dir.

E-mail: info@wffmail.com

Type of Grant Maker: Foundation

Description

Founded: 1987

Operating Locations/Geographic Preferences: Some funding limited to northwest AR and the Mississippi River's delta region of AR and MS

Financial Summary

Assets: $1,282,168,113
Total Giving: $1,479,636,053
Number of Grants: 967
Grant Ranges: $800,000,000–$100

Grants Information

GRANT TYPES

Program development, continuing, general and operating support, matching, investments and loans, management development

TYPICAL RECIPIENTS/SUBJECTS OF INTEREST

Systemic reform of primary education (K–12) and the environment as it relates to marine and freshwater conservation.

Also funds Public Charter Startup Grant Program for school developers who primarily serve low-income children in target geographies.

PAST GRANT RECIPIENTS

General

- Crystal Bridges Museum of American Art, Bentonville (AR), $50,000,000
- Walton Arts Center, Fayetteville (AR), $1,000,000
- Children's Scholarship Fund, New York (NY), $15,400,000
- Museum of Northern Arizona, Flagstaff (AZ), $10,000

REQUIREMENTS AND RESTRICTIONS

Educational funding is limited to charter schools. No support for medical research programs. No grants to individuals, or for endowments for operations, church-related construction projects, travel expenses for groups to compete or perform, or business-related activities such as start-up costs, or expenses related to groups or individuals participating in non-curricular programs.

APPLICATION PROCEDURES

Organizations interested in applying for a grant must first send a brief letter of inquiry. The letter should succinctly describe the organization and the proposed project, specify and briefly explain its relevance to a particular funding area and initiative, and provide an estimate of the funds that would be requested. If the project appears to match our funding criteria and priorities, the applicant may be invited to submit a formal grant proposal and budget.

Deadlines: None

Warhol, Andy Foundation for the Visual Arts

Headquarters

65 Bleecker St., 7th Fl.
New York, NY 10012-2420
Phone: 212-387-7555
Fax: 212-387-7560

www.warholfoundation.org

Contact: Rachel Bers, Acting Prog. Dir.

E-mail: info@warholfoundation.org

Type of Grant Maker: Foundation

Description

Founded: 1987

Operating Locations/Geographic Preferences: Giving on a national basis

Financial Summary

Assets: $316,547,132
Total Giving: $12,456,738
Number of Grants: 188
Grant Ranges: $1,500,000–$2,350; average: $50,000–$100,000

Grants Information

GRANT TYPES

Program development, conferences

TYPICAL RECIPIENTS/SUBJECTS OF INTEREST

The advancement of the visual arts

PAST GRANT RECIPIENTS

General

- Andy Warhol Museum, Pittsburgh (PA), for general support and Time Capsule Cataloguing Project, $325,000
- Hyde Park Art Center, Chicago (IL), for exhibition program support, $150,000
- New Museum of Contemporary Art, New York (NY), for Free Culture exhibition, $150,000

REQUIREMENTS AND RESTRICTIONS

No grants to individuals.

APPLICATION PROCEDURES

A full proposal for funding should include the following:

A letter of approximately 3 pages describing the activity for which funds are being requested; if applying for the first time, give a brief description of the organization's mission, purpose and goals.

A project budget

A copy of the organization's 501(c)3 ruling from the IRS A letter of support from the sponsoring organization's director (for Curatorial Research Fellowship applicants only).

Please do not send any additional material with your proposal. Proposals may be submitted either by mail or by e-mail. Please select only one method of application and send only one copy.

If submitting by mail, address the proposal to:

Rachel Bers, Program Director
The Andy Warhol Foundation for the Visual Arts
65 Bleecker Street, 7th Floor
New York, NY 10012

If submitting by e-mail, send to deadline@warholfoundation.org and attach all materials as Word documents, Excel documents or PDFs. Please do not call to confirm your proposal has arrived; notification of receipt will be sent in the mail. Grant requests are reviewed twice a year.

Deadlines: March 1 with notification on July 1 and September 1 with notification on January 1.

Washington State Library

Headquarters

Washington Secretary of State
Point Plaza East, 6880 Capitol Blvd. SE, Tumwater
PO Box 42460, Olympia WA 98504-2460
Phone: 360-704-5200

www.sos.wa.gov/library/libraries/grants/

Contact: Anne Yarbrough, LSTA Grants Manager

E-mail: anne.yarbrough@sos.wa.gov

Phone: 360-704-5246

Type of Grant Maker: Government

Grants Information

LSTA Grants

Awards fund the development of library programs and services.

REQUIREMENTS AND RESTRICTIONS

Libraries in Washington State eligible for funding under the LSTA are those libraries included within item 1 or 2 below, and that also meet the criteria identified within item 3.

1. Libraries identified in the legislation, as further defined below.
2. Libraries operating as not-for-profit entities (i.e., 501(c)(3) status or a similar nonprofit designation), or as part of not-for-profit entities.
3. Those libraries that report to a governing body and have:
   Written mission statement
   Fixed location
   Established and posted hours of service
   Organized collection accessible to its clientele
   Designated staff with authority and responsibility for library operations and services
   Adopted policies consistent with accepted library practices
   Budget with a defined, ongoing revenue source
   Legal basis for operation
   Clearly defined governance structure

Libraries eligible to apply for LSTA funds are public libraries, academic libraries, research libraries and special libraries or information centers, school libraries, and library consortiums.

APPLICATION PROCEDURES

Contact:

Anne Yarbrough
LSTA Grants Manager
anne.yarbrough@sos.wa.gov
360-704-5246

Continuing Education Grants

Members of Washington State's Library Community who need financial assistance to attend or receive instruction (individuals) or provide a workshop (organizations) may be eligible for Continuing Education (CE) grants. A portion of the State Library's federal Library Services and Technology Act (LSTA) funds have been allocated specifically for supporting Continuing Education.

REQUIREMENTS AND RESTRICTIONS

Those eligible include:

Individuals: Librarians and all categories of support staff working ten or more hours per week (paid or volunteer) in a library or library consortia which is eligible to receive LSTA funds. Trustees, managers, and supervisors are eligible if benefit to the library's customers can be shown.

Organizations: Institutions whose primary role is to provide or support library and information services and who are eligible to receive LSTA funding may hire a trainer to present a CE event to their own staff or another group whose primarily duties are working in libraries. Organizations may also complete an application to cover multiple staffs' attendance at the same outside CE event that fits one or more of the seven national priorities.

APPLICATION PROCEDURES

Use the application appropriate to your situation and download. Mail your application to:

CE Grants Program
Washington State Library
PO Box 42460
Olympia, WA 98504-2460

Deadlines: Must be postmarked no later than 30 days prior (and preferably not more than 3 months prior) to the CE event

Information Technology Continuing Education (ITCE) Grants

Members of Washington State's library community who need financial assistance to attend to specific technical classes and other specialized courses not normally available to the library IT community may be eligible for Information Technology Continuing Education (ITCE) grants. Digital resources and information technology have become a crucial component in the delivery of information. The ITCE grants were created to provide up-to-date training for the Washington State's library community. Library Services and Technology Act (LSTA) funds will offset 50 percent of registration fees for the technical training of library and IT support staff.

Grant Amount: Individuals are limited to a total of $2,000 in grants per calendar year; grants to staff of any library system may not exceed a combined total of $4,000 for any calendar year.

REQUIREMENTS AND RESTRICTIONS

Eligibility for ITCE grants is limited to staff members of Washington State's LSTA-qualified libraries and IT staff who directly support these libraries a minimum of 10 hours per week.

APPLICATION PROCEDURES

Send application to the address below.

ITCE Grants Program
Washington State Library
PO Box 42460
Olympia, WA 98504-2460

Deadlines: Submit the signed original of your ITCE Grant Application form plus one copy, postmarked no later than 30 days prior (and preferably not more than 3 months prior) to the ITCE event.

Weinberg, Harry and Jeanette Foundation, Inc.

Headquarters

7 Park Center Ct.
Owings Mills, MD 21117-4200
Phone: 410-654-8500

www.hjweinbergfoundation.org

Contact: Rachel Garbow Monroe, C.O.O.

E-mail: info@theweinbergfoundation.org

Type of Grant Maker: Foundation

Description

Founded: 1959

Operating Locations/Geographic Preferences: Giving nationally, primarily in MD, HI, northeast PA, NY, and internationally to Israel and the Former Soviet Union

Financial Summary

Assets: $2,072,697,349
Total Giving: $86,059,465
Number of Grants; 620
Grant Ranges: $3,390,000–$250

Grants Information

GRANT TYPES

General and operating support, building and renovation, capital campaigns, matching

TYPICAL RECIPIENTS/SUBJECTS OF INTEREST

Giving Programs include:

Baltimore Weinberg Fellows Program

Basic Human Needs

Disabilities

Education, Children, Youth and Families, supporting
Early childhood education
K–12 education
Out of school time—at-risk population
Family safety and development

General Community Support: supporting some types of Jewish causes/issues and community development in low-income neighborhoods.

Israel Mission Alumni Scholars

Maryland Small Grants Program: For qualified non-profit organizations

Older Adults

Workforce Development

PAST GRANT RECIPIENTS

Library or School Related

- SEED Foundation, Washington (DC), to support site acquisition, design and construction for SEED School of MD, $1,000,000

General

- Resources for Human Development, Philadelphia (PA), to support pilot program to match the homeless with jobs, $50,000
- YWCA of the Greater Baltimore Area, Baltimore (MD), to support services for females, $40,000

REQUIREMENTS AND RESTRICTIONS

No support for political organizations, colleges, universities, think tanks, or for arts organizations. No grants to individuals, or for deficit financing, annual giving, publications or for scholarships.

APPLICATION PROCEDURES

See website for guidelines. Initial inquires must be submission of letter of inquiry.

Deadlines: None

Weingart Foundation

Headquarters

1055 W. 7th St., Ste. 3050
Los Angeles, CA 90017-2305

Phone: 213-688-7799

Fax: 213-688-1515

www.weingartfnd.org

Contact: Fred J. Ali, C.E.O. and Pres.

E-mail: info@weingartfnd.org

Type of Grant Maker: Foundation

Description

Founded: 1951

Operating Locations/Geographic Preferences: Giving limited to 7 southern CA counties: Los Angeles, Orange, Santa Barbara, Riverside, San Bernardino, Ventura and San Diego

Financial Summary

Assets: $718,445,607

Total Giving: $33,378,659

Number of Grants: 670

Grant Ranges: highest $750,000

Grants Information

GRANT TYPES

General and operating support, program development, seed money, building and renovation, investments and loans, capital campaigns, matching, investments and loans, management development

TYPICAL RECIPIENTS/SUBJECTS OF INTEREST

Past Grant Recipients

Community and social services, education, health care with emphasis on programs for children and youth

General

- Exceptional Children's Foundation, Culver City (CA), for capital support for repairs to headquarter facility, $75,000
- Community of Friends, Los Angeles (CA), for core support, $200,000
- Century Villages at Cabrillo, Culver City (CA), for capital support to construct Family Shelter Project, $200,000
- Serving People in Need, Costa Mesa (CA), for core support, $100,000

REQUIREMENTS AND RESTRICTIONS

No support for religious programs, political refugee or international concerns, federated fund-raising groups, or national organizations that do not have chapters operating in Southern California. No grants to individuals, or for endowment funds, annual campaigns, emergency funds, deficit financing, fellowships, seminars, conferences, publications, workshops, travel, surveys, films, medical research, or publishing activities.

APPLICATION PROCEDURES

See website for application criteria and form.

Deadlines: See website

Wells Fargo Foundation

Headquarters

1800 Central Pk. E., 12th Fl.

Los Angeles, CA 90067-3033

www.wellsfargo.com/donations

Contact: Timothy G. Hanlon, Pres.

E-mail: thanlon@wellsfargo.com

Type of Grant Maker: Corporate Foundation

Description

Founded: 1979

Operating Locations/Geographic Preferences: Giving primarily in areas of company operations (see online map for locations)

Corporate Foundation Information: Supported by:

- Norwest Corp
- Wells Fargo & Co.
- Norwest Ltd.

Financial Summary

Assets: $657,954,906

Total Giving: $96,423,419

Grants Information

GRANT TYPES

Program development, continuing, general and operating support, annual campaigns, management development, employee volunteering

TYPICAL RECIPIENTS/SUBJECTS OF INTEREST

Education, job creation and job training, housing, financial literacy, human services, and community economic development.

PAST GRANT RECIPIENTS

Library or School Related

- University of Nevada Reno Foundation, Reno (NV), $2,300

General

- Habitat for Humanity International, Americus (GA), $2,250,000
- Exploratorium, San Francisco (CA), $500,000
- New Economics for Women, Los Angeles (CA), $250,000

REQUIREMENTS AND RESTRICTIONS

No support for religious organizations not of direct benefit to the entire community, lobbying organizations, or fraternal organizations. No grants to individuals, or for political campaigns, advertising purchases including booths and tickets, fund-raising dinners, video or film production, club memberships, or endowments.

APPLICATION PROCEDURES

See website for procedures.

Deadlines: Vary

Western North Carolina Community Foundation, Inc.

Headquarters

The BB&T Bldg., Ste. 1600
1 W. Pack Sq., PO Box 1888
Asheville, NC 28802-1888
Phone: 828-254-4960

www.cfwnc.org

Contact: Virginia Dollar, Prog. Admin.

E-mail: dollar@cfwnc.org

Type of Grant Maker: Community Foundation

Description

Founded: 1978

Operating Locations/Geographic Preferences: Giving limited to Avery, Buncombe, Burke, Cherokee, Clay, Graham, Haywood, Henderson, Jackson, Macon, Madison, McDowell, Mitchell, Polk, Rutherford, Swain, Transylvania, and Yancey counties, NC

Financial Summary

Assets: $144,534,145
Total Giving: $10,863,115
Number of Grants: 273

Grants Information

GRANT TYPES

Program development, endowments, matching, management development, equipment

TYPICAL RECIPIENTS/SUBJECTS OF INTEREST

Giving Programs include:

Asheville Merchants Fund Grants: Supporting economic growth and improve quality of life in Buncombe County.

Biltmore Lakes Charitable Fund Grants: Supporting projects in the Enka-Candler area.

Capacity Grants: For nonprofit organizations

Learning Links Grants: Supporting public schools in Avery, Graham, Jackson, Madison, Mitchell, Polk, Rutherford and Swain counties.

Melvin R. Lane Fund Grants: Supporting organizational development and collaborative approaches for human service nonprofits.

Pigeon River Fund Grants: Providing grants of up to $25,000 to nonprofits in Haywood, Madison and Buncombe counties that are working to improve water quality.

Ramble Charitable Fund Grants: Supporting projects in southern Buncombe communities.

Scholarships

Summertime Kids Grants: Supporting organizations in the region that provide disadvantaged children with enriching summer activities.

Women for Women Grants: Offering grants of up to $100,000 to improve the lives of less fortunate women and girls in the region.

PAST GRANT RECIPIENTS

Library or School Related

- Veritas Christian Academy, Fletcher (NC), for Land Acquisition Fund, $268,000
- All Hallows High School, Bronx (NY), for scholarships, $2,000

General

- North Carolina Arboretum Society, Asheville (NC), for Bent Creek Institute, $50,000
- Black Mountain Pastoral Care and Counseling Center, Black Mountain (NC), $8,000

REQUIREMENTS AND RESTRICTIONS

No support for religious organizations or sectarian purposes (except from designated funds). No grants to individuals or for capital campaigns, endowment funds, start-up funds, or debt retirement.

APPLICATION PROCEDURES

See website for application guidelines.

Deadlines: Vary

WHO (Women Helping Others) Inc.

Headquarters

c/o W.H.O. Foundation
2121 Midway Rd.
Carrollton, TX 75006-5039
Phone: 972-341-3080

www.whofoundation.org

Contact: Cindy Turek, Exec. Dir.

E-mail: who@beauticontrol.com

Type of Grant Maker: Foundation

Description

Founded: 1993

Operating Locations/Geographic Preferences: United States and Puerto Rico

Financial Summary

Assets: $379,370
Total Giving: $354,300
Grant Ranges: $40,000–$1,000

Grants Information

GRANT TYPES

Program development, building and renovation, general and operating support

TYPICAL RECIPIENTS/SUBJECTS OF INTEREST

Women and children, especially addressing health, education, and social service needs. Also of interest to the foundation are free after-school and literacy programs.

PAST GRANT RECIPIENTS

Library or School Related

- Single Parent Scholarship fund of Northwest Arkansas, Fayetteville (AR), for low-income scholarships for mothers, $22,500

General

- Youth on Their Own, Tucson (AR), for gradation support for homeless youth, $15,000
- Military Women in Need, Los Angeles (CA), for resources for female veterans, $20,000

REQUIREMENTS AND RESTRICTIONS

No support for religious organizations, educational institutions, political causes or campaigns, endowment funds, sports organizations, or foundations that are grant-making institutions. No grants for salaries, specific events, galas, conferences, personal request loans, or scholarships.

APPLICATION PROCEDURES

Download application form. Applicants should submit:

1. Copy of IRS Determination Letter
2. Brief history of organization and description of its mission
3. Copy of most recent annual report/audited financial statement/990
4. Listing of board of directors, trustees, officers and other key people and their affiliations
5. Copy of current year's organizational budget and/or project budget

Deadline: Second Tuesday in September

Widgeon Foundation, Inc.

Headquarters

PO Box 278
Wye Mills, MD 21679-0278
Fax: 410-827-8081
Contact: Richard Robinson, Pres.
Type of Grant Maker: Foundation

Description

Founded: 1963
Operating Locations/Geographic Preferences: Giving on a national basis.

Financial Summary

Assets: $2,813,860
Total Giving: $232,335
Number of Grants: 31
Grant Ranges: $29,791–$450

Grants Information

GRANT TYPES

Program development, building and renovation, continuing support, conferences, equipment, seed money

TYPICAL RECIPIENTS/SUBJECTS OF INTEREST

Medical and educational organizations

PAST GRANT RECIPIENTS

Library or School Related

- Indiana University, Indianapolis (IN), $13,700
- Virginia Tech, Blacksburg (VA), $15,300
- Wright State University, Dayton (OH), $13,600
- University of Pittsburgh, Pittsburgh (PA), $29,700

General

- Smithsonian Institution, Washington (DC), $30,000
- Center for Child Protection, Austin (TX), $20,000

REQUIREMENTS AND RESTRICTIONS

No support for supporting organizations or to individuals.

APPLICATION PROCEDURES

Send letter
Deadlines: None

Wiegand, E. L. Foundation

Headquarters

Wiegand Ctr.
165 W. Liberty St., Ste. 200
Reno, NV 89501-2902
Phone: 775-333-0310, ext. 112
Fax: 775-333-0314
Contact: Kristen A. Avansino, Pres. and Exec. Dir.
Type of Grant Maker: Foundation

Description

Founded: 1982
Operating Locations/Geographic Preferences: Giving primarily in NV and adjoining western states, including AZ, ID, OR, UT and WA; public affairs grants given primarily in Washington, DC, and New York, NY.

Financial Summary

Assets: $118,934,457
Total Giving: $1,775,339
Number of Grants: 37
Grant Ranges: $250,000–$500

Grants Information

GRANT TYPES

Program development, building and renovation, equipment

TYPICAL RECIPIENTS/SUBJECTS OF INTEREST

Educational institutions in the academic areas of science, business, fine arts, law, and medicine
Health institutions in the areas of heart, eye, and cancer surgery, treatment and research, with priority given to programs and projects that benefit children
Emphasis on Roman Catholic institutions

PAST GRANT RECIPIENTS

Library or School Related

- Saint Olaf Catholic School Library/Media, Bountiful (UT), $87,700
- Our Lady of the Snows, Reno (NV), Classroom school additions, $1,000,000
- Creighton University, Omaha (NE), for pediatric simulation equipment, $340,433

General

- Nevada Museum of Art, Reno (NV), for Cowboy Poetry exhibit, $256,000
- Magic Valley Arts Council, Twin Fall (ID), Equipment and furnishings, $110,000

REQUIREMENTS AND RESTRICTIONS

No support for organizations receiving significant support from the United Way or public tax funds or federal, state, or local government agencies or institutions. No grants to individuals, or for endowment funds, fund-raising campaigns, debt reductions, emergency funding, film or media presentations, operating funds or loans.

APPLICATION PROCEDURES

An informational booklet outlining the Foundation's grant criteria is available upon request for organizations within geographic areas served. After reviewing the booklet, prospective applicants should submit a Letter of Inquiry that briefly describes the organization and the proposed request. The Letter of Inquiry is reviewed by staff to determine if the proposal warrants further consideration by the Foundation. If, after staff consideration, it is determined that the proposal warrants further review, a numbered Application for Grant form is forwarded to the applicant. The applicant completes the application in accordance with instructions included in the informational booklet and returns it to the Foundation for more detailed consideration. Applicants are notified of specific submission deadlines upon receipt of an Applicant for Grant form.

Deadlines: None

Wild Ones Natural Landscapers, Inc.

Headquarters

PO Box 1274
Appleton, WI 54912-1274
Phone: 920-730-3986

www.for-wild.org

E-mail: info@for-wild.org

Type of Grant Maker: Foundation

Description

Founded: 1979 (Seeds for Education founded 1996)

Operating Locations/Geographic Preferences: National giving

Financial Summary

Assets: $1,085,333

Grants Information

GRANT TYPES

Program development

TYPICAL RECIPIENTS/SUBJECTS OF INTEREST

The Lorrie Otto Seeds for Education Grant Program gives small monetary grants to schools, nature centers, and other nonprofit and not-for-profit places of learning in the United States with a site available for a stewardship project. Successful nonschool applicants often are a partnership between a youth group (scouts, 4-H, etc.) and a site owner. Libraries, government agencies and houses of worship are eligible subject to youth participation.

Established by Wild Ones in 1996, the Seeds for Education (SFE) Program honor the late Lorrie Otto, our "philosophical compass." Money for the grant program comes from donations from Wild Ones members, chapters and other benefactors.

Examples of appropriate projects are:

- Wildflower gardens with habitat for butterflies or other pollinators
- Rainwater gardens that capture run-off and feature native plant communities
- Groves of trees or native shrubs that support birds and other wildlife

Larger-scale projects that may receive funding include:

- Design, establishment and maintenance of a native-plant community such as prairie, woodland, wetland, etc., in an educational setting such as an outdoor classroom.
- Developing and maintaining an interpretive trail landscaped with native plant communities.
- Developing a wetland area to study the effect of native vegetation on water-quality improvement.

Cash awards range from $100 to $500. Funds are restricted to the purchase of native plants and seed for the grant-award year.

PAST GRANT RECIPIENTS

Library or School Related

- North Shore Community School, Duluth (MN), for Rain Garden Swale Planting, $300
- Wauwatosa West High School, Wauwatosa (WI), for Tosa Prairies and Woodlands, $300

General

- Winnemucca Community Garden, Winnemucca (NV), for Nevada Basin and Range Plant Demonstration, $300
- River Revitalization Foundation, Milwaukee (WI), for Brown Deer Riparian Woodland Restoration Project, $210

REQUIREMENTS AND RESTRICTIONS

Project goals should focus on enhancement and development of an appreciation for nature using native plants. Projects must emphasize involvement of students and volunteers in all phases of development, and increase the educational value of the site. Creativity in design is encouraged, but must show complete and thoughtful planning. The use of, and teaching about, native plants and the native plant community is mandatory, and the native plants must be appropriate to the local ecoregion and the site conditions (soil, water, sunlight). The Project Coordinator should be knowledgeable and committed.

APPLICATION PROCEDURES

To be considered for the annual award, applicants must submit an electronic application

Deadline: October 15 of the year prior to the grant year.

Wildermuth, E. F. Foundation

Headquarters

1014 Dublin Rd.
Columbus, OH 43215-1116
Phone: 614-487-0040

Contact: Robert W. Lee, Treas.

Type of Grant Maker: Foundation

Description

Founded: 1962

Operating Locations/Geographic Preferences: Giving primarily in OH and contiguous states

Financial Summary

Assets: $4,382,015
Total Giving: $194,031
Number of Grants: 14
Grant Ranges: $50,000–$1,000

Grants Information

GRANT TYPES

General support

TYPICAL RECIPIENTS/SUBJECTS OF INTEREST

Higher education, including optometry programs at colleges and universities, human services, children's hospitals

PAST GRANT RECIPIENTS

Library or School Related

- Ohioana Library, Columbus (OH), $2,500
- Indiana University, Bloomington (IN), $5,000

General

- Wildermuth Memorial Church, Carroll (OH), $51,000
- OhioHealth Foundation, Columbus (OH), $17,000
- Ballet Metropolitan, Columbus (OH), $10,000

REQUIREMENTS AND RESTRICTIONS

No grants to individuals.

APPLICATION PROCEDURES

No form required. Send proof of tax-exempt status.

Deadline: July 1

Wilson, Anne Potter Foundation

Headquarters

c/o Bank of America, N.A.
231 S. LaSalle St., IL1-231-10-05
Chicago, IL 60697-1411

Type of Grant Maker: Foundation

Description

Founded: 1996

Operating Locations/Geographic Preferences: Giving primarily in Nashville, TN

Financial Summary

Assets: $20,189,754
Total Giving: $854,876
Number of Grants: 17
Grant Ranges: $393,876–$5,000

Grants Information

GRANT TYPES

General support

TYPICAL RECIPIENTS/SUBJECTS OF INTEREST

Education and human services

PAST GRANT RECIPIENTS

Library or School Related

- Vanderbilt University, Nashville (TN), $394,000
- Montgomery Bell Academy, Nashville (TN), $15,000
- Tennessee Charter School, Nashville (TN), $5,000
- East End Prep Charter School, Nashville (TN), $50,000

General

- Cumberland Trail Conference, Crossville (TN), $135,000

REQUIREMENTS AND RESTRICTIONS

No grants to individuals.

APPLICATION PROCEDURES

Send letter.

Deadlines: None

Wilson, H. W. Foundation, Inc.

Headquarters

950 University Ave.
Bronx, NY 10452-4224
Phone: 718-588-8400

Contact: William E. Stanton, Pres.

Type of Grant Maker: Foundation

Description

Founded: 1952

Operating Locations/Geographic Preferences: National giving

Financial Summary

Assets: $14,441,442
Total Giving: $645,473

Grants Information

GRANT TYPES

General support

TYPICAL RECIPIENTS/SUBJECTS OF INTEREST

Accredited library schools for scholarships, cultural programs, historical societies, and library associations

PAST GRANT RECIPIENTS

Library or School Related

- American Library Association, Chicago (IL), $50,000
- Boston Public Library, Boston (MA), $20,000
- Sweet Briar College, Sweet Briar (VA), $30,275
- ARK Link Library Consortium Inc., $21,000
- Central New Jersey Regional Library Cooperative, $25,000
- Special Library Association, $6,000
- Stanford Free Library, $5,000
- Rockland Community College, $12,000
- New York Public Library, $7,000
- San Francisco Public Library, $5,000
- Simmons College, $10,000

REQUIREMENTS AND RESTRICTIONS

No grants for building or endowment funds or operating budgets

APPLICATION PROCEDURES

Send a description of the organization (library) and proposed use of proceeds to:

William Stanton
950 University Ave.
Bronx, NY 10452
718-588-8400

Deadlines: None

Windgate Charitable Foundation, Inc.

Headquarters

PO Box 826
Siloam Springs, AR 72761-0826
Phone: 479-524-9829

Contact: John E. Brown, III, Exec. Dir.

Type of Grant Maker: Foundation

Description

Founded: 1993

Operating Locations/Geographic Preference: Giving on a national basis with emphasis on the Midwest and Southwest

Financial Summary

Assets: $90,821,442
Total Giving: $20,992,049
Number of Grants 277
Grant Ranges: $2,543,032–$158; average: $1,500–$100,000

Grants Information

GRANT TYPES

Program development, matching

TYPICAL RECIPIENTS/SUBJECTS OF INTEREST

Art and craft education, marriage and family relationships. Focus on programs that serve children and Christian higher education.

PAST GRANT RECIPIENTS

Library or School Related

- Bard Graduate Center for Studies in the Decorative Arts, Design and Culture, New York (NY), $26,000
- George Fox University, Newberg (OR), for Marriage and Family Relationship, $2,500
- Penland School of Crafts, Penland (NC), for Resident Artist Program, $2,500,000
- John Brown University, Siloam Springs (AR), for Dr. Gary Oliver Endowed Chair, $1,000,000

General

- Fort Smith Art Center, fort Smith (AR), for Art Center Renovation Project, $500,000

REQUIREMENTS AND RESTRICTIONS

No support for private religious schools or churches. No grants to individuals, or for undesignated annual funds, debt retirement, completed projects, or group travel for performance or competition.

APPLICATION PROCEDURES

Applicants should submit a two-page letter with:

1. Copy of IRS Determination Letter
2. Brief history of organization and description of its mission
3. Copy of most recent annual report/audited financial statement/990
4. Listing of board of directors, trustees, officers and other key people and their affiliations
5. Detailed description of project and amount of funding requested
6. Copy of current year's organizational budget and/or project budget

Deadlines: None

Wisconsin Department of Public Instruction Division for Libraries and Technology

Headquarters

State Superintendent of Public Instruction
125 S. Webster Street
PO Box 7841
Madison, WI 53707-7841
Phone: 800-441-4563

http://pld.dpi.wi.gov/pld_lsta

Type of Grant Maker: Government

Grants Information

LSTA GRANTS

The Library Services and Technology Act (LSTA) is the federal grant program for libraries in Wisconsin. The Wisconsin Department of Public Instruction's Division for Libraries and Technology implements the "Grants to States" program on behalf of public libraries in Wisconsin. The LSTA program is administered at the federal level by the Institute of Museum and Library Services (IMLS). The program builds on the strengths of the LSTA program but sharpens the focus on technology, resource sharing, and targeted services.

REQUIREMENTS AND RESTRICTIONS

Eligible organizations are listed with each grant category. Some LSTA categories are restricted to certain libraries or organizations.

APPLICATION PROCEDURES

Grant application forms and the LSTA Information and Guidelines for Wisconsin are found on the DPI Public Library Development website listed under LSTA (dpi.wi.gov/pld/lsta.html).

Applicants must use the LSTA online application form that will be available on the DPI website.

For more information, contact:

Terri Howe
LSTA, Public Librarian Certification and Continuing
    Education
608-266-2413
teresa.howe@dpi.wi.gov

Deadline: September 16

Wish You Well Foundation

Headquarters

12359 Sunrise Valley Drive, Suite 360
Reston, VA 20191
Phone: 703-476-6032

www.wishyouwellfoundation.org/founders/

E-mail: info@wishyouwellfoundation.org

Description

Operating Locations/Geographic Preferences: None stated

Financial Summary

Grant Ranges: $10,000–$200

TYPICAL RECIPIENTS/SUBJECTS OF INTEREST

Family literacy in the United States and development and expansion of new and existing literacy and educational programs

PAST GRANT RECIPIENTS

Library or School Related

- Fairfax County Public Library Foundation, Inc., Fairfax, (VA)

General

- Book Buddies, Charlottesville (VA), for tutorial program that supports reading instruction in the classroom
- Catherine McCauley Center, Inc., Cedar Rapids (IA), for free adult English language education for immigrants and refugees
- Children's Literacy Foundation, Waterbury Center (VT)

REQUIREMENTS AND RESTRICTIONS

No support to individuals, candidates for political office, building or construction projects, debt reduction, capital campaigns or research.

APPLICATION PROCEDURES

Application form available for download. Information should include:

- Organization's history, mission, and contact information
- Amount requested
- Program or event to be funded.

Deadline: None

Wood-Claeyssens Foundation

Headquarters

PO Box 30586
Santa Barbara, CA 93130-0586

www.woodclaeyssensfoundation.com

Contact: Noelle Claeyssens Burkey, Pres.

E-mail: wcf0543@gmail.com

Type of Grant Maker: Foundation

Description

Founded: 1980

Operating Locations/Geographic Preferences: Giving limited to Santa Barbara and Ventura counties, CA

Financial Summary

Assets: $149,384,745
Total Giving: $15,415,667
Number of Grants: 330
Grant Ranges: $1,000,000–$1,000; average:
    $10,000–$100,000

Grants Information

GRANT TYPES

General, operating and continuing support, annual campaigns, building and renovation, capital campaigns

TYPICAL RECIPIENTS/SUBJECTS OF INTEREST

Education, housing, youth, health care and the arts

PAST GRANT RECIPIENTS

General

- Youth Connection of Ventura County, Camarillo (CA), $366,000
- California Association of Resource Specialists, Roseville (CA), $184,000
- YMCA, Simi Valley Family, Simi Valley (CA), for child care center renovations and computers, $26,000
- Girls Inc. of Carpinteria, Carpinteria (CA), for after-school programs, $25,000
- New West Symphony, Thousand Oaks (CA), for Masterpieces Series Concerts and music education, $20,000

REQUIREMENTS AND RESTRICTIONS

No support for tax-supported educational institutions, government-funded organizations, religious or political organizations, or for medical research. No grants to individuals.

APPLICATION PROCEDURES

Application form required. See website.

Deadlines: June 30

Wyoming Community Foundation

Headquarters

313 S. 2nd St.
Laramie, WY 82070-3611
Phone: 307-721-8300
Fax: 307-721-8333

www.wycf.org

Contact: For grants: Samin Dadelahi Sr., Sr. Prog. Off.

E-mail: wcf@wycf.org

Type of Grant Maker: Community Foundation

Description

Founded: 1989

Operating Locations/Geographic Preferences: Giving primarily in WY

Financial Summary

Assets: $70,948,399
Total Giving: $2,513,775
Number of Grants: 144

Grants Information

GRANT TYPES

Program development, conferences/seminars, continuing, general and operating support, management development, matching, seed money, technical assistance

TYPICAL RECIPIENTS/SUBJECTS OF INTEREST

Current statewide areas of need from the foundation's unrestricted funds are children and youth and civic projects

PAST GRANT RECIPIENTS

Library or School Related

- Natrona County Public Library Foundation, Casper (WY), $6,700 and $6,500
- Niobrara Community Library Foundation, $26,000 and $11,000
- Sue Jorgensen Library Hued, Laramie (WY), $7,500
- Northern Wyoming Community College Foundation, Sheridan (WY), $30,000
- Sweetwater One Public School Foundation, Rock Springs (WY), $15,000

General

- Buffalo Bill Historical Center, Cody (WY), $50,000
- Cheyenne Botanic Garden, Cheyenne (WY), $50,000
- Green River Valley Land Trust, Pinedale (WY), $50,000
- YMCA of Sheridan County, Sheridan (WY), $50,000

REQUIREMENTS AND RESTRICTIONS

No grants to individuals or generally for block grants, capital campaigns, annual campaigns, or debt retirement.

APPLICATION PROCEDURES

Online application required. See website.

Deadlines: March 1, July 1, and November 1

Yawkey Foundation II

Headquarters

990 Washington St., Ste. 315
Dedham, MA 02026-6716
Phone: 781-329-7470
www.yawkeyfoundation.org
Contact: Nancy Keilty-Brodnicki
Type of Grant Maker: Foundation

Description

Founded: 1983

Operating Locations/Geographic Preferences: Giving primarily in MA, with emphasis on the greater metropolitan Boston area

Financial Summary

Assets: $411,004,678
Total Giving: $26,114,350
Number of Grants: 218
Grant Ranges: $3,000,000–$1,500

Grants Information

GRANT TYPES

Program development, general support

TYPICAL RECIPIENTS/SUBJECTS OF INTEREST

Giving programs include:

- Arts and Culture
- Conservation
- Education
- Health Care
- Human Services
- Youth and Amateur Athletics

PAST GRANT RECIPIENTS

Library or School Related

- Fund for Catholic Schools, Boston (MA), for renovation and support of Pope John Paul II Academy and youth center serving inner-city students, $4,000,000
- Emmanuel College, Boston (MA), for athletic field improvements, $1,000,000

- Esperanza Academy, Lawrence (MA), for scholarship program for disadvantaged students, $25,000

General

- Children's Museum Fund, Boston (MA), for renovation of museum space, $1,000,000
- Isabella Stewart Gardner Museum, Boston (MA), for education and access programs for children, $25,000

REQUIREMENTS AND RESTRICTIONS

No support for private foundations, political, fraternal, trade, civic or labor organizations, religious organizations for sectarian purposes, public schools or districts, charter schools, community or economic development corporations or programs, advocacy groups, pass-through or intermediary organizations, or workforce development programs. No grants to individuals. No grants for operating deficits, retirement of debt, endowments, capital campaigns, events, conferences, seminars, group travel, awards, prizes, monuments, music, video, or film production, feasibility or research studies.

APPLICATION PROCEDURES

See website for grant guidelines. Applicants should submit:

1. Population served
2. Copy of IRS Determination Letter
3. Brief history of organization and description of its mission
4. How project's results will be evaluated or measured
5. Detailed description of project and amount of funding requested
6. Copy of current year's organizational budget and/or project budget
7. Listing of additional sources and amount of support

Deadlines

- March 1 for Arts and Culture, Conservation, and Health Care
- June 15 for Human Services
- September 1 for Education
- November 15 for Youth and Amateur Athletics

Zarrow, Anne and Henry Foundation

Headquarters

401 S. Boston Ave., Ste. 900
Tulsa, OK 74103-4012
Phone: 918-295-8004

www.zarrow.com/ahz.htm

Contact: Bill Major, Exec. Dir.

E-mail: Bmajor@zarrow.com

Type of Grant Maker: Foundation

Description

Founded: 1986

Operating Locations/Geographic Preferences: Giving primarily in the Tulsa, OK, area

Financial Summary

Assets: $94,522,168
Total Giving: $7,396,616
Number of Grants: 481
Grant Ranges: $1,000,000–$150

Grants Information

GRANT TYPES

General and operating support, annual campaigns

TYPICAL RECIPIENTS/SUBJECTS OF INTEREST

Education, social services, Jewish causes, health programs, medical research and mental health programs

PAST GRANT RECIPIENTS

Library or School Related

- University of Tulsa, Tulsa (OK), to help build a research building on the grounds of Gilcrease Museum, $1,000,000
- Saint Gregory's University, Shawnee (OK), for operating funds, $150,000

General

- Jasmine Moran Children's Museum Foundation, Seminole (OK), for operating costs, $5,000
- Center for Individuals with Physical Challenges, Tulsa (OK), for operating grant, $12,000

REQUIREMENTS AND RESTRICTIONS

No grants to individuals.

APPLICATION PROCEDURES

See website for application information and guidelines.

Deadlines: January 15, April 15, August 15, and October 15 for grants.

GRANT-RELATED ORGANIZATIONS AND RESOURCES

The list of Grant-Related Organizations and Resources provides the next step for grant seekers. And it is hoped there will be a next step. Few seekers of library money have as their goal to *identify* grant sources. Rather, the goal is to *obtain* grant funding by submitting a successful proposal.

For those overwhelmed by the idea of actually developing the grant proposal (and who isn't?), finding a grant writer may be the step that comes next. Resources listed under library grant writers or grant professional associations may be helpful for this purpose. Library grant writers includes consultants that have indicated a specialty in library grants. Another source of grant writers is the listings under grant professional associations. Many of these groups maintain listings of or referrals to grant writers.

Updating and verifying grants information, which was encouraged in the introduction, is another next step to securing grant funding. Consulting the sources under grant databases or Fund-Raising/Donor/Nonprofit Organization Associations will enable the grant seeker to make sure the information about grant opportunities and funding sources is current and accurate.

For some, taking a grant development class may be helpful before attempting to craft a grant request. For them, resources will be found under Grant Training/Workshops.

Those lucky enough to land a grant may want to use the Grant Software or Grant Evaluation resources to administer and/or evaluate the project.

Finally, those who want to learn more about the world of grants in general are encouraged to consult Grant Publications for useful sources to consult.

Inclusion, Exclusion, and Method of Compilation

Several sources were used to compile these listings, but inclusion or exclusion should in no way be seen as an endorsement or lack of same from the American Library Association or the editor of this publication.

The goal of this list of resources is to provide a starting point for library grant seekers. Care was taken to include the major sources for each category. However, invariably some excellent sources have been overlooked. Likewise, it is possible some less-than-helpful resources may have been included here.

Among the major sources consulted for this compilation were the American Library Association, the Grant Professionals Association, nonprofit organizational resources, literature reviews, and consultation with key grant professionals. The categories included for each resource are intended to reflect the predominant activity or activities for each, but should not be assumed to be comprehensive or exclusive. Some organizations may engage in activities that are not noted, while others may have been incorrectly omitted from certain categories.

As much as possible, the information provided here is the most current information that could be located. However, as with all of the information in this publication, updating and verifying is mandatory.

CATEGORIES

Fund-Raising/Donor/Nonprofit Organization Associations
    Grant Databases
Grant Evaluation

Grant Professionals Associations
Grant Publications
Grant Software
Grant Training/Workshops
Library Grant Writers

American Evaluation Association

Headquarters

16 Sconticut Neck Rd #290
Fairhaven MA 02719
Phone: 888-232-2275, 508-748-3326

info@eval.org

www.eval.org

Operating Locations: AEA has approximately 7,300 members representing all 50 states in the United States as well as over 60 foreign countries.

Description

The American Evaluation Association is an international professional association of evaluators devoted to the application and exploration of program evaluation, personnel evaluation, technology, and many other forms of evaluation. Evaluation involves assessing the strengths and weaknesses of programs, policies, personnel, products, and organizations to improve their effectiveness.

CATEGORIES

Grant Evaluation
Grant Professionals Association

American Funding Innovators (AFI)

Headquarters

AFI, Inc.
710 South Myrtle Blvd., #133
Monrovia, CA 91016
Phone: 800-580-7146

info@afisystems.com

www.afisystems.com/index.html

Description

AFI works within the grant community to solve complex problems with simple, innovative software solutions.

ONLINE PRODUCTS INCLUDE

GrantNavigator Premium, a comprehensive project management and reporting tool
GrantNavigator Express, a project-based grant tracking and communication tools
GrantNavigator Pre-Award, for direct access to federal funding information and communication and application tracking.

CATEGORIES

Grant Databases
Grant Software

Association of Fund-raising Professionals (AFP)

Headquarters

4300 Wilson Blvd, Suite 300
Arlington, VA 22203
Phone: 703-684-0410, 800-666-3863

afp@afpnet.org

www.afpnet.org

Operating Locations: Association of Fund-raising Professionals (AFP) represents more than 30,000 members in 230 chapters throughout the world.

Description

AFP works to advance philanthropy through advocacy, research, education and certification programs. The association fosters development and growth of fund-raising professionals and promotes high ethical standards in the fund-raising profession.

CATEGORIES

Grant Professionals Associations
Fund-Raising/Donor/Nonprofit Organization Associations

American Grant Writer's Association

Headquarters

AGWA
PO Box 8481
Seminole, FL 33775
Phone: 727-596-5150 or 727-366-9334

customerservice@agwa.us

www.agwa.us

Operating Locations

AGWA Regional Offices

Southern Office: Customer Service and Membership, Largo, Florida

Midwest Office: Member Newsletter, Dayton, Ohio

DESCRIPTION

Association's members work as grant consultants or employees of State or Local Government Agencies, institutions of Higher Education, Native Tribes, and Nonprofit Organizations throughout the United States. Promulgates AGWA's Professional Standards and Code of Ethics and offers online courses and workshops on grant researching, proposal writing, grant consulting, and grant management. Awards the Certified Grant Writer® Credential and holds an Annual Grant Conference.

CATEGORIES

Grant Professionals Association
Grant Training/Workshops

American Publishing Inc.

Headquarters

7025 County Road 46A, Suite 1071
Lake Mary, FL, 32746-4753
Phone: 800-610-4543
Fax: 877-722-4008

grantsinfonet@gmail.com

www.grantsinfo.us/index.html

DESCRIPTION

Produces American Grants and Loans Catalog and American Grants and Loans Database that provide information leading to financial help in the form of subsidies, grants, loans, joint ventures, or any funding program offered by the US government or private corporations.

CATEGORIES

Grant Databases
Grant Publications

Association of Small Foundations

Headquarters

1720 N St., NW
Washington, DC 20036
Phone: 888-212-9922, 202-580-6560

asf@smallfoundations.org

www.smallfoundations.org/about

DESCRIPTION

Association of Small Foundations (ASF) is a membership organization for donors, trustees, employees and consultants of foundations that have few or no staff. At ASF small relates to staff size, not to assets. Members range in assets from under $1 million to more than $50 million, with most member foundations operating with fewer than two paid staff and volunteers.

CATEGORIES

Grant Professionals Associations
Fund-Raising/Donor/Nonprofit Organization Associations

Bishoff (The) Group LLC

Headquarters

31157 Lewis Ridge Rd
Evergreen, CO 80439
Phone: 303-679-0201, 303-908-6736 (cell)

DESCRIPTION

Library consultant that provides library grant writing services. Other areas of expertise include digitization, facilitation, policy development, strategic planning, surveys, technology planning and training.

CATEGORIES

Library Grant Writers

Bolt, Nancy & Associates

Headquarters

9018 Ute Dr.
Golden, CO 80403
Phone: 303-642-0338, 303-905-9347 (cell)
Fax: 303-642-0392

nancybolt@earthlink.net

DESCRIPTION

Library consultant that provides library grant writing services and evaluation. Other areas of expertise include focus groups, management, needs assessment, planning for results, staff development, and team building.

CATEGORIES

Grant Evaluation
Library Grant Writers

CD Publications

Headquarters

8204 Fenton St.
Silver Spring, MD 20910
Phone: 301-588-6380, 800-666-6380
Fax: 301-588-6385

E-mail: See website

www.cdpublications.com/index.php

DESCRIPTION

CD Publications provides news and reporting from Congress, federal agencies, and communities across the country. The newsletters cover a wide range of key domestic issues, including housing, health care, children, seniors, minority business, community development, welfare, and education.

CATEGORY

Grant Publications

Chronicle of Philanthropy

Headquarters

1255 Twenty-Third St., N.W.
Seventh Floor
Washington, DC 20037
Phone: 202-466-1200

editor@philanthropy.com

http://philanthropy.com

DESCRIPTION

The *Chronicle of Philanthropy*, available in print and online, provides news and information to nonprofit leaders, fund-raisers, grant makers, and other people involved in the philanthropic enterprise. Areas covered include health, education, religion, the arts, social services, and other fields. Along with news, it offers lists of grants, fund-raising ideas and techniques, statistics, reports on tax and court rulings, summaries of books, and a calendar of events.

CATEGORY

Grant Publications

Cohen, Aaron Cohen Associates, LTD

Headquarters

159 Teatown Rd
Croton-on-Hudson, NY 10520
Phone: 914-271-8170, 914-271-2434 (cell)

aca2010@acohen.com

www.acohen.com

DESCRIPTION

Library consultant that provides library grant writing services and evaluation. Other areas of expertise include accessibility, archives and preservation, board development, communication development, community analysis and GIS, continuous improvement, facilitation, facilities planning, focus groups, fund-raising and development, management, needs assessment, organizational design, planning for results, program planning, staff development, strategic planning, surveys, team building, technology, and workflow analysis.

CATEGORIES

Grant Evaluation
Library Grant Writers

Council on Foundations

Headquarters

2121 Crystal Dr., Suite 700
Arlington, VA 22202
Phone: 800-673-9036

resrchdept@cof.org

www.cof.org

DESCRIPTION

The Council on Foundations is a national nonprofit association of more than 1,700 grant-making foundations and corporations. They serve community foundations, corporate grant makers, those in family and global giving and independent consultants. Programs and services cover the areas of legal and public policy information, professional development, career information, and conferences and seminars. Also publishes a variety of publications.

CATEGORIES

Fund-Raising/Donor/Nonprofit Organization Associations
Grant Professionals Associations
Grant Publications
Grant Training/Workshops

Cuesta MultiCultural Consulting

Headquarters

6648 Lake Park Dr.
Sacramento, CA 95831
Phone: 916-395-1688

yjcuesta@mindspring.com

DESCRIPTION

Library consultant that provides library grant writing services. Other areas of expertise include communication development, focus groups, Hispanic services, needs assessment, planning for results, program planning, staff development, and strategic planning.

CATEGORY

Library Grant Writers

E-Civis

Headquarters

418 N. Fair Oaks Ave., Suite 301
Pasadena, CA 91103
Phone: 877-232-4847
Fax: 626- 578-6632

info@ecivis.com

www.ecivis.com

BRANCH OFFICE

11044 Research Boulevard, Suite B-530
Austin, TX 78759

DESCRIPTION

eCivis Grants Network includes the products and services in the following areas:

Grants Network: Research—This suite provides professional research and review of all grant funding and uses the most sophisticated search engine to find grants.

Grants Network: KnowledgeBase—This suite provides professional online training and information to help organizations learn about grants at every stage of the grants lifecycle.

Grants Network: Tracking & Reporting—This suite is a grants management software solution designed to doctor down costs, improve efficiency, and provide transparency for grants organizations.

CATEGORIES

Grant Databases
Grant Software
Grant Training/Workshops

Foundation Center

Headquarters

Foundation Center
79 Fifth Avenue/16th St.
New York, NY 10003-3076
Phone: 212-620-4230, 800-424-9836

order@foundationcenter.org

http://foundationcenter.org

Operating Locations: Five regional library/learning centers and network of more than 450 funding information centers are located in public libraries, community foundations, and educational institutions nationwide and around the world.

DESCRIPTION

The Foundation Center provides information about philanthropy worldwide through data, analysis, and training. Supported by more than 500 foundations, the Center maintains databases on US and global foundations and donors and their grants. Operates Library/Learning Centers and Cooperating Collections and offers research, education, and training programs on philanthropy.

The Foundation Center produces several grants databases, directories and publications, including the Foundation Directory Online and Foundation Grants to Individuals Online, among others.

CATEGORIES

Grant Databases
Fund-Raising/Donor/Nonprofit Organization Associations
Grant Publications
Grant Training/Workshops

FundBook

Headquarters

1707 St., NW, Suite 560
Washington, DC, 20036
Phone: 202-643-0525

editor@fundbook.org

http://fundbook.org

FUNDBOOK PROJECT

2123 Maple Ave., Suite 2
Evanston, IL 60201

DESCRIPTION

FundBook is a nonpartisan, independent, privately held company that provides local leaders with free access to grants, loans, and other forms of federal assistance available to their communities. Organization also provides information on grant-related consultants.

CATEGORIES

Grant Databases
Grant Publications

Fund-raising Success

Headquarters

1500 Spring Garden St., 12th floor
Philadelphia, PA 19130
Phone: 888-889-9491

magazinecs@napco.com

www.fund-raisingsuccessmag.com

DESCRIPTION

Fund-raising Success provides nonprofit organizations information to raise money for and interest in their organizations' missions. Publications include monthly magazine, *Fund-raising Success,* covering topics such as: e-philanthropy, direct response, direct mail, annual appeals, capital campaigns, planned giving, special events, corporate fund-raising, major gifts, endowments, cause-related fund-raising, fund-raising software, and grants.

Organization also provides access to philanthropy and grant-related books, seminars, and other publications.

CATEGORY

Grant Publications

Grant Professionals Association

Headquarters

1333 Meadowlark Lane, Suite 105
Kansas City, KS 66102
Phone: 913-788-3000

info@grantprofessionals.org

http://grantprofessionals.org

Operating Locations: Group maintains network of local chapters, which can be found at http://grantprofessionals.org/about/chapters

DESCRIPTION

Grant Professionals Association (formerly American Association of Grant Professionals-AAGP), is a nonprofit membership association representing all aspects of the grant profession. GPA provides professional development, maintains a job service, holds an annual conference, publishes the *GPA Journal* (published semiannually), and sponsors a formal credentialing process. Grant Professional Certification Institute (GPCI), an affiliate organization, oversees the development of granstmanship standards.

MEMBERS INCLUDE

Grant proposal developers
Grant administrators and program managers
Directors of development
Program development directors and specialists
Grant-makers and funders
Proposal and program evaluators
Independent consultants
Grantsmanship trainers and other service provider
Executive directors and board members of public and
    private organizations

CATEGORIES

Grant Professionals Association
Grant Publications
Grant Training/Workshops

Grant-makers for Education

Headquarters

720 S.W. Washington St., Suite 605
Portland, OR 97205
Phone: 503-595-2100
Fax: 503-595-2102

information@edfunders.org

www.edfunders.org/about/index.asp

DESCRIPTION

Grant-makers for Education (GFE) is a membership organization for private and public philanthropies that support improved education outcomes for students from early childhood through higher education. GFE promotes dialogue, inquiry, and learning to strengthen practice within the field of education philanthropy, by enhancing grant-makers' knowledge about effective education strategies and effective grant-making strategies.

CATEGORY

Fund-Raising/Donor Association

Grants Managers Network

Headquarters

1666 K St., N.W., Suite 440
Washington, DC 20006
Phone: 888-GMN-1996
info@gmnetwork.org
gmnetwork.org

Operating Locations: GMN's regional networks offer educational and networking events to grants management professionals.

DESCRIPTION

GMN has 2,000 members from 1,200 grant-making organizations who represent the breadth of the philanthropic community, including small family foundations, national foundations, grant-making public charities, and socially responsible corporations.

Members span various titles, including grants administrators, grants managers, directors of grants management, financial officers, and program officers/

associates. The organization provides professional development, produces publications, holds an annual conference, and collaborates with grant makers and grant seekers to improve grant application and reporting practices.

CATEGORIES

Grant Professionals Association
Grant Publications
Grant Training/Workshops

Grantstation

Headquarters

GrantStation.com, Inc.
3677 College Road, Suite 11B
Fairbanks, Alaska 99709
Phone: 877-784-7268, 907-457-6601

info@grantstation.com

www.grantstation.com

DESCRIPTION

GrantStation is an online funding resource for organizations seeking grants. The searchable database provides access to private grant-makers, federal grants, links to state funding agencies, and a database of international grant-makers. In addition, GrantStation publishes two e-newsletters: the weekly *GrantStation Insider*, which focuses on opportunities for US nonprofit organizations; and the monthly *GrantStation International Insider*, which focuses on international funding opportunities.

CATEGORIES

Grant Databases
Grant Publications

Grantsmanship Center

Headquarters

Mailing Address
PO Box 17220
Los Angeles, CA 90017

Physical Address
350 South Bixel St., Suite 110
Los Angeles, CA 90017
Phone: 213-482-9860
info@tgci.com
www.tgci.com

Operating Locations: Trainings are held in various locations across the country.

DESCRIPTION

Grantsmanship Center offers more than 150 workshops annually in grantsmanship training and earned income strategies for nonprofits. The Center produces publications, an online database of funding sources, and daily grant announcements. The Center maintains an archive of *The Grantsmanship Center Magazine*, and indexes of funding sources at the local, federal and international levels.

CATEGORIES

Grant Databases
Grant Publications
Grant Training/Workshops

Grantwriting USA

Headquarters

Located in Las Vegas, but workshops are held in various locations.
Phone: 800-814-8191
cs@grantwritingusa.com
http://grantwritingusa.com

Operating Locations: Classes are held in a variety of locations. For a listing, see http://grantwritingusa.com/grants-training/grant-workshops-by-state/state.html.

DESCRIPTION

Grantwriting USA offers classes in grant writing that cover how to write grant proposals start to finish and how to locate and track relevant grant opportunities. Federal, state, local and nongovernmental, private-sector grants are covered. The grant management classes are available for government grant recipient organizations.

CATEGORY

Grant Training/Workshops

Guidestar

Headquarters

Two Locations

4801 Courthouse St., Suite 220
Williamsburg, VA 23188

1730 Pennsylvania N.W., Suite 250
Washington, DC 20006
Phone: 866-989-4511

libraryservices@guidestar.org

www.guidestar.org

DESCRIPTION

The goal of Guidestar is to revolutionize philanthropy and nonprofit practice by providing information that advances transparency, enables users to make better decisions, and encourages charitable giving.

Guidestar maintains a database where a nonprofit organization can update information about its mission, programs, leaders, goals, accomplishments, and needs for free. GuideStar also produces several products, including GuideStar for Libraries and GuideStar for Higher Education. A list of all services and products are available at www .guidestar.org/rxg/products/index.aspx.

CATEGORIES

Fund-Raising/Donor/Nonprofit Organization Associations
Grant Databases
Grant Publications

Kaliwell, Inc.

Headquarters

Nancy Kalikow Maxwell
Plantation, FL 33322
Phone: 954-260-7696

kaliwell@kaliwellinc.com

librarygrants.org, kaliwellinc.com

DESCRIPTION

Library consultant that provides library grant writing services and evaluation. Founder and President Nancy Kalikow Maxwell is the editor of this publication and the author of *Grant Money through Collaborative Partnerships* (ALA, 2102).

Kaliwell, Inc., specializes in library, education, and nonprofit organization grant development. Other areas of expertise include grant identification, proposal development, grant evaluation, program assessment, grant research, and grant writing.

CATEGORIES

Grant Evaluation
Library Grant Writers

Maack, Dr. Stephen C.

Headquarters

REAP Change Consultants
2872 Nicada Dr.
Los Angeles, CA 90077
Phone: 310-384-9717
Fax: 310-474-4161
consultant@reapchange.com
www.reapchange.com

DESCRIPTION

Library consultant that provides library grant writing services and evaluation. Other areas of expertise include community analysis and GIS, continuous improvement, facilitation, facilities planning, focus groups, needs assessment, organizational design, planning for results, strategic planning, and surveys.

CATEGORIES

Grant Evaluation
Library Grant Writers

Management Concepts

Headquarters

8230 Leesburg Pike
Tysons Corner, VA 22182
Phone: 888-545-8571

E-mail: See website
www.managementconcepts.com

DESCRIPTION

Management Concepts provides courses, organizational development, professional services, and publications to federal, state, and local agencies; associations; and nonprofit organizations. Management Concepts also offers consulting services and a certification program.

Course *topics include:*

- acquisition and contracting
- analytics
- business analysis
- federal financial management
- grants and assistance
- leadership
- professional skills
- project management

Publications cover topics such as:

- federal acquisition and contracting
- federal financial management
- federal travel
- leadership and management
- project management
- public administration

CATEGORIES

Grant Publications
Grant Training/Workshops

Metasoft Systems Inc.

Headquarters

300-353 Water St.
Vancouver, BC V6B 1B8
Canada
Phone: 604-683-6711, 888-638-2763
Fax: 604-683-6704 (Canadian Clients), 604-699-0071 (US Clients)

support@bigdatabase.com (customer support), info@ bigdatabase.com (general inquiries)

www.bigdatabase.com

DESCRIPTION

Source of fund-raising information, opportunities and resources for charities and nonprofits. Produces BIG Online database—comprehensive, keyword and field searchable database with detailed information and profiles on 25,000 foundations, corporate donors, matching gift programs, in-kind donations, and government grant-makers.

Also offers writing tools, including a step-by-step guide and templates for the writing of highly professional funding proposals and letters of inquiry and client support by assisting with product training, advice and direction for maximizing usage of the BIG Online database.

CATEGORIES

Grant Databases
Grant Training/Workshops

National Center for Charitable Statistics

Headquarters

The National Center for Charitable Statistics
The Urban Institute
2100 M St. NW, 5th Floor
Washington DC 20037
Phone: 866-518-3874
Fax: 202-833-6231

nccs@urban.org

http://nccs.urban.org

DESCRIPTION

NCCS is the national repository of data on the nonprofit sector in the United States. Its mission is to develop and disseminate high-quality data on nonprofit organizations and their activities for use in research on the relationships between the nonprofit sector, government, the commercial sector, and the broader civil society.

Working closely with the IRS and other government agencies, private sector service organizations, and the scholarly community, NCCS builds compatible national, state, and regional databases and develops uniform standards for reporting on the activities of charitable organizations.

NCCS's web tools offer more than 200 data files, including data on the finances and activities of nonprofit organizations going back as far as 1989 as well as the latest zip code–level giving data for households that itemize their IRS income tax forms, and much more.

CATEGORIES

Fund-Raising/Donor/Nonprofit Organization Associations
Grant Databases
Grant Publications

National Grants Management Association (NGMA)

Headquarters

2100 M St., NW, Suite 170
Washington, DC 20037
Phone: 202-308-9443

info@ngma.org

www.ngma.org

DESCRIPTION

Membership association for grants professionals to support high levels of grants management competency and establish standards of excellence for grants managers.

Organization provides grants management training, professional certification, continuing professional education, resources, and a forum for networking for grants industry professionals. NGMA serves all levels of government (federal, state, local, tribal), nonprofit organizations, foundations, institutions of higher education, and affiliated private sector organizations. Collectively, NGMA members are responsible for the management of billions of dollars in grants.

CATEGORIES

Grant Professionals Association
Grant Training/Workshops

Sage

Headquarters

6561 Irvine Center Dr.
Irvine, CA 92618-2301
Phone: 866-996-7243
E-mail: See website
www.sagegrantmanagement.com

DESCRIPTION

Sage Grant Management helps nonprofit and government organizations maximize funding potential and provide transparency at the organization, program, and grant levels. The web-based grant receiving solution combines development, contact, and financial data to improve grant pipeline oversight while optimizing success tracking.

CATEGORY

Grant Software

StreamLink Software

Headquarters

812 Huron Road, Suite 350
Cleveland, OH 44115
Phone: 866-423-1113, 216-377-5500
E-mail: See website
http://streamlinksoftware.com/

DESCRIPTION

StreamLink provides nonprofit organizations with web-based management software and helps solve different management challenges including board member and leadership volunteer management. Products are offered in the areas of board management, communications, and reporting.

CATEGORIES

Grant Software

TaxExemptWorld.com

Headquarters

Online only
www.taxexemptworld.com

DESCRIPTION

Provides an information service to search and download information on nonprofit/tax-exempt organizations (e.g., asset amounts, income amounts, EIN, form 990 PDF files, etc). Monthly and annual subscriptions are available for searching the database of all nonprofit/tax-exempt organizations.

CATEGORIES

Fund-Raising/Donor/Nonprofit Organization Associations
Grant Databases

Thompson Publishing Group

Headquarters

Customer Service Center
PO Box 26185
Tampa, FL 33623-6185
Phone: 800-677-3789

service@thompson.com

www.thompson.com

DESCRIPTION

Publisher of several grant-related publications, including *Grantswire, Guide to Federal Funding for Governments and Nonprofits*, and *Local/State Funding Report.*

CATEGORIES

Grant Databases
Grant Publications

Young Nonprofit Professionals

Headquarters

Group operates through local chapters.

E-mail: See website

http://ynpn.org/

Operating Locations: YNPN chapters operate across the country; currently numbering more than 30. See website for list.

DESCRIPTION

The Young Nonprofit Professionals Network (YNPN) promotes an efficient, viable, and inclusive nonprofit sector to support the growth, learning, and development of young professionals. Organization offers an opportunity for future nonprofit and community leaders through professional development, networking, and social opportunities designed for young people involved in the nonprofit community.

CATEGORIES

Fund-Raising/Donor/Nonprofit Organization Associations
Grant Professional Association

GRANTORS BY TOTAL GRANT VALUE

$1,000,000–$25,000,000

$500,000–$1,000,000

$100,000–$500,000

Under $100,000

GRANTORS BY STATE

NAMED GRANTS/PROGRAMS

PROFESSIONAL LIBRARY ORGANIZATION GRANTORS